W9-CDC-044

ECCLESIAL REFLECTION

ECCLESIAL REFLECTION

AN ANATOMY OF THEOLOGICAL METHOD

EDWARD FARLEY

FORTRESS PRESS
Philadelphia

COPYRIGHT © 1982 BY FORTRESS PRESS

All rights reserved. No part of this publication may be reproduced, stored in a retrieval system, or transmitted in any form or by any means, electronic, mechanical, photocopying, recording, or otherwise, without the prior permission of the copyright owner.

––––––––––

Library of Congress Cataloging in Publication Data

Farley, Edward, 1929–
  Ecclesial reflection.

  Includes index.
  1. Theology—Methodology. I. Title.
BR118.F35   230′01′8   81–43088
ISBN 0–8006–0670–1   AACR2

––––––––––

9023D81   Printed in the United States of America   1–670

to
Charles Austin Farley, Jr., Laura Lee Farley,
David Kimbel Nichols, James Edward Nichols
and
in memory of Lisa Caldwell Farley

Contents

Contents

Contents

Contents

Contents

Contents

xii

Preface

The present work is a sequel to *Ecclesial Man* (1975), the two together adding up to a prolegomenon to theology. Hence, some account of the division of labor between the two works is called for. That there is little consensus among theologians concerning the task and content of prolegomena should come as no surprise. Not only is there an enormous variety of motifs taken up in the theological literature, there are widely differing versions of the task itself. In other words, theological prolegomena have a historical character. They mirror the confessional tradition, the religious community of the theologian, and the historical situation in which the work is occurring. Thus works of prolegomena range from descriptions of sacred Scripture as the *principium* of dogmatic theology to accounts of the anthropological conditions of the knowledge of God.

Four features of this two-volume prolegomenon constitute a response to the current situation in theology and call for comment. First, the prolegomenon does not begin with the problem of "authorities," criteria, or methods but with the problem of reality in faith. Such was the task and inquiry of *Ecclesial Man*.[1] That work and the present one constitute the two major parts of the prolegomenon: the first part concerns the problem of foundations, the ways in which realities are pregiven to theology; the second concerns the judgment, the ways in which those realities lay claim to truth. The task of foundations is that of describing faith, the faith-world, the community of faith (ecclesial

1. Edward Farley, *Ecclesial Man: A Social Phenomenology of Faith and Reality* (Philadelphia: Fortress Press, 1975).

existence) as the matrix of reality-givenness. The primary instrument of this description as it was carried out in *Ecclesial Man* was social phenomenology. The present task of describing theological judgment (criteriology) involves the remaining features of prolegomena as a response to the present situation.

The second feature of this prolegomenon is its major focus on the legacy of theological method, called in these pages the house of authority. Two factors propelled this archaeology and critique of the house of authority comprising Part One of the present work. First, most contemporary theological work continues to appropriate elements from that legacy, such as the Scripture principle, with the result of incoherence. This is not unexpected since these elements continue in some sense to be operative in most modern forms of Christianity. And yet what it means to make and ground theological judgments within the house of authority is simply incompatible with what it means to make such claims outside the house. And clarity about the second alternative requires detailed, presuppositional analysis and critique of the legacy of authority, a theological counterpart to what Heidegger calls the "destruction of the history of ontology." The careful student of the history of Christianity will surely be suspicious of what looks like outrageous historical generalizations in this depiction of the house of authority. The method used here glosses over the real differences between branches of Christendom, historical periods, and theological figures and movements. It does not pretend, therefore, to be a straightforward history of theological method or the use and interpretation of Scripture in the church. The analysis in no way does justice to the many and profound variations in the use of Scripture in both Judaism and Christianity. Both traditions, even when they retained the meaning strata of the Scripture principle, frequently transcended the narrow hermeneutics which the principle itself would put forth. There are, then, serious differences on these questions between Luther and later Protestant scholastics, between the scholastics and later denominational traditions.

It is important at this point to clarify that this archaeology of the house of authority is not offering uniform, historical generalizations but an uncovering of strata of meaning. It offers, in other words, a skeleton, not an enfleshed historical entity. There are characteristic presuppositions about what meaning content goes into "holy Scripture" in the house of authority, and these presuppositions can be operative even when at other levels a figure makes statements about or interprets Scripture in ways that contradict the presuppositions. Further, it does seem that the historian can find figures and movements in the history of Christianity which depart from these presuppositions. I would, however, argue that these departures (for instance, W. E. Channing, the Chicago school, Schleiermacher) for the most part represent a time when the house of authority has come under criticism and begun to erode.

Third, this prolegomenon offers an uncharacteristic stress of what may be called a phenomenology of tradition, that is, of ecclesial process and its bearers. *Ecclesial Man*'s focus on knowledge anticipates this approach to theological criteriology. It should be clear that this move from foundations and pregivenness to theological judgment is not simply a move into philosophy of religion nor from the determinacy of faith to the generic level of ontology. Theological judgments are made from a historical faith-community which has a determinate corporate memory carried in a determinate network of symbols. The bearers of that determinacy, even written collections from the past, play some role in judgment. And the nature of that role is established not by authority but by the structure of ecclesial process itself. This is why a phenomenology and even sociology of tradition plays such a central part in this prolegomenon.

Fourth, the goal and culminating focus of this prolegomenon is the problem of truth. This is partly because of the radical way in which the truth question is modified in theology when the house of authority is abandoned and partly because of contemporary theological tendencies to reduce the question of truth to the question of interpretation. There may be hermeneutic theologies in which the truth question is still operative. Yet insofar as hermeneutic theology is a type of theology which contends that references and units addressed by theology are texts, bearers of linguistic forms of tradition such as myths, symbols, stories, and metaphors, that the interpretation of these linguistic forms is the unifying and culminating activity of theology, and that theological method means the rules for such interpretation, the problem of truth has been obscured. Nor is this remedied by adding a "front porch" of transcendental theology to the interpretation, since this merely offers anthropological grounding and orientation toward determinate, historical, linguistic expressions whose truth status remains obscure.

Having summarized the major distinguishing features of this prolegomenon, we can indicate what the prolegomenon does not expect to accomplish. It should not be necessary to point out that a theological prolegomenon cannot itself mediate the realities and references of theology. It cannot itself be ecclesial existence, the transforming power of redemption, the manifesting appresence of the transcendent. Such a view makes the category mistake of identifying theology with faith and the faith-world which propels it. In its clearest, most insightful expressions, the best that a theological prolegomenon can do is to describe the "world," environment, or typical situation in which theology's realities appear and the criteria they evoke when judgments are made about them.

Second, the theological prolegomenon does not offer to the believer, the student, or the inquirer a single, definitive theological procedure that, when put into operation, solves problems, clarifies obscurities, or produces understanding. To formulate the problem of theological method in this way is seriously misleading for it sets the theologian on a treasure hunt, a search for *the* hidden, definitive method. But when the elements of theological reflection come into view, we realize immediately that there is no single, definitive procedure waiting to be discovered. This model of a definitive procedure may be at work in many who have become disillusioned with theology's pluralism and seeming inability to make real headway. Failing to discover the treasure, many students of theology abandon the field for quasi-theological activities of polemic, book-reading, reporting on the theological scene, and technical scholarly projects.

The notion of a definitive procedure simply falsifies the historicality that attends all the moments of theological reflection. For theology always occurs in a situation, and its fields of evidence are mediated within that situation. Theology, for instance, is always carried on in connection with the attempted discernment of ecclesial existence. But ecclesial existence itself is not a single treasure to be unearthed once for all but is a living, changing reality portrayable through many types of inquiries. Even that which is grasped as an enduring feature has a historical character. Thus, we glimpse the universal references of ecclesial existence at one time through Paul, again in Augustine, and again in Luther or Barth. But the common feature (universality) is not simply an essence which someday some theologian will formulate completely, perfectly, and for all time. Further, although the making of judgments in theology may have certain describable features, they do not amount to a single procedure. For even if they employ the universal insights of ontology, as is argued in the final chapter, these insights themselves come forth in ontologies that have historical elements. Hence, the question of truth is perpetually being recast and reattempted. Instead of a single, definitive procedure, the theologian has available pregiven, manifesting realities of ecclesial existence experienced corporately and historically, and these realities evoke postures and categories proper to them. And though these postures and categories may yield insight, they do not establish the one and only valid procedure.

A final comment is called for. It concerns the paradoxical relation of this prolegomenon to traditional, historical Christianity. A glance at the table of contents will disclose that the critique of the classical criteriology (the house of authority), is a radical one. Furthermore, the house of authority is the historical form in which ecclesial existence has occurred. Historical Christianity and the house of authority are more or less identical. The loci of divine–human identity (the Scriptures, for instance) and various doctrines derived therefrom define what "Christianity" is, at least as belief-ful contents. It is the case, then, that in describing the demise of the house of authority, I am at the same time describing the demise of "Christianity" as the mode of authority's historical actualization in Catholicism and Protestantism.

On the other hand the radicality of the critique does not occur solely in the name of some world epoch, worldview, mode of human existence, science, or philosophy. The critique of the Scripture principle found in these pages may, accordingly, appear to be merely one more Enlightenment-prompted iconoclasm. The reader, it is hoped, will reserve judgment on this matter until Part Two has been read. Because the approach to the literature of the ecclesial community is one which attempts to uncover a correlation between the meaning and proper function of that literature and the nature of ecclesiality and its duration over time, it is not without parallel to both Luther's and Barth's discernments of the primacy of Christology in the approach to Scripture. My own quarrel with these figures is that they added the christological approach onto the inherited and essentially antiecclesial Scripture principle without subjecting the principle itself to either analysis or criticism. According to the approach undertaken here, when the collection of authoritative writings is submitted to ecclesiality, the resulting function of that collection in the community bursts the Scripture principle altogether.

Thus, the radicality of this critique does not originate in Enlightenment, science, or philosophy. It simply distinguishes ecclesial existence as a mode of corporate existence from "Christianity".[2] Historical Catholicism and Protestantism, the two major enduring historical actualizations of ecclesiality, both retain and contradict the social structure and symbolic universe of ecclesiality. To those for whom ecclesial existence and the house of authority ("Christianity") are identical, this prolegomenon will no doubt appear as either a philosophy of religion or a heresy. The fact that it proceeds from the pregivenness of ecclesial existence gives it a theological character and disqualifies it as a philosophy of religion. Furthermore, it is part of several centuries of interpretive effort which, if it found institutional and cultic expression, would amount to a post-Catholic, post-Protestant, third epoch and type of ecclesiality. Post-Vatican II Catholicism, isolated parts of non-Catholic Christendom, and liberation theology, especially in its South American version, may all be anticipating a third Christendom.

Because of considerations of length, two important topics which fall within the task of theological prolegomena are not included in these explorations. The following analysis argues that theological reflection has three dimensions: the depiction of ecclesiality (portraiture), the truth question, and reflective praxis. The third dimension is theology as it occurs in and toward specific biographical and social situations. The present work explores portraiture (chapters 9 through 12) and truth (chapters 13 and 14) but does not offer an equivalent account of the third dimension.

Because it is in connection with this third dimension that reflection on praxis occurs, this is a serious omission. Given the omission, the work may appear to either ignore or contradict the insights and claims of liberation theology. Such a conclusion is, however, inaccurate on three counts. First, since the three dimensions of theological reflection (portraiture, truth, and praxis) are constitutive of that reflection, the description of any one of them is necessarily an isolating and abstracting act. I do not, in other words, see the first two dimensions as alternative approaches to praxis reflection but as grounding strata to that reflection. Second, because the three strata or dimensions amount to a morphology of theological reflection, they do not necessarily repudiate liberation theology's insistence that true theology is always

2. We recall that "Christianity" was a historical and relative and not a normative term for Karl Barth, *Church Dogmatics* (Edinburgh: T. & T. Clark, 1956), vol. I, 2, pp. 280 ff.

situational and contextual. That situational primacy can coexist with the claim that reflection on praxis requires both portraiture and the truth question. Third, the analysis of the house of authority (chapters 1 through 7) uncovers an approach to theology which the liberation theologies regard as a ready vehicle for ideology. Because liberation theologies themselves retain many elements of the house of authority, and because they are prone to formulate theology's relation to praxis in such a way as to obscure both the portraiture and the truth dimensions, this work is related to such theologies by way of criticism and supplementation. By implication, this analysis criticizes the biblicism and neoorthodoxy present in this literature and suggests that its adoption of a pragmatic theory of truth is inadequate to its own theological purposes.

Finally, this work appropriates a distinction developed in *Ecclesial Man* between theological realities that are directly present and those that are only indicated, appresented: for instance, divine being, ultimate human destiny, and even the historical reality of the Christ. In the explorations of the way the truth question enters theology, the examples are restricted to matters available to immediate confirmation. The second topic unexplored in this work, then, is the very complex issue of what it means to move to the question of truth in matters that are only appresented, for instance, the transcendent. Admittedly these are serious lacunae in a work whose approach to prolegomena is to some degree comprehensive.

Two comments remain. I have tried to use sex-inclusive language throughout, thus avoiding use of the term *man* for human being. The generic usage was still in vogue when *Ecclesial Man* was written but has since been seriously challenged. The exception to sex-inclusive language in the present work is the use of the masculine pronouns to refer to God in the description of the house of authority. Second, I would like to express my gratitude to both the Association of Theological Schools and the Research Council of the Graduate School of Vanderbilt University for making possible through fellowships an extended sabbatical leave during which much of this work was written. In addition, I would like to thank Walter Harrelson of Vanderbilt Divinity School and George Kehm of Pittsburgh Theological Seminary for their criticism and commentary on this work in its manuscript stage.

PART ONE

AN ARCHAEOLOGY AND CRITIQUE
OF THE
HOUSE OF AUTHORITY

1

The Religious Matrix

We begin this critique of theological judgment with what may seem to be a lengthy detour. This detour is a seven-chapter "archaeology" and critique of the classical criteriology. We use the word *criteriology* instead of *method* self-consciously. Church theologians throughout the history of Christianity have been attentive to method in varying degrees. However methodologically self-conscious they were, they did engage in theological disputes and make theological judgments, and they did these things under criteria. Criteria (authorities, norms) functioned in theological work whether it was methodologically self-conscious or not. The term *classical* refers simply to Christianity as it developed into its major epochal and global forms (Eastern Orthodoxy, Roman Catholicism, Protestantism), each of which in some sense came to regard its own historical branch as normative. There are, to be sure, countless diversities, even heterodoxies, in these global branches of Christendom; yet through these variabilities persists a certain unity, even doctrinal unity, which sets them all within one historical form of Christianity for which the doctrinal development of the church in the patristic period remains decisive. Thus, none of these major branches of Christendom in their classical periods seriously questioned incarnationalist Christology, trinitarian theism, the universality of both sin and guilt, and a dual (heaven–hell) eschatology. Furthermore, a consensus marks classical Christianity concerning the sources and criteria for religious truth. Because of this consensus, we can speak of the classical criteriology and that consensus is the subject of our "archaeological" or layered investigation.

We appropriate Foucault's metaphor of archaeology to indicate that

3

this is not a historical investigation in the usual sense of the word. Most of the questions of a causal explanatory and sequential sort which occur to the historically minded are passed over. Yet what is before us is a historical phenomenon, the Christian religion in its classical form and its attendant criteriology. Positively, the term archaeology suggests an investigation of the strata which underlie beliefs, symbols, actions, and institutions.[1] I would not do justice to the metaphor if I restricted it to strata analysis. The science of archaeology works with strata in order to reconstruct the events and processes of the prehistorical past. Likewise, this archaeology of the classical criteriology will have a sequential or developmental reference. It begins with that which the faith of Israel supplies to the classical criteriology, then proceeds to look at synagogal Judaism and the origin of the Scripture principle, and then the doctrinalization of the resultant criteriology in Catholic Christianity. The primary effort, however, is to expose the strata themselves, the various levels of presupposed symbols and axioms taken for granted by the classical criteriology.

Why the detour at all? Why must a theory of theological judgment cut a path through this jungle of complexities on its way to a constructive proposal? The legacy of the classical criteriology is still very much with us. Almost all theologians acknowledge this legacy and its problematic status and limitations. Yet rare is the theological enterprise which obtains a clear sense of the theological task by way of a critical response to the classical criteriology as a whole.[2] More typical is the prolegomenon which offers a ritual acknowledgment of the effect of historical-critical method on the authority of Scripture or tradition followed by the search for a different location of authority in

1. "Archaeology" in this sense is a mode of thought and analysis devised by Michel Foucault for various inquiries into the history of science. His own account of archaeology as a method is the best introduction. See his *The Archaeology of Knowledge*, trans. A. M. S. Smith (New York: Harper & Row, 1972), pp. 135–40, 192 ff. Thus he says, "by questioning the sciences, their history, their strange unity, their dispersion, and their ruptures, . . . the domain of positivities was able to appear" (p. 195). It is just this that the archaeology of the house of authority will also try to accomplish.

2. Paul Althaus devotes one chapter of his dogmatics to a critique of the classical Protestant doctrine of Scripture. See *Die christliche Wahrheit* (Gütersloh: Gerd Mohn, 1962), chap. 20. Helmut Thielecke in the first volume of his prolegomenon subjects what he calls "Cartesian theology" to extensive analysis and criticism. The target here is more post-Schleiermacher theology than the classical criteriology. See *The Evangelical Faith*, vol. I: *Prolegomena: The Relation of Theology to Modern Thought Forms*, trans. G. W. Bromiley (Grand Rapids: Wm. B. Eerdmans Publishing Co., 1974), part one.

Scripture or a different hermeneutic of the texts. The effect of post-Enlightenment critical modes of thought on the classical criteriology *as a whole* is passed over. The result is the uncritical retention of the Scripture principle, the concept of canon, and therewith a host of underlying presupposed strata. Rather than a selective response to the classical criteriology, archaeological inquiry amounts to a psychoanalytic purge of the theological consciousness. Or, to put it differently, it represents a theological parallel to Heidegger's beginning his philosophical program with a negation, the "destruction of the history of ontology."[3] It is only when the founding strata of the classical criteriology are brought to the surface that the problematic which attends any contemporary theological appeal to specific norms can be experienced in its radicality. The classical criteriology tends to be of one piece, or, to change metaphors, a pattern created by a long series of upright dominoes. The archaeology will attempt to disclose the pattern. Interpreters of the Christian faith will have to decide whether or not to flick the first domino. Historically speaking, the row was toppled centuries ago.

This archaeology concentrates on expressions of the classical criteriology occurring in more or less completed form, in methodologically self-conscious, sophisticated theological expressions. We find versions of this criteriology in the Church Fathers, in both medieval and Protestant scholasticisms, in contemporary "neoorthodox" Catholic (Rahner) and Protestant (Barth) theologians. We find its non- or premethodological strata in the piety, liturgy, cultus, and individuals of the Catholic and Protestant faiths. However, the actual description of the criteriology does not begin with its extant, specific expressions but with its less visible foundations. Accordingly, the analysis moves from the dominant metaphors of the religious matrix to founding axioms and their middle axioms, and finally to church doctrines and theological arguments. The analysis occurs in five major steps: (1) the religious matrix in Israel and early Christianity (chapter 1); (2) the founding axioms of salvation history and the principle of identity (chapter 2); (3) the secondary axioms, the *locations* of divine–human

---

3. It may not be too far-fetched to suggest that this theological effort has some resemblance to Heidegger's very self-conscious destruction of the history of ontology as a way to the ground of metaphysics. See Martin Heidegger, *Being and Time*, trans. Macquarrie and Robinson (London: SCM Press, 1962), Introduction, vol. II, p. 6.

identity, in Scripture (chapter 3) and (4) definitive doctrines and the definitive institution (chapter 4); and (5) the concept and method of theological understanding and its self-legitimation (chapter 5).

The founding axioms of salvation history and the principle of identity (chapter 2) originate in the historical religious communities of Israel and early Christianity. I shall not at this point attempt to assess these founding axioms in relation to the so-called essence of these historic faiths. Nevertheless, the basic mythos, the family of symbols, the unifying motifs of self-understanding which constitute these faiths will preside over this attempt to discern a theological criteriology. This is why I begin with a shorthand (some would say, no doubt, slight of hand) account of themes from these religious faiths that are relevant to the task.[4]

THE FAITH OF ISRAEL

Since the Christian faith is the matrix and context of any prolegomenon to Christian theology, discernments and proposals about its criteria are not possible apart from reference to that faith's material content. And yet that content did not appear *de novo* in Jesus of Nazareth. The Christian religion is clearly one of the historical outcomes of Israelite religion (Judaism and Islam being other major outcomes), and Christian faith, like the Jewish faith, is continuous with the faith of Israel. More specifically, Christian faith is both a perpetuation of and departure from the faith of Israel. The faith of Israel provides what C. H. Dodd calls the "theological substructure of the New Testament," hence the description of Christian faith begins with the faith of Israel.[5]

Historically speaking, the faith of Israel begins to form in Israel's premonarchical period (patriarchs and judges) and persists until the rise of Judaism after the exile. Its classical period is that of the

---

4. The initial volume of this prolegomenon, *Ecclesial Man* (1975), anticipates this approach to theological criteriology. In that work I argued that the cognitive dimension of faith, reality-apprehensions, occurred in the determinacy of a religious community, in the shaping of a social self by certain intersubjective and mutual intentionalities. If theology is the attempt to grasp the matter of those apprehensions in the mode of understanding, some of its criteria would be generated out of that determinacy itself. For material criteria, in other words, we are referred back to the historic religious faith and not simply to generic structures of being or evidences or to individual subjective experiences.

5. C. H. Dodd, *According to the Scriptures* (New York: Charles Scribner's Sons, 1953), chap. 1.

monarchy including the protest literature of the writing prophets.[6] The standard descriptions of the faith of Israel organize the material into major periods and the literature which attends them and into major themes of Israel's faith as it concerns God, human being, world, cult, and so on. I find no serious difficulty with such an approach. It does, however, reflect the theological *loci* which have become standard in Christian systematic theology. I shall pursue another closely related course, one which attempts to discern a family of interdependent primary symbols that express the identity and coherence of Israel's faith. But what is it which makes these symbols interrelated and part of the same thing? Students of the matter have made a variety of proposals concerning the unique contribution, the distinctive essence of Israelite religion.[7] The faith of Israel, like most historical faiths, embraces a complex or family of interdependent symbols. It refers minimally to a discrete community's developing historical experience of being guided toward salvation through the activities of a world-creating, kinglike deity. Five essentially interrelated symbols or families of linguistic expressions comprise the major themes of this faith.

First, it is a Yahwism, a faith in the kingly lordship of a personal deity who originally was a tribal deity worshiped initially in a henotheistic framework but eventually as the world maker and the disposer of

6. My account here is especially dependent on two studies: Helmer Ringgren's *Israelite Religion*, trans. D. Green (Philadelphia: Fortress Press, 1966), and Max Weber's *Ancient Judaism* (New York: Free Press, 1952). Brief but penetrating summaries by scholars who are not Old Testament specialists have also been helpful. See Rudolf Bultmann, *Primitive Christianity in Its Contemporary Setting*, trans. R. Fuller (New York: Meridian Books, 1956, Reprint ed. Philadelphia, Fortress Press, 1980), part I; Henri Duméry, *Phenomenology and Religion: Structures of the Christian Institution* (Berkeley: University of California Press, 1975), chap. 2; John B. Cobb, Jr., *The Structure of Christian Existence* (Philadelphia: Westminster Press, 1967), chap. 9; and Talcott Parsons, *Societies* (Englewood Cliffs, N.J.: Prentice-Hall, 1966), chap. 6. In addition, see Y. Kaufmann's comprehensive study, *The Religion of Israel from Its Beginnings to the Babylonian Exile* (Chicago: University of Chicago Press, 1960).

7. Cobb describes "prophetic existence" as a multiplicity of themes which are unified by self-conscious concern for the self-responsible individual or personhood. See *Structure*, chap. 9. Reflecting a more sociological approach, Parsons finds distinctiveness in a community of people who ground their *raison d'être* and the telos of their existence in the will of a deity with whom they make an agreement (*Societies*). Duméry sees the chief contribution of Israel in its experience of history as revelatory, that divine revelation and theophany occur by way of moments, events, and epochs of history itself (*Phenomenology and Religion*, p. 6). Although he does not pretend to offer an account of the distinctiveness of the faith of Israel, Paul Ricoeur's position appears to be one which regards the Adamic myth, a comprehensive interpretation of the problematic of human being in the world before God, as the real legacy of Israelite faith (*The Symbolism of Evil*, trans. E. Buchanan [Boston: Beacon Press, 1967], pp. 47–150).

human history. The shorthand expression of this first symbol is the *shema,* the confession of the one and only Lord. In the later (prophetic) stages of Israel's faith the central implication of Yahweh as world maker and disposer of all history is drawn out, namely universalism. The main symbols of Israel's faith (people [nation], land, Torah) are particularistic and even nationalistic. Yet Yahweh is the one God of the one world, and this communicates a universalistic quality to his revelation and Torah. Thus Torah righteousness is not simply righteousness for Israelites but righteousness as such. This combination of universalistic monotheism with geographical and national particularism is one of the distinctive features if not paradoxes of the faith of Israel.[8]

Second, the primary symbol of Israel's self-interpretation is the people of Yahweh. This means that they owe their origin and very existence to Yahweh's elective activity. As that elected social entity they have a place and mission in the ongoing drama of history, a place and mission willed by Yahweh. It also means that as the people of Yahweh their very existence is bound up with a continuing obligation of loyalty and obedience to the God-king and continuing life under Yahweh's direction and providential care. This relation, initiated by Yahweh but able to be violated by the people, is symbolized in the notion and narratives of the covenant.

Third, the people of Yahweh do not understand themselves simply as a migratory people. What Yahweh willed for them was the occupation of a specific territory, and it is on this territory that they will fulfill their function in the stream of history. In other words a correlative symbol to "covenant people of Yahweh" is the land, promised, given, taken away, and restored. This is the space in which the social entity willed by Yahweh comes to actualization, the territory which receives or is denied God's blessings, from which they go into exile, to which they return.[9] Thus, the covenant with Yahweh includ-

---

8. See Duméry, *Phenomenology and Religion,* p. 27.

9. Many students of Israel and Judaism have stressed the land as a major element in these faiths. The fullest and most recent study is W. D. Davies, *The Gospel and the Land: Early Christianity and Jewish Territorial Doctrine* (Berkeley: University of California Press, 1974). See also B. Z. Bokser, *Judaism: Profile of a Faith* (New York: Alfred A. Knopf, 1963), chap. 13, "The People, the Book, and the Land"; Abraham J. Heschel, *Israel: An Echo of Eternity* (New York: Farrar, Straus & Giroux, 1967), chap. 2; W. P. Eckert, N. P. Levenson, and M. Stöhr, eds., *Judaisches Volkgelobtes Land* (Munich: C. Kaiser, 1970). See especially R. Rendtorff's essay. Walter Brueggemann, *The Land* (Philadelphia: Fortress Press, 1977). For an extensive bibliography of studies of the land motif in Israel and Judaism see Brueggemann, p. 190, n. 15.

ing requirements, promises, guidance, and destiny all concern the life of the people on the land.

Fourth, Yahweh's guidance of the people embraces many kinds of activities: judgment and punishment, the raising up and casting down of political leaders both inside and outside Israel, blessing the fertility of the land. But these activities are unified by a central activity of assisting the people to keep the covenant and covenant righteousness by means of the Word, the disclosure of Yahweh's will to the people. This revelation is the earlier and broader meaning of Torah. Yahweh saves the people not only from their enemies but from themselves, from the hardness of hearts set in disobedience. Although Torah means instruction, it gradually took on the connotation of moral and cultic laws, regulations for the corporate life of the people of Yahweh. In later Judaism, Torah becomes the very telos of salvation-history, and covenant and land are given as a setting for the study of Torah.

This fourth element of the faith of Israel is, then, the revelatory instruction Yahweh gives to the people for their well-being. Instruction (Torah) becomes the norm which measures the people's keeping or breaking of the Covenant. Furthermore, Torah, land, and elected people-on-the-land are interdependent elements of one complex. This is why Torah can also mean the specific instructions for individual and corporate life on this land, not simply universal moral truths. Because the content of Torah is not simply cultic regulations but commandments pertinent to the moral life of individuals and the community, Torah presupposes what Ricoeur calls the Adamic myth, a vision of the legacy of universal human sin which originates in a primordial act of human disobedience against God, the consequences of which pervade and dispose all of history. In the framework of this myth, Torah is a gift to a frail, mortal, and sinful race which lives a perpetually rebellious and guilty existence before Yahweh. Hence, the faith of Israel includes the cultic practice of sacrifice as a propitiation for sin.

These motifs of people, land, and Torah are brought together in Israel's social structure as a nation; territorially bounded, linguistically unified, with specific, even if changing, forms of self-government. This social structure is presupposed by the fifth component of the faith of Israel, tradition. Tradition may not have obtained expression in a single unified symbol such as covenant, Yahweh, or people of God. Yet there are linguistic expressions which disclose a distinctive view of the persistence of the past, found especially in the language of remembering.[10]

Linguistic expressions which communicate Israel's remembering are one aspect of a mode of social perpetuation which distinguished the faith of Israel from ancient Near Eastern faiths. What made this possible was Israel's self-understanding as a people elected by and in covenant with the world-maker God who placed them on a territory and disclosed to them the requirements for righteous life. All these notions are in some sense historical. The land is not simply a space, a bounded territory, but a space which had a historical origin in the activity of Yahweh and which has a remembered history. Yahweh is thought of as the one responsible for certain events and persons in the past and one who effects the destiny of Israel and the nations now and in the future. Israel's identity occurs, therefore, in connection with its covenant loyalty to Yahweh, which means specifically its keeping of the Torah. And for this to happen, covenant and Torah must be remembered, deposited, and institutionalized in such a way that new generations can obey Yahweh. Hence, the vehicles of duration found in most religions (a leadership, cultus, cultic festivals, the recital of myths) function in Israel as the carriers of a historical self-understanding. Torah is remembered but in the setting of recital of Yahweh's past activities in Israel's history.[11]

It would be anachronistic to speak of a Scripture principle as part of the faith of Israel. This is because Israel's major vehicles of duration were events and institutions through which a landed, territorial people endured; for example, the conquest of Canaan, the kingship, the building of the temple, the centralization of the cult in Jerusalem, the priesthood, and so on. Scriptures, in the sense of a collection of inspired writings, entered into Israel along with a new set of postexilic vehicles of duration.[12] Nevertheless, the faith of Israel endured in the

10. See Brevard S. Childs, *Memory and Tradition in Israel* (Naperville: A. R. Allenson, 1962), especially chap. 4. See also the recently published collection of essays edited by Douglas Knight, *Tradition and Theology in the Old Testament* (Philadelphia: Fortress Press, 1976), and Peter R. Ackroyd, *Continuity: A Contribution to the Study of the Old Testament Religious Tradition* (Oxford: Oxford University Press, 1962).

11. See James A. Sanders, *Torah and Canon* (Philadelphia: Fortress Press, 1972), pp. 15–17; Walter Eichrodt, *Theology of the Old Testament*, trans. J. A. Baker (Philadelphia: Westminster Press, 1961), vol. I, p. 123; Childs, *Memory and Tradition*, chap. 6.

12. This thesis assumes that the history of the accumulation of a *literature* of tradition in Israel's history, recently called canon criticism, is not a history of the Scripture principle or of a literature regarded as Scripture in every period. Important writings

Jerusalem cultus, its festivals, and the kingship by way of the primary symbols of that faith—Yahweh, people (covenant), land, Torah—as well as event-symbols (Exodus), figure-symbols (Abraham, David), and story-symbols. And the specific means through which these functioned in Israel's social duration was the memory of Israel, deposited in lines of tradition and recited regularly in the cultus. Israel therefore not only remembered Yahweh, but did so through cultic repetition of segments of Israel's own past. These in turn became the tradition appealed to and utilized in later stages, as in the prophets.[13]

Accordingly, it may be accurate to speak of an incipient Scripture principle in the faith of Israel insofar as the remembered and recited past was a major means of Israel's self-perpetuation. It is this I am calling tradition, the fifth major element of Israel's faith. It, too, is closely bound up with the other four. For what is remembered and recited is a story of *Yahweh's* activities with his elected and covenant *people* as they keep or violate his revealed instructions (*Torah*) given for the life of a *nation* on a designated *land*.

Tradition in this sense may be one of Israel's contributions to subsequent Western religion. It is a term for the distinctive social duration of Israel. We should keep in mind, therefore, the interrelation, the correlation of tradition with the other symbols of Israel's faith. *What* is perpetuated is the memory (and the events and persons) of a national and territorial people. Hence, the vehicles of duration (priesthood, temple, festivals, sacrificial cult, cultic recitals) all occur in the framework of not only a land given by Yahweh but a land whose center is Jerusalem, the definitive locus of Yahweh's presence to the people. This identity through time is carried by Jerusalem-related entities, the monarchy, the priesthood, and temple. Needless to say, when these institutional vehicles are destroyed or dispersed, when the nation, the larger framework for these vehicles, is lost, the re-

---

functioning as vehicles of tradition are "Scripture" only in a very broad and loose sense, not in the specific sense of the sacred Scriptures since that concept arose as part of Judaism's solution to the problem of its survival. Nor is Josiah's reform necessarily evidence of a functioning Scripture principle in the later Judaic sense. The subjection of the corporate life of the people to the code of an ancient document anticipates but is not synonymous with the full concept of sacred Scripture.

13. Sander's *Torah and Canon* is an excellent account of this accumulation of tradition and the building up of the literatures of what came to be Jewish Scriptures through the process of continued reinterpretation of former deposits of tradition.

ligious community must find other means of duration or else cease to exist.

THE BEGINNINGS OF CHRISTIANITY

If not strictly historical, this archaeology of the classical criteriology does concern a historical entity. If we are to understand the basis of the founding axioms of that criteriology, we need to locate their source in the actual religious communities behind them. And this means primarily the religion of Israel and of early Christianity. Although a detailed account of the historical origins of Christianity is unnecessary, we do need at least a summary account of what persisted from the faith of Israel into Christianity—what of the faith of Israel was rejected and what was modified. The selective principle of the summary will be that which came to play a role in the development of the classical criteriology.

The Christian movement of the first three centuries appears to have three distinct phases. The first is composed of the events which led to and mark the ministry of Jesus, including his death and the effecting by these events of a self-conscious religious movement among Palestinian Jews. Here we are concerned with the ministry and teachings of Jesus and the early Palestinian kerygma. Needless to say, we are dependent on sources from the second period for the retrieval of the first period, on authors writing from the situation of the Gentile mission. In this first period, Christianity is one among various Jewish sects and there is little or no self-conscious repudiation of the temple or Jewish authorities.

The great event initiating and characterizing the second period is the Gentile mission. It covers roughly the period of writings of that collection of writings called the New Testament (50–130 C.E.), and at the end of the period the new faith is primarily a Gentile faith. As the writings of the New Testament authors indicate, the Christian movement in this period is one of great diversity. Nevertheless, the Christian community did accomplish in that eighty or so years a fairly unified theological symbolism which discloses both retentions and departures from the religion of Israel and Judaism.

The third stage is the movement which led to the Catholicizing of the new faith. Its roots are in the second period. Its accomplishment is the institutional and doctrinal unification of the church, thereby overcoming the fragmentizing effects of the Enthusiast, Gnostic, and religiously syncretistic movements of the Roman Empire. What I am calling the classical criteriology obtained its earliest expression in this third period. The problem now is to locate its background in the second period when Christianity was separating from Judaism and developing an identifiable symbol system of its own.

The Christian movement from the beginning was unified and centered in some relation to Jesus of Nazareth. His teaching, example, ministry, and death had such an impact on his followers that they experienced in him the individual modification of human life as might occur through a new, controversial, and insightful teacher and prophet. More than that, they experienced something which they interpreted in the inherited language of apocalyptic. Jesus himself appears to have employed the apocalyptic framework in his preaching of the impending kingdom. The post-Easter kerygma proclaimed that the kingdom had been inaugurated and humankind was living in the new epoch of the promised reign of God and that the ministry, teaching, wonder working, death, and continued presence (understood in the apocalyptic notion of resurrection) of Jesus are that through which the kingdom had finally appeared. Thus, Jesus himself is the very center of the preaching of the second period, and to express his centrality as the inaugurator of the kingdom, the fulfillment of Israel's expectations, the term *Messiah* is applied to him to give expression to his centrality and finality.[14] We have, then, prior to the second period a human figure, Jesus of Nazareth, whose life and death effected a following which continued after his death and which made him the center of a new eschatological preaching. The environment of this movement is Judaism and Palestine. The community of people who responded to this preaching appears to be an end-time community, and this conviction of living in the end-time persisted into the early period of Paul's writings.[15]

14. For a compact description of four types of terms and phrases applied to Jesus in primitive Christianity, see Helmut Koester's "The Structure of Early Christian Beliefs" in Koester and James Robinson, *Trajectories Through Early Christianity* (Philadelphia: Fortress Press, 1971).

15. John C. Gager, following the line of Albert Schweitzer and Martin Werner but using social world analyses and categories, finds the earliest Christian community to have the standard features of a millenarian community. Since one of the features of that type of community is a short period of existence in its millenarian form, the church's survival depended on successful transition into a stable and enduring community, which means developing vehicles of generation-bridging duration. See the

What are the major themes and features of the second period of Christianity, the period of the transplanting of the Jesus movement onto Hellenistic soil? The initial task and problem of the Jesus movement was to formulate its relation to its Israelite-Jewish past, and this occurred in the context of the struggle and polemic between the Pharasaic party and the Christian sect. As the Gentile mission proceeded, the new Christian sect was also challenged by non-Jewish religiously syncretistic movements, a challenge which is present in the second period and which becomes the major problem of the third Catholicizing period. The problem of the Israelite-Judaic heritage persisted in the second phase and may be clarified through the posing of three questions. (1) What was the Judaism which was the immediate environment of the origin of the Jesus movement, and what is its relation to the faith of Israel? (2) What are the dominant features of the gospel or kerygma as it occurs in the second phase and how did they originate? (3) What was retained, rejected, and modified from the legacy of the faith of Israel and Judaism?

The Judaic Environment Behind the Jesus Movement

The faith of Israel was not present to Jesus, to his disciples, and to the first Christians in the form it took in the period of the Jewish monarchy or the prophets. Between that period and the time of Jesus had occurred the destruction of the first temple, the exile, the return, and the renewal of the temple cult in Jerusalem. In addition Israel had experienced hellenization and secularization of its religion, the Maccabean revolt, reactions against adaptive and syncretistic strategies of survival, and the rise of the Hasidim, the bearers of the strategy of segregation and legalism. The outcome of these events, described in Chronicles, Nehemiah, Ezra, and Old Testament inter-testamental writings, was synagogal Judaism.[16] The diaspora set a new

---

Appendix on general structures of social duration for an account of these vehicles. In the scheme offered here, the second or "apostolic" period is the transition period into the third period of early Catholic forms of consolidation. See John C. Gager, *Kingdom and Community: The Social World of Early Christianity* (Englewood Cliffs, N.J.: Prentice-Hall, 1975).

16. I am following Samuel Sandmel's terminology which avoids the expressions Pharisaic Judaism and rabbinic Judaism and prefers to distinguish between temple Judaism and synagogal Judaism. See *Judaism and Christian Beginnings* (New York: Oxford University Press, 1978), p. 16.

problem for the people and religion of Israel: how to survive and maintain its faith-world under the conditions of occupation of the homeland and under conditions of life outside the homeland. The varieties of Judaism in the first century C.E. indicate that the response and solution to this problem were not uniform. And this is one outstanding feature of the environment of early Christianity, the preservation of the faith of Israel in different types of social and religious Jewish groups: the continuing Jerusalem temple cult and priesthood, the end-time community of Qumran, the Pharisaic party, and the philosophically disposed Hellenistic Jews.

Yet this pluralism should not obscure the commonalities of synagogal Judaism, the new institutions and themes, which, if not all-pervasive, were widespread and highly influential. Four features are especially prominent. The first and most prominent feature of diaspora Judaism is a new means of world maintenance which is not dependent on the physical existence of the temple or even the existence of the Jewish homeland. This new way involves vehicles of duration other than the temple, the priesthood, and the ritual sacrifices. Instead of the temple came a local gathering and building, the synagogue. In place of sacrificial rites came a reading of the inherited writings in a posture of seeking guidance in the local situation. In place of the priesthood came a new class of leaders, the *sopherim*, who study the old writings and become authoritative interpreters of them. Descending from them are masters with pupils, teaching in schools for the study of Torah.[17] Important as the monastic community is in the environment of Christianity, the isolated, millenarian community is not the typical alternative for social duration in diaspora Judaism.

Second, the Jews of the diaspora faced a problem not present when the faith of Israel endured by means of the land and nation. In the diaspora Jews live in an alien culture with foreign language, customs, religions, and cultures, and this foreign element, particularly Hellenism, was not simply a threat but an attraction. The solution to this perpetual possibility of the minority religion being assimilated into the

---

17. While it is generally acknowledged that the synagogue itself was a center for instruction, disagreements continue over whether there were in Babylonian Judaism Talmudic *academies* for the teaching and dissemination of the oral Torah or, instead, simply teachers with their apprentices. David M. Goodblatt finds evidence only for the latter. See his *Rabbinic Judaism in Sasanian Babylonia* (Leiden: E. J. Brill, 1975).

larger alien culture was to maintain the identity of the exiles by means of meticulous cultic and legal regulation of everyday life, creating and maintaining a culture within the larger culture. This being the case, the writings, always respected and revered as the authoritative history of the people of the covenant, now become *the* decisive means for maintaining the minority culture. Torah as revelation or divine instruction obtains a definitive location in the writings (the written Torah). And what unifies these writings is not simply their function as a deposit of the traditions of Israel, a narrative of Yahweh's activity with his people, but rather their function as the divinely given source for regulating the everyday life of the people. The interpretation of the writings takes the form of *halakah* and *hagadah*. In short, diaspora Judaism had given birth to the *sacred Scriptures*. And this in turn brought about a new piety and a new myth; Torah piety (the end for which the Jew is created is to study the Torah), and the Torah-myth (the origin of the Torah in Divine inspiration).

Third, a new literature, symbolism, hermeneutic, and world outlook arose in some movements of postexilic Judaism. This is the modification of prophetic eschatology into apocalyptic. As a literature it is present in the canonical Book of Daniel and in noncanonical books such as 2 Esdras and 1 Enoch. The Qumran community appears to be the major Jewish community organized around the dualistic and end-time outlook of apocalyptic. Its distinctive hermeneutic is the interpretation of the Scriptures with the purpose of indicating that the older writings speak in veiled ways of what is now fulfilled in the one, true, end-time community. Such a hermeneutic draws upon one of the central features of apocalyptic, the periodizing of world history.[18]

Fourth, diaspora Judaism actualized to a considerable degree the universalism inherent in the faith of Israel.[19] While the faith of Israel

18. Martin Hengel finds the periodization of history characteristic of apocalyptic in the Book of Daniel. *Judaism and Hellenism*, trans. John Bowden (Philadelphia: Fortress Press, 1974; reissued 1981 as one volume), vol. I, p. 189. He locates the roots of this in Babylonian and Iranian mythology and claims that by the fourth century B.C.E. the Iranian eschatology had a linear outline of history (p. 193).

19. Three very illuminating treatments of Jewish universalism are the following. Duméry, *Phenomenology and Religion*, pp. 27 ff. Duméry attempts to express the uniqueness of Jewish universalism in his notion of "concrete universality," which means a universal religion "confined to a particular mode of expression" (p. 27). Leo Baeck's *The Essence of Judaism* (New York: Schocken Books, 1948) is an extensive and eloquent argument for Judaism as the paradigm case of universal religion and as the origin of all

occurs in an ethnic-nationalistic setting and symbolic framework, it testifies to a deity who is the world maker and the monarch of world history. Hence, the self-understanding of Israel includes a reference beyond itself, to the nations and its role among them. The apocalyptic movement intensified this self-understanding in its visions of a world-historical end involving all nations and all history. It is not clear what the relationship is between these universalistic tendencies and Jewish missions of the diaspora period.[20] The fact is that diaspora Judaism did become a missionary religion.[21] Such "missions" were not the result of a unified, officially sponsored effort by temple or synagogue. Non-Jews were attracted to Judaism and associated themselves with the synagogue, and individual Jews engaged in proselytizing efforts. The result was that some non-Jews, a small number, became full proselytes, submitting to circumcision, and others associated themselves with the synagogue as "god-fearers." Although these occurrences indicate the actualizing of universalistic tendencies, they do not amount to full or consistent universalism. What the non-Jew was converted *to* was both the universal God, the world maker, a universal myth of the human problem, the Adamic myth, and a universally applicable moral requirement, the Torah. At the same time the non-Jew was converted to the institutional and linguistic bearers of these things which remained symbolically national and ethnic. Thus conversion was both a religious and a political decision.[22]

This account of the Judaic environment of the Christian movement

---

other universal religions and of the missionary idea. He argues that universality is an unavoidable consequence of the idea of election and of ethical monotheism (pp. 68–69). Hans Joachim Schoeps's *The Jewish-Christian Argument: A History of Theologies in Conflict*, trans. D. E. Green (New York: Holt, Rinehart and Winston, 1963), goes even farther than the others in discovering grounds for universalism in Judaism. Thus he finds universalism in the Jewish attitude toward the stranger, the theme of grades of proselytes, and the category "devout Gentiles" (chap. 2).

20. Hengel cites as background of Jewish missions the new expansionism which succeeded the Maccabean revolt and which engaged in forcible conversion of adjacent areas (*Judaism and Hellenism*, vol. I, p. 307). Some stress the attractiveness of Jewish monotheism to middle and upper classes of non-Jews. Y. Kaufmann affirms that the written Torah as the embodiment of the religion of Yahweh after the destruction of the temple was the "seed of an ultimate liberation of the religion of Israel from ethnic and territorial limitations" (*The Religion of Israel*, p. 448).

21. Joachim Jeremias calls it the first great missionary religion in the ancient world. *Jesus' Promise to the Nations* (rev. Eng. ed.; London: SCM Press, 1967), p. 11. For treatments of postexilic Judaism as a missionary religion, see ibid., pp. 11–19; G. Bornkamm, *Paul* (New York: Harper & Row, 1971), chap. 1; Duméry, *Phenomenology and Religion*, p. 27; Hengel, *Judaism and Hellenism*, vol. I, pp. 307 ff.

22. Hengel, *Judaism and Hellenism*, vol. I, p. 307.

has centered on features of diaspora Judaism which are innovations to the faith of Israel: the new institutions of duration (synagogue, teachers, Torah liturgy), the sacred Scriptures and their application, apocalyptic, and Jewish missions. These themes should not obscure Judaism's continuity with the faith of Israel.[23] The founding symbols are certainly retained. Yahweh as the world creator and disposer of history, grasped especially through the monarchical metaphor of his relation to the world, continues and is even strengthened in the emphasis on God's transcendence and the reticence in using the sacred name. The larger setting for the royal metaphor is the *heilsgeschichtlich* view of history, a legacy from the religion of Israel. The people as the people of Yahweh, maintained by his activity, continues as a theme as does the connection between the people and the land of Israel.[24] Yet there were modifications. On the one side there is realistic acceptance of the people as a dispersed people, evidenced in the creation of strategies and institutions which relate a minority people to the alien culture in which they live. On the other side, the dispersed communities maintain their identity through a perpetually growing oral *halakah* which applies and adapts the written Torah to new situations. The reference, therefore, was still to the land, history, and nation of Israel, whatever the present political and empirical situation in the land happened to be. Dispersed Judaism still thought of its past in relation to the nation-land. It centered the world in Jerusalem and Zion, and its future hope, be it expressed in traditional prophetic mode or apocalyptic symbols, referred to the land. And this association of the people of God and the land continues in Judaism to the present day.

The Kerygma of the New Testament Period

The most prominent social feature of the Christian movement of the second phase, the period from the beginning of the Gentile mission to the establishing of the Catholic institution, is its transition from a Jewish to a Gentile constituency but with a religious content retaining much of the faith of Israel and of Judaism. The separation

---

23. For an account of the continuity of rabbinic Judaism and Old Testament religion, even on such themes as *halakah* and midrash, see Jacob Weingreen's essay, "Oral Torah and Written Records," in F. F. Bruce and E. G. Rupp, eds., *Holy Book and Holy Tradition* (Manchester: Manchester University Press, 1968).

24. Davies, *The Gospel and the Land*, pp. 108 ff.

from the synagogue, the successful Gentile mission, and the theological struggles which attended these occurrences, mark the transition to this Jewish-Gentile faith. This transition, and the subsequent existence of the ecclesial community as a universal community, is the setting of the kerygma as it is given expression in the literature of the second phase, the collection now called the New Testament. Insofar as a kerygma is recoverable from the first phase, from Jesus' own preaching itself, it appears to be an announcement of the impending reign of God, the signs of which are already present and the response to which should be repentance and belief-ful, joyful anticipation. Elements of the later universalism are present in Jesus' conflict with the established Jewish leadership, both the temple priesthood and the Pharasaic party. The issue of a universal redemption is posed by Jesus' association with "sinners and tax collectors," an association prohibited by the Pharasaic *halakah*. There does seem to be a real conflict between Jesus and the established religious leadership which is not simply read back from the Gentile mission, and the heart of that conflict is one of the main foundation stones of diaspora Judaism, the strategy of survival and social continuity through the oral Torah especially focused in *halakic* regulations. Jesus' preaching and teaching indicate that the oral (*halakic*) Torah does not describe life suitable to the reign of God nor is it the appropriate preparation for the kingdom.

However we reconstruct Jesus' actual preaching from the New Testament collection, the fact that faces us in the second phase is an accomplished universalization of the faith of Israel. In what way is this related to the kerygma?[25] We propose the following five items as a summary of the convictions taken for granted by the authors and compilers of the New Testament collection.

1. The kingdom announced in the preaching of Jesus of Nazareth has arrived, inaugurated by the life, death, and resurrection of Jesus. The end of all things, the return of Jesus, may be imminent (as the

---

25. I realize how historically simplistic and misleading it is to speak of *the* gospel as present in such a multiplicity of writings, geographical regions, and periods of time in what I have called the second phase. In the most specific sense Paul's "gospel" will not be identical with Mark's or the author of Hebrews. Yet it does seem legitimate to ask for whatever unity these writers do share. After all, it is clear that none of them is simply a Platonist, a Hellenistic Jew, or a loyal member of an Essene community. In some sense they are part of the Jesus movement in the second half of the first century. I am using *gospel* as the term for whatever unity we discover among them that expresses the distinctiveness of the new corporate existence, ecclesiality.

earlier period believed) or delayed. Whichever is the case, the eschaton is the culmination of the aeon of the kingdom which has already begun.

2. This kingdom is not simply an innovation which cancels the past but is a *fulfillment* of both specific prophesies found in texts and the entire historical aim and promise of Israel's faith and its role among the nations.

3. With the kingdom has come the community of the kingdom (the ecclesia), which is the instrument of the fulfillment and the true Israel. This community is a universal community in the sense that entrance into it sets no ethnic-national or cultural requirements or conditions. Specifically, this means that the nonuniversalizable aspects of the Torah, the *halakic* oral tradition of regulations for the Jewish diaspora community, are not a priori attendants of salvation.

4. Jesus of Nazareth is the one through whom God has inaugurated the kingdom. The ancient promises are, accordingly, fulfilled in him, hence he is the promised Messiah. As the one whose resurrection inaugurates the new aeon, he is the present lord of the new community.

5. Salvation means participation in the final, eschatological act of God free from his punishment and being in that state of forgiveness and the higher righteousness, ever ready for death or the Parousia. Participating in the community of the kingdom (thus believing in its cultic Lord and what God offers through him) is the only necessary condition for salvation.

As far as I can determine, no New Testament writer or apostolic father would reject any of the above five assertions, although they would not all express them in the same language.[26] Further, different writers expressed this gospel in different kinds of summary phrases (such as "Jesus is Lord") and different thematic emphases (justification by faith, light as opposed to darkness). We have here a kerygma which announces a new aeon of history, the arrived kingdom, brought about by the appearance of the Messiah, who founds and becomes the cultic lord of a salvific community which is the heir of the covenant community of Israel, through whom salvation is available from deserved punishment of God for sin and for eschatological fulfillment

---

26. It may be argued, however, that the author of the Fourth Gospel would have a very different (nontemporal) version of item five, the final eschatological act of God.

in the presence of God. We can see the close correlation of such a gospel with the new kind of social entity Christianity became, namely, a pan-ethnic group of local communities whose authority, memory, and tradition are the faith of Israel, certain elements of Judaism, and the apostolic kerygma about Jesus.

THE RETENTION AND MODIFICATION OF THE FAITH OF ISRAEL AND OF JUDAISM

The gospel or kerygma summarized above is by no means simply a shorthand form of all the things that early Christians and their leaders held in common. The focus of gospel is on what they shared as a preachment. In addition to that preachment, early Christianity appropriated from its Jewish past a theological substructure which the gospel presupposed.

Taken for granted throughout early Christian literature is what Paul Ricoeur calls the Adamic myth.[27] Adamic myth refers to that comprehensive account of the human problem and predicament characteristic of the faith of Israel. Its classical canonical expression is the Adam story of the early chapters of Genesis. The elements of the myth include monotheism, one God who is without qualification good, who is the source of the existence and the constitutive rightness and legitimacy of all creatures. Second, it sets forth the human problem in the notion of a primal and rebellious act of the first human pair from which sin has spread throughout all human times and places. Because of the constitutive goodness of created being, sin has a voluntary element and has the nature of distrustful rebellion. We have then in the Adamic myth, the world maker, the dependent but good creation, the sinful human being exiled from his or her proper place in the presence of God.

Also taken for granted by first-century Christians is the overarching *heilsgeschichtlich* framework of the faith of Israel.[28] Israel's recital of the stories of its past, its self-understanding of its own role, its theology of past and future all occur in this framework. One element in such a

---

27. Ricoeur, *Symbolism of Evil*, pp. 47–150 and 232–305.
28. Duméry identifies a number of features of Christianity as having their roots in Judaism. The fundamental feature is historical revelation or history as revelatory. From this he traces other elements: the concept of revelation itself, the historical self-consciousness of the Hebrew people, the humanism of Israelite religion, and the iconoclasm which replaced the religion of images. See *Phenomenology and Religion*, chap. 2.

view is the royal or kingly metaphor of God's relation to what is other than himself. This metaphor appears in a variety of themes in Israel's faith, but it is a foundation stone of salvation history, since salvation history is history as God is disposing it, bringing it to the end he himself wills. Thus *all* of history, even the fall of nations and civilizations, even the destruction of God's own temple and the exile of his own people, is due to God's activity. This continued to be the framework when the early church applied interpretive titles to Jesus of Nazareth (such as Messiah) and when it interpreted its own origin and existence in the scheme of promise and fulfillment.

When we ask what persisted from synagogal Judaism into early Christianity, we need to distinguish the many details which we discover by studying the use of sources by New Testament writers from the larger, more foundational elements. It is clear that the apocalyptic worldview formed in postexilic times had a powerful influence on early Christianity.[29] One author, John Gager, reflecting the tradition of Albert Schweitzer and Martin Werner, sees early Christianity as a millenarian movement with all the social characteristics of such a movement. Jesus' own preaching used apocalyptic categories (kingdom of God). The church applied apocalyptic terms to interpret the significance and event of Jesus (resurrection, Son of man). It used the *pesher* type of exegesis of the Qumran community to interpret the Scriptures. One writer, the author of Revelation, used the literary tradition of apocalyptic to propound a Christian theodicy in the situation of persecution.

A second major element taken from Judaism is the Scripture principle. Early Christianity's survival as a community required more than simply the cultic recital of the past sacred events. Modeling on the synagogal congregation, the Christian congregation read the "Scriptures" in their weekly meeting and appropriated various Jewish hermeneutic traditions to interpret them.

Two other features of synagogal Judaism functioned as models for the practices of early Christianity. Bornkamm argues that Paul's own missionary efforts in behalf of the church were only a continuation of missionary efforts he had engaged in as a Jew.[30] In addition to Jewish missions and their correlative universalism is the kind of social unit in

29. See Paul Hanson, *The Dawn of Apocalyptic* (Philadelphia: Fortress Press, 1975), for an excellent account of the origin of apocalyptic.
30. Bornkamm, *Paul*, p. 12.

which diaspora Judaism resided, namely, the synagogal congregation. Here we have a social unit where God's presence is located in the continuing activities of a relatively independent community of people. They can symbolically refer themselves to the past, to the land, to Jerusalem, to the temple, but the fact remains that God's Word is heard not in the sacrifices but in the study of the Torah. Here too is a model for the kind of unit which arose as the social bearer of early Christianity, the congregation.

More significant for the distinctiveness of the Jesus movement are the features of the faith of Israel and Judaism which are either absent altogether or strongly modified. The general cosmic and historical frameworks of the Adamic myth and salvation history with the royal metaphor of God's relation to history continue more or less unaltered. However, a new form of periodizing history attends the kerygma, a scheme which makes use of apocalyptic and which centers history in the appearance of the Messiah, expressed in such phrases as new covenant, new Israel, and new aeon.[31]

I have previously described the distinctive bearers of Israel's social persistence (the temple, the priesthood, and the sacrificial cultus) and their displacement in synagogal Judaism by the synagogue, the teachers, the written Torah with continuing oral commentary.[32] Not only are these features different modes of social persistence, they represent different understandings of the way God is present to his people. In the period of the origins of Christianity the temple cult had not disappeared though there was growing tension between the ever more powerful Pharasaic party and the priesthood. Although universalism of a sort characterized synagogal Judaism, it was a qualified universalism, for even Pharasaic (and later rabbinical) Judaism never

31. Technically speaking, apocalyptic represents a different way of relating God and the world from the preapocalyptic religion of Israel. Arising out of primarily theodicy problems, apocalyptic does not attribute all of history's happenings to the judging activity of God. Instead, history is a disputed territory with evil powers in temporary command. Rectification, therefore, does not occur in history but in the final judgment and resolution. One finds both prophetic and apocalyptic views in the literature of the New Testament and in some cases a synthesis of the two. The Lucan scheme that finally came to dominate Christian theology exemplifies such a synthesis. There, salvation history receives a center (the coming of the Messiah), history is periodized in a new way, and apocalyptic resolution is indefinitely postponed to the end. I shall elaborate this theme of periodization in the next chapter.

32. For a comprehensive account of the institutions of Judaism, see Sandmel, *Judaism and Christian Beginnings*, pp. 131 ff. He lists six institutions of Judaism after 50 B.C.E.: the temple, sanhedrin, the patriarch, the local courts, the academy, and the synagogue.

abandoned that mode of corporate memory in which the land of Israel, Jerusalem, and Zion are paramount.[33] The written Torah, the Scriptures, are in Judaism the deposit of revelation for the people on the land. The dispersed people who continue to study, interpret, and obey the written Torah are dispersed from the land, hence they retain the language and customs of the land and their future hope and telos includes a return to the land. The corporate space of Judaism is a space structured by alien land and home land, and the corporate time of Judaism is structured by a definite past period of revelation and sacred history in which the Torah was given to the covenant people on the land and a subsequent period which lives in perpetual application of that revelation.

The Jesus movement originated with many more affinities with the Pharasaic party than with the temple cult. Strikingly absent is the motif of the land in the Israelite sense of a definitive territory given to the elect people as a nationally defined entity.[34] The qualified universalism of synagogal Judaism had become, after the Gentile mission, an unqualified universalism. Thus, the trilogy of elements of Judaic social persistence (synagogue, teacher, Torah) are all modified. The presupposition of the replacement is a nonland, nonnation under-

33. See Martin Buber, *Israel and the World* (New York: Schocken Books, 1948), pp. 227 ff.

34. The Davies (*The Gospel and the Land*) and Brueggemann (*The Land*) studies of the land motif in the New Testament are not in total harmony with each other. Brueggemann argues against Davies that the New Testament and Old Testament are "dialectical" in their interactions. The case he would argue is against a total spiritualization and existentialization of the land theme in the New Testament. Thus he maintains that the New Testament theme of the kingdom and the new age refers to a new political-historical arrangement, not simply a spiritual state. And this inevitability includes land, thus a renewal of the promise of land to the landless. I have no quarrel with this. It does, however, disguise an equivocation and for this reason does not confront Davies head on. "Land" means different things in different frameworks. In a universal, phenomenological sense, place, space, or territory is a human necessity, closely bound up with stability, safety, economic resources, freedom, and so on. In this universal sense *land*lessness can be a comprehensive symbol of human poverty and oppression and *landedness* a symbol of salvation. "Land" can also be a symbol occurring within a particularistic framework of salvation history in which a specific territory is promised and given to an elect people, thereby becoming *the* place of revelation, *the* place of the history of salvation, and the place for the institutions of social duration, which then take on the status of necessary units of divine presence. It is this second sense which disappears from the symbolic universe of the authors of the New Testament. Brueggemann's exegesis and "dialectic" has to do with land in the first sense. By so universalizing it, he passes over the second sense and thus obscures the way in which the Christian movement with its message of the kingdom was a radical departure on the very issue of the land.

standing of the people of God. In the pre-Catholic second phase of the Christian movement, roughly the second half of the first century, we find in place of the synagogue, synagoguelike congregations. In place of masters of the Torah, we find missionary preachers who have charismatic authority plus leaders of local congregations. In place of Torah and Torah piety we find the Jesus kerygma and Jesus piety.

At the same time the Jesus movement follows Judaism in retaining the Scriptures, the Law and the Prophets, as authoritative. The Jesus movement seems at first to have used the Scriptures primarily as an apologetic resource in controversies with Judaism. Eventually, the Scriptures become a source for the institutionalization of the Jesus movement necessary to its survival. At this point Catholic Christianity becomes much more a synthesis of elements in Pharasaic Judaism and the temple cult. Sacrificial imagery plays an ever-greater role in interpreting the significance of Jesus' death and the believer's appropriation of this event. Furthermore, the delayed Apocalypse, though always a formal part of the Christian creed, becomes transformed into an ever-present dual destiny (heaven and hell) faced by each human individual, a destiny determined in this life and by the mediation of the benefits of the once-for-all sacrifice. The result was a new set of vehicles of duration, the church as a local temple, the priesthood, the rituals of sacramentally mediated salvation.

To summarize, elements of the faith of Israel (salvation history, the Adamic myth) provided the theological substructure of the new faith. The territorial-ethnic element present in both the faith of Israel and Judaism was eliminated. Features from Judaism were appropriated (apocalyptic, the Scripture principle, the sacrificial motif, the synagogal congregation), but they all underwent transformation, especially in the second and third centuries of Christian institutionalization. Such, in brief outline, is the event and community which is the matrix of the classical criteriology.

2

The Founding Axioms

The terms criterion and criteriology, like all terms, depend on contexts and frameworks for their meaning. In a rather general and neutral sense *criterion* is simply a standard to which self-conscious inquiry appeals in the making of true judgments. It would not do, however, to simply assign that meaning to the classical criteriology, for we cannot assume that the overall *genre* of the classical criteriology is that of an open *inquiry*. Because this is the case, there is at certain key points very little methodological consciousness and concern with method in the classical criteriology. This is not to say that theologians within the classical framework did not engage in controversies, make judgments, and engage in disputes. It is to say that what settled the disputes and grounded the judgments were not so much evidence-gathering inquiries as appeals to some entity, place, or person which was regarded as authoritative. For this reason *criterion* has a special significance in the classical criteriology. It means authority, not regions of or types of evidence. The framework of the classical criteriology is a framework of authority.[1]

Nor would it be historically accurate to say that the church first obtained clarity about its criteria (authorities) and then constructed the patristic incarnationalist-trinitarian theology. The classical criteriology and the classical Catholic theology evolved together, and neither can be considered complete without the other. This is because the church came to regard its own substantial doctrinal accomplishments themselves as criteria or authorities. The road from faith to under-

1. The thesis here is in harmony with Auguste Sabatier's interpretation of classical Christianity in *Religions of Authority and Religions of the Spirit*, trans. L. S. Houghton (New York: McClure, Phillips, 1904).

standing was not a road from something in dispute to cognition but from an already doctrinalized assertion to the rational grasp of its necessity. It is thus misleading to speak of a criterion or norm *for* the establishing of church doctrine since church doctrine itself is a criterion. In the classical criteriology, criterion and accomplished doctrinal formulation coincide. The story of the developing of the classical criteriology, therefore, is a story of the Christian movement undergoing institutionalization by assigning entities the status of definitive expressions of divine truth. These definitive entities are the new bipartite canon of Scripture, the patristic doctrinalization of the apostolic tradition, and the authoritative institution. To list these items is to start at the end, to focus on the outcome. The archaeological task is rather to explore the route from the religious background to these three loci of authority. What connects the religious background and the developed criteriology are a number of foundational presuppositions, axioms universally present in the church but rarely thematized and explicated. These foundational presuppositions fall into two major classes, those which attend the church's retention (from Israel, Judaism, and its own period of origins) of salvation history as a category of self-understanding, and those which attend what we shall call the principle of identity.

THE FIRST PRESUPPOSITION: SALVATION HISTORY AND ITS MIDDLE AXIOMS

Salvation History

Salvation history as a comprehensive interpretative framework is present in some way in the religion of Israel, Judaism, and Christianity.[2] Although apocalyptic may be seen as an alternative framework to

---

2. According to historians of the religion of Israel, the salvation historical framework is not merely an occasional motif. It is the overall unifying viewpoint in every major section of the Old Testament. This is Gunnar Östborn's conclusion in *Cult and Canon* (Uppsala: Lundequistska, 1950). In addition, see G. E. Wright, *The God Who Acts* (London: SCM Press, 1952), chaps. 2 and 3; Helmer Ringgren, *Israelite Religion* (Philadelphia: Fortress Press, 1966), chaps. 2–5; Y. Kaufmann, *The Religion of Israel from Its Beginnings to the Babylonian Exile* (Chicago: University of Chicago Press, 1960), pp. 61, 132–33, 266; Brevard S. Childs, *Myth and Reality in the Old Testament* (Naperville: A. R. Allenson, 1960), pp. 76 ff.; Gerhard von Rad, *Old Testament Theology*, trans. D. M. G. Stalker (New York: Harper & Brothers, 1962), vol. I, pp. 121–35; Walter Eichrodt, *Theology of the Old Testament*, trans. J. A. Baker (Philadelphia: Westminster Press, 1961), vol. I, pp. 490 ff.

salvation history because of its assignment of history to the control of evil powers, it is more a refinement and qualification of the salvation history view. The main elements of the salvation history framework are the people (nation), whose history is a sequence of significant past and future events, whose significance is a result of the activity of God. Salvation history interprets the past, present, and future of the people as a sequential story whose development and outcome is determined by God.

The third element of the salvation history scheme, the divine agent, is provided by the Adamic myth. God, the transcendent world maker, on whom the world itself depends, is the agent of the historical process. His righteous will establishes the desired telos of the people or peoples and his activity moves the people toward that telos. At this point there are variations in the literature of Israel and Christianity which amount to an ambivalence on the issue of determinism. Thus interpretations range from a thoroughgoing deterministic version of God's sovereign rule in which the catastrophes of history are wrought by his hand to an acknowledgment of contingencies for which God is not responsible and which includes God's own continuing modification of his plan.

The very essence of this third element is the royal or kingly metaphor of God's relation to the world which in the faith of Israel and Christianity is primarily expressed as a relation to history.[3] As the righteous and powerful world maker, God is the monarch or king over the realm he has made. This metaphor, taken from an ancient political pattern, is what is behind several specific conceptions of God's relation to the world in the faith of Israel and Christianity. First, as the world maker, God is the world governor. Creation, the sun, the moon, and the stars, the beasts on earth, and humankind are all his subjects. He is the source of the law of their being, and their proper response is to honor him as the one sovereign being deserves to be honored and to obey him when he commands. Like the better earthly monarchs, this monarch can have compassion on his subjects and exercise mercy. But the mercy is a mercy in the face of violations of his own kingly rule.

---

3. One philosopher-theologian whose very agenda is marked by the exposure of this royal metaphor as a metaphor and by an unambiguous repudiation of the metaphor is Nicolas Berdyaev. See *The Destiny of Man,* trans. N. Duddington (New York: Harper & Row, 1960), p. 27; and *Slavery and Freedom,* trans. R. M. French (New York: Charles Scribner's Sons, 1944), chap. 2.

The second element of the metaphor, or at least one which draws on the metaphor, flows out of the governing relationship. As the world king (or king of the people) God exercises governance, and this means he exercises a causality in the affairs of his people. In apocalyptic views this causality is greatly reduced and even postponed to a final cataclysmic interference which balances the scales and sets things right. In prophetic religion God exercises decisive interventions which are causally responsible for global historical events. In addition, his interventions can and do occur in detailed theophanies, miracles (such as healing), acts of inspiration, and punishments and rewards of individuals. The two themes, governance and interference, are interconnected. Governance requires activities of governance and thus some capacity to intervene: to punish, to correct, to offset.

Such is the salvation history framework. Its elements are corporate historical entities (not just individuals), their temporality teleologically interpreted, and the kingly deity who governs through causal interventions. This framework characterizes the Israelite and Jewish religion and continues as an immanent feature of early Christianity.[4]

The Middle Axioms Between Salvation History and the Classical Criteriology

Although the classical criteriology finds definitive expression in locations of divine authority which do presuppose salvation history, it does not found its authorities directly on salvation history. Mediating the two are certain middle axioms.[5] These middle axioms are not, like salvation history, characteristic features of the religion of Israel, but

4. Thus Hans von Campenhausen writes, "In essence, of course, a salvation-history pattern of thought was bound up with belief in Christ from the very first; for one of the presuppositions of such belief is that, under the guidance and dominion of the ancient God, a new and final salvation has been inaugurated, at once the end and the predicted consummation of the ages." *The Formation of the Christian Bible,* trans. J. A. Baker (Philadelphia: Fortress Press, 1972), p. 36.

5. The term *middle axiom* comes from John C. Bennett's *Christian Ethics and Social Policy* (New York: Charles Scribner's Sons, 1946), chap. 4. Needless to say, I am using the term somewhat differently. For Bennett middle axioms are somewhat like what philosophers are now calling warrants. They are translations of very general value units into guidelines specific enough to function in policy making and in decisions. I am using the term to call attention to a stratum of presupposition which mediates the founding stratum and the explicit criteria or authorities appealed to in self-conscious reflection or disputation.

they do occur in some form in Judaism. The focus here will be not on their Judaic but on their Christian form, with occasional observations concerning their counterparts in Judaism. Three middle axioms appear to be especially important as presuppositions of the classical criteriology: the periodization of history, the marking off of the era of revelation, and eschatological dualism.

The Periodization of History

It may be argued that salvation history itself is an implicit periodization of history. Even if this is the case, periodizing is an interpretative act which goes a step beyond salvation history.[6] We do find the roots of that act in the way the faith of Israel remembered, recorded, and transmitted its traditions. According to Sanders, the Torah story of Israel from creation through David was recited at annual Israelite festivals. Such recitals played a crucial role in the social persistence of the Jews after the destruction of the second temple and provided a legitimation of the laws as originating in the oracles of God himself. These recitals of the Torah story were made possible by the unification of Israelite faith in Jerusalem and the temple cult, and they reflected the Moses-David tradition of the south. This founded the later inclination to locate the origin of the laws in Moses the law giver.[7] This is a step toward periodization, since it establishes the divine origin of the Torah by locating it in an ancient, definitive time of divine activity.

Periodization occurs explicitly in apocalyptic literature's notion of world epochs and also in synagogal Judaism's notion of the period of revelation (the prophets) which is thus the period of sacred Scriptures. With the Jesus movement a self-consciously new periodization of history occurs. In the first period centered on the activity of Jesus and his followers, the movement follows the standard periodization of apocalyptic accompanied by the claim that the end-time has begun. In the second period (50–130 C.E.) expectation of an imminent Parousia is replaced by a new periodization, a two-aeon doctrine which seems to

6. The term *periodization* occurs in nineteenth-century idealist historiography. See F. C. Baur, *On the Writing of Church History*, trans. Peter C. Hodgson (New York: Oxford University Press, 1968), pp. 253 ff., 309; and also Peter C. Hodgson, *The Formation of Historical Theology* (New York: Harper & Row, 1966), p. 123. It is also used by Martin Hengel, *Judaism and Hellenism*, trans. John Bowden (Philadelphia: Fortress Press, 1974; reissued 1981 as one volume), vol. I, p. 189.
7. James A. Sanders, *Torah and Canon* (Philadelphia: Fortress Press, 1972); pp. 28–30.

be the work of Paul but which obtains schematization in the two works of Luke. The periods are two, the time of promise-preparation and the time of the church, the dividing line being the coming of the Messiah.[8]

Such is the beginning but not the end of Christian periodization. Judaism came to distinguish between the period of revelation with its literary deposit, the written Torah, and the subsequent period with its written expression, the oral Torah. Similarly, Catholic Christianity came to distinguish between the apostolic period and its literature (eventually to be regarded as canonical) and the patristic period of fathers and councils whose texts were the definitive commentary on the former.[9] The Alexandrian fathers, especially Origen, who spoke of Israel, the church, and the kingdom, and Augustine's *City of God*, offer the fullest, most explicit periodizations in the patristic period. Although at the level of detailed formulation Christian writers offered varying versions of the periods, the Pauline–Lucan scheme of old covenant, new covenant, eschaton, becomes pervasive and normative. The Christian movement thus amounted to a new way of periodizing history which became a foundation stone in the development of the Scripture principle and dogma principle as the definitive locations of divine authority.

Two concluding observations remain to be made. To the degree that the standard scheme is an apocalyptic one, the periods take on cosmic or world-historical significance. They are not simply periods in the history of the holy nation. Second, the periods are not secular but sacred entities, effects of God's own activity. Thus the royal metaphor of God's sovereign disposal of history is an important foundation of periodization.

The Fixing of the Time of Revelation

There is nothing in the nature of revelation as such which necessarily restricts it to specific periods of time. In fact, the opposite is closer to the truth. For if revelation is a disclosive activity of God, one would

---

8. For an exposition of this Lucan scheme, see Hans Conzelman, *The Theology of St. Luke*, trans. G. Buswell (London: Faber & Faber, 1960), see especially p. 150.

9. Thus Hugh of St. Victor speaks of three parts of the New Testament: the Gospel, the Apostles, the Fathers. See George H. Tavard, *Holy Writ or Holy Church: The Crisis of the Protestant Reformation* (London: Burns and Oates, 1959), p. 16.

expect that activity to be rooted in God's very nature and therefore characteristic of the ongoing relation between God and being. If revelation is a concomitant of God's redemptive activity, it has no independent or primary status in theology. If this is the case, revelation will occur as long as redemptive activity occurs. Revelation-redemption describes a constant relation between a loving and merciful God and a fragile and fallen world.

Contrariwise, the classical criteriology presupposes not only the periodization of revelation-redemption but the restriction of revelation to a past period. Revelation occurred in the past in connection with a definitive epoch. There is then a time of revelation that is normative for all times. This notion originated not in the Christian but in the diaspora Jewish community as a presupposition of the Scripture principle. Even though the Council of Jamnia is dated at the end of the first century, canonical thinking, the notion of sacred Scriptures, long preceded that period. If the collection of writings regarded as sacred and inspired is obtained by an act of limitation to a specific group, the prophets, there had to be a *last* prophet, an era of prophecy. Similarly, to draw a circle around the Christian collection viewed as revelation to a specific group, the apostles, there had to be a *last* apostle who ended the era of apostles, that is, the era of revelation.

The Christian version of this act of limitation differed from the Jewish version for the reason that it was bound up with the new periodizing of salvation history. In the Jewish version, at least the Pharasaic-rabbinic movement, *what* is definitely revealed is the Torah interpreted as the instructions for the life of the community. And God's complete Torah is disclosed to the prophets. For the Christian church Jesus himself is the central event-person of revelation and the establisher of the new, final epoch of revelation. Those who describe that person-event from within its temporal center and formulate it in a kerygma or preachment are the new prophets, namely, the apostles. They are, like the prophets, unique recipients of God's revealing word. When their period ends, revelation ends. Thus, the for-all-times valid and sufficient disclosure of God occurred in an identifiable and now completed period in the past. The church, like the synagogue, now lives in a different time, the time of applying and interpreting the past definitive revelation.

The Criteriological Function of Individualized
Eschatological Dualism

Those who describe Christianity in its earliest period as a millenarian movement are persuasive.[10] In this period Jewish apocalyptic offers the framework in which the significance of Jesus is understood. We have here a corporate, social outlook. Individuals are urged to be ready, to repent, but the expected event itself is cosmic and corporate. In spite of the community's transition from millenarian, end-expecting community to a stable, institutionalized community, the notion of the Parousia was never totally dropped. As an element in the apostolic symbol and most later creeds, end-expectation became a doctrine about the individual's destiny and the world's telos rather than about an imminent occurrence. But the making of the eschaton into an ever-possible yet remote event was not the only result of the church's handling of this apocalyptic heritage. The gospel had always been in some sense a gospel of salvation for the individual. What happened in early Christianity was the merger of the notion of individual salvation with the apocalyptic theme of the saved and the lost in the final judgment. The result is that the physical death of each individual is the event which fixes the individual's eternal destiny. Instead of an imminent Parousia presiding over the community and rendering it temporary and short-lived, death presides over the individual in the community and with it the perpetual possibility of an occurrence which seals the individual into hell or heaven (or, eventually, purgatory). This quasi-eschatology functions as an important middle axiom in one of the three loci of authority, the definitive institution, or the church catholic. For it functions in a crucial way in the maintenance of the criteriology and its definitive doctrinalizations.[11]

THE SECOND PRESUPPOSITION: THE PRINCIPLE OF IDENTITY

One of the striking features of the writings (Fathers, Councils, Reformers) of classical Catholicism and Protestantism is the acknowl-

10. John C. Gager, *Kingdom and Community: The Social World of Early Christianity* (Englewood Cliffs, N.J.: Prentice-Hall, 1975).
11. Hannah Arendt is one of the few philosopher-historians of Western culture who has thematized the enormous political import of the church's use of eschatological dualism. See *Between Past and Future* (New York: Viking Press, 1968), chap. 3, p. 5.

edgment of the divine status of the truths for which they are contending. Given the powerful persistence of the Adamic myth and its distinction between the world maker and the world, one would think that the term *divine* would be used for predicates applicable to God alone. Yet we hear of divine truths, the divine law, the holy church, the divine Jesus, the sacred Scriptures, and the sacred dogmas. This language may merely suggest that the faith of Israel and the religions it spawned are not deistic faiths but "religions of revelation." Yet its import is much stronger. Convinced by the royal metaphor that God accomplishes what he wills, and convinced that he has willed to reveal his law, his gospel with its saving truths, the church affirmed that what God himself knew as God he communicated to human beings. And if God knows infallibly and inerrantly, and communicates what he knows, then we have human beings receiving, obeying, and believing what has the status of infallibility and inerrancy. The subjective, personal counterpart to infallibility as a feature of a mediating entity is "certainty." So sounded the language of Catholics and Protestants when they spoke about the church, the Councils, the dogmas, the Scriptures, or the papacy. Our task is to push beneath this language to its founding presupposition and middle axioms. We shall call this founding presupposition the principle of identity. Briefly defined, it affirms an identity between what God wills to communicate and what is brought to language in the interpretative act of a human individual or community. Before breaking this definition down into its constituents, we shall briefly explore the origin of the principle.

The Origin of the Principle of Identity

In one sense the principle of identity is a general, history-of-religions phenomenon, the disposition of all religious faiths to regard their beliefs, myths, or practices as divinely originated and communicated. Yet there is a significant difference between mythical religions whose deities are immanent worldly powers and the religion of Israel and its successors. The primary and unifying feature of the former is mythological world maintenance through ritual activity. The myths have to do with world origin, the activities of immanent worldly powers.[12] Something quite different arises with Yahwism and the faith

12. Hinduism is a religious faith whose very essence involves the principle of iden-

of Israel. Here we have what Schleiermacher called a teleological religion and what G. F. Moore called a nomistic religion. As summarized in the previous chapter, its main notions are the existence of a personal and righteous world maker who covenants with a specific people as part of a world plan. Monarchlike, he discloses the law to be followed by that people and requires obedience to that law as their part of the covenant. Here we have the principle of identity. The deity wills a content to be understood and obeyed by the people loyal to him. Yet the general claim that the law is in fact Yahweh's willed law does not fully exemplify the principle of identity. In addition, the community must be able to locate where the divinely willed content is given, the available bearers of the message. Thus, in the history of Israelite faith are specific occasions in which the will of God is communicated: theophanies, dreams, visions, signs occurring to individual patriarchs, prophets, or kings.[13] The objective side of the principle of identity is God's disclosed will for the corporate life of his people. The agential side is the specific process of divine communication expressed later in the notions of "prophets" and "inspiration."

Postexilic Judaism extends and refines this principle by a very specific location of the *place* of identity, namely, the sacred Scriptures. The will of God for the people is not simply available in occasional theophanies to prophets. The prophet's primary significance is not a specific historical accomplishment for his or her time but the recording of a valid-for-all-time word, and there is an identity between what God wills the people to do (for all time) and what the prophet records. Hence, certain *writings* become the locus of identity.

Early Christianity continued the principle of identity although with some modifications and some new refinements. It never questioned the fact of identity as it was laid claim to in the narratives of the religion of Israel. Furthermore, it appropriated Judaism's location of identity in written deposits, the Law and the Prophets. Over and above this appropriation Christianity not only propounded a new, decisive location of identity, the Christ, and a new collection of

---

tity. Because it is an ontological identity between the true self of human being and reality (Brahman), this form of the principle is very different from the epistemological identity of a religion of revelation.

13. The prophets' formulation of the locations of identity appears to have its background in the hieratic presence of God in local sanctuaries, in sacred objects (the Ark), and definitively in Zion, the temple, and the temple culture.

"prophets," its emphasis on what is identical between divine intention and human interpretation shifts from Torah, the willed behavior and collective life of the people of God, to faith, eventually interpreted as revealed, doctrinal content.

The Concept of the Principle of Identity

Having considered a rather general definition of the principle of identity, we turn now to a more detailed analysis of its main elements. These elements come into view when we grasp the act of meaning directed toward the *bearer* of identity and which attributes to that bearer qualities of divinity such as inerrancy, infallibility, absolute truthfulness, and the like.[14] It would be more accurate to say that these qualities are attributed to the bearer's accomplishments: claims, sayings, commands. "Divine," then, are the claims of the scriptural passage, the magisterium, or the ecumenical council. Four elements are especially prominent in the principle of identity.

The first element is a certain relation between the two main actors involved: on the one side, God, and on the other side, the creaturely, human recipient or medium. The creaturely recipient's role in this relation is an ersatz presence of God himself. The recipient is not merely God's messenger or representative if that means that the representative has enough autonomy to block the message. Psychologically or sociologically speaking, this is obviously a possibility. But recall that we are looking at an *act of meaning* in which the bearer is an already accomplished identity.

The second element is likewise due to an act of meaning which has the character of a synthesizing of two things. The ingredients of this synthesizing act are more specific than simply God and a creaturely ersatz divine presence. On the one side is God, a personal being who wills a communication; on the other side is a variety of events and

14. The term *meaning-act* or *act-of-meaning* is used here somewhat specifically and technically. It does not refer to the utterly individual, privatistic, and subjective experiences of meaning according to which one person finds something meaningful and another does not. Instead, the term refers to a content (meaning) which a particular object or kind of object evokes and requires. Once something becomes manifest as itself, Mozart's *Requiem* for instance, it cannot be "meant" (grasped, intended, experienced) as simply anything the person desires it to be such as a sunset, a bicycle, or a galaxy. Granting the inevitability of all sorts of variations, interests, and subjective meanings we bring to the manifest item, its manifestness still sets before us a certain necessary content. And once it becomes manifest, the principle of identity likewise presents to us certain requirements if it comes into view at all.

relations comprising and surrounding a human being interpreting those events. These interpretations occur in language and in different genres of language: predictions of catastrophe, specific regulations for everyday life, cultic regulations, myths, legends, and sagas, narratives or stories about people or epochs, theological reflections, polemics. What are synthesized are God's willed or intended communication and the particular interpretation of the representative. Such a synthesis is not always directed merely toward the content of a human interpretation. Many are the claims made that such and such is God's very will and truth. My point is that when the principle of identity is operative, this double-sided act is part of it.

The third element accompanies the meaning or interpretative act which synthesizes God's willed communication with human interpretation. In this act the occurrence of the divine–human synthesis is explained, accounted for, as causally effected by God. The identity of content which the synthesizing act posits is effected by God. This is a step beyond the second feature insofar as the mere fact that A and B coincide does not mean necessarily that the coinciding is causally rooted in the activity of A. This is just what the third act of meaning does. Presupposing salvation history and the royal metaphor of God's relation to the world, it interprets the presence of divinely willed instruction or doctrine as effected by God. If we are talking about one specific bearer of identity, the sacred Scriptures, that which exemplifies and thematizes this third element is the doctrine of inspiration. Inspiration accounts for the coinciding of divine communication and human interpretation as grounded in divine causal efficacy.

To summarize, the principle of identity involves interpreting the creaturely entity as the ersatz presence of the divine, a synthesis of divine intention and human interpretation into one content, and the explanation of that content by divine causal efficacy. The result is an *identity* of content between what is divinely willed (revealed) and what is humanly asserted. The question is, identity in what sense?

The fourth element in this act of meaning addresses this question, and its nature is that of a predication. Predicated of the creaturely act or some aspect thereof is "divinity," something shared with God himself. Here the principle of identity can easily elude us. For its religious background remains the Adamic myth, a myth which forbids any ontological identification between the world maker and the world.

This suggests that the synthesized identity is a cognitive identity, a truth or reality known by God and, resulting from an act of communication, now known by human beings.

The element of transcendence in the Adamic myth, especially as it was doctrinalized in the *via negationis*, prompts a refinement. A cognitive identity shared by God and humanity does not require that God and human being grasp that content in the same cognitive mode. God knows things as God—timelessly, comprehensively, pan-relationally, essentially. Human beings know things through their finite mode of world participation and in postures pervaded by sin.[15]

The refinements which occur in the fourth element show that the principle of identity does not attribute divine qualities (eternality, omniscience, omnipresence) to either the bearer of identity or the creaturely forms of expression. Nor does it make divine the cognitive processes of human beings. The identity is a content presented to those processes initially willed, intended, known by God. Willed and known by God and grasped by human beings are the commandment to observe the sabbath, the doctrine that Jesus of Nazareth is the Logos made flesh, and the doings of the first parents. That an ancient religion came to observe the sabbath as a day of rest and worship is an empirical and historical fact. The principle of identity is present when that observance is identical with a command originating in divine intention. That the unknown author of the Fourth Gospel asserted that in Jesus the Logos was made flesh is a historical-exegetical assertion. The principle of identity is applied when that assertion takes on the predicate of truth initially known and then communicated by God. Such truths are "divine" not as predicates of God's very being but as contents of his actual knowledge.

This principle of identity with its four elements is the basis for attributing infallibility and inerrancy to what appears to be human and creaturely. Given the assignment of commands and truths to God's agency, the synthesis of divine and human contents, the objective quality of infallibility and the subjective quality of certainty are inescapable.

---

15. Thus the Reformed scholastic theologies were always careful to distinguish God's own mode of knowing the divine things of theology (*theologia archetypa*) and all creaturely modes, angelic and human (*theologia ectypa*). For instance, A. Polanus, *Syntagma Theologiae Christianae* (Hanover, 1615), book one, chaps. 3 and 4; and J. H. Alsted, *Praecognitorum Theologicorum* (1614), book one, chaps. 2–5.

The Middle Axioms of the Principle of Identity

Even as salvation history originates certain mediating principles which function in the classical criteriology, so does the principle of identity. Likewise, as the middle axioms of salvation history are specific translations of that overall scheme, so are those of the identity principle refinements, particularizations, and extensions. All three axioms function in the classical criteriology itself, and an analysis of the major themes of that criteriology (the Scripture principle, the teaching authority of the church) uncovers these axioms as presuppositions. The three prominent middle axioms which attend the principle of identity are the axiom of secondary representation, the axiom of leveling (the equal distribution of truth in the vehicle of communication), and the axiom of immutability.

The Axiom of Secondary Representation

The notion of a *secondary* representation depends on the element of representation constitutive of the principle of identity. We recall that the principle of identity involves two main actors, God and some recipient of his disclosed will, a bearer of his communication which becomes his *ersatz* presence, *the* place where his word and will are to be found. Insofar as this initial recipient is simply a charismatic individual—a prophet, for instance—we have sufficient conditions for a claimed identity between what God wills to be understood and performed and what the prophet understands and says, but we do not have sufficient conditions for the *perpetuation* of that identity. We have a vehicle of reception but not one of generation-bridging duration. Involved here may be a history-of-religions principle that in order to survive the originating, individualistic, and charismatic phase of a religious faith must transmute itself into a socially stable, enduring entity.[16] However that may be, we find in fact such transitions in the religion of Israel, Judaism, and Christianity, and these transitions from an original representative of God (Moses, Jeremiah, Jesus) to

16. See Adolf Harnack, *The Origin of the New Testament* (New York: Macmillan Company, 1925), "The Needs and Motive Forces that Led to the Creation of the New Testament," question 4. See also S. G. F. Brandon, "Holy Book, Holy Tradition, and Ikon," in F. F. Bruce and G. Rupp, eds., *Holy Book and Holy Tradition* (Manchester: University of Manchester Press, 1968), pp. 1–19. Brandon argues that the first step in the developing of the authoritative book is the embodiment of an authoritative tradition in some revered or respected person (p. 3).

subsequent *secondary* representatives or vehicles, manifest this first middle axiom.

The initial and most basic extension to a secondary representative occurs in the transition from a living, charismatic, authoritative figure to its persistence or revival in ongoing tradition. A second extension of representation occurs in the transition from oral tradition and its characteristic mode of duration (in cultic recital, in memorization) to written deposit. A third extension of representation occurs in the transition from written deposit to a definitive commentary on or interpretation of that deposit. A fourth extension, which can also take place concomitantly with other extensions, occurs in the emergence of an institution whose role is to maintain, protect, and purify the tradition and its ongoing interpretation. In all of these transitions, the original locus of identity between divinely willed content and human recipient is extended to entities (institutions, writings, oral traditions) that represent the original *ersatz* divine representative and thus have a secondary status.

The secondary representative does have features all its own. First, it is secondary only in the sense that it is not the chronologically original locus of identity. In actual authority it tends to replace the original locus and presides over the original locus in a definitive way. Therefore, when Fathers and Councils finally conceptualized logos Christology in a trinitarian framework, the written expressions thereof came to be more definitive for true doctrine than Scripture itself even though Scripture was formally acknowledged as the prime authority. The reason for this becomes clear only when we consider the second middle axiom, the axiom of leveling. Second, that which is extended into the secondary representative is the identity occurring in the original representative. As the series of substituted representatives develops, identity between what God intends and what is humanly claimed is not left behind. Each new representative is also a new locus of such identity. Thus, what God wills the community to be, do, or believe is not only present in the vehicle of reception but in the vehicle of duration; not only in Jesus but in the Gospel of John; not only in the Gospel of John but in the church's official christological definitions which interpret the Gospel of John.

Third, the secondary representative is a generation-bridging vehicle of the community's social persistence. This means that there is some accessibility to it on the part of the total religious community.

The charismatic prophet's original theophanous visions are accessible only as the prophet communicates them to his or her contemporaries. But they are inaccessible to future generations unless they obtain some form of social persistence. In other words the prophet's communication must be incorporated into cultic recital or holy writings for it to endure in the community. Accomplishing this incorporation is the function of the secondary representative. Its function, in other words, is to provide social perpetuity. That perpetuity is the result of traditionalization and institutionalization in which the divine–human content is given a generation-bridging form.

What has been under discussion is the transition from an originating revelatory event and time to ongoing tradition. This transition indicates a close relation between this extension of identity to a secondary representative and periodization. In some cases periodization is simply the symbolic sanction of this extension; thus Prophets, Apostles, and Fathers not only are comprehensive symbols for authoritative periods but express the extension of identity into secondary representatives. The dominant tone of this analysis has been sociological, hence the focus on vehicles of social persistence which maintain and give continuing access to the original revelation. Yet sociological categories do not sufficiently grasp the dynamics of this axiom. In a neutral and sociological sense these secondary representatives are vehicles of duration: in the community's faith experience they are places where God's actual will becomes visible. Thus, to believe and obey the secondary representative is to believe and obey God himself.

What propels the community to give a secondary representative divine status? The answer is the salvation history framework. Salvation history sets in motion an inexorable teleological logic of fulfillment. If God wills his Torah and Gospel not only for the generations of Moses and the Christ but for all subsequent generations, an ongoing line of representatives is required to perpetuate that end, and in each one of these representatives the identity of his intended communication and what is heard must continue. Thus, the principle of identity and its middle axioms of secondary representation are rooted in this first major principle, salvation history.

The Axiom of Leveling

The first middle axiom concerned the extension of identity to a secondary representative functioning as a vehicle of social persistence.

This extension thus has an intrinsic chronological element. The believer interprets the chronologically succeeding entity as a locus of divine–human identity. The second middle axiom also has the characteristic of extending the identity, but in this case the scene of the operation occurs within the vehicle itself. The second axiom presupposes the first axiom, the extension of divine–human identity to a secondary representative. We note now that this representative as a generation-bridging vehicle has a different function from the original recipient of the word. That function is to preserve and maintain the word, to be a place of deposit of that word whatever the fate of the original recipient and whatever the historical situation. This means that the secondary representative, the generation-bridging deposit, must be comprehensively valid and significant. Thus the focus of the community shifts from the content of the original identity to the vehicle itself. In this shift the original historical situation of the divine communication is lost or at least is incorporated in a distancing act as an aspect of the vehicle.

The result of this shift is that something different becomes the bearer of identity. Two elements in the shift are responsible for this. First, in the original historical situation, the message from God was specifically addressed to the people in their situation. Hence, it was clear that the identity resided in the prophecy itself, or the law, or the good news. The unit and content of the identity was not the recipient itself or the recipient's specific language. But once a new situation replaces the original one and the focus is shifted from the *message and its validity* to the *vehicle and its validity,* the grounds for distinguishing between the content as divine and the vehicle as divine are removed.

The second element accompanies the shift of focus to the vehicle itself and results from the requirement that the vehicle function validly in a variety of continuing historical situations. To function in this way the vehicle must be comprehensively and not just provincially trustworthy and valid. At this point a new extension occurs, not chronologically to a secondary representative, but interiorly in the vehicle itself. The identity of the divine will and creaturely interpretation is extended to the detailed parts of the vehicle. If the vehicle is a written work, the tendency is to attribute divinity, the identity, to the words, even syllables and vowel points. If it is a doctrinal settlement, divinity is attributed to the propositions which comprise it. The result of this shift of focus and new extension is a new synthesis of the two

43

elements identified, namely, the divine intention (willed, known content) and the content of the vehicle as a whole and in its details. The effect of this new synthesis is that contents of the vehicle are regarded as equally divine. The divine instruction or truth is *equally* distributed throughout the vehicle, thus all parts of the vehicle (the Scripture, the creed, the encyclical) are given the same status.[17] The logic which drives this extension of identity to the parts of the vehicle is simply that the vehicle will not be qualified as a location of divine communication if some parts are relative and errant.

It goes without saying that the leveling out of the contents of a vehicle dehistoricizes the vehicle. Thus, once this axiom develops, a religious faith is much more vulnerable to historical modes of thought, which unavoidably place a historical bearer of social persistence back into its historical context including its interior parts.

The Axiom of Immutability

The immutability of the content of revelation is a highly visible, even argued, element in the classical criteriology, even in those later versions of it which acknowledged the development of dogma in the face of factually evident doctrinal changes over the centuries. According to some interpretations, the motif of immutability is a Hellenistic contribution to early Christianity and represents a mode of thinking about revelation foreign to Semitic (Israelite and Judaic) religion. Contrariwise, it appears that the middle axiom of immutability originates as the offspring of the other middle axioms of the principle of identity, and its original historical matrix is the religion of Israel and Judaism. At best, Hellenistic modes of thought offered a new conceptual apparatus in which this was expressed.

Why does immutability attend the other middle axioms of identity? Immutability does not seem to be a priori to the principle of identity as such. According to the principle of identity, there can be a coincidence of content between what God wills or knows and what

---

17. I repeat that I am setting forth a presupposition on which the classical criteriology is built. It is clearly not a principle which the religious person can consistently apply and abide by. Hence, there are many exceptions and qualifications to the principle in both the theologies and pieties of the religious community that are unavoidably selective in their use of their authoritative vehicles of tradition. I shall pursue these qualifications in more detail in the next two chapters.

creatures do and understand. But there is nothing about such an identity which prevents it from being occasional or provisional. God may command one thing for one period, and, as the situation changes, something else for another. The impetus toward the axiom of immutability comes from the axioms of secondary representation and leveling. For these axioms reflect the problem not just of identity between divine and humanly received content but the problem of preserving what is given. They express concern that the given revelation be ever present and accessible to the religious community. Thus we have extensions of the identity into subsequent secondary vehicles which carry the revelation and into their detailed parts. This added concern takes identity beyond provinciality to universal applicability. What was given as true to the charismatic prophet is in fact universally valid for future generations. The original Hebraic version of this was centered in Torah. Not only is there identity between what God intends and wills as the Torah and the Law of Moses, it is an identity given for all times. Its content is an unchanging set of requirements. In fact historical situations do change and this gives tradition the character of a continual application of the ever-valid, unchanging Torah to new times and places, an application which in turn called forth ever more ingenious hermeneutical crafts. But persisting through those times is the immutable content and its axiom. Early Christianity continued the axiom but in the form of its own content of gospel, apostolic faith, and apostolic doctrine.[18]

The axiom of immutability attends the axiom of leveling and goes beyond it. The vehicle in which divine communication is deposited is not just a provisional bearer of valid divine truths; it is an *immutably* valid bearer for the total future preeschatological time of the church. The axiom of immutability is thus the following: *the bearers which give social persistence to the divinely communicated content* are, in their *detailed parts, valid and true for all time*. The immutability refers both to the bearers (vehicles) themselves, such as Scripture and conciliar creed as

18. R. L. Wilken's *The Myth of Christian Beginnings* (Garden City, N.Y.: Doubleday and Co., 1971) presents extensive documentation for the axiom of immutability as an intrinsic feature of Catholic and Reformation forms of Christianity. Wilken describes the church as idealizing and unifying its own beginnings as a period of pure and revealed truth, a period in which occurred the unchanging deposit of truth agreed upon by all Christians. His thesis is simply that there never has been such a period or phenomenon.

divinely given means of the community's persistence, and to their contents as unchanging laws or truths for the guidance of the community.

The three middle axioms of the principle of identity are not always visible in self-conscius, precise formulation in the classical criteriology. Yet they have come to expression in a motif familiar to both Protestant and Catholic theologies, the motif of inerrancy. Inerrancy is a way of conceptualizing the adequacy of the units of authority, their qualification to fulfill the function described in the three middle axioms. It is a predicate of the bearers or location of divine–human identity, and resident within it are the notions of secondary representation, leveling, and immutability. A phenomenology or eidetics of inerrancy in its historical setting within the house of authority would yield these middle axioms.

Such are the founding presuppositions of the classical criteriology. Their origin is primarily the religion of Israel and Judaism and the logic of sovereignty generated by the conviction that a kingly deity rules history and that the church is an outcome of that rule. I have set these presuppositions out in two major strata. The most foundational level comes from the general conviction that the God-king controls history and has disclosed the contents of his will to human creatures (salvation history and the principle of identity). The second stratum is composed of specific axioms which connect the general convictions and the bearers and locations of identity which occur in the Christian church. These locations of identity themselves comprise a third and much more visible stratum to be uncovered by this archaeology in the following two chapters.

3

The Locations of Identity:
Sacred Scripture

Continuing this upside-down archaeology which begins at the bottom levels and moves upward, we come now to a third stratum, a level which Christian theology has traditionally viewed as the foundations, the unquestionable *principia* of theological method and knowledge.[1] The preceding chapters have uncovered the fundamental presuppositions, salvation history and the principle of identity, on which this third stratum rests and it draws acts of meaning and interpretation which were described as the middle axioms between salvation history and identity and the third stratum. The first-level presuppositions have an impetus, a teleology, of their own. This teleology is generated both by the religious community testifying to its God and reciting the story of God's activities with his people and by developing ways of social persistence, passing on the recital to future generations. Thus from the time of Israel to the present, the inheritors of Israel's faith have persisted in forms of institutionalization in which tradition was preserved. The direction set by this teleology is from the salvific experience to its recording and preservation in enduring vehicles. The divinely given message finds its way into visible, enduring entities. Giving visibility, access, and temporal duration is the function of

---

1. *Principia* (principles) is the language of sixteenth- and seventeenth-century school theology of Protestantism. The term, a Latin translation of Aristotle's *archai*, refers to self-manifest or self-evident truths or realities with which demonstration begins. This implies that the *principia* themselves are undemonstrable, for instance, the law of noncontradiction. But the Protestant school theologians, especially on the reformed side, did make attempts to demonstrate that Scripture was divinely given. Whether one uses this language or not, or follows the school theologians in their Aristotelian approach to the grounding of theology, there still seems to be a stratum of classical theology, Catholic and Protestant, which serves as the place or location of divine truths. It is this which is now under consideration.

secondary representation. But when we move to the third level, we move beyond the mediating axioms to their fulfillment in actualized locations of God's unchanging truth and law. We have, in other words, sacred writings, official conciliar declarations, and an official institution of teaching and interpretation. These actual bearers of divine revelation occur in the life of the church not just as presuppositions but as actual, visible, and specific realities. They occur in the self-conscious thought and the depth piety of the religious community, functioning in its worship, political controversies, and the theological disputes. The church self-consciously appeals to these entities in their status as bearers of the original divinely revealed content. In other words, they are the church's authorities, the criteria of its polity, theology, and religious life.

According to our archaeological inquiry, the background of the specific locations of identity is the religion of Israel and postexilic Judaism. The very nature of Israel's tradition and traditioning, its distinctive corporate memory, propelled the move to secondary representatives of revelation, the extension of identity to generation-bridging locations. In the oral tradition stage, new epochs with their authoritative figures were added to old. Thus the prophetic faith reinterpreted the exodus tradition.[2] A qualitatively different extension occurs with the writing down of tradition. With this step revelation obtains a new kind of location, sacred writings. Furthermore, once tradition is centered in writings, as occurred in postexilic Judaism, a process of application and reapplication is begun, giving rise to commentary on the written Torah. Thus in commentary a new post-Torah location of identity between God's will and human interpretation occurs.[3] In other words, Israel and Judaism offer the Christian movement not only founding presuppositions of salvation history and the principle of identity but also specific locations of the identity of divine intention and human interpretation. The central

2. This cumulative process of interpretation building on and altering previous interpretation is well described in James A. Sanders, *Torah and Canon* (Philadelphia: Fortress Press, 1972); in James Barr, *Old and New in Interpretation* (London: SCM Press, 1966), chap. 1. See also Brevard S. Childs, *Memory and Tradition in Israel* (Naperville: A. R. Allenson, 1962), especially chap. 6; and Peter R. Ackroyd, *Continuity: A Contribution to the Study of the Old Testament Religious Tradition* (Oxford: Oxford University Press, 1962).

3. G. G. Scholem argues for the a priori necessity of this post-Torah commentary once revelation has obtained written form. See "Tradition and Community" in Jacob Neusner, ed., *Understanding Jewish Theology: Classical Issues and Modern Perspectives* (New York: KTAV, 1973).

and most visible location is sacred Scripture. A second location is the previously mentioned commentary on Scripture. Thus in Judaism the *heilsgeschichtlich* logic impels it to identify the content of the prophets' message with God's message. Then the written record of the prophet's message (a vehicle of social persistence), is so identified. The same logic assigns the same status to the *halakah* arising out of the interpretation of the writings. Manifest here are all the middle axioms of the principle of identity: identity extended to secondary representatives, identity extended to the interior details and parts of the vehicle, and the immutable validity and permanence of the divine content.

This logic continues to function in the Christian spheres of divine–human identity. The places where God's will and truth are manifest and the presuppositions of the logic (salvation history and the identity principle) were never questioned by the Jesus movement. But it did foster a new primary locus of identity, Jesus himself as the very presence of God. We shall not attempt a historical account of the emergence of the locations of authority in early Christianity. Suffice it to say that three major locations of identity developed in the early centuries of the Christian movement with the later locations being secondary representatives of the earlier ones. First, the identity of God's word and Jesus' word obtains an oral, then written testimony in his followers. Thus it can be claimed that the conclusion to holy Scripture, the new covenant, has occurred and been recorded. In the internal struggle of the church with the religious eclecticism introduced by gnostic types of interpretation, the church develops a definitive doctrinalization of the "apostolic" testimony recorded in the New Testament, and this too takes on the status of God's own communicated truth. Third, developing simultaneously with the other two, a definitive institution arises as the perennial guardian and interpreter of prophets and apostles (Scripture), and of Fathers and Councils (the orthodox dogma), namely, the episcopal, papal, and magisterial church. All three locations of identity have counterparts in synagogal Judaism. Further, all three continue in some sense in Reformation and post-Reformation forms of Christianity, even the notion of a definitive, divinely willed ecclesiastical institution. While the interconfessional controversies disclose major differences of interpretation of the nature, primacy, and interrelation of the three locations, all the major branches of Christendom retain these ways of understanding divine presence. Our task is to describe these three locations of divine–human identity, that is, the three entities of authority which ground the theological judgments in the classical criteriology. The present chapter on the Scripture principles attempts two inquiries: the origin of the Scripture principle in postexilic Judaism, and the appropriation and modification of the Scripture principle by the early Christian movement.

We attempt now a rather comprehensive description of the Scripture principle which includes the following: (1) a depiction of the origin of and need for a "sacred scriptures" on the part of a specific religious community and its social–historical conditions. We are less concerned here with the literary history of a developing canon than with the motivations of a religious faith toward having a "scripture"; (2) a setting forth of that about the particular religious faith which is correlative to having a "sacred scriptures," the main themes or symbols which form the family of symbols that defines scripture for that faith; (3) a more focused analysis of what the religious community *means* by sacred scripture. This would include both the genre which unifies the notion (Torah, testimony, wisdom, narrative) and the essential attributes (inspired origin, inerrancy, closed collection); (4) a description of the *function* of scripture in its setting in the religious community. This will include the community's use of its scriptures and the rules which preside over its use. It also includes the community's second-order attempt to legitimate its scripture in such mythological or theological interpretations as the Torah myth of Judaism or the apostles myth of Christianity. Needless to say, I shall not attempt to cover all four elements in this chapter. However, the preceding descriptions of Israel and early Christianity and their general principles are pertinent to this comprehensive account of the Scripture principle. The following exploration concentrates on the first three features and pays little attention to the fourth theme, the hermeneutic dimension. The heart of the exploration occurs in the third step, having to do with what constitutes scripture for a religious community.[4]

---

4. I am distinguishing here the descriptive analysis of the Scripture principle, Scripture as it is meant and functions in the religious community, and the theological problem of the use of Scripture in the complex process of making theological judgments. It is the latter which has been the focus of some excellent recent studies, for example, David H. Kelsey's *The Uses of Scripture in Recent Theology* (Philadelphia: Fortress Press, 1975).

THE JUDAIC ORIGINS OF THE SCRIPTURE PRINCIPLE

From a history-of-religions point of view it appears that many religious faiths have sacred scriptures and therefore have embraced the Scripture principle. In a general sense the Vedas, the Pali canon, and the Confucian classics are all scriptures. For in that general sense "scripture" refers to a collection of writings which is in some way normative or authoritative and which functions as a vehicle of social persistence of a religious community. There is usually a close correlation between the *function* of those writings as a bearer of social persistence and the *kind* of persistence (social time) marking that community. Since each religion means or interprets its writings within its own universe of symbols, it is misleading to say that all religions with special writings share the Scripture principle. My thesis is that the Scripture principle is shared by religions that have some dependency on synagogal Judaism (Islam, Christianity, Mormonism) and that it is Judaism which is the real origin of that principle.

Furthermore, since the Scripture principle in its fullest sense is a correlate of canon and the canonizing process, we should distinguish between the periods of a religious faith when it has authoritative writings and when such become canon. Accordingly, I shall distinguish between the prehistory of the Scripture principle (canonical Scriptures) and the history of the making of the canon. I shall not pursue either in any great detail since the purpose of this chapter is to understand what finally Judaism and Christianity meant by "Scripture" and how they came to see it as such. The emphasis is therefore on the essential meaning and function of Scripture in these communities.

The Prehistory of the Scripture Principle in Israelite Religion

A major thesis of this chapter is that *canonical* Scriptures originated in synagogal Judaism not in Israelite religion. The major Jewish sects or parties in the first century c.e., the Qumran community, Hellenistic Judaism of Alexandria, and Pharasaic Judaism, pluralistic though they are in hermeneutical principles, all shared certain convictions about the Scriptures.[5] Longenecker argues that all the major parties

5. For a summary of the hermeneutic principles and exegetical methods of the major

presuppose a collection of inspired writings, the Scriptures, whose words originate in God, that such Scriptures contain the entire truth needed to guide the community, that there are levels of plain meanings and deeper, hidden meanings, and that the task of interpretation is to apply these truths to the present.[6] Yet in pre-Ezra times, we find a written literature functioning in the cultus and regarded in some sense as authoritative. But we do not find the views of the later Jewish community guiding that function. To put it in straightforward terms, what came to be normative Judaism was a religion of the book and Israelite religion was not such a religion.

Yet there was much about the religion of Israel that anticipated the Scripture principle and that created its required presuppositions. Religiously speaking, both salvation history and the principle of identity are present in the religion of Israel. Constitutive of the faith of Israel was the conviction that God the world maker was the world governor. His activity called forth Israel's very existence, and his act of giving Israel the Law set the terms for its covenantal obedience and the measure of its disobedience. Convinced that its history was a story of God's activities, Israel remembered and recorded not only the Law but the narrative which indicated the divine origin of the Law. That story, the Torah story, was recited in the cultus, and in pre-Ezra times the Pentateuch functioned as an authoritative record of Israel's history.[7] The very existence of a collection like the Pentateuch, an accumulation and synthesizing of a plurality of traditions, shows Israel constantly reinterpreting and recording the Torah story under an ever-more unified *heilsgeschichtlich* view. This literature had more than just a ceremonial function in the cultus because it exercised control over the narrative recitals which occurred there. Thus in monarchical times major elements of the religion of Israel contribute toward but do not obtain a sacred Scripture. These elements include

---

Jewish sects of the period, see Richard Longenecker, *Biblical Exegesis in the Apostolic Period* (Grand Rapids: Wm. B. Eerdmans Publishing Co., 1975), chap. 1; and the longer study of Daniel Patte, *Early Jewish Hermeneutic in Palestine* (Missoula: Scholars Press, 1975).

6. Longenecker, *Biblical Exegesis*, pp. 48–50.

7. Thus Israel's seasonal festivals were times of celebration of past events. For this motif of the recital of the Torah story, see Childs, *Memory and Tradition in Israel*, chap. 6; Walter Harrelson, *From Fertility Cult to Worship* (Garden City, N.Y.: Doubleday and Co., 1969), chap. 6; and Gunnar Östborn, *Cult and Canon* (Uppsala: Lundequistska, 1950), chap. 5.

Israel's self-understanding as a covenantal and national people located on a territory given to them by Yahweh and governed by Yahweh through his revealed Torah.

A second decisive element in the prehistory of the Scripture principle is provided by the prophetic movement. First, there arises the figure and therefore the concept of the prophet of Yahweh, the messenger who utters Yahweh's word to the people. Here we have a significantly new interpretation of Yahweh's presence, an ersatz presence which occurs outside the temple and sacrificial cult to a charismatic and morally insightful individual. Further, the message of the prophetic movement made explicit what is always implicit in a salvation history view, namely, a periodization of history.[8] Technically speaking, there may not be a prophetic eschatology. Yet the prophets tried to awaken Israel's conscience by appealing to its covenantal obligation to God and God's past acts on its behalf. They interpreted Israel's present corruption and interpreted impending world-political events as signs of God's future activity. Ambivalently, they proclaimed future judgment and future hope for Israel. Such modes of thought do not obtain the clear periodizations of world history found in apocalyptic or in self-conscious canonizing activities, but they do suggest past and future periods of Israel's history correlated with Israel's obedience.

A third element in the prehistory of the Scripture principle provides the background for the axiom of immutability and its closely related motif of universalizability. When the divine communication is viewed as addressed not simply to the generation of the original theophany but to subsequent generations, its status is not provisional and provincial but enduring and universal. Whenever a set of writings is claimed to be applicable to subsequent times and varying places, universalism has replaced the provincialist view of revelation. Thus the universalist aspect of the religion of Israel is an indispensable foundation for the Judaic Scripture principle. Of universal import is the Adamic myth with its monotheism and its vision of corruption and exile of the human race. Torah itself, even in the narrower sense of a righteousness-defining Law, sets requirements on human beings as

---

8. Jürgen Moltmann, *The Theology of Hope*, trans. J. W. Leitch (New York: Harper & Row, 1967), chap. 2, p. 6.

such. Thus, if the religion of Israel had been totally and consistently nationalist and ethnic, it could never have claimed for its tradition and its literature revelation which is abidingly valid even when the nation and its institutions collapse.

These elements in the prehistory do not altogether amount to a Scripture principle. The crisis of Israel's very existence in the exile and the rise of a new mode of social perpetuity was the specific occasion for that. But the religion of Israel provided many key elements. It had originated a literature—History, Wisdom, and Prophets—which, if not actually used in the oral recitals of the cultus, helped control those recitals. It provided Judaism with notions necessary to viewing that literature as Scripture, the notion that God himself rules the nation of Israel and is active in a revelatory way in its history. The Torah of Israel originates in God, not human beings. Further, the notion of the charismatic prophet was later to become one of the criteria for settling what was and was not Scripture, and the minimal kind of periodizing of history found in the prophetic movement provided Judaism with a way of thinking about revelation as itself having a period which can come to an end. Finally, the universal applicability of revelation and Torah helps a later generation, removed from its provincial setting and its institutions of duration, to find nonprovincial and enduring validity in a collection of past writings.

The Occasion and Motivation of the Judaic Origin of Sacred Scripture

Sanders has argued persuasively that the crises in Israel's history were the occasions of new solidifications of its tradition and of various stages of the rewriting of tradition.[9] The Scripture principle originated as a solution to the major crisis in Israel's history, that series of events which modified Israel's institutions of social persistence and separated a portion of its population from those institutions. The result was what Max Weber called a pariah people.[10] Once the tribal amphictyony was unified into northern and southern monarchies, the

---

9. Sanders, *Torah and Canon*, pp. 7–9, 29–30, 48.

10. Max Weber, *Ancient Judaism* (New York: Free Press, 1952), chaps. 13–14. Actually, Weber sees some anticipations of the ritualistic segregation and exclusiveness of a pariah community in Israelite prophecy and priestly ritualism prior to the exile (p. 336).

entity that persisted was a territorially bounded people. When this is the case, the institutions and elements of social persistence function to maintain just that entity: central governorship (kings), military power and its symbolic legitimation, the synthesis of disparate past traditions into a common tradition and common symbolism, centralized cultus. Israel is not an ordinary nation but a religious-political entity. The territory is unified not just by a governing center, the seat of the king, but by a cultic center, Jerusalem, which is the location of the temple, the priestly leadership, and even the divine presence. Mythological versions saw Jerusalem as the very center of the world itself.[11] In the temple cult with its priests, seasonal festivals, and sacrificial rituals, the traditions endured through the recitals of Israel's history of salvation. Thus, even when written interpretations of salvation history were produced, they did not function as a decisive element in Israel's social persistence.

With the destruction of the first temple and the exportation of a portion of the population and its leadership to Babylonia begins the situation in which Jews have lived until the twentieth-century creation of the state of Israel. That situation involves both life in Palestine under a succession of foreign rulers and life beyond Palestine as a minority religious-ethnic community. In both cases the monarchy is lost and with it autonomy over the land and its inhabitants. Lost are the traditional modes of survival and perpetuity and in their place comes the threat of cultural and religious assimilation into the foreign cultures which dominate their land or in which they are living. The very existence of Israel was therefore at stake and a new mode of social persistence was required. Such a mode did occur. It was long in coming and the end result was Judaism. An account of the origins of Judaism is not in order here, and yet the major elements of the birth of Judaism are the matrix of the Scripture principle and call for a brief summary. More specifically, we are concerned with the transition to the new institutions which constitute synagogal Judaism in the first century C.E. and which finally overcome Jewish pluralism in the victorious rabbinical movement of the second half of the second century C.E.

Expressed succinctly, the diaspora Jews, lacking the land, the

11. W. D. Davies, *The Gospel and the Land: Early Christianity and Jewish Territorial Doctrine* (Berkeley: University of California Press, 1974), p. 7.

temple, and the priesthood as institutions of social duration, created a new institution of social persistence, the synagogue.[12] The synagogue was the solution to the problem of how the Jewish people could remember Zion in the absence of the traditional institutions of memory. Yet this symbolic language does not fully capture the problem. More elaborately, how could the Jewish people, removed from the territorial environment and thus from the institutions which ensured the keeping of the ceremonial laws, survive in an environment (such as Babylonia, Egypt, Asia Minor) where other religions, cultures (Hellenic), and laws are the cultural majority and norm? The first generation may successfully remember Zion and remain Jews. But it is well known that subsequent generations of an emigrant people tend to fade into the culture.[13] Thus the synagogue as the new institution of salvation had elements about it which enabled the diaspora community to retain its separateness.[14] What were those elements? The major problem of the diaspora community was simply survival and the retaining of religious identity. National festivals at Jerusalem and the temple-based cultic recital of the history of salvation were no longer possible. To survive the exiled community needed both remembrance of Zion (tradition) and specific institutions of self-regulation. The continuing necessity of the Torah, the instruction from Yahweh to his covenant people, was never questioned. Taken for granted were the obligations to keep the sabbath, to obey the commandments, and to celebrate the festivals. Exercising these obligations posed a new and complex problem partly because of the absence of traditional institutions of traditioning and partly because the foreign culture raised difficult questions as to exactly what the Torah required—questions of intermarriage, of accepted occupation, of ceremonies and rituals. Therefore, careful study, interpretation,

12. On the role of the synagogue in the origin of the Jewish canon and the Scripture principle see James W. Parkes, *The Foundations of Judaism and Christianity* (London: Vallentine-Mitchell, 1966), chap. 1, secs. 2 and 3; Samuel Sandmel, *The First Christian Century in Judaism and Christianity: Certainties and Uncertainties* (New York: Oxford University Press, 1960), pp. 32–34; Patte, *Early Jewish Hermeneutic,* chap. 2.

13. See Will Herberg, *Protestant, Catholic, and Jew* (Garden City, N.Y.: Doubleday and Co., 1960), chap. 3.

14. I realize that the history of diaspora Judaism from the beginning of the Babylonian exile on was a history of tension, conflict, and self-conscious struggle *within* the Jewish community itself on just this issue and that the Jewish community spanned a larger spectrum ranging from very purist, separatist postures to very adaptive if not assimilative postures. Something of that spectrum is present in the major types of Judaism even today.

and application of the Torah were required. Isolated from the land and temple, the diaspora Jews needed more than oral traditioning for their survival and persistence. As a cognitive minority in an alien culture they needed specific social regulations. They required some authoritative reference by which they could answer the questions perpetually raised by life in a strange land, and this resulted in a new focus on written Torah, writing which had existed in Israel even from premonarchical times. That new focus called forth masters of Torah, individuals whose acumen and diligence in interpretation made them leaders of the community at the point of its central need of living the Torah in an alien culture. In written Torah and its masters was the key to the nature and function of the synagogue. The synagogue was a gathering of Jews under authoritative teachers for the hearing and interpretation of the written Torah. In this temple-replacing institution the Scripture principle was born and with it a new set of vehicles of social identity and social persistence.

Constitutive Features of "Scripture" in Early Judaism

The preceding sections offer an outrageously oversimplified account of the elements in the religion of Israel which anticipate and provide the presuppositions for the Scripture principle as well as a summary of the new diaspora institutions which were the matrix and occasion of the birth of the Scripture principle. We offer now an even more outrageous simplification, an account of the essential meaning of *Scripture* in Judaism.[15] The focus is on what Daniel Patte calls the basic convictions about Scripture which underlie beliefs and doctrines about Scripture[16] We are not exploring the hermeneutical rules for

15. It seems impossible methodologically to have a clear-cut period in view in this description. The actual origins of the synagogue and therefore of the social matrix of Scripture are obscure. The discovery of a portion of Deuteronomy in the reign of Josiah and the subsequent reform is clearly not the "origin" of Scripture but a specific incident of political-religious reform on the basis of an older and written tradition. Because of the difficulty of speaking about the Judaism of the synagogue in a specific reference to origin, I shall have in mind the period from roughly 200 B.C.E. to 200 C.E. which climaxes at about 140 C.E. and maybe before with the victory of synagogal Judaism. I am regarding, therefore, synagogal Judaism as the central and most developed example of the Judaic Scripture principle, but would apply most of the features of that principle to other major sects and parties of Judaism of the first century. For a summary of the convictions that major Jewish parties shared about Scripture, see Longenecker, *Biblical Exegesis*, chap. 1.
16. Patte, *Early Jewish Hermeneutic*, Introduction.

interpreting Scripture or its function in the synagogue. Ours is the phenomenological question. What elements of meaning are present essentially when a collection of writings is "meant" as *Scripture?*

We begin with a preliminary definition. In Judaism *Scripture* means a *written deposit of the definitive and completed revelation of Yahweh to his people, the primary function of which is to be the source of community cultic and moral regulations (halakah).*[17] The primary elements in the definition are evident. Scripture is (1) a written collection, (2) of divine origin (from Yahweh), (3) communicating his will and truth to his covenant people, (4) to function as an enduring source of regulations for the corporate and individual life of that people. Some of these elements are simply appropriated from the religion of Israel, such as the God-king's revelation or instruction (Torah) to his covenant people. Scripture arises in Judaism by a synthesis of these elements with the requirements of the new situation. We distinguish, therefore, that which accounts for this synthesis (the origin of Scripture in the sense of the definition), and the *convictions* that determine the essential meaning of Scripture.

We recall that preexilic Israel had written records of its tradition which exercised some control on the traditioning process and the cultic activities of recital but not as a canon of sacred Scripture. How do these written deposits of tradition end up as sacred Scripture? Decisive are both the various elements of the religion of Israel necessary to sacred Scripture and the shift that occurs when the writings which preserve the Torah story take on a new function in the preservation of Jewish identity in the absence of land and temple. The dispersed and landless Jews could avoid assimilation into the alien culture only if they regulated their corporate life so as to retain their identity in the new land and if they found ways of adapting those regulations to the new environment. Fulfilling the first need was a written source of regulations, Scripture; fulfilling the second need was *gemara*, commentary which interpreted and applied Scripture to the present. Both occurred in the synagogue and were the reason for its existence.

The interpretation of Israel's written deposits of tradition as sacred

---

17. I realize that the term *Scripture* in rabbinic Judaism is sometimes used in a broader sense to cover both written and oral Torah, thus both canonical writings of Law, Prophets, and Writings, and Mishnah and Talmud. For the various terms for Scripture, see the article, "Bible," in the *Encyclopedia Judaica.*

Scripture carried with it the acts of meaning described earlier as the founding and middle axioms of the Scripture principle. The principle of identity is present in the sense that what God knows and wills to communicate to this people is in fact communicated and received, except that now the locus of that communication is a *written* vehicle. The meaning nucleus of the Scripture principle is thus the interpretation of a written deposit of tradition as a locus of divine–human identity. Second, the Jews of the diaspora period not only remembered that God had spoken to patriarchs and prophets in visions and dreams but possessed written deposits of that speaking. But when the editors, recorders, and redactors of the traditions fix them in writing, we do not have the prophet himself as the representative of God speaking directly to Israel in a living situation. We have secondary representation, a representation of Abraham, Moses, David, and Isaiah by the recorders of the tradition. The secondary representative is thus a new ersatz presence of God, Scripture.

Third, the prophets themselves viewed and represented revelation in a different way. In the actual faith and experience of Israel Yahweh could be and was continuously active in the nation through various kinds of prophets and their literature, prophets of Israel's story, songs, law, corruption, and hope. As long as Yahweh was active in the world, one could expect prophets to arise and forthtell his Word. The only periodizing involved here concerns various historical times of Israel's history and the final culmination and fulfillment of Yahweh's promises. But in diaspora Judaism comes a new understanding of the relation between the prophets and revelation. Revelation becomes something in the past, and since prophets are its messengers, the *time* of the prophets is in the past. This new periodization of salvation history thus distinguishes between the time of revelation and the time (before the fulfillment) of the interpretation of revelation. And this distinction is necessary to any idea of canon, that is, a collection which by its very nature is closed. Of course, the religious community's determination of what is and is not in the canon can go on for centuries. But that does not contradict the canonical idea, built as it is on a new periodization which can speak of the end of the time of revelation and "death of the last prophet."[18]

18. See G. F. Moore, *Judaism in the First Centuries of the Christian Era* (Cambridge: Harvard University Press, 1927–30), vol. I, p. 237, n. 2.

Fourth, that which presides over these shifts and developments is the actual function of the authoritative writings in the community. Like preexilic Israel, dispersed Israel needed to remember its past, to tell and retell the Torah story. It needed to sing the songs of Zion in the language of Zion in a strange land. But more than corporate piety was needed to maintain an identifiable community. The community, removed as it was from the environment and structure of authority, needed binding regulations which made clear the duties and prohibitions toward marriage, diet, sabbath, criminal acts, and so on. When social persistence occurs on the land and through its institutions, these fundamental areas of social life are managed and ordered. Removed from land and its institutions, the dispersed community's existence and identity depend on some successful retention of this ordering, its mealtime customs, its seasonal celebrations, its rites of passage for youth. In short, it needed law, and law in the distinctive sense of ordering regulations for a cultural minority. Lacking governance over the alien culture or nation, it needed an institutionalization of law which somehow would generate its own self-monitoring. The result was some new locations of divine–human identity. Torah, the revelation and instruction Yahweh gives to Israel, comes to mean primarily law. Further, the term *Torah* is now applied to the writings of Israel, first and especially the Pentateuch. Hence, the genre of the writings of Israel becomes law. This description of global acts of meaning does not do justice to the richness of the function of the Scriptures in the history of Judaism as a resource for charismatic renewals, individual inspiration and piety, liturgical celebration and mourning. In addition, much in the literature of Judaism, especially the midrash, indicates broader concerns. Nevertheless, the central meaning of "sacred Scripture" as *halakah* corresponds to a new requirement of dispersed Israel for the ordering of its collective life in alien cultures. *Halakah* posed the main issues of interpretation and application. *Sacred Scripture* in diaspora Judaism refers to a written source of divinely given regulations for the life of the community. This central meaning of Scripture is manifest in the specific convictions about Scripture which reigned and eventually triumphed in rabbinic Judaism.

We have before us a general definition. Sacred Scripture means a collection of writings reflecting a period of revelation whose genre and function concern divinely given regulations for the life of the

60

community. This definition is presupposed by the more specific hermeneutic rules and basic convictions about the written Torah which became dominant in Judaism. Three of these convictions stand out.

According to the first conviction, the Torah is the *exhaustive* location of God's divine communication in that it contains all the instructions and guidance the elect community will ever need. Because the written Torah is a Torah for all time (see the principle of immutability), there is an answer in the Torah for every need and crisis of God's people. This conviction provides the basis for the multiple-meaning hermeneutics common both to Jewish apocalypticists (Qumran) and the rabbis. The distinction at work here is not between a valid kernel in a disposable husk but simply between plain and hidden meanings. The hidden or implied meanings may be secrets about the future grasped only by the authentic Judaism of the end-time (Qumran) or a multiplicity of references to be discerned in different equally valid interpretations (rabbinic Judaism).

The second principle follows the logic of the first into the detailed parts of the written Torah. The written Torah is totally and equally valid and true. According to Jacobs's exposition of Maimonides's eighth principle, the divinity of the Torah, all verses originate equally in divine revelation and belong equally to the law of God.[19] Admittedly, Maimonides represents a more scholastic and even Aristotelian type of Judaism. Yet, Maimonides is merely giving expression to the Mishnah discussions of *halakah* which take for granted that the written Torah is a collection of equally valid and true statements. In other words, the axiom of leveled authority, the equal distribution of divine–human identity throughout the vehicle, is now at work. We have here the textualizing of the authoritative writings, an act of meaning in which the writings are viewed as a collection of specific texts, each one authoritative and available for interpretation and application. This development is not an arbitrary one. Once the writings are grasped *en bloc* as of divine origin and then used to found *halakah*, specific texts must be the authoritative, functioning units of interpretation. This in turn requires that authority be distributed equally to every part of the collection.

19. See Louis Jacobs, *Principles of the Jewish Faith* (London: Vallentine-Mitchell, 1964), chap. 9.

The third feature of Scripture which reflects its genre as law (source of community regulations) results from elements in the religion of Israel. Those elements include Yahweh, the God-king and world maker, the covenant people, the revealed instruction (Torah) for life on the land and carried by tradition. Added to these elements by synagogal Judaism was a new form of social persistence and maintenance through institutions independent of the nation, land, holy city, and temple. It would be a serious mistake, however, to suppose that synagogal Judaism eliminated all reference to these entities. Historically, diaspora Judaism and the synagogues looked back to Jerusalem authorities and made pilgrimages to Jerusalem.[20] And even though a struggle developed between the post-Maccabean Pharisaic party and the priesthood, the ever-more-dominant Pharisees and their successors, the rabbis, never abandoned symbolic reference to the nation and land. Judaism continued the religion of Israel's way of connecting memory and hope with the land. Thus no matter where the dispersed people settled, their past was contained in the Torah story of Abraham, Moses, David, and the prophets, and their future was a future story about restoration to the land.

Yet the themes of land and nation not only persist in Judaism in a generalized sense but are foundational to the Scripture principle.[21] Land and nation do function in the very meaning and essence of Scripture. The divinely willed law recorded in Scripture or occurring as Scripture occurred as a law for the covenant people, and this meant a landed and national people. The Torah story, the ceremonial and dietary laws, the sabbath laws, and the festivals all functioned in land

---

20. S. Safrai and M. Stern, *The Jewish People in the First Century* (Philadelphia: Fortress Press, 1974), p. 186. Jacob Neusner points out that in the pre-70 Pharasaic party as treated in the Gospels, we have a primarily cult-centered piety whose main focus is keeping the *temple* laws at home; see *Early Rabbinic Judaism: Historical Studies in Literature and Art* (Leiden: E. J. Brill, 1975). Sandmel's summary of major institutions of synagogal Judaism in Palestine shows the continuing function of the temple and the priesthood at least in the first century c.e. (*The First Christian Century*). We note that Neusner and Sandmel are describing the period in which Judaism is still in transition from preexilic temple Judaism to synagogal Judaism, a period in which there is a mixture of elements and the characteristic institutions of social persistence of later rabbinic Judaism are functioning along with survivals of earlier patterns. Once the transition is effected, land, nation, and temple are still retained but as imagery which interpret social identity, not as frameworks of actual institutions.

21. For an explicit treatment of the relation between Scripture and the land see Abraham J. Heschel, *Israel: An Echo of Eternity* (New York: Farrar, Straus & Giraux, 1967), pp. 44 ff. To quote, "To abandon the land would be to repudiate the Bible" (p. 44).

and nation institutions. Thus is established an intrinsic relation between the content of a nation-land revelation to a nation-land people and the meaning of Scripture as the written Torah. Thus if the written Torah became a substitute temple, an ersatz divine presence and entity of the community's duration, what endured was a people whose self-understanding remained that of a dispersed nation, a quasi-political and religious entity. Scripture, then, as a written collection functioning in the social persistence of Judaism and as a divinely given law for the dispersed nation is correlative to the ideas of land and nation. The dispersed nation has as its regulative and normative law what was originally given for the life of the nation on the land. This is not to say that Scripture as Torah has no universalizable aspects. As previously noted, the universalistic import of the content of Torah made it possible to adapt in a variety of historical situations. Nevertheless, the *meaning* of Scripture and the Scripture principle has intrinsic to it a divinely given Torah to a dispersed but symbolically and memorially landed-national people.

In our original definition, Scripture was said to refer to a written deposit of the definitive and completed revelation of Yahweh to his people which functions as the primary source of community cultic and moral regulations. We now append to this definition the following. The written collection was *meant* as Yahweh's exhaustive word, equally valid throughout the variety of its texts, as the Torah for his dispersed but ethnically self-interpreted people. We find in the Judaic Scripture principle the two founding presuppositions and their middle axioms: salvation history and the periodization of history, the principle of identity with its principles of secondary representation, leveling, and immutability. Sacred Scripture thus becomes *the* locus of divine–human identity, the divinely given thing to which to listen is equivalent to listening to God, which to read is equivalent to reading the words of God.[22]

---

22. These principles are rarely conceptually expressed as such. But they clearly come to expression in what Jacob Neusner calls the Torah myth and the Moses myth. According to the Moses myth, Moses received the oral and written revelation at Sinai, the totality of which is the design for the universe. According to the Torah myth, God himself was the teacher of Moses, and Moses himself is the archetypal rabbi. Thus not only is there a heavenly study of Torah by Moses but God himself studies and lives by Torah. See Jacob Neusner, *Understanding Rabbinic Judaism: From Talmudic Times to the Present* (New York: KTAV, 1974), Introduction. See also Neusner, *There We Sat Down: Talmudic Judaism in the Making* (Nashville: Abingdon Press, 1972).

THE CHRISTIAN APPROPRIATION AND MODIFICATION OF
THE SCRIPTURE PRINCIPLE

Like their Jewish forebears and contemporaries the early Christians claimed an identity between what God knew, willed, and intended to reveal and what was proclaimed as Gospel. The causality operative in the origin, ministry, death, and resurrection of Jesus is a divine causality. The words of teaching handed on from Jesus, the sayings of the Lord, are divine words. The divine or revelatory origin of the content of the Gospel was never in question. In synagogal Judaism the specific location of divine–human identity was clear and explicit. It is to be found in the divinely inspired Scripture. And while it never seriously questioned the divine nature of the Jewish Scriptures, Christianity did not originate with an accomplished notion of the location of identity in hand. The specifically Christian version of the locations of revelation (divine–human identity) was a historical accomplishment. And like the origin of the Scripture principle in Judaism it had a social and historical context. Even as Judaism came to locate God's revealed will in the written Torah as a response to the crisis of exile and dispersion, so Christianity came to claim definitive locations of the divine will in the situation of its own internal struggles to maintain itself in the face of a cultural pluralism and religious syncretism. Christianity, like Judaism, eventually identified the place where human words are in content divine as sacred Scripture. Our task then is to discover, if possible, how it was that the Jesus movement ended up with the Judaic Scripture principle. The final aim of such an inquiry is to grasp what "Scripture" *means* in Christianity, what claims and presuppositions go into the term *sacred Scripture*.

The Development of the Scripture Principle
in Early Christianity

After 200 c.e. sacred Scripture in the Christian church was a two-part collection of writings comprised of the "Scriptures" of Judaism and the collection known now as the New Testament. Two fundamental accomplishments were necessary to this bipartite canon. First, the Scripture principle of Judaism had to survive in this largely Gentile religious community. Second, certain early Christian writings had to be appropriated as canonical, as part of sacred Scripture.

The Earliest Christian Scripture

It would be a misstatement to say that at some time in its early history the Christian movement appropriated the Scripture principle from Judaism. The fact is that there is no period of early Christianity in which the Scripture principle was absent. As an originally Jewish movement, the Christian sect always had Scripture, a collection of authoritative writings regarded as being of divine origin. That collection, the Scripture of early Christianity for the first century or so of its existence, was roughly the Jewish Scripture.[23] Hence, the Scripture principle and its presuppositions entered Christianity as an aspect of its retention of the written Torah of Judaism. Yet we need to press beyond this Jewish matrix of Christian Scripture if we are to understand the motivations behind Christianity's eventual location of identity in sacred Scripture. The Christian retention of the Judaic Scripture principle was not a historical inevitability. Other major elements of Judaism (such as the oral Torah) had simply been abandoned by the Christian movement. We need to distinguish, therefore, the appropriation and use of the Jewish Scriptures by Christian writers of the first century of the Christian movement and the later self-conscious retention and confirmation of the Scripture principle which occurred in the face of serious difficulties.

That a sect which originates in the framework of a specific religious faith retains the sacred writings of that faith comes as no surprise. The earliest controversies and polemics of the Jesus movement were with Judaism. Those controversies and their issues dominated the first generations of Christianity. And the major apologetic weapon in that struggle was the Jewish Scriptures. The Jesus movement was persuaded that the end-time, the time of the reign of God, had begun, that Jesus' death and resurrection were the inaugurating events, that Jesus was thus the expected Messiah, and that they, the community which confessed his messiahship, were the true Israel and the fulfillment of the prophetic hope. Reflecting these convictions, the dominant mode of interpreting the Jewish Scriptures in the Jesus movement was the *pesher* exegesis of the Qumran community. The

---

23. I say "roughly" because the exact list of canonical Scriptures was not settled for either Christians or Jews in the first century. Certain works of the *Writings* continued for some time in dispute.

focus of such exegesis is not on Scripture as the source of *halakah* regulations (see rabbinical exegesis) but as a foreshadowing and anticipation of a time of fulfillment. Even as the Qumran community saw itself as the only valid heir of the promise and thus the only community prepared for the end-time, so the Christian sect saw in Jesus and the subsequent community the fulfillment of the salvation-story described in the writings of Israel.[24]

However, we should not so stress the fulfillment exegesis of New Testament writers that their retention of the basic convictions of Jewish hermeneutics is minimized. We have hitherto maintained that beneath the several hermeneutics attending the major parties of Judaism (rabbinical, apocalyptic, Hellenistic), are certain common convictions about Scripture.[25] According to these convictions Scripture is inspired, of divine origin, meaningful and authoritative throughout (see principle of leveling), self-consistent, and a record of the now-ended time of revelation (see periodization). Thus, when early Christian authors appropriate the Jewish term *Scripture*, when they utilize Jewish modes of interpretation and formulas of citation, we can assume that they *mean* by Scripture what the Jewish parties mean. The one shift of emphasis is from Scripture as a source of *halakah* to Scripture as anticipation and promise of the messianic community of the end-time.

Such is the *inherited* Scripture principle present in writers of the New Testament period. Yet this inherited usage would not by itself explain the survival of the Scripture principle in Christianity. The context of the Christian *pesher* interpretation of Scripture was controversy with Judaism. But as Christianity became a Gentile movement and controversy with Judaism receded into the past, the unit of that controversy (Scripture) might have also receded. In Judaism itself Scripture and its interpretation had become an indispensable vehicle of social persistence. But if Scripture functions in the Christian

24. For a description of *pesher* exegesis see Patte, *Early Jewish Hermeneutic*, chap. 8; and Longenecker, *Biblical Exegesis*, chap. 1. Krister Stendahl's study of Matthew stresses Matthew's use of the Jewish Scriptures as *pesher* midrash. He finds Matthew's quotations to resemble in form those of the Habbakuk commentary of the Qumran community. See *The School of St. Matthew and Its Use of the Old Testament* (Philadelphia: Fortress Press, 1968); for a summary of the principles of *pesher* interpretations see pp. 191 ff.

25. Daniel Patte lists the major convictions common to these parties. See *Early Jewish Hermeneutic*, Introduction. Cf. Moore, *Judaism in the First Centuries of the Christian Era*, vol. I, chap. 4.

movement primarily as an apologetic weapon in a single period of controversy, it does not seem to be a vehicle necessary to Christian social persistence. In fact the Jewish Scriptures were not functioning in the Christian congregation as they were in the synagogues.

Over and above this seeming dispensability of Scripture to the Christian movement, the Jewish Scriptures also posed a serious problem for early Christianity.[26] This problem emerged initially not as the problem of Scripture as such but as the issue of the validity and authority of the law. The occasion of the problem was the success of the Gentile mission which confronted the church with the undeniable fact that salvation through Jesus could occur outside the conditions necessary for full proselytes to Judaism. The problem of Scripture follows directly on this issue. How can the church acknowledge these writings as Scripture (as God's inspired, sufficient, self-consistent, inerrant word), as the church in fact did in its Jewish controversies, without also acknowledging the Torah disclosed therein as binding. In Judaism these writings communicate God's very will and command, and acknowledging this is an act of obedience.

The earliest Christian solution was to distinguish between the abrogated Law and the written vehicle of the Law, the Scriptures. It was Marcion who saw the problem in its full and radical sense, and it was his very scholarship and knowledge of Scripture which made this possible. For he approached the Jewish Scriptures literally, one might even say historically. He sensed that the vengeful God of Israel was not reconcilable with a deity who was simply a loving redeemer and that the required Torah pertained to a different kind of religious community from the universal ecclesial community. Marcion is trivialized and mythologized if he is approached simply as someone who believed in two deities or who posited unbridgeable alienation between creation and redemption. Marcion knew well the principles of leveling and identity necessary to Scripture. If a writing is Scripture, it is the location of God's very communication to his people. And the communications in the Jewish Scriptures simply cannot coexist consistently with the Gospel. This then is the question in radical form: Can Christians acknowledge the Jewish canon as *Scripture*? His answer was a clear-cut negative, and this forced the church to justify explicitly

---

26. For a summary of the problems the Jewish Scripture created for the Christian movement, see Ernest C. Colwell, *New or Old: The Christian Struggle with Change and Tradition* (Philadelphia: Westminster Press, 1970), pp. 29 ff.

what it had hitherto taken for granted, namely, that its sacred writings are the Jewish canon.

The response to this challenge on the part of Apologists and Fathers was not a uniform one. To some, allegorical method offered a way out. Closely related to this was the approach of non-Marcionite gnostic movements which, because of their levels-of-truth approach, could acknowledge both that the Jewish Scriptures are Scripture and that it is not totally consistent with the Gospel. By rejecting the principle of leveling involved in the Scripture principle, this solution can thus relativize much of the content of Scripture.[27] What won the day was an approach proposed by Justin and elaborated in Irenaeus. It retained the Jewish Scriptures as Scripture in the full sense of the word—a divinely given, self-consistent book. At this point the salvation history scheme of Paul and Luke is used to establish different epochs of revelation and with them the notion of provisional validity. Thus Christians can say that the ceremonial law is literally commanded by God but it was a law for Israel, not for the epoch of Christ and his church. With this solution we have the first major step in the retention and justification of the Jewish Scripture principle. The church not only inherits that principle from its Jewish matrix, initially employed as an apologetic weapon in its early preaching and writing; it now faces the difficulty created for the Scripture principle by the church's rejection of the written Torah as binding and by its own affirmation of a Gospel which is the center and fulfillment of revelation. The solution is a reperiodization of salvation history which lays the ground for a two-part Scripture, one pertaining to the old covenant, the other to the new.

The Completed Christian Scripture

In the second step in the development of the Christian Scriptures, a collection of early Christian writings is added to the Jewish Scriptures. In other words, Gospels and Epistles are drawn into the general notion of sacred Scripture. Christians have lived so long in a symbolic universe which presupposes this step that they have difficulty seeing it as anything but a historical inevitability, the development of some-

27. See Hans von Campenhausen, *The Formation of the Christian Bible* (Philadelphia: Fortress Press, 1972), chap. 3, for a summary of the church's response to the crisis of the Old Testament as Scripture.

thing a priori to Christianity itself. Yet the Christian movement existed for almost two centuries without this bipartite canon.[28] Other alternatives were open to it. It is only when this is granted that we can grasp the continuation of the Scripture principle in Christianity as a historical contingency.

There are several ways of describing the emergence of the New Testament as canonical Scripture. The most external way is simply a literary history, a detailed account of the developing lists of books offered by Marcion, Irenaeus, and others. Somewhat deeper is a social history which attempts to account for the canon as a solution to crises in the church.[29] More adequate yet is the attempt to trace the key steps in embracing the axioms and presuppositions necessary to meaning a collection to be *Scripture*. In what follows I shall give no attention to the first way, some attention to the second, and most attention to the third.

We begin by recalling what Scripture came to mean in the normative Judaism which won out sometime in the second century C.E. Scripture is the written deposit of the definitive and completed revelation of Yahweh to his people, the primary function of which is to provide a source for the cultic and moral regulation of the community. While the *literary* genre of Scripture appears to be a narrative or story, the *functional* genre of Scripture is Torah. The narrative or Torah-story provides the setting in salvation history for the Torah, thereby indicating its divine origin. And because the narrative and the Torah concern a landed, national people, the Torah is given for the life of that people living on or exiled from the land. We have in this definition the various axioms of the Scripture principle: *identity* (it is God's very communication), *secondary representation* (a series of extensions of identity to ever-new traditions of interpretation), *periodization* (history and revelation occurring in the past),

---

28. Following some historians of the New Testament canon, I am distinguishing between writings regarded as authoritative by the community and writings regarded as Scripture. Thus, the Gospels and Paul's letters had some "authority" from very early times, as is indicated by oblique references to a collection of Paul's letters (2 Pet. 3:15). Yet they are not meant as Scripture until the various axioms of the Scripture principle are applied to them and hermeneutic methods regarded as appropriate for the Jewish Scriptures come into play.

29. Adolf Harnack's *The Origin of the New Testament* (New York: Macmillan Company, 1925) is just such an approach.

leveling (the equality of authority distributed in literary units), and universal applicability of an *immutable*, everlastingly valid content. These elements of Scripture's meaning help show why the Christian movement did not easily and automatically appropriate the Scripture principle and what is involved when it does.

First, the general historical setting in which the New Testament came to be regarded as canonical Scripture is not unlike the diaspora setting of postexilic Judaism where the Scripture principle was born. The problem faced by both diaspora Jews and second-century Christians was that of social identity and social duration. For the Jews that meant maintaining their corporate identity in a situation where the traditional institutional vehicles of duration were no longer available. The solution was the development of new institutional bearers of tradition: synagogue, teachers, Scripture. For second-century Christians the problem was maintaining the identity of the Jesus movement in a situation where institutional controls over the tradition were largely absent and in which tradition itself was a plural phenomenon. Like the diaspora Jews, second-century Christians were looking for institutional, generation-bridging means of social perpetuity.

Second, the Christian community of the second century self-consciously embraced the Scripture principle by retaining the Jewish Scriptures. Thus the various axioms of the Scripture principle survive in the Christian interpretation of the Law and the Prophets. This retention of the Jewish Scriptures was not without its ambivalence, since another location of revelation and tradition besides the "Old Testament" Scriptures existed in the Christian community, namely the *regula fidei*, the Apostolic tradition. And, the Christian community obviously did not interpret the Jewish Scriptures in the functional genre of Torah for the people on or exiled from the land. Scripture is thus retained and yet does not function as *the* vehicle of duration as it did in Judaism.

Third, a new religious content and symbolism occurred in the Christian movement. Its Gospel message proclaimed that the Messiah had come, his death and resurrection signaled the inauguration of a new aeon (interpreted apocalyptically in the first generation of Christianity), and that eschatological salvation was available through belief in him and participation in the community of his continuing presence. Everything in the tradition other than this Gospel of salvation was either abandoned (the oral Torah) or given secondary status.[30] A new tradition is thus born, centered in the events surrounding Jesus of Nazareth and his teachings and interpreted in writings associated with the period of those events. In other words, the ecclesial community's preaching and teaching, its ongoing tradition, had a norm other than "Scripture," the living presence of the Lord and a nucleus tradition of early testimony to the Lord. Jesus of Nazareth is thus the triumph and culmination of salvation history. Both foundational presuppositions of the Scripture principle are present in this norm although in a new way. First, the salvation history framework is present but in the form of a new periodization which makes the coming of Jesus of Nazareth the center of history, thus establishing the epoch of Israel and the epoch of the church. We have then the groundwork for a new version of the "period of revelation." Second, the identity principle is retained but is applied to a new entity, the person and event of Jesus. In Jesus' acts and teachings we have the decisive, salvific presence of God and the disclosure of his will and purpose. This creates the groundwork for an extension of identity to new secondary representatives through whom the identity present in Jesus continues to be available.

To summarize, the Christian movement, like Judaism, needed to solve the problem of its own generation-bridging duration. It had committed itself somewhat ambivalently to the Jewish Scriptures. It had a nonscriptural authoritative tradition which gathered around Jesus and early testimony to him. Accordingly, several of the presuppositions of the Scripture principle are either established or anticipated prior to the explicit struggle with the question of an extended Christian canon of Scripture. That struggle occurred in the middle of the second century C.E. Its general occasion was the internal disparities in the Christian movement created by a plurality of traditions.[31] This plurality extended beyond the material interpretations of the Gospel to the terms or rules of the disputes themselves. Each group could claim to have *the* authentic tradition. Some could base their judgments on a secret tradition. Appeal to the Jewish Scriptures had

30. I am assuming here that the Gospel message retains a certain theological substructure persisting from the religion of Israel and necessary to it. But while the Christian preaching took this for granted, the Adamic myth, for instance, it did not thematize the total legacy in its preaching.

31. Indicative of an approach which attempts to probe this multiplicity are the essays in Helmut Koester and James Robinson, *Trajectories Through Early Christianity* (Philadelphia: Fortress Press, 1971).

been pertinent in the earlier polemics with the Jews, but this could not settle disputes about the Jesus tradition itself.

It is at this point that the second-century church faced a crossroads. It could attempt to sort out and assess its own written deposits of tradition, distinguishing therefore between authentic first-century works such as the collection of Pauline epistles and later imitations. In this approach the community would be exercising some control over proliferating and ever more speculative traditions by means of a literature which has the genre of testimony to the Lord. The fact that Jesus of Nazareth and the birth of the Christian movement refer to an actual historical person and event establishes a distinction between literatures which contain early testimonies to that event within the community in which it occurred and literatures which occur outside any relation to such communities and where historical reference exercises little or no control on tradition. The second-century community was not always either clear or correct in its historical judgment as to whether a given work was connected in fact with an apostle or even the apostolic period, but its effort to control the proliferation of tradition by locating the earliest deposits of testimony expresses a valid inclination. It is clear that this way of ordering and controlling tradition is not the Scripture principle. In this alternative the genre of literature in question is not divinely given Torah or truth but early authentic human testimony to the Lord and to the events of origin of the ecclesial community. Even if this literature is gathered into a collection, functioning in the religious community as a control on tradition, that collection would not necessarily function as a canon of sacred Scripture. Prior to Marcion and the church's response to his proposal, the church was, in fact, pursuing this first alternative. Its disputants did cite the Gospels, the writings of Paul, and other works, not in the technical formulas reserved for Scripture, but in debates over what is and is not the authentic Christian tradition. Individual Gospels and the Pauline collection did have authority of some kind in specific geographical areas.[32]

But this first alternative did not suffice. Instead, the church, already propelled by its early retention of the Jewish Scriptures with the attending basic convictions, took a second course, the canonizing of

32. On the difference between New Testament writings regarded as authoritative and those regarded as canonical, see Robert M. Grant, *The Formation of the New Testament* (New York: Harper & Row, 1965), p. 145.

early Christian writings as inspired Scripture. According to von Campenhausen this took place in two major steps.[33] First, Marcion proposed to solve the problem of controlling the pluralism of traditions by an official list of acceptable writings. The church's response was "no" to Marcion's own list and "yes" to the idea. There followed a period in which the number of acceptable books was expanded. The key influential figure in this search for an alternative list to Marcion is Irenaeus. Marcion's proposal of a canon of writings from the apostolic period is a critically important step because its result is a new sphere of secondary representatives. Not only is Jesus a location of divine identity and a representative of God himself. Those who testify to Jesus in the apostolic period are meant now as representatives of the revelation in Jesus and an extension of that identity. Thus, the divine communication has obtained a new secondary location, apostles. Second, the Montanist controversy created a fear of a limitless canon and the issue became how to limit the list of books. By 200 c.e. the New Testament canon as it is today was largely determined, a language for the collections was forged (Old and New Testaments), and a self-conscious doctrine of a bipartite inspired Scripture was formulated by Origen. The Christian movement thus embraced the Jewish Scripture principle not just as a legacy of its past and a useful tool in polemics with the Jews but as a new, divinely given canon of literature embracing the two epochs of revelation.

The Meaning of "Scripture": The Ambivalence of Christianity Toward the Scripture Principle

The question indicated by the title of this section is, What did the Christian community finally come to mean by *Scripture?* What are the elements of meaning operative when certain writings are meant by the Christian church as *holy Scripture?* In its most comprehensive sense this question has a variety of levels of answers which include the function of Scripture as an entity in the community's social duration, the presuppositions and middle axioms of the Scripture principle, and the specific functional genre of Scripture. The question is also complex because the interrogation of Christian literature and practice yields two incompatible answers to the question. One answer either rejects the middle axioms of the Scripture principle or so transforms

---

33. Campenhausen, *Formation of the Christian Bible,* chaps. 5 and 6.

them that the Christian community seems to break with the Scripture principle. The other answer appropriates the Judaic Scripture principle and permits it to dominate and determine what the Christian community means by Scripture. To express this twofold meaning of Scripture in the Christian community historically, Christianity came very close to rejecting or transcending the Judaic Scripture principle, but finally adopted it in revised form. I offer the following analysis in support of this thesis.

The Christian Modification of the Scripture Principle

The authoritative writings of all religious communities function as a control of tradition by preserving the corporate memory and by referring new developments and contemporary situations to that memory. But this statement is too general to capture the distinctive way Scripture functions in the social persistence of diaspora Judaism. Jewish social maintenance as a social-outcast, ethnic people in alien cultural environments was by means of the detailed religious and social regulation of private and public life. By this means there could continue not only a distinctive Jewish cultus but a distinctive education, language, sex ethic, leadership, religious calendar, and so forth. The institutional entities of this regulation were especially the synagogue, the teachers (of Scripture), and Scripture as source of *halakah* and *hagadah*. We recall this distinctive institutionality of Judaism to help make clear that Scripture had a different function in the Christian community of the first three centuries. Even when the Jewish Scripture was retained as Scripture, its genre was not primarily Torah but prefigurative narrative. And when the two-testament Scripture was obtained, it was not primarily the source from which the teacher, using specific hermeneutical rules, could determine the community's *halakah*. The Christian community's problem of social persistence was not the threat of an ethnic group's cultural assimilation but the threat of how a multiplicity of interpretive traditions will affect an already culturally diverse community. The bipartite Scripture, especially the New Testament, came to function as the one ancient and authoritative deposit of tradition and the criterion for assessing all other traditions. Furthermore, the chief concern was not community regulation, the interpretation and application of Scripture as Torah, but the community's confession, the interpretation and application of Scripture as Gospel. Thus Scripture in the Christian community functioned as a control of tradition in the specific sense of designating the authoritative testimony to Christ, the cultic Lord.

Yet from the beginning the Christian movement had retained the writings of Israel as Scripture. This retention, a matter of religious heritage in the first century and self-conscious decision after Marcion, mediated the Jewish Scripture principle to the Christian community. With it came the presuppositions (salvation history, divine–human identity), the middle axioms (periodization, leveling, immutability), and exegetical practices of Judaism (*pesher* exegesis, allegory, rabbinical rules). Thus the groundwork was laid to apply these concomitants of the Scripture principle to the early writings of Christianity.

The Christian movement came to regard its own earliest and most authentic writings as Scripture, but not without some crucial changes in the Scripture principle. The first modification concerns the new Christian periodization of salvation history. The incorporation of a second collection (the New Testament) into Scripture could be done only on the basis of a new periodization of history in which the epochs of salvation are centered in the coming of the Messiah. In this periodization the time of revelation is not over with the last prophet. It extends through Jesus of Nazareth, and hence the founding of the church closes with the last apostle. This new periodization provides the basis for making the Jewish Scriptures coincide with the old covenant and the early Christian writings with the new covenant. The result was a certain ambivalence toward the Old Testament which has characterized the Christian movement throughout its history. The two-covenant solution of the interrelationship of the two collections helped explain the Christian rejection of the Mosaic law as authoritative and gave expression to a historical sense on the part of the early church which could acknowledge the relativity of the religion of Israel and therefore of its literature. Thus is grounded an exegetical approach to the Old Testament which is primarily a discovery of prefigurations of later fulfillments. On the other hand the Old Testament, meant as Scripture, the divinely given word for all time, was seen as an authoritative source of belief and practice and was appealed to as such.

The second modification of the Jewish Scripture principle concerns the *functional genre* of Scripture. We distinguish here between the literary and functional genres of a community's authoritative writings. In the literary sense the writings of Israel and early Christianity

75

contain many genres; legal codes (the covenant code), visions (the Book of Daniel), aphorisms of wisdom, narrative, and so on. Some have argued effectively that the overall literary genre of Old and New Testament Scripture is narrative.[34] The functional genre concerns the way the *function* of the collection in the community determines how its unity is conceived. In Judaism the functional genre of Scripture is that of Torah. That is, because the primary function of Scripture in the community is to regulate individual and community life, its overall unity is grasped as Torah. But the Christian two-testament Scripture modifies the functional genre from Torah to doctrine. The term *doctrine* does not, of course, express the historical intentions of the original authors or the literary genres. It expresses what came to be the primary function of Scripture in the church. First, that which unified early Christian literature and grounded its authority even before it was proposed as canon was that which unified Christianity itself, the Christ. Some of the earliest strata of tradition describe his ministry, teachings, death, and what happened as the result of these events. If the term *Gospel* had not become associated with a particular literary genre, it could have been an appropriate inclusive term for the whole literature. *Apostles* in contrast to prophets also summarized this early literature, and this too is a christologically derived term, describing as it does an initial generation of witnesses to and proclaimers of the Messiah. The *regula fidei*, that canon of belief which constitutes the distinctive and indispensable elements of the Gospel, was itself one of the criteria for the qualification of a writing as canonical.[35] This, too, suggests that the unity of these writings is the Messiah's appearance translated into a message of salvation to be proclaimed to the world.

Second, the situation which produced the bipartite canon was a controversy in the Christian movement engendered by a plurality of traditions, with Roman Christianity coming to be orthodoxy and other forms of Christianity, heresy.[36] The main struggle between these two lines was the setting for the emergence of the New Testament canon.

34. Hans Frei, *The Identity of Jesus Christ* (Philadelphia: Fortress Press, 1975), p. xv. See also his *The Eclipse of Biblical Narrative* (New Haven: Yale University Press, 1974), Introduction.

35. See Kurt Aland, *The Problem of the New Testament Canon* (London: A. R. Mowbray, 1962), pp. 16–17. See also Willi Marxsen, *The New Testament as the Church's Book*, trans. J. E. Mignard (Philadelphia: Fortress Press, 1972), pp. 27–29.

36. See Walter Bauer, *Orthodoxy and Heresy in Earliest Christianity*, ed. R. Kraft and G. Krodel (Philadelphia: Fortress Press, 1971).

The canon of the New Testament came into being not so much through official, institutional acts of the church as through the orthodox party's identification of a deposit of the authentic apostolic tradition and therefore the expression of the original, divinely given truth. Given this setting, the writings *functioned* primarily in the settling of theological, doctrinal disputes. This is what we mean when we say that the functional genre of the New Testament is doctrine. Its function is not to provide authority for regulating the life of the community but authority for right teaching, belief, and confession. Its unity is thus not law but a Gospel message intended as true. While the church did speak of the Jewish Scriptures and the New Testament as the law and the gospel, it actually unified the two under the category, gospel, in the sense that the Old Testament prefigured the Christ and the New Testament explicitly records his accomplishment. Thus both testaments could and did function as a source of doctrine.

The third modification is based on the new Christian periodization of salvation history and concerns the corporate referent of Scripture, that to which and for which Scripture is given. In the Judaic sense, Scripture is the divine word of instruction and commandment to the people of Yahweh, Israel. Granting various senses in which there is an incipient universalism in the faith of Israel and in diaspora Judaism, the fact remains that the postexilic struggle for survival and identity is the social setting of the birth of the Scripture principle, and Scripture as Torah is Torah for the regulation of the corporate life of an ethnic people. This, too, is modified in the Christian two-testament Scripture. The literature of the New Testament is written from the time and perspective of Hellenistic Christianity, and it takes for granted transplants of the faith of Israel onto Gentile soil. This universalization of the faith of Israel is seen as the fulfillment of the faith of Israel. Those for whom salvation is available through the coming of the Messiah are the nations. The new community of the Messiah is drawn from all nations, to form not a new nation but a universal religious community. The telos of the events recorded in the writings of Israel is the universal community. Thus, that to which Scripture is Scripture, the divine word of gospel, is the world.

The Christian Adoption of the Scripture Principle

The new periodization of history and the new collection, the functional genre of gospel and doctrine, and the world-orientation are not frivolous but fundamental alterations of the Scripture princi-

77

ple. If "Scripture" means a collection of prophetic writings that serves as the divinely given Torah for the landed-national but dispersed people of Yahweh, then the new messianic community has replaced Scripture wtih a two-part collection of writings which record the saving gospel intended for a worldwide hearing. But could these modifications be simply changes within a general Scripture principle shared by both Judaism and Christianity? Whether or not the Christian movement retains the Jewish Scripture principle in the full sense of the word depends on whether it applies the principle of identity and its middle axioms to the new two-testament collection. When the claim is made that God's knowledge, will, and intentions and the content of a human expression are identical, we have articulated a major presupposition of the Scripture principle. From this come middle axioms that claim the words of the authors of the books to be secondary representatives of the divine presence and communication to the original prophet, that the validity and truth of the prophet's communication is as trustworthy at one point as at another point in the writings (leveling), that all the writings are immutably valid and applicable. These middle axioms altogether add up to the view of Scripture as an absolute authority, removed from all possible error. They are also the presuppositions for atomistic exegesis which sees Scripture as composed of so many equally infallible units (texts) so that the work of God offers itself for interpretation in the form of these units. The Christian movement has taken into itself the Judaic Scripture principle only if it takes over this principle and its middle axioms. Did it in fact do so? It is just at this point where a clear-cut answer is not possible, where there seem to be two ways in which Scripture persists in the Christian religion.

When we consider the proper function of these ancient writings in ecclesial duration and how the ecclesial community modifies the very meaning of Scripture, the middle axioms of the principle of identity turn out to be incompatible with a proposed Christian Scripture. The writings of early Christian authors were first cited as the earliest, most trustworthy deposit of tradition about Jesus of Nazareth and the origins of the church. Here "Scripture" is functioning as a control of tradition running rampant. The unity of such writings is this event of Jesus the Christ and the outcome of that event. Insofar as the church proclaims an identity between God's act and word and Jesus's ministry and teaching, it should be unable to extend that identity to a literary substitute. The identity is between God and Jesus as the revelatory and saving event, not between God and the words of Mark and Paul. This is borne out when we consider that the functional genre of the early writings was doctrine. This could be taken in an oracular sense of divinely communicated aphorisms. In fact, the apostolic doctrine is a matter of the gospel, the remembering and recording of the saving event and person, a message of salvation of worldwide import. This is simply incompatible with the middle axiom of leveling where every literary unit takes on the character a priori of a divine communication. Scripture as Torah lends itself to such leveling since Torah does exist in discrete units to be interpreted and applied.

Furthermore, the fact that these writings pertain not simply to a designated historical people but to all nations means that their content is authoritative only to the degree that is is universalizable. Content relative only to specific situations, be it the Mosaic law, cultic prescriptions, or advice given to a local group, could not be the divine word for all human beings. Further, the fact that the Jewish Scripture is retained as the old covenant, implying relative and provisional validity, suggests that the Scripture's total unity is not a leveled, equally distributed truth. These several Christian modifications of the Judaic Scripture principle add up to a new definition of Scripture. Scripture means a two-part collection of writings which prefigures (the Old Testament) and describes (the New Testament) the central event of salvation history, the coming of the Messiah and the beginnings of the universal messianic community, which functions to control and measure the continuing traditioning event and proclaiming of that event to all nations.

This, of course, is not the whole picture. I indicated earlier that the Christian community answers the question of the meaning of Scripture in two contradictory ways. Even a cursory look at the Christian movement of the early centuries discloses that Scripture is being interpreted and appealed to in ways that presuppose the Judaic Scripture principle in the full sense. We find atomistic exegesis practiced on both Old and New Testaments, the ahistorical citation of single sentences and passages as if each one was a direct communication from God. Somewhere along the way, regardless of the incompatibilities created by the Christian modifications of the Scripture principle, the middle axioms of identity have persisted, with the result that the new bipartite canon is now a sacred Scripture in the sense of synagogal Judaism. How can we account for this? I shall offer at this point only some historical surmises which need further historical work for their confirmation.

First, the Jewish Scripture principle in the full sense of the principle of identity was never really repudiated by the Christian movement. The church took into itself from the beginning the exegetical practices and principles of Judaism.[37] When the early Christian literature was incorporated into Scripture, it was natural for the church to extend the middle axioms of identity to the New Testament.

Second, insofar as the two-testament canon was accomplished in the setting of controversy, we can expect the kinds of appeals made in the controversy to be a major influence in determining the functional genre of Scripture. In the trinitarian and christological controversies of the third and fourth centuries, the orthodox party saw itself defending the one, universal faith, established and disclosed by God. The heretics were introducers of novelties into the ancient and authentic tradition and as such were in opposition to God himself. God's word, will, and truth are easily identified with the apostles' symbol, the *regula fidei*, the gospel, and its ancient bearer the New Testament. Given such identifications, citing God and his truth and citing Paul came to coincide.

Third, the Christian movement never abandoned one element in the faith of Israel, the royal metaphor for God and his relation to the world. Its logic was always the logic of sovereignty. And this logic requires that that which occurs in salvation history as a means of promoting God's reign (such as the church, the New Testament) carries with it whatever is necessary for successful completion. This is why the view of the New Testament authors as ordinary, fallible human beings who gave their witness could not hold very long if this meant that their fallibility might have so distorted the original event that it becomes lost behind impenetrable traditions. Such a notion was inconceivable. If God has willed the event and its outcome, surely he will ensure whatever is necessary for its continued presence. To question the trustworthiness of Mark or Paul is thus to question God himself. The final resting place of this logic is the view of a supernaturally guaranteed trustworthiness of the testimony to Jesus, a testimony

37. Thus the apostolic fathers proclaimed "the words of the Bible to be the very words of the Holy Spirit." F. W. Farrar, *History of Interpretation* (New York: E. P. Dutton, 1886), p. 115.

not subject to the fallibilities and errors of ordinary human acts. Since this logic of triumph pervades the total criteriology of Christendom, it is difficult to conceive of its absence at the birth of canonical Scripture. And it is this logic of triumph which pushes the church to extend the middle axioms of identity to the New Testament collection. Jesus himself is the very Word of God. But to continue salvifically present in the church, there must be a trustworthy reduction of the event and person of Christ to verbal testimony. That testimony takes on the status of a secondary representation of the divine will and word, a place where revelation is deposited.[38] As such it assumes the features of equally distributed truth (leveling) and universal applicability and infallibility. Here we have the Jewish Scripture principle applied to New Testament authors, which means the origin of the writings in divine inspiration. Driven by this logic the church extended the Jewish Scripture principle to its own modified Scripture.[39]

In this second meaning of Scripture, the Judaic Scripture principle has triumphed. Scripture is "sacred Scripture," the divinely inspired, bipartite collection of writings which are God's very words to the world, thus having the character of errorlessness, self-consistency, and applicability of every unit to the task of discerning the truth. Obviously, the formal features of Scripture as defined by the Judaic principle of identity and its middle axioms dominate this definition. The material characters, the christological unity, the new functional genre, the role in ecclesial duration, are all in the background. Once this occurs, once Scripture is retained in the Judaic sense, Christianity itself changes, for this means that the vehicle of Christian social persistence is an infallible collection. This lays the groundwork for a specific kind of relation between the collection and liturgy, piety, teaching, and theology. It does not in itself make Christianity into a

---

38. A very clear example of this extension of the Lord's authority to the apostles is the following. "After his resurrection the Lord transmits to his Apostles . . . the authoritative power of his own word and deed of salvation. Since the fate of the disciples is the same as that of their Lord, and since their word is accepted or rejected as that of their Lord . . . ., their claim to announce God's salvific will is also the same." Paul Neuenzeit, "Canon of Scripture," in Karl Rahner et al., *Sacramentum Mundi* (New York: Herder and Herder, 1968), vol. I.

39. Thus Origen argued explicitly for the equal inspiration of both Testaments. See Campenhausen, *Formation of the Christian Bible,* chap. 7. According to F. W. Farrar, Origen "held in its strongest form the theory of verbal inspiration. Not one iota, he said, of Scripture is empty." And, "Every clause of the Bible is infallible." *History of Interpretation,* pp. 190, 196.

book religion, but it creates the possibility if not even the probability of forms of Christianity emerging as book religions, for instance, Protestantism in all of its forms. Thus the classical criteriology, both Catholic and Protestant, rests on a foundational location of divine–human identity, a place where God's very truth can be discerned as identical with the multiplicity of truths offered by human authors of the two testaments. This, however, is only the cornerstone of the foundation. More than just divine–human identity in Scripture was necessary if doctrinal certainty was to be procured. And this brings us to the second and third locations of identity in the classical criteriology.

4

The Locations of Identity:
Dogma and Church

The criteriology of classical Catholic and Protestant theologies subjects itself not just to a collection of ancient writings but to specific divinely revealed contents or doctrines. The preceding chapter attempted to uncover one of the definitive places where these contents occur, sacred Scripture. According to that account the Christian movement, after some hesitation and resistance, appropriated the Judaic Scripture principle with its presuppositions and middle axioms and extended it to a collection of early Christian writings. But a description of the classical criteriology cannot limit itself simply to this single foundation, Scripture. The classical criteriology is not reducible to that single criterion. The identity between divine intention and human words is not restricted to the words of the authors of Scripture. Scripture itself, the original and foundational location of identity, continues in the life of the church as something to be interpreted, studied, and applied. But this ongoing process cannot be turned over to human or satanic autonomies, corruptions, and contingencies. Among the many possible distorted interpretations of Scripture is a definitive one which comes to expression and achieves fixation in a second location of the divine–human identity, the dogmas of the church.

It seems that both the Scripture principle and definitive dogmas presuppose the continued divine activity in the structure and processes of the church. Whether this is the case or not, both the Scripture and its definitive interpretation persist into ever-new historical situations which call for continuing responses and declarations of the church. Here too the logic of teleology and triumph is operative. It is accordingly inconceivable that Scripture and dogma might be endangered by a disobedient church. Thus God continues to be active in the life and structure of the church thereby guaranteeing the proper deployment of Scripture and dogma. The very existence of Scripture and dogma imply this divine activity insofar as they themselves are effects of the divine presence in the church. Thus, we have a third location of identity between divine intention and human acts, the church itself.

Three locations of divine–human identity structure the classical criteriology. We would misread their relation to each other if we arranged the three locations in chronological sequence. From a more formal and theoretical point of view, Scripture has a certain primacy, since both dogma and church are by nature dependent on the deposit of revelation centered in Christ. From a more sociological perspective, the church is the primary location since the written Scriptures, the making of the canon, and the definitive doctrinal formulation are all (divinely guided) ecclesiastical activities. Further, *the* church can identify and propose certain writings of past tradition as Scripture only if it grasps what is essential and definitive about the tradition. In other words the *regula fidei* is an immanent aspect of the church from the very beginning and has a certain primacy in relation to both Scripture and the church's actual life and process. In this sense dogma is primary. Accordingly, all three locations of identity presuppose and require each other. This is confirmed by the historical fact that the church's proposal of the two-testament canon, its articulation of the classical, orthodox theology, and its awareness of the divine activity in its own structure and processes all occur more or less simultaneously.[1]

DIVINE–HUMAN IDENTITY IN DEFINITIVE DOGMAS

The following exposition proceeds in three steps: the background of the principle of dogma in the Scripture principle, the occasion and impetus for the rise of a definitive interpretation, and the essential elements of the principle of dogma.

---

1. More specifically, however, the period in which the church settled on most of the books in the New Testament as canonical (the last part of the second century) precedes the great trinitarian and christological controversies of the third and fourth centuries in which the major dogmas of the church were formulated and approved.

The Scripture Principle as the Background of the
Principle of Dogma: The Parallel with Judaism

There appears to be a consensus in some circles that dogma became central to Christianity in contrast to Judaism because Christianity had to form its identity and its modes of self-perpetuation in a culture pervaded by Hellenism. We begin with this well-known emphasis of Harnack not to reject it but to supplement it with another theme, the role the Scripture principle itself plays in the origin of the dogma principle. Our overall purpose is to uncover the nature, basis, and function of the dogma principle in the classical criteriology.

Widespread is the inclination to interpret dogma, belief, and creeds as Christian innovations in total opposition to Judaism.[2] Such an approach tends to bypass the central clue to the impetus toward and nature of dogma. This clue comes into view only when we recognize that dogma and the occurrence of a definitive tradition of interpretation closely parallels a similar element in Judaism. This element rises from a problem created by the Scripture principle itself, by having a period of revelation and authoritative writings limited to that period. The problem is created by two features of the Scripture principle: Scripture's absolute authority and Scripture's continuing function in subsequent generations of the religious community. The two together mean that Scripture is never self-sufficient but always requires interpretation and application, in other words, *gemara* or commentary.[3]

These two features which require commentary call for exploration. First, the principle of leveling requires that every unit (text) of Scripture be a deposit of divine truth. On the other hand, as a

---

2. See Franz Rosenzweig, *The Star of Redemption*, trans. W. W. Hallo (New York: Holt, Rinehart and Winston, 1970), p. 342; Samuel Sandmel, *We Jews and You Christians* (New York: J. B. Lippincott Company, 1967), pp. 62–65; Martin Buber, *Two Types of Faith*, trans. N. P. Goldhawk (London: Routledge & Kegan Paul, 1951).

3. G. F. Moore maintains that once a religious faith grants authority to revelation as *written*, its whole notion of tradition takes on the character of interpretation and supplementation of those writings. *Judaism in the First Centuries of the Christian Era* (Cambridge: Harvard University Press, 1927–30), chap. 3. Scholem makes the same point emphasizing that once revelation is seen as a *written* tradition the new problem is how that can be applied to new situations and historical times. See G. G. Scholem, "Tradition and Commentary," in Jacob Neusner, ed., *Understanding Jewish Theology* (New York: KTAV, 1973).

collection of writings by different authors from different historical situations, Scripture is not an ahistorical system but a religious and moral pluralism. This disproportion between a leveled, equally distributed authority and historical pluralism within the collection itself engenders the hermeneutic problem distinctive to Scripture. Interpretation is challenged to overcome Scripture's constitutive and actual pluralism. The result is a unification of Scripture in such a way that it can be a basis for appeals. Second, Scripture is an absolute authority which at the same time reflects its historical settings. Thus the regulations, policies, and pieties of the texts cannot be literally imitated in every age. We have here a second disproportion. This is between Scripture's times and situations and subsequent situations, and it too calls for a special hermeneutic. The first problem calls for the resolution of the essential ambiguity of Scripture created by its own time-boundedness and pluralism. The second adapts the results of the first to the plurality, novelty, and situation of the religious community. The first is a hermeneutic of synthesis, the second of application.[4]

We find these hermeneutics at work in the development of rabbinic Judaism. We have described sacred Scripture as originating (with the synagogue and teachers) as diaspora Judaism's solution to its problem of social survival created by exile. But to function at all as Scripture in Judaism's social persistence, it must be interpreted. Attending Scripture are teachers who study it and comment on it. Some find this midrashic activity as early as Ezra and the men of the great synagogue.[5] Once commentary occurs, it tends to persist beyond its own time. It is learned by disciples and passed on in a chain of tradition with the result that future generations interpret both the written Torah and the received commentary. Therefore, in addition to the written Torah a massive oral Torah accumulates in Babylonia and

---

4. A very specific example of the second hermeneutic, the hermeneutic of application, occurs in Maimonides's fourteen principles for interpreting positive and negative commandments. For example, "The enumeration is not to be based on the number of times a particular negative or positive injunction is repeated in Scripture, but instead is to be based upon the nature of the action prohibited or enjoined." See Maimonides, *The Commandments,* trans. Rabbi C. B. Chavel (New York: Soncino Press, 1967), vol. II, p. 397.

5. James W. Parkes, *The Foundations of Judaism and Christianity* (London: Vallentine-Mitchell, 1960), p. 13.

Palestine in the Tannaitic and Amoratic periods. And much of this commentary material survives in written form in the Mishnah and Talmud.

So far we have simply noted the fact that written Scripture is attended by commentary. We have yet to explore and understand the distinctive way Judaism exemplifies this fact. We recall that the functional genre of Scripture in Judaism is Torah, that Scripture's decisive function in the community is as a source of divine legislation. Judaism thereby solved its problem of survival and social maintenance in the face of the threat of assimilation in alien lands by specifying and enforcing the community's corporate life. Since Scripture was the authority for that ordering, the primary function of the commentary on Scripture was the adaptation of Torah to corporate life. Commentary, then, and the oral Torah took on the character of *halakah*.[6] In every period the teachers (commentators) confronted the same general problem. What shall we do in this situation given the fact that Scripture says such and such? Filling the pages of the Talmud are minute struggles with interpretive problems as they concern the ritualistic and moral life of the community.

Finally, the principle of identity was extended from the Scriptures to their commentary. The impetus for this extension is the logic of sovereignty or victory according to which God accomplishes what is necessary to complete his salvific and revelatory work.[7] What would be accomplished if a Scripture were given to the community which remained ambiguous, antiquarian, or inaccessible? To make Scripture work, commentary is required. But what is gained if the commentary itself is merely an ambiguous and fallible phenomenon? The logic is inescapable. Commentary, like Scripture, is a locus of divinely given truths.

Reflecting this extension of divine authority to commentary, the term *Scripture* sometimes encompassed both written and oral Torah. The oral Torah as well as the written Torah was attributed to Moses

6. See Daniel Patte, *Early Jewish Hermeneutic in Palestine* (Missoula: Scholars Press, 1975), chap. 3, for the notion that *halakah* was the most important expression of the oral Torah.

7. See the first section of chap. 1, and the analysis of the ingredients in the notion of salvation history for an elaboration of the logic of sovereignty. See also my article, "Jesus Christ in Historical and Non-historical Schemes," *Perspective*, 9, no. 1 (Spring 1968): 63 ff.

himself.[8] God's word and will for the community are to be found not only in the text of the written Torah but in the teachings of the masters.[9] And because the oral Torah eventually obtained written form, Judaism came to have two authoritative collections that function in its social persistence and that are regarded as deposits of the divine will, namely, written Scriptures and their commentary. To account for the authoritative status of commentary, the "second Scripture," a new periodization occurs, the period of definitive commentary, the literature of which is indispensable to Scripture and is the key to Scripture. In Judaism we have no definitive *dogma* but we do have an extension of divine–human identity to a definitive postscripture tradition of interpretation.

The Impetus Toward the Principle of Dogma

Since Scripture requires by its very nature ongoing interpretation and application to unify its inner pluralism and to overcome its historical provinciality, it is not surprising that Christianity, once committed to the Scripture principle, requires a supplementary commentary. In a strict historical sense oral tradition in both Judaism and Christianity does not succeed but precedes Scripture as that which becomes Scripture when it is reduced to writing. But once that has happened, continuing oral tradition becomes subject to the written tradition and takes on the character of commentary on Scripture. We recall that Christianity's earliest Scriptures were the Scriptures of Judaism. In this period the Christian movement rejected the oral Torah of Judaism and substituted for it Jesus and the apostolic tradition. Jesus and the Gospel are seen as the true fulfillment of the written Torah and the key to and unity of the total narrative. If the Christian movement's canon-making impulses had stopped at this stage, the early writings pertaining to Jesus and the origin of the church would have become the Christian postscriptural counterpart to the Mishnah and Talmud. As it was, the writings of the New Testament were given the status of sacred Scripture in the full

8. See Moore, *Judaism in the First Centuries of the Christian Era,* p. 239. According to Neusner the Torah myth includes the claim that both written Torah and oral Torah were originally delivered by Moses himself. *There We Sat Down: Talmudic Judaism in the Making* (Nashville: Abingdon Press, 1972), p. 73.

9. See Jacob Neusner, *Understanding Rabbinic Judaism: From Talmudic Times to the Present* (New York: KTAV, 1974), p. 8.

sense of the Scripture principle. When this occurred the Christian movement faced a problem similar to that of diaspora Judaism but complicated by the inclusion of two testaments which did and yet did not share the same status. The problem originates in the unavoidable discrepancy between the insights and claims of writings occurring in one cultural setting and the everchanging situation and historicity of the religious community.

This does not mean that the ancient Scriptures are completely obscure until the church clarifies them, a position which Protestants attributed to Catholics. It does mean that Scripture's own internal pluralism and antiquity made it ambiguous as an authority pertinent to subsequent generations of Christians.[10] This sets for the Christian movement a complex hermeneutical problem. Given the pluralism, historical situatedness, and ambiguity of these collections, how can Scripture function as a standard for what the church would confess and a measure against schismatic movements of the true religion? Hermeneutically, this is a more complex problem than that which confronted diaspora Judaism. By unifying the collection under the functional genre of Torah, and using it as a source of community regulation, Judaism at the same time unified and simplified the interpretation of Scripture. Hermeneutic rules could all serve the single purpose of discerning commandments and prohibitions in the texts of Scripture. In contrast, Christianity saw the New Testament as a deposit of the one authentic tradition concerning the coming of the Messiah. The collection, then, must be able to ground belief, valid proclamation, and right teaching. Instead of exploring the text's possibilities for community ordering, the interpreter stands under each and every text as an authority for right belief. The texts in all their pluralism and historical situatedness must be able to fund right belief.

10. This is the main point of Ernst Käsemann's article, "The Canon of the New Testament and the Unity of the Church," in *Essays on New Testament Themes* (London: SCM Press, 1964). He argues that the plurality of the forms of Christendom merely reflects the essential plurality of the New Testament itself and that the New Testament's own internal plurality makes it impossible for a religious community to unify itself at a belief level simply on the basis of its own literature. For a reply to this position, see Hans Küng, " 'Early Catholicism' in the New Testament as a Problem in Controversial Theology," in *The Living Church*, trans. Hastings and Smith (London: Sheed and Ward, 1963).

The church's solution, developed into a self-conscious hermeneutic over several centuries, was to propose a hermeneutic key to the meaning and use of Scripture which transforms pluralism and ambiguity into clarity and definiteness. Without that key, one can make anything and everything of Scripture. With it, the unity and meaning of Scripture is unambiguously clear. This key is the structure of the Gospel itself, called in the early period the *regula fidei* and in later periods simply the teaching, *doctrina*, of the church. In spite of the church's "apostles myth" parallel to Judaism's Torah myth, this essential teaching developed gradually. The importance of this solution is not just that an oral tradition is added to Scripture but that it took a written form whose status and function is that of a definitive commentary on Scripture. It is the key unlocking the mysteries of the text. Like the Mishnah and Talmud this literature has a period, the time of the Church Fathers. Unlike the Jewish commentary, the Christian commentary's main concern is not *halakah,* the regulation of daily life for the pariah community and its individuals. Because of its focus on grounding the continued testimony of the Messiah in the authentic tradition, the commentary literature offered and disputed about the definitive *truths* of revelation. How did this happen?

Instead of attempting a historical account of the rise of dogma in the history of Christianity, we shall describe the major impetus toward dogma internal to Christianity itself and the primary external occasion of its emergence. We recall that the functional genre of Scripture in Christianity is not Torah, oriented toward *halakic* application, but gospel which is oriented toward belief. This difference carries with it an altered view of revelation. Both Judaism and Christianity gave the contents of written Scripture the status of divine communication. This did not mean simply that the divine presence attended the prophetic message but that the very contents (of the Scriptures) originated in the divine knowledge and will. They represent a sufficient communication of what God requires and offers for the salvation of his people and the world. The Jewish version of this emphasizes revelation as Torah, the revealed instructions for the corporate and individual life of the people. Thus revelation is ordered toward salvation, the condition and consequence of which is corporate obedience.

In the New Testament writings the emphasis is still on salvation, the meaning of which is belief-ful participation in the conditions of salvation, in the thing God has done to make salvation possible. More specifically, salvation is an individual's trustful laying hold of the accomplishments and effects of the Messiah's death and resurrection. In some early Christian writings this response occurs in the apocalyptic situation of the imminent end of history as we know it, thus salvation is procured by that event. This apocalyptic element was eventually attached to the motif of individual salvation, the result being a perennial eschatological situation for the individual, the double destiny of heaven and hell.[11]

Pressed by ongoing controversies over who Jesus was and what was accomplished through him, the church more and more insisted that the faithful response to Jesus cannot occur in a distorted act of belief evoked by a distorted representation of Jesus himself. The emphasis thus shifts from faith as the trusting response to Jesus occurring through participation in the messianic community to correct belief in a correctly proclaimed Jesus. And this correct belief becomes the condition of salvation in a scheme of double destiny. Therefore, revelation's relation to salvation is altered. Revelation now becomes the very center of salvation. The proper discernment of revelation's content determines what is Christian. Revelation comes more and more to mean the communication of the truths of the *regula fidei* which are constitutive of belief in Christ and determinative for salvation. Thus, what had been brief formula-type summaries of the Gospel in the New Testament period become in the second century lists of necessary contents to be confessed, carried by such vehicles as the Apostolic Symbol. Thus we have here an internal impetus in Christianity toward dogma, that is, toward truths definitive of the Gospel and expressing the consensus of the church.

This impetus was not in and of itself sufficient to actually accomplish the gradual articulation and conceptualization of key dogmas. That required an actual historical occasion and crisis in the Christian movement. I have in mind here the church's centuries-long struggle with its own syncretism, the result of a universal religious faith attempting to evangelize and exist in a religiously pluralistic time and empire. It seems unnecessary at this point to decide whether Bauer's

---

11. See Rudolf Bultmann, "The Transformation of the Idea of the Church in the History of Early Christianity," *Canadian Journal of Theology*, I, no. 2 (1955). He describes the transformation of the idea of the church from an invisible, unified end-time congregation of God to a sacramental community with its focus on the salvation of the individual soul.

thesis is correct that classical trinitarian orthodoxy is simply that party of Christendom which happened to be the political victor.[12] The fact remains that religious syncretism did occasion a genuine crisis in early Christianity. Expressed sociologically, the survival of the Christian movement depended on successful differentiation from both its Jewish matrix and the plurality of popular gnosis religions which were so widespread in the empire. The new intellectual class that began to come into the church in the second and third centuries brought with it sophisticated schemes of religious and philosophical categories in which the Gospel was interpreted.

The history of the resolution of this crisis is well known. It includes the Christian appropriation, already begun in the New Testament itself, of the vocabulary, modes of argument, and objectifying cosmologizing levels of interpretation whose origins are the great philosophical movements of Greece and Rome. Directing these interpretative instruments toward materials in Scripture and toward the inherited ordering of Scripture in the *regula fidei*, the church attempted to articulate a comprehensive and self-consistent objective doctrinalization of certain elements of the tradition. These doctrinalizations (the Logos Christology, the trinity) originated in polemical writings of individuals but eventually were incorporated into overall unitary accounts of Christianity such as we find in Augustine, Origen, and John of Damascus. Formulated originally by individual church fathers, these doctrines finally obtained the status of official churchwide declarations. The result was dogma, the official teaching of the church deposited in the writings of the church fathers and councils, and the hermeneutical key to the interpretation of Scripture.

The Presuppositions and Constitutive Features of Dogma

By observing a thing's backgrounds, parallels, and even genesis one does not necessarily grasp its essential, constitutive components. All discerned presences have components of meaning which constitute their unity and attend their distinctiveness and which make up the

---

12. Walter Bauer, *Orthodoxy and Heresy in Earliest Christianity*, ed. R. Kraft and G. Krodel (Philadelphia: Fortress Press, 1971). Bauer's thesis is expounded and criticized by H. E. W. Turner, *The Pattern of Christian Truth* (London: A. R. Mowbray, 1954), lect. II.

objective pole of acts of meaning in which those presences exist. Dogma is no exception. Briefly defined, dogma is an officially sanctioned comprehensive proposition which articulates some article of faith and which has the character of freedom from error. This definition permits the distinction between the dogma and the variety of historical expressions in which it can reside yet retains its propositional nature, thus distinguishing it from a symbol. Jesus Christ is not a dogma: "Jesus as the Logos assumed flesh" is.

The foundational motivation behind the presence of dogmas in the Christian movement is provided by one of the presuppositions of the classical criteriology, the royal metaphor of God's relation to the world and the "logic of triumph" of the salvation-history scheme. This impetus toward dogma is not simply the impetus toward *gemara* or commentary, the need for postscriptural interpretation which attends the Scripture principle itself. What the motivation accounts for is why the postscripture commentary is given the status of *dogma*, the immutable and infallible proposition. The answer is that the classical criteriology works from what it regards as the successfully accomplished end of God's historical salvific activity. In relation to the eschaton, it is a penultimate end. As a penultimate end, the divine act and presence in Christ constitutes a de facto salvation occurring in the world in and through the church. This de facto accomplishment of salvation in history sweeps along with it everything necessary to that accomplishment. Thus, the event does not end with the death and resurrection of Jesus as if God accomplished that much and then permitted the whole event to go unnoticed. Rather the event is carried forward by the apostolic witness which must be adequate to and not merely distortive of the event if the event is not to be lost. Nor does God abandon the story with the apostles, that is, with written Scripture whose amorphous character may invite such a disparate response that the salvific event will be lost in a babble of human wrangling. God continues to be a living presence in the church, granting, in addition to Scripture, a definitive commentary and to the church a definitive structure and interpretive power to keep doctrine pure. If one grants the end—God's accomplished salvific operation in the church—one should then grant the means necessary to prevent that being turned over to Satan or to contingency. Such is the logic of the triumphant church. It assumes the royal metaphor of God's relation to the world in which patriarchs, prophets, exile, incarnation, apostolic witness, and dogma all occur as God's teleological disposal of history. Thus the logic of triumph is the temporal aspect of the salvation history scheme.[13]

The royal metaphor and the logic of triumph provide the presuppositions of dogma by first founding the middle axioms of the principle of identity, periodization, and secondary representation. Since dogma as commentary arises from and depends on the Scripture principle, it appropriates these middle axioms. But when applied to dogma, these axioms undergo further refinement. First, dogma involves a refinement of periodization. The Christian movement had divided salvation history into two periods, setting the end of the time of revelation with the apostolic witnesses.[14] With the commentary principle a new period is necessary to *fix the interpretation* of those writings which had translated the event of Christ into narrative and symbolic form. Thus the various writings representing the church's attempt to overcome internal and external syncretism are brought together into a category, the church father, and with that a new period.[15]

Second, "Fathers and Councils" are grouped as constituting a new postscriptural, definitive period of commentary. The identity principle presses the church to acknowledge a type of secondary representative. God's will and word are located in Jesus the Logos of God. That same will and word obtain reincarnation and continued presence in the words of the apostolic witness, Scripture. This scripturalized word

13. In stressing the logic of victory as the fundamental principle behind the doctrine of timeless and definitive dogma, I do not want to ignore the fact that this "logic" found confirmation and expression in the legacy of Platonism. Platonism and philosophies like it created what Wiles calls a metaphysical confidence which makes possible theology's capacity to give "descriptive accounts of ultimate realities in the spiritual world." See Maurice Wiles, *The Making of Christian Doctrine* (Cambridge: Cambridge University Press, 1967), pp. 117–18.

14. Karl Rahner argues just this point in an attempt to make "apostolic" into an immanent and necessary category of the history of salvation. See *Inspiration in the Bible* (New York: Herder and Herder, 1966), part II.

15. George Tavard speaks of the "conventional way of looking at Sacred Scripture as the sum total of the Bible and its commentaries in the Church," arguing that this was narrowed to the biblical canon only later. *Holy Writ or Holy Church: The Crisis of the Protestant Reformation* (London: Burns and Oates, 1959), p. 29. I am not entirely persuaded by this thesis, established as it is primarily by citations of linguistic conventions and the use of the term *writings*. The early church's inclusion of the Fathers in "sacred Scripture" in the full Judaic sense of that collection does not seem to be firmly established by Tavard. His view does exemplify in a very strong way what I am trying to maintain here, the special, authoritative, position given to the makers of dogma in the period of the great ecumenical Councils.

and will are again reincarnated in those who offer the definitive key and interpretation of the apostolic witness, the makers of dogma. The principle of divine–human identity is thereby extended beyond Scripture to Scripture's commentary, an extension which is also found in rabbinic Judaism.[16] Thus, the doctrinal formulations of Nicea and Chalcedon take on the status of God's very communication and wisdom.

Third, the middle axioms of the principle of identity are also extended from Scripture to dogma. Because dogma (the definitive commentary) like Scripture is a location of divine communication, its status of authority and truth equals and even displaces Scripture. Therefore, a repudiation of the trinitarian theology of the Athanasian creed has the same status as the repudiation of Scripture itself. Since dogma as a whole is a location of divine communication, we cannot selectively sift through the vehicles of dogma (such as a creed) for the true items and false items. Truth is thus present in dogma, not in the more indeterminate units of narratives, motifs, and the like, but in atomistic or literary units of propositions. Dogmas by nature tend to lend themselves to the literary form of the definition which, as "truths," are leveled into equal status as authoritative deposits of divine communication.[17] Insofar as dogma occurs in the mode of equally authoritative propositions (leveling), there is impetus to attach the predicates of divine truth to those propositions. The dogma is therefore "true" in the classical Hellenistic sense of an ahistorical, immutable essence.[18]

16. It is not necessary that the literature of Fathers and Councils be *in fact* valid commentary on Scripture either in form (as was the Mishnah and Talmud) or in content. Maurice Wiles correctly points out that the more typical use of Scripture in the Fathers was illustrative not exegetical. He argues that actual church practice, for instance the cultic worship of Christ, was more determinative for the content of dogma. See Wiles, *Making of Christian Doctrine,* chap. 3. My only point is that the church, not being able to simply repeat Scripture, developed a postscripture and an extrascripture tradition of belief and practice which was perceived as rooted in Scripture or the apostolic tradition.

17. The use of the Fathers as authorities in the history of Christian theology displays some ambivalence. On the one hand, the full hermeneutical apparatus used on Scripture and its individual texts was not applied to the Fathers. Furthermore, certain doctrines of individual Fathers (Origen) could be the object of church condemnation. On the other hand, the church could make use of the writings of the Fathers as if they were aggregates of individual authoritative units, and we find this especially in the collections of Sentences in medieval scholasticism.

18. The classical criteriology regarded the content of divine communication as it was voiced by apostles and Fathers as true and therefore true for all time, true as such. This

These extensions of the middle axioms of identity from Scripture to dogma all come together in the notion of dogma's inerrancy. If a dogma *is* a divine communication whereby divine activity so pervades the human propositions that their content is identical with divinely held truth, it will be without error. Like the writings of prophets and apostles, the works of fathers and councils are inerrant.[19]

To summarize, in the classical criteriology dogma, like commentary in Judaism, obtains the status of a second locus of divine communication in which divinely intended revelation and human formulation coincide. Dogma originates in a problem created by the Scripture principle itself—the need for a definitive key that will render Scripture perpetually applicable and resolve its ambiguities. Dogma obtains its status as a second locus of identity when acts of meaning which carry the middle axioms of the Scripture principle are extended to include dogma. When this happens, dogmas become criteria. Creeds, confessions, and writings of church theologians constitute more than just a literature produced by the church's application of Scripture to its actual life. As bearers of dogma these writings are, with Scripture, criteria for all future applications. Accordingly, dogma is not theology or even the product of a theological process but a material norm presupposed by theology. It has become part of the theological given and, as such, an authority.

---

content, unlike the ritual Torah of the Old Testament, could not be relativized. It is simply what the believer grasps and affirms in the course of salvation. It is divine communication a priori to salvation itself. Some qualification of the concept of dogma's immutability has occurred in Catholic theology in the concept of dogma's development (Newman et al.) and in recent Catholic neoorthodoxy (Rahner). The result is that *something*, dogma, is immutable even if its finite expression can undergo development. In this case development does not mean the transition of one thing into another but the realization of inherent potentialities in the original thing. Yet that immutable something may be distinguished from the actual verbal expression it obtains in any given period. Thus Catholic theologians can acknowledge a certain relativity of expression that attends, for instance, the creed of Chalcedon or the papal bull, *Munificentissimus Deus*, which defined the dogma of the Assumption of Mary. Yet the dogma itself, the Assumption of Mary, is a proposition, not just a symbol, and it is immutably true.

19. Contemporary neoorthodox Catholicism, reflecting historical and critical modes of thought, has searched for reformulations of the classical criteriology on this point. From Abelard (*Sic et Non*) through Jean Daillé (*A Treatise on the Right Use of the Fathers*) to the present, contradictions in the patristic writings have been recognized. Reminiscent of postcriticism response to evidence against the inerrancy of Scripture itself, contemporary interpreters have responded by rendering the concept of dogma ambiguous. The search is on to locate that *about* dogma, that element *in* dogma, beneath the relativity and errancy of the time-bound and human formulations, which is inerrant. Obviously, the identity principle is beginning to fade in such efforts, but continued commitment to it is still what prompts them.

DIVINE–HUMAN IDENTITY IN THE
ECCLESIASTICAL INSTITUTION

Our archaeology has so far uncovered two locations of divine–human identity in the classical criteriology, the two-testament Scripture and dogma. These locations function in classical Christianity not simply in its theological criteriology but as vehicles of its social duration. With the help of these vehicles the Christian movement shifted from a charismatic and millenial community to an institutionality stable enough to bridge generations. However, Scripture and dogma were not sufficient in themselves to procure social survival and identity. For tradition, oral and written, exists in a living social entity, the community. They exist as the traditions persist in the community's interpretive, liturgical, and self-ordering activities. In short, the bridging of generations requires institutionalization. Nor did the process of institutionalization chronologically succeed Scripture and dogma. Scripture, dogma, and institution evolved together. If there is a chronological order, institutionalization appears to be primary since the overcoming of the local allegiances of congregations is presupposed by a unified canon or *regula fidei*. Far from being unusual or even a corruption, institutionalization is an inevitable accomplishment of any social movement which endures over time. What is significant is not the fact of the institutionalization of Christianity but the role the institution plays in the classical criteriology. What made that role distinctive was the church's extension of the principle and middle axioms of identity to itself and its own institutionalized structure. That being the case, the church itself becomes a third location of divine communication and of divine–human identity.

The institutionalization which took place in the formative centuries of Christendom does not depend as closely on Judaism as does the Scripture principle. Even so there remains a parallel between synagogal Jewish and Christian institutions, between the synagogue and the rabbis and apostles and their successors.[20] Another parallel goes deeper, the conviction of Israelite religion that God is not only the author of the Torah but of a specific social entity, the holy nation with its institutions. The Christian movement continued this conviction in

---

20. Jacob Neusner has drawn attention to this parallel in *There We Sat Down: Talmudic Judaism in the Making* (Nashville: Abington Press, 1972), p. 25.

the form of the claim that God is the author of the church's specific institutional structure. In addition, the religion of Israel provided Christian institutionality with such specific elements as the priesthood and the theme of sacrifice.

In addition to the religion of Israel, Roman culture, along with its modes of government, was an important historical matrix of Christian institutions. Hannah Arendt argues persuasively that the authority (*auctoritas*) of the Roman system must be distinguished from the coercive power of the despot and slave owner or the rule of reason of a philosopher-king. It is an "obedience in which men retain their freedom." Since authority is carried by those who represent, serve, and confirm the founders and foundation of Rome, it is closely tied to tradition. These carriers have the ability to bear the weight of the past, and their function was to promote development toward the past and toward similarity with the ancestors.[21]

Israelite religion, Judaism, and the Roman Empire all shared certain common elements which the Christian movement appropriated. They highlighted the importance of a geographical center (the land, the holy city, the founding city) as the symbol and source of the institution. They stressed central governance. Even the synagogue attempted to be subject to the central authorities in spite of the tendency toward autonomy in the rabbinical schools. And the priestly, senatorial, and military elements of Rome were a hierarchical structure which distributed authority through strata of leadership. An additional feature common to the whole ancient world is the unreflective consensus that one's own religion or civilization is the definitive form of human culture. The great social forms of existence (Hebrew, Greek, Roman) thought it self-evident that their own form was an unchanging, divinely sanctioned, and valid-for-all-time accomplishment. To such a conviction the cultural relativism which comparative anthropology, history, and sociology have fixed into contemporary consciousness is foreign and inconceivable. This claim to a definitive cultural accomplishment and therefore to a definitive institutionalization was in the air, so to speak, something to be taken for granted by Christendom as it obtained a unified institution. And this conviction is behind the church's ahistorical claim to a valid-for-

21. Hannah Arendt, *Between Past and Future* (New York: Viking Press, 1968), chap. 3.

all-time language, polity, law, dogma, ritual, and system of governance.

The Social-Historical Occasion for
Christian Institutionalization

Dogma is ordered toward Scripture as its interpretative key and commentary, and both dogma and Scripture are functions of an institutionalized community. John Gager's work on the sociality of the origin of Christianity offers historical confirmation of this general rule. According to Gager charismatic leadership marks a movement's initial stage and this becomes transformed into enduring institutions of leadership if the community is to last. This does not exclude the possibility of charismatic periods and leaders reappearing later in moments of renewal, for instance Montanism or the Reformation.[22] Gager follows Werner, Wilken, and others who characterize the transition from charismatic period to stability as the transition from a millenarian community expecting the imminent end of all things to a nonmillenarian, institutionalized community. Symptomatic of the early Christian response to the delay of the Parousia is the Lucan reperiodization of salvation history which depicted a time of the church and therefore set the task of recounting the origin and spread of the church.

Although institutionalization begins with this adaptation to a time of the church, its decisive and originating occasion is the same as that of dogma, the situation of early Hellenistic syncretism and pluralism and the challenge of the so-called heresies. Gager and even Karl Barth have pointed out the positive, even providential function of heresy in the church.[23] The heresies, especially the several forms of Christian gnosticism, evoked a constant barrage of criticism from the orthodox party, and this orthodox-gnostic theological warfare was crucial in

22. John C. Gager, *Kingdom and Community: The Social World of Early Christianity* (Englewood Cliffs, N.J.: Prentice-Hall, 1975), chap. 3. See also Gerd Theissen, *The Sociology of Early Palestinian Christianity*, trans. J. Bowden (Philadelphia: Fortress Press, 1977); Robert M. Grant, *Early Christianity and Society* (San Francisco: Harper & Row, 1977); and A. J. Malherbe, *Social Aspects of Early Christianity* (Baton Rouge: Louisiana State University Press, 1977).

23. See Gager, *Kingdom and Community*, pp. 79 ff. See also Wiles, *The Making of Christian Doctrine*, pp. 32 f.; and William Reiser, *What Calls Forth Heresy?* (Nashville: Vanderbilt University, diss., 1977), pp. 198 ff.

the origin of Christian-Catholic institutionalization. The institution emerges from the way in which the orthodox party rooted its claims in the authentic tradition. We can safely say that for the earliest Christian community there was a twofold authority, the Jewish Scriptures and the Lord. But even by the time of Paul access to the Lord was by way of different deposits of tradition: the Eucharist tradition, the earliest kerygma, certain confessional formulas.[24] And these authoritative units of tradition eventually obtained written vehicles in Gospels and the writings of Paul. Thus the writings of "apostles" give access to the authority of the Lord. Because the Gospel referred to an actual historical person and set of events (the passion and resurrection), we are not surprised that it becomes connected to tradition-bearing writings that record those events. From this comes the principle taken for granted by the church in later periods—the earlier, the more authentic.[25] The way to settle a theological dispute and confute heresy was, therefore, to trace the dogma in question to the original period. Some congregations claimed to go back to the apostolic period. Congregations as early as the latter part of the first century had local leaders (presbyters, bishops) who were primarily teachers. Thus when it became of critical importance where the ancient, apostolic tradition was to be found, the continuity of the churches with the Lord and the apostles emerged as a crucial issue. Since the teachers (bishops) had local authority already, they were obvious candidates as bearers of that continuity. This understanding of the way the authentic tradition persists requires an institution, a succession of bishops which goes back to apostolic times.

The term and concept of *apostle* is not an unambiguous one. Originally the apostles were a rather large group of missionaries with charismatic qualities, and only later was the term reduced to the small circle of officially appointed followers of the Lord, virtually the

24. Goppelt's account of authorities in early Christianity is more complex than the usual twofold Scripture and the Lord analysis. Studying Pauline writings he finds available to the author specific authorities or units of tradition which include the Gospel tradition (the picture of Jesus), the apostolic kerygma, confessional formulas (such as 1 Cor. 15:3), classical ethical instructions. See Leonard Goppelt, *Apostolic and Post-Apostolic Times*, trans. R. A. Guelich (London: Adam and Charles Black, 1970), chap. 5.

25. Wilken offers an account of the origin of the principle (*The Myth of Christian Beginnings* [Garden City, N.Y.: Doubleday and Co., 1971], chap. 2). In his view it is aided by the myth of the uncorrupted original church which only later undergoes corruption.

Twelve.[26] The local bishops trace their lineage to the Twelve and lists of successions of bishops arise, the earliest being that of Hegesippus in the second half of the second century. We have here the primary occasion for Catholic institutionalization. Doctrinal and organizational pluralism in the church develops into doctrinal and organizational unity with the victory of the orthodox party. The result is a definitive dogma and a definitive institution (bishops as successors of apostles and deposits of apostolic tradition). The final step in this process is a new unit of divine–human identity. Because of his place in the succession, the bishop becomes an *authority*. The movement is from the authority of the Lord, to the apostles and their writings, to dogma as containing and expressing that authority, to representatives of apostles regarded as authoritative bearers of the dogma.

Theological Grounds for the Classical Catholic Institutionalization

The historical occasion for the church's initial institutionalization is only one aspect of that accomplishment. Exploring that occasion does not explain why the church came to view its own institutionalization as a locus of divine–human identity. Therefore, we move to a new question. Granting the general need of any enduring social movement to undergo institutionalization, and presupposing that early controversies were the occasion of Catholic institutionalizing, what is there about early Catholic Christianity itself that would prompt it to extend the principle of identity beyond Scripture and dogma to the church itself? We find a number of convictions operative in the church in the period of its initial institutionalization which explain clearly why the church interprets itself as a locus of divine communication.

We should first clarify exactly what we are talking about when we say the church interpreted itself as a locus of divine–human identity. An explicit expression of this occurs in a later period when the church articulated this self-understanding into the form of dogma. We are referring to the first Vatican Council (1870) which attributes infallibility to the church's teaching office and to its embodiment, the vicar of

---

26. On the "Twelve" and "apostles" see R. Bultmann, *Theology of the New Testament,* trans. K. Grobel (New York: Charles Scribner's Sons, 1951), vol. I, pp. 58 ff. According to Bultmann the "Twelve" is a symbol of the eschatological congregation, the true Israel. On "apostles" see vol. II, pp. 104 ff.

Christ. Thus, in addition to a primary location of divine communication in sacred Scripture and the divinely given key to the Scripture in dogma, we have a divinely instituted infallible institution whose articulations under certain carefully specified conditions have the status of divine truth itself. Obviously at work here is the principle of identity, now extended again to another locus, the teaching office of an institution. The episcopal college and the papacy become secondary representatives, ersatz entities of the divine itself, whose declarations concerning Scripture and dogma express God's very will and truth. What theological convictions so guided the church's response to its internal pluralism that this view was the result? Four themes are especially prominent in the church's solution to the problem of conserving the tradition.

First, in the period of controversy with Judaism the Christian movement came to understand itself as the true Israel and thus the telos of salvation history. This self-interpretation presupposes the Christian periodization of history occurring in Luke, Paul, and subsequent Christian writers. But what exactly does this "true Israel" refer to? Minimally, we are talking about an actual, historical community responding to external and internal threats to its existence by institutionalizing itself. This community did not distinguish itself as an ideal, ecclesial reality from its developed institutional vehicles. Instead, it claimed its total, actual historical reality to be the true Israel authored by God, and that included its institutional structure. Because it identified its total actuality with God's willed teleological community, the church saw its developed institutionality as definitive. This is the first theme and it obtained a specific theological expression. On the basis of this synthesis of institution and the divinely intended salvific community, the church saw itself as the locus of the continued presence of Christ, in fact, an extension of the incarnation itself, the very body of Christ whose head is Christ's vicar.

Anticipating the second theme, we recall that the church articulated fundamental dogmas, the knowledge of which was necessary to salvation and the denial of which means disqualification from the church and from salvation. Yet definitive dogmas do not exist in isolation but in a social matrix of activities which make the dogmas and their language available to new generations. Furthermore, the problem that attends Scripture and which pushes a religious community beyond Scripture to commentary also attends dogmas themselves. For like Scripture dogmas have their origin in historical contexts and occur initially as responses to specific issues, crises, and controversies. Like Scripture they are formulated in the languages (Greek, Latin), philosophical frameworks (Platonic, Aristotelian), and the general *Weltanschauung* of their setting. Further, their content is the mystery and complexity of divine being and human historical being, which always gives them the status of attempts. For these reasons dogmas are not absolutely clear, cognitive expressions, self-evident to every human culture and epoch. Dogmas, too, have a certain amorphousness about them which requires continued translation and definition. Their truth may be immutable but this immutable truth always requires interpretation. Accordingly, dogmas can be misunderstood and misused. And this is why these fundamental, necessary articles of faith require an institutional guardian. So when we press the question as to why God's new Israel must be an institutionalized authoritative hierarchy, part of the answer is the necessity of transmitting and protecting the dogmas necessary to salvation.

Third, we have listed as one of the presuppositions of the classical criteriology the dualistic eschatology of heaven and hell as setting the ultimate destiny of the individual soul. This presupposition is not merely an object of belief but has a function in ecclesiastical, political, and liturgical practice, for participation in the church's cultic mediations of sacramental power is the necessary condition of salvation. The church's specific function as the teleological community of salvation is to preside over the *process of salvation,* to hold the keys to the kingdom. The church has authority both to define and guard the saving dogmas and to determine participation in the saving sacraments where Christ's sacrifice is available for appropriation.

These three convictions about the church, its legacy as God's newly elected people, its guardianship of dogmas necessary for salvation, and its presiding over the individual's ultimate destiny, all come together in a new extension of the logic of victory. According to the logic of victory, presupposing as it does God's monarchical disposal of history, God not only wills the end toward which creation and history move, he executes all the necessary means to the end. At no point can any of these means be vulnerable. The incarnation must be carried on in the apostolic witness (Scripture) which obtains definitive interpretation in dogma, which is preserved by an infallible, ongoing institution of salvation, the church. Without the last step, salvation is turned over to the failures, sins, and fallibilities of human beings or to the contingencies of nature and history.[27] God thus equips the church to exercise its task as the guardian of dogma and as a vessel of salvation. The equipment itself is an institution which preserves through succession the authentic tradition and which continues to direct the enterprise of the church through an infallible, hierarchical institutional order. The result is bishops as successors of apostles, congregations unified by a hierarchical structure ranging from laity through successive levels of clergy, and the papacy, the vicar of Christ himself and the seat of infallibility. Present here are the middle axioms of the principle of identity, secondary representation, and immutability. For the original truth and authority are now extended to an institutional representation, and this institution as *the* divinely established institution of salvation has an immutable character.

Because of these theological convictions, the particular solution of the problem of disunity and instability represented in Catholic Christianity (episcopacy, papacy) is one which appropriates the principle of identity. Since the institution has been granted the gift of infallibility, its voice is the voice of God himself. God himself has created the church as his representative vehicle of salvation, and what he has to say he says through the activities of the institution. Needless to say, this Catholic institutionalization was a formidable, almost inconceivable accomplishment of the early church, this obtaining of a unified testimony and order in the face of dismembering pluralism. Its effect was to make the church, along with Scripture and dogma, a third location where the voice of God could be heard and where, in human words, divinely willed content was accessible. Thus, in addition to the fundamental dogmas formulated in the ecumenical councils, the details of polity, liturgy, and moral practice, obtain the status of divinely given contents. The church not only passed through its own

---

27. Hans Küng, probing for the arguments that justify the Catholic claim for an infallible teaching office, summarizes the way Scripture enters into matter. Citing Ott's *Fundamentals of Catholic Dogma* (1960), he finds an appeal to the promise of Christ to remain with the apostles, ensuring the "purity and integrity of the proclamation of faith by the apostles and their successors as assured forever." Thus, "the infallibility of the promulgation of faith is a presupposition of the unity and of the indestructibility of the Church." Needless to say, this is not Küng's own position, but it clearly exemplifies the logic of victory argument, the claim to infallibility on the basis of what is necessary *if* the church is to be a triumphant actualization of God's will. See Küng's *Infallible? An Inquiry* (Garden City, N.Y.: Doubleday and Co., 1971), p. 68.

early charismatic and millenarian phase toward institutional stability; it found a way to sanctify that institution as a location of God's communication. The church's institutionality became part of the theological given, that which must be attended to as normative by those who would discover what is to be believed, taught, and practiced. With Scripture and dogma the church too is an authority.[28]

28. Thus we have three locations of divine–human identity: Scripture, dogma, and the church's teaching authority. This threefold location of identity is clearly stated in the second Vatican Council. "It is clear, therefore, that sacred tradition, sacred Scripture, and the teaching authority of the Church, in accord with God's most wise design, are so linked and joined together and each in its own way under the action of the one Holy Spirit contribute effectively to the salvation of souls." "Revelation," Article 10, in Walter M. Abbott, ed., *The Documents of Vatican II* (New York: American Press, 1966).

5

Theological Method in the
Classical Criteriology

We move now to the uppermost stratum of the classical criteriology, the traditional Catholic and Protestant way of understanding how theological judgments are grounded. Three presuppositional strata of that understanding have been uncovered. The deepest one, religious faith itself, includes both retentions and modifications of the religions of Israel and Judaism. The second consists of the founding presuppositions and axioms presupposed by the locations of authority. The third is the locations themselves, places where the divine communication obtains specific articulation (Scripture, dogma, the teaching office). The fourth and uppermost stratum is simply the interpretative work itself, the theological thinking (in disputation, antiheresy polemic, systematic exposition, philosophical apologetic) which we find recorded in the church's theological and conciliar literature. The term *criteriology* centers on how criteria are constructed and employed in that thinking. The term *theology* may, however, mislead us. It can be used so broadly as to refer to every genre of interpretative activity in the church: liturgies, prayers, biographies, and canon law proposals. While these activities do reflect theological postures, theology is used here in the narrower sense of a self-conscious attempt to arrive at critical and constructive interpretations (judgments) of the faith in the church.

Even with this narrower definition, is it possible to describe a criteriology which stretches over eighteen or so centuries of the church's thought and embraces both Catholicism and Protestantism? Does this not do violence to the variety which has marked every period of the church and even characterizes the phases of thought of

individual theologians—Augustine, for example? We cannot but acknowledge these perils and risks. Furthermore, the violence which
generalization works on historical particulars is more manifest in the
uppermost stratum of actual theological thinking. Here there are
enormous differences from age to age, church group to church
group, individual to individual on how theological thinking is conceived and performed. Martin Luther and Martin Chemnitz, a
Lutheran scholastic, may agree at the level of the deeper strata,
salvation history, the Scripture principle, and yet pursue theological
work with widely divergent convictions and styles. On the other hand,
it would be a mistake to so focus on the evident variety which
differentiates branches of Christendom, periods, and theologians as to
miss what they do have in common. It is this common element in the
theological thinking of classical Christianity which we would portray
in this final archaeological step.

The common elements tend to recede from view when we restrict
ourselves to the methods and styles of individual theologians and are
more clearly manifest when we address what seems to be a consensus
in classical Christianity on how one properly establishes or defends a
theological position. Furthermore, even the individual theologians
who seem to be exceptions to this classical method and who transcend
it in attitude and procedure (Abelard, Luther, and Pascal) participate
in these common elements. Their oneness with the classical criteriology would be exposed by an interrogation of their theological reasons
for retaining the doctrines of the trinity or the Logos Christology.

THEOLOGICAL THINKING IN THE MODE
OF AUTHORITY

We begin our account with a summary thesis which has negative
and positive aspects. This thesis is neither startling nor original.
*Theological thinking in the classical criteriology is a method of authority and is
therefore not a "science" in either the ancient or contemporary sense of the word.*
We make this distinction between science and authority as alternative
modes of understanding and methods of procedure simply neutrally
and descriptively. Stating the thesis comes easy; specifying its meaning presents complexities. We try to avoid making the thesis depend
on the successful procuring of universal agreement on what "science"
is. Philosophers of science continue to debate what science really is,
and in its broadest sense, the question is simply *the* philosophical

question of knowledge and reality. An initial glance at theology's history discloses that theological thinking has, in varying degrees, appropriated certain general features of science—reality-reference, coherence, rationality, interpretation, pregiven foundations. At the same time, certain features which appear to be unavoidable to any science—natural, social, or humanistic—are either absent or highly reduced in the theological thinking of the classical criteriology. When we discover what these features are and how they are displaced in theology, classical theological method as a way of authority begins to come into view. Summarily expressed, this way of authority locates *evidences* for judgments in vehicles of social persistence (authorities) rather than in immediate manifestation; it is in style and genre *citation* rather than *inquiry*; and, it restricts the question of *truth* to very formal operations.

Vehicles of Duration as the Locations of Evidence

To call classical theological method a way of authority is not an unambiguous statement. The reason is that "authorities" attend all cognitive enterprises. We are faced, then, with the meaning of "authority" in the natural, humanistic, and a priori sciences, and in the "way of authority." In the former, authorities are present in the sense of experts or cognitive specialists. Authorities as specialists are needed because the vastness and complexity of reality require a distribution of areas of knowledge. No single person or group can so master the enterprises of science that he or she knows everything there is to be known at the level of the immediacy of data and the specificity of experiment. The scientist, historian, mathematician, or philosopher "knows" immediately what comes forth in his or her own investigation. The larger portion of available knowledge is known mediately or indirectly by way of social processes of knowledge-mediation which the scientist has good reason to trust. "Authorities" function in this process as deposits of knowledge grounded immediately by specialists and mediately available to the rest of the community. The point to emphasize here is that the area over which the expert presides is at some point a region of immediate or evidential manifestation. The expert does not make his or her own expert judgments "on authority." Thus the area is, in principle, open to inquiry by other experts or in some cases even nonexperts.

Needless to say, "authority" in the way of authority does not refer to this sociology of knowledge insight on the distribution of knowledge, the parceling out of areas of expertise. Authorities are the places where divine communication can be found, the locations of divine–human cognitive identity. These locations may contain descriptions of immediate reality presentations, such as the burning bush. In this instance the immediacy is available only to Moses. It is present contemporaneously only through the written deposit and Moses' immediacy can never be transferred to contemporary immediacy. More to the point, immediate presentation and confirmation is not a central element in the acts of meaning directed to an authority. Rather, the logic of triumph, salvation history, the principle of identity with its middle axioms propel the impetus toward Scripture, dogma, and church. The location as a deposit of divine truth is an *authority* precisely because it replaces immediacy and renders it superfluous. If one is persuaded, on the basis of leveling the Scripture into equally trustworthy and true texts, that the words of the authors express what God himself willed to communicate, that is sufficient basis for knowing that there are angels and demons and that the walls of Jericho collapsed at the sound of Israel's trumpets. Immediate experience of angels or the historical weighing of evidence may be confirmatory, but they are not decisive. We conclude that *the locus of divine–human identity, the authority, is itself the evidence or the location of evidence for religious belief and theological judgment.* Accordingly, evidence for the judgment that astrologers presented gifts to the infant Jesus is the event's recorded presence in the authoritative location (Scripture). That is, presence in the location constitutes a content as evidence and as evidential grounds for judgment. We can see that something much more specific is at stake here than the general acknowledgment that God or even revelation is the ultimate authority. Rather we have a rendering of those general claims into the acts of meaning and presuppositions of the Judaic Scripture principle and its extension into definitive commentary (dogma).

The scholastics offered their own version of this synthesis of evidence and authority. Every science has *archai* or *principia* which themselves are indispensable, unrevisable, and beyond criticism or demonstration. The science works *from* these principles and is not possible without them. A principle of logic, for instance, the law of noncontradiction, though itself unprovable, is the self-evident and necessary basis of all logical demonstration. In the classical criteriology *the principium* is revelation, but this means specifically (because of the various underlying presuppositional strata of the criteriology) human-historical deposits of revelation: Scripture, dogma, tradition. Accordingly, the theologies, historical recollections, pastoral advice, and editings by known and unknown authors of Scripture as well as of the Fathers and Councils are not seen as relative historical and human attempts to interpret the faith but as principles, unrevisable and undemonstrable starting points of theology. These historical efforts become the theological givens from which theology works and to which theology goes for evidence. Further, because of the middle axiom of leveling, the principles are not just Scripture or dogma as totalities but their discrete parts and passages. In other words, specific texts are the *principia* of theology. Thus the contents of those texts, the responses of the authors of Scripture and Church Fathers to their situations, obtain the status of inerrant and unrevisable givens for interpretation. They are transferred from *attempts to interpret* to *that which is to be interpreted,* the revelation itself. And this is the feature of the way of authority which founds all the others, the genre of theology as citation and the formal role of the truth question.

Since Scripture, dogma, and ecclesiastical institutions are all solutions to the problem of the church's social persistence, a sociological description of the way of authority discovers that classical Christianity's vehicles of social persistence are at the same time the principles and givens of its theology. Scripture and dogma are not simply that through which the religious community retains its continuity with the past and remembers its period of origins; they are locations of evidence for judgments about God and his communications. And this is the very essence of the way of authority. The vehicles of social persistence thus displace the sphere of immediate evidence, the sphere of reality presentation. This is what the authority refers to in the way of authority. What better expression is there for the way of authority than the words of the children's song, "Jesus loves me, this I know, for the Bible tells me so."

Citation as the Genre of Theological Argument

It is characteristic of the contemporary scientific mentality, scientific in the broad sense of all cognitive enterprises, to think of cognitively grounded judgments as following a process of inquiry. Science as both a corporate and individual effort has the character of inquiry or investigation. Conclusions, however tentative, occur after the data are gathered, sorted, evaluated, and tested. This is as true of social and humanistic sciences as of natural sciences. This scientific mentality is almost invariably puzzled whenever it concerns itself with theology. The source of that puzzlement is probably that theology *appears* to be science but does not settle its problems in processes of investigation. Theology seems to be knowledge without inquiry. If inquiry means that the issue is open and is settled in the course of the investigative process, theology does not seem to refute heresy and settle disputes by inquiry. We must acknowledge that something that looks like inquiry does in fact attend theology throughout its history. But in the classical criteriology inquiry does not determine whether or not God's being is triune. The reason for this has already been stated earlier in this chapter. The criteria, evidences, and givens for theological work reside in dogmas or doctrinalizations. The problem before the church theologian, therefore, is not whether the dogma is valid. The validity of the dogma is a given, a first principle. This means that the theologian relates to the location of divine–human identity not by *inquiry* but by *exposition*. The intellectual work which attends the church's teaching office is primarily setting forth, understanding, and clarifying the doctrinal given. When new questions and issues do occur, the way they are settled is by citation of the authority: a scriptural text, a Church Father, Church Council, or papal declaration.[1] The theologian's relation to the authority is hermeneutical in character. The agenda which the authority sets is to interpret and apply, not to assess. The authority can generate different hermeneutical activities: strict exegesis, homily, allegorical interpretation, moral

1. We must acknowledge that *in fact* many kinds of reflection and interpretation besides the citation of authorities occur in the life and thought of the church. The great variety of historical types of Christianity, multiple agendas, strata, and functions of institutional life make this unavoidable. Furthermore, a variety of interpretation can and does occur even when the linguistic form is dominated by citation. This can occur because the citation of an authority can occur under many different sets of hermeneutic rules. The ambiguity, unclarity, multiple strata, and antiquity of authoritative texts can easily be exploited by eisegetic techniques which serve hidden or not-so-hidden agendas. Accordingly, citation can be simply the external form of persuasion behind which function political, pietistic, philosophical, and other criteria. However, in the theoretical self-understanding of the classical criteriology, the one legitimate way to settle theological questions is by the citation of the proper authority.

application. What it cannot abide is assessment as to its validity or truth.

Accordingly, in most of the periods of classical theology there is little second-order reflection on "theology." What reflection there is has a hermeneutical character, pertaining to the proper ways to use or cite authorities. Because the doctrine, the substance and content of Christian faith, is a settled matter, there is no such thing as "theology" in the nineteenth-century sense of an enterprise whose end and telos is doctrinalization. *Sacra doctrina* is not "theology" in this sense. Theological inquiry as a process of assessing and revising the doctrine present in the locations of divine–human identity simply cannot occur in the framework of the classical criteriology.

Furthermore, because of the extension of middle axioms of the identity principle to all the locations of divine communication, each unit (text) of the authority is authoritative. Texts are isolatable passages in Scripture, Fathers, and Councils. Citation, therefore, has an atomistic character. Its hermeneutic rules may vary considerably depending on what strata of meanings in the text (literal, allegorical, and so on) it acknowledges and selects. But none of these varying hermeneutic postures questions the atomistic understanding of how the text is authoritative. Citation therefore means citing *this* specific text or saying from the authority. It is, thus, by citation that the doctrinal positions of Catholic and Protestant confessional gatherings are justified, including the theological Declaration of Barmen of 1934.

The Formal Role of the Question of Truth

Our account so far maintains that the classical criteriology displaces evidence with authority and inquiry with citation. This account would be misleadingly incomplete if it resulted in the claim that classical Christian theology was indifferent to the question of truth. No theologian or church group would have acknowledged that the gospel was simply a lie or deception thereby capitulating to Christianity's external critics. Yet the Christian concern for truth has a deeper basis than simply apologetic requirements. That concern may be intensified by and formulated in the general ethos of Hellenism, but its rootage is in Israelite faith and the Christian mythos, for the elements of that mythos are the one God, author of everything other than himself, bestowing reality and unity on the created world. And this founds a reality-oriented posture toward the world which is uncomfortable with deception and falsification and which cannot be utterly indifferent to questions of truth.

The question of truth does, therefore, attend classical theological thinking. But to understand what theological thinking is in the way of authority, we need to discern how the truth question is present. What price does truth pay for its admission? On the basis of the middle axioms of the identity principle, we anticipate delimitations of areas in which the truth question can operate. If the content of the locations of divine–human identity is "divine"—an unrevisable *principium,* the *terminus a quo,* the "from which" thinking begins—then the question of truth cannot be directed toward that content. That is, the judgments which bring the content to expression are not assessed as to their truth or falsity. This in itself is an essential feature of the way of authority. As we have seen, the content of the Christian faith is given in the form of doctrinalization, and the places where it is given are the locations of authority. This content, or at least judgments expressing it, has the character of truth, but it is established as true by the authority functioning as evidence. If we cannot apply the question of truth to the historical-human expressions found in the locations of divine–human identity, what areas remain open to interrogation by truth? Classical theological thinking goes beyond mere exposition and citation to the question of truth in at least two ways.

Both ways raise the question of truth by attempting to grasp the *necessity* of the judgment in question. Rational understanding goes beyond mere *assensus* and the acknowledgment of the truthfulness of the truth by apprehending why the truth is necessarily true. The term *necessity* is not unambiguous. And that ambiguity is clarified in the two ways in which truth is understood in classical theology. The *necessity* of a doctrine can mean that it is logically required by other truths present in the authority or in the already apprehended system of doctrine. Second, the necessity of a doctrine can mean that the doctrine exists in and is required by a transauthority, universal framework. It is required by how the world is.

In the first sense, truth in theological thinking means a grasping of the overall coherence of the objects of belief. Christian theology has never settled for a mere atomism of texts or doctrines. Rooted as it was in the faith itself, theology's legacy from the religion of Israel and the Jesus story, the gospel was not a mere incoherence. It was this initial coherence of mythos and narrative that was given summary expression in early gospel formulas and the *regula fidei*. This coherent mythos and primacy of the gospel could only be in tension with the leveling or atomistic approach to the authority of Scripture. And this was only partly resolved in the rise of the dogma as the definitive key and commentary on Scripture. By the close of the patristic period theology was committed to an atomistic understanding of authority of Scripture and dogma. But the mere exposition of truths distributed in separate propositions in inherited writings does not constitute understanding. Because there is a gospel, a faith of the church, and because truth is one and not self-contradictory, coherence and consistency are a priori features of the relationship between these truths.

The truth question in this first sense enters theology at the point of grasping the coherent relation between truths in the deposit of revelation. Thus is engendered theology as dogmatics, the building of a house of dogma out of the bricks and boards of scriptural texts and church doctrines. There is, accordingly, in Scripture one view of God, Jesus, sin, salvation, church, time, the soul, and creation. Atomism is thus overcome by organizing motifs. But it continues in operation in the method of establishing these motifs, a text-by-text construction of each locus of doctrine. The coherence occurs, then, at more than one level. It is a consistency within Scripture itself which means between the texts or passages of Scripture. And it is a unity and harmony of the motifs or loci of doctrine. Discerning and expressing this overall harmony constitutes one sense of theology's responsibility to truth. Its first moment is exposition and citation. Its completing moment is the formulation of the motifs (for example, the nature of God) and their elements (such as, omnipresence, eternality, mercy) in order to disclose their internal connection.

The second way in which truth enters classical theological method is more apologetics than dogmatics. Here, too, the move is toward understanding in the sense of discerning "necessary" relations. But in this second sense the relations are between a doctrine received as true and universal rationality or its products. The first role of the truth question (internal coherence) clearly dominates classical theological method. The second role is only occasionally present in the history of theology, in the writings of Augustine and Anselm, for example. Their interpretations are indicative. Given the self-evident phenomenon of human rationality, is there in sacred doctrine (the motif of God, for instance) something required for the very existence of that rationality, for the very possibility of knowledge?[2] Given the structure and processes of the cosmos and their status as non-self-explanatory, is there a theological motif whose necessity is established when it is shown to be necessitated by the cosmos? Some periods distinguished fairly sharply between those doctrines whose necessity could be demonstrated in this way (God as the world-author) and those whose necessity could not (the doctrine of the trinity).

Since both of these approaches restrict the role of truth to internal or external coherences, and since they do not apply questions of facticity or reality to the contents of the doctrinalized given, these functions of truth in theological thinking are formalistic. It could be argued that the second or apologetic way goes beyond formalism since it attempts to demonstrate the necessary existence of the referent of the doctrine. But this enterprise nevertheless occurs as a faith seeking understanding. The doctrine itself is never in question and therefore is never investigated. The procedure is to start from the doctrine as a given and then to discover its rational necessity. In neither approach is the critical principle applied to doctrinal content itself. The formulation of these two approaches gives theological thinking the character of demonstration. We recall, however, that theological judgments (and contents) themselves are established not by demonstration but by citation, by appeal to authority. Demonstration enters as a postdoctrinal moment to explore and disclose internal harmony or general rational necessity. To summarize, theological thinking in the classical criteriology is primarily a hermeneutic. Thus, the kinds of activities which characterize it are: (1) citation (*Do* the Scriptures and the fathers affirm that the Logos assumed flesh?); (2) exposition (What does "the Logos assumed flesh" mean?); (3) harmonizing (Is the Logos as incarnate consistent with the immutability and impassibility of God?); and (4) rational grounding (Is there any way that the Logos assuming flesh is necessitated by the nature of the human predicament as creature and sinner or the nature of God's relation to the world?). What is not pursued is the question whether the Logos as incarnate is itself a true doctrine. This is because the theological, doctrinal accomplishment itself has been given the status of criterion, given, and evidence. Furthermore, once the classical criteriology

2. Augustine, *On the Freedom of the Will*, Book II.

(method) was itself doctrinalized and given authoritative legitimation, it too becomes a criterion and a given. The effect of this is to make the way of authority itself immune to criticism, inquiry, and the truth question. In this way classical theology insulated itself from any possible self-criticism not only in its doctrinal content but in its way of establishing that content, its method. This is not to say that self-criticism never occurred. Individual theologians through the ages transcended this criteriology and method in varying degrees. But these individuals are idiosyncratic and not representative figures in the theological tradition at large.

The thesis with which we started may now be clearer; classical theological thinking occurs not in the mode of science but in the mode of authority. This thesis does take for granted certain general features of science. A science is a genre of real inquiry, not just citation. It must make its judgments and draw its conclusions, however revisable these might be, on the basis of evidence which has *some* immediate, experiential presentation. The fact that a content resides in a vehicle of a community's social persistence does not make that content evidential. And it must direct the question of truth to whatever contents are the subject of judgments. Because it eschews these features, replaces the evidence with authority, and limits and formalizes the question of truth, classical theological thinking is a method of authority. Many will acknowledge this thesis as obvious and will go on to defend the classical criteriology on the grounds that the way of science is a correlate of a human autonomy which has control over its content whereas the way of authority is an inevitable feature of any religion of revelation. Whether that is or is not the case, whether the way of authority is a priori to Christian faith or is one among various possible historical modes of self-interpretation available to Christianity, is the question we shall pursue in the chapters which conclude this archaeology.

THE DOCTRINAL LEGITIMATION OF THE CLASSICAL CRITERIOLOGY

Our archaeology of the classical criteriology began with faith of the religious community, then moved on to the foundational presuppositions of salvation history and identity and their middle axioms, the more visible locations of authority in Scripture, dogma, and church, and finally theological thinking itself, the actual enterprise of thought

117

in which the church offered and defended judgments. Even though the presuppositions and authoritative locations are foundational strata of this enterprise, they are not simply hidden. The church has self-consciously evoked commitment to and belief in the authorities, yet it is not entirely unaware of the strata which they rest on. And the church has brought this self-awareness to expression in its *doctrinal justification for the classical criteriology itself.* The church has not only formulated and defended the doctrines of the faith but has developed a secondary theological rationalization and institutional enforcement of its own criteriology. Thus, the elements of the classical criteriology (the Scripture principle, the dogma principle, the magisterium) obtain the same status as revelation itself. With this, the concepts in which these authorities are interpreted also take on the status of contents of revelation.[3] The criteriology itself becomes an article of faith.[4] Thus, heresy can mean a departure from the presuppositions and concepts of the classical criteriology. Sociologically speaking, this doctrinalizing of the way of authority is part of the Christian movement's attempt to survive the dispersive effects of historical change. But by making its criteriology into dogma it absolutized for all time the particular historical accomplishment and solution of a specific epoch. Inerrancy and immutability are not only predicates of the contents of faith and their vehicles but of the methods and hermeneutics of their interpretation. Thus the elements of the classical criteriology are moved into the gospel itself. The Protestant version of this was to make Scripture a locus of doctrine. This doctrinal absolutizing of

3. The point is well expressed by Hans Küng. "What is meant by 'religiously guarding' the deposit of divine revelation? 'The words, *sancte custodiendum,* imply that the object of infallible authority includes *truths which form a safeguard for the deposit of revelation strictly speaking,* even though these truths are not formally revealed (implicitly or explicitly).' And what is there that cannot be part of the safeguarding of the deposit of revelation properly so-called? On the basis of such a definition the Roman teaching office has never hesitated to take up a position 'authentically' on almost all questions in any way relevant—from particular questions of exegesis and history to those of natural science, politics, economics, culture, schools, and thus of course to that of birth control—in all of which the limits of 'infallible' were often fluid." Küng, *Infallible? An Inquiry* (Garden City, N.Y.: Doubleday and Co., 1971); p. 74. The quote within the citation is from Karl Rahner; the italics in the citation are mine.

4. For a brief but good account of the thematizing of "theology" itself in Protestant dogmatics of the seventeenth century, see Johannes Wallmann, *Der Theologiebegriff bei Johann Gerhart und Georg Calixt* (Tübingen: J. C. B. Mohr [Paul Siebeck], 1961), pp. 5 ff. As Protestant dogmatics developed out of the sixteenth century, "Scripture" became itself a locus of doctrine, even as Scripture, tradition, councils, authority of the church all are thematized in the Protestant and the Catholic confessions.

the classical criteriology is not utterly arbitrary since it too represents another extension of the logic of triumph. According to this logic, if God provides certainty about saving doctrine, he surely provides, as part of that, certainty about the criteria for its interpretation.

We shall not attempt an elaborate account of the church's doctrinalization of its own criteriology.[5] Instead, we propose in what is no doubt an oversimplification two identifiable stages of development, the first being mythical-historical and the second conceptual-theological.

The church's self-conscious legitimation of its developing criteriology originated in its internal polemics between "orthodox" and heretical parties. The controversy was over the nature and content of the true and authentic gospel, the gospel promoted by the Lord himself and the apostles. The orthodox party saw the heretics as propounding what was recent and innovative, not early and original, what was local rather than universal, and what was diverse and incompatible rather than what was unified. Thus the period of origin was idealized as the time when the church had one unified message throughout. The one thesis which guides this early legitimation of the classical criteriology is that Christianity, in its originative period, possessed a pure, unified, and completed deposit of doctrine, and the role of all later periods is to preserve, interpret, and guard that deposit.

Such is the thesis. To ground and defend that thesis a "historical" myth, the myth of apostolicity, developed.[6] It is historical in the sense that its referent is a historical state of affairs, the coincidence of present dogma and institutions with apostles' doctrine. According to the apostolic myth Jesus and the apostles (the Twelve), instituted the articles of faith (dogma) and the vehicles of the classical criteriology. In fact, the myth breaks down into several myths and includes the following.[7] The twelve apostles not only received the commission

5. One of the best accounts is Yves Congar's *A History of Theology*, trans. H. Guthrie (Garden City, N.Y.: Doubleday and Co., 1968).
6. The generation of an apologetic myth to legitimate the identity principle occurs in rabbinic Judaism. There, the Torah myth and the Moses myth lay claim to the antiquity (and therefore validity) of the written and oral Torah by tracing it back to Moses himself. This is a clear parallel to the function of the apostles' myth in early Catholic Christianity.
7. For summary accounts of the apostles' myth see Auguste Sabatier, *Religions of Authority and Religions of the Spirit,* trans. L. S. Houghton (New York: McClure, Phillips, 1904), chaps. 4 and 5; R. L. Wilken, *The Myth of Christian Beginnings* (Garden City, N.Y.:

from the Lord to carry the gospel into all nations but actually did evangelize the world; hence the key areas of Christendom (Rome, Asia Minor, Egypt) can trace their origin and tradition to an apostle. The apostles left with their successors formulas to interpret the Gospel which have endured without alteration through succeeding generations. And the Apostolic Symbol is their most important expression. The *regula fidei*, therefore, comes from the apostles, and, according to the story, the Apostle Peter brought the Apostles' Symbol to Rome. The New Testament writings, canonized by the church, go back to the apostles who either wrote the works themselves or had their message recorded by a disciple or companion. The specific way in which the tradition of the apostles was transmitted from generation to generation comes from the consecration by apostles of their successors, bishops. Hence, the succession of bishops in the major churches is the means by which we have a chain of tradition which goes back to the apostles. When the bishop of Rome became the bishop of bishops and the repository of ecclesiastical authority, the apostles' myth again legitimated that development. Accordingly, Peter is said to have established an episcopal see at Rome early in his career, to have exercised a papal rule there, become martyred, and left the Roman See to succeeding bishops. Such is the legend of the *Cathedra Petri,* or Peter's Chair.[8] What is happening here is that the notion of an original, uncorrupted, universal, and unchanging dogma and institution finds expression in legends of origin. These legends then take on quasi-scientific or rational form in the apologetically motivated Christian historians who record spurious events (for example, the Donatian of Constantine) and who propose the apostles' myth as the very foundation of church history.[9]

The theological justification of the classical criteriology translates

---

Doubleday and Co., 1971), especially chaps. 2–4; and Walter Bauer, *Orthodoxy and Heresy in Earliest Christianity,* ed. R. Kraft and G. Krodel (Philadelphia: Fortress Press, 1971), p. xxiii. Wilken closely documents the way the apostles' myth is given "historical" confirmation from Hegisippus's lists of bishops through Eusebius. He sees Eusebius as the key figure who synthesized the assumptions of the apostles' myth into the great themes of immutable church and immutable dogmas present in the church from the very beginning.

8. See Sabatier, *Religions of Authority,* chap. 5.

9. See Wilken's summary of Eusebius as initiating the historiography which interprets the past from the perspective of the uncorrupted, pure time of beginnings, thus assuming the completion of the key dogmas in apostolic times. Later historians, Sozumen, Socrates, and Theodoret, all follow Eusebius on this point. Wilken, *The Myth of Christian Beginnings,* chap. 3.

the major elements of the apostles' myth into a self-consistent system and rationale. This is not to say that the church fathers gave a great deal of systematic attention to such matters. On the contrary, they were more preoccupied with the heterodox challenges to substantial doctrines than with method. Yet the ongoing controversy did engender a family of interrelated concepts which obtained in the Christian movement the status of self-evidence, for instance, authority, orthodoxy-heresy, dogma, rule of faith, canon, inerrancy (of writings), infallibility (of office and persons), succession, the keys, inspiration. Some of these concepts came to specific expression in key writings such as Cyprian's *De catholicae ecclesiae unitate* and in key controversies from the Donatist controversy through the Reformation and Counterreformation. Many simply arose as self-evident implications of preconceptual commitments to the locations of authority and as expressions of the historical-mythical apologetic.

Protestantism, engendered in part at least in a controversy over authority, marked the Christian movement's most explicit formulations of the Scripture principle. And in the course of the seventeenth century this formulation included a specific defense of the middle axioms of identity. Thus, Scripture, the primary location of authority, was expressed in a doctrine of Scripture which included in both Lutheran and Reformed confessions concepts of verbal inspiration, dictation theory, amanuensis, plenary inspiration, inerrancy, and so on.[10] In sum, the classical criteriology did obtain conceptual, theological expression, an official doctrinalization, and to challenge that was to challenge something divinely given. Identity thus is extended beyond the locations of authority to the doctrinalizations which express and defend the classical criteriology. Divine–human identity has thus been claimed for the work of theology itself.

THE PROBLEM OF PROTESTANTISM

This archaeology of the classical criteriology has found its historical examples primarily in the periods of primitive and patristic and therefore Catholic Christianity. However, even though the Protestant

---

10. On the Lutheran side, the fullest historical studies of the seventeenth-century theologians on Scripture are Robert Preus, *The Inspiration of Scripture* (London: Oliver and Boyd, 1955), and *The Theology of Post-Reformation Lutheranism* (St. Louis: Concordia Publishing House, 1970). For the Reformed side see Heinrich Heppe, *Reformed Dogmatics* (London: Allen and Unwin, 1950), chap. 2.

movement made certain departures from Catholic Christianity, it remained within the way of authority. No one would dispute this if it refers to the Scripture principle. But does the Protestant version of the classical criteriology extend also to the second and third locations of identity, dogma, and church? Are these "Catholic" themes eliminated by the Protestant *sola scriptura*? There is no doubt that these themes do express fundamental differences between Protestantism and Catholicism on questions of Scripture, tradition, and magisterium. And it seems evident that Protestantism, especially in some of its branches, is much more a religion of the Book than the sacramental Christianity of Catholicism. Furthermore, Protestantism did formally and theoretically renounce the authority of the fathers for the primacy of Scripture.[11]

De facto, the difference between Catholicism and Protestantism is not as great as their controversies make it appear. Because Protestantism appropriated the Scripture principle with even more emphasis than Catholicism, it could not avoid the amorphousness and pluralism of Scripture and the need for unified interpretation and contemporary application. In anti-Catholic controversies, confessions, and textbooks, Protestant writers insisted that Scripture was sufficient, plain, and evident. Yet Protestantism retained in several ways something like the Jewish commentary and Catholic dogma to help it interpret, apply, and even control the "perspicacious and clear" Scriptures.[12] First, Protestant theology never repudiated the content of that first great Christian commentary literature, the Church Fathers. The great theological-doctrinal scheme produced in the period of the Fathers and expressed in the early ecumenical Councils of patristic, trinitarian, and Logos christological theology was never questioned. The doctrines of the impassible deity, the trinity, incarnational Christology, and original sin continued in Protestant theology as if the formulations of the Church Fathers were simply direct restatements

11. For instance, The Second Helvetic Confession, chap. II; The Belgic Confession (1561), art. VII; The Scotch Confession of Faith (1560), art. XX; The Tetrapolitan Confession of 1530, chap. XIV; The Formula of Concord, Introductory Epitome.

12. For Lutheran sources on the perspecuity of Scripture, see Heinrich Schmidt, *The Doctrinal Theology of the Evangelical Lutheran Churches*, 3rd rev. ed. (Minneapolis: Augsburg Publishing House, 1961), pp. 72–79; and Preus, *Inspiration of Scripture*, chap. 8. The theme is found throughout the classic Lutheran textbooks of theology. Thus, Hutter, *Compendium Locorum Theologicorum*, loc. I, 7; *Hutterus Redivivus* (1842), nos. 47, 48; Baier's *Compendium Theologiae Positivae*, 2nd ed. (1694), chap. II, p. xxiii. For the Reformed sources see Heppe, *Reformed Dogmatics*, pp. 32–36.

of Scripture itself. Occasionally, the normative status of the Church Fathers was formally acknowledged. Reformed and Lutheran branches of Protestantism explicitly expressed allegiance to early ecumenical creeds and incorporated these into their confessions.[13]

Second, the early Lutheran confessions take on the status of dogmatic guides to the interpretation of Scripture. The Lutheran churches adopted three confessional expressions of the Lutheran faith as criteria against internal schism and in external debate: the Augsburg Confession of 1530, the Smalcald Articles, and Luther's Smaller and Larger Catechisms. The Larger Catechism, in fact, was called "the Bible of the laity."[14] The Formula of Concord, like all Protestant confessions, distinguishes between Scripture as the only judge and the Confessions which "merely give testimony to our religion." Our point, however, is that a secondary literature has now arisen which functions as the authoritative, hermeneutical key to Scripture.[15]

13. According to the Formula of Concord, "And inasmuch as immediately after the times of the Apostles, nay, even while they were yet alive, false teachers and heretics arose, against whom in the primitive Church symbols were composed, that is to say, brief and explicit confessions, which contained the unanimous consent of the Catholic Christian faith, and the confession of the orthodox and true Church (such as are the Apostles', the Nicene, and the Athanasian Creeds): we publically profess that we embrace them, and reject all heresies and all dogmas which have ever been brought into the Church of God contrary to their decision." Introductory Epitome, II. Hutter's *Compendium* lists the Apostles', the Nicene, and the Athanasian Creeds as the three great Catholic creeds and affirms them as representing the confessions of the Christian faith against heretics both in and after apostolic times. According to *Hutterus Redivivus*, the Lutheran church receives these three creeds which demonstrate the harmony of the Lutheran church with genuine Catholicism (loc. VI, no. 50). We note that Quenstedt, one of the cited sources, lists in addition to the three, the creeds of Ephesus, Constantinople, and Chalcedon. On the Reformed side, the First Helvetic Confession says, "When the holy fathers and early teachers, who have explained and expounded the Scripture, have not departed from the rule, we want to recognize and consider them not only as expositors of Scripture, but as elect instruments through whom God has spoken and operated" (no. 3). The Belgic Confession of Faith, like the Lutheran confessions, lists three ancient creeds (Apostles', Nicene, Athanasian) as "in accordance with the Word of God" (art. I, V). The Thirty-nine Articles of the Church of England urges Apostles' and Nicene creeds to be "received and believed" (art. VIII).

14. Formula of Concord, Introductory Epitome, III.

15. Hutter's *Compendium* lists as the symbols of the Lutheran church the Augustana Confession, the Apology (Melanchton), the Smalcald Articles, Luther's Catechism, and the Formula of Concord, loc. I, no. 14. *Hutterus Redivivus* follows the same list. We note that, according to Schmid citing Hollaz, some theologians speak of the confessional books as inspired since they "contain and expound the Word of God, formerly communicated by immediate inspiration to prophets and apostles," and because they reflect as "mediate illumination," a special influence of God on the minds of those who wrote them (*Doctrinal Theology*, p. 101).

Third, the authority of symbols or confessions is closely bound up with the concept of fundamental articles of faith. These fundamental articles are "dogma" in the sense of objective propositions the beliefful knowledge of which is necessary to salvation.[16] And these articles are the contents of the confessions. At work here is an understanding of the locations of identity closely parallel to early Catholicism and within the framework of the classical criteriology. According to this confessional Protestant view, God is not only the author of Scripture in the full sense of the Scripture principle, in which Scripture is *the* locus of divine communication, he has further provided the church with a clear apostolically originated consensus about the meaning and essential contents of Scripture, the knowledge of which is necessary for salvation. These contents are definitively formulated in the early ecumenical creeds and are present again in the confessions of Protestant Christianity. Scripture has a postscriptural literature which is its hermeneutical key, the confessions of the church. Therefore, not merely is theology individual exegesis of Scripture but it has a confessional role.

Some of the Protestant churches were not confessional. Left-wing, free-church Protestantism was aggressively anticonfessional and for self-conscious biblicist reasons. This anticonfessionalism does qualify the participation of these churches in the classical criteriology, but not totally. The nonconfessional churches remained in the framework of patristic Christology and theology, even if at a more literal and folk religion level. They took their place in the Reformed tradition, retaining many of its characteristic themes. In addition, these free-church Protestants generated for themselves a specific tradition of interpretation on such things as baptism, church order, the use of Scripture, and the Christian life. And this tradition functioned as their postscriptural hermeneutical key to Scripture. They never officially claimed this patristic-Protestant-sectarian tradition to be a second locus of divine communication. It was perceived, in fact, as simply coincident with Scripture. De facto, these churches had an extrascriptural tradition that included a moral casuistry, a church structure and polity, liturgical practices, and beliefs, all of which were thought of as contents that God himself had willed and communicated. Here, too, the principle of identity is extended, without ac-

16. Schmid, *Doctrinal Theology*, p. 92.

knowledgment and without second-order theological legitimation, to tradition (commentary). And, as in Catholicism and confessional Protestantism, this tradition functioned as the key to the interpretation and application of Scripture. Accordingly, the free churches of the Reformation are more inside than outside the classical criteriology.

The controversy, it seems, between Catholic and Protestant churches was not over the existence of dogmas as valid expressions of divine truth and normative for theological work. Both churches operated with concepts of orthodoxy and heresy and could excommunicate those who embraced heresy. The controversy rather concerned how dogmas were identified. The reformers insisted that dogmas are expressions of that primary deposit of revelation, Scripture. Catholicism, pushing the logic of triumph a step farther, maintained that God equipped the church with the capacity to recognize and define truth over against heresy and both Scripture and the interpretation of Scripture are expressions of that capacity and gift. The difference is a subtle one, and it raises the issue of whether and how the third locus of identity functions in Protestantism.

Where does Protestantism stand regarding the third locus of divine–human identity, the teaching office of the church itself? On this issue the two branches of Christendom appear to be at polar opposites. The nucleus of most Protestant–Catholic controversies was the nature of the institutional church's authority. And it is clear that Protestantism rejected the external features of Catholic institutionalization and its attendant theological themes and justifications: the hierarchy of bishops, the bishops as successors of apostles, the bishop of Rome as the successor of Peter, the doctrine of the keys, the church's claim to infallibility, and its claim to authority over Scripture's interpretation. On the other hand, Protestantism like early Catholicism needed an institutional setting for the interpretation of Scripture and the enactment of salvific means of grace. Furthermore, it participated in some of the foundational theological convictions which pressed Catholicism into viewing the institution as divinely originated and a locus of divine communication.

The most foundational conviction was the logic of triumph. Protestantism with its *heilsgeschichtlich* framework and its doctrines of election and glorification could not conceive of God acting salvifically in Christ and then letting the outcome be determined by human autonomy or historical contingency. Rather, God's work in Christ is followed by God's work at Pentecost and the creation of the new Israel. This salvific work continues in the inspiration of the apostles, the result being the New Testament Scriptures. God's special providence continues with the church in its early elaboration of trinitarian faith in the ecumenical councils. Further, in addition to providing objective conditions of salvation (justification), God creates subjective and social conditions in the internal testimony of the Spirit and in the gifts to the church of ministry and the means of grace (preaching and sacraments). Like Catholicism, Protestantism affirmed that God did not abandon the church but equipped it for its missionary task. The dialectic of the church visible and invisible, militant and triumphant, the concept of the *ecclesia semper reformanda*, the description of confessions as "exactions and impositions of Faith," the formal doctrine that Councils can err, and the principle of *sola scriptura* prevented Protestantism from embracing any formal doctrine of the church's necessary infallibility.[17] Yet the various branches of Protestantism did not see themselves as contingent historical forms of Christianity but as that specific institutionality required by Scripture and necessitated by the gospel. Aided by the notion of a definitive form of history and culture and the Judaic Scripture principle, Protestantism could claim divine sanction for practices, polities, and organization structures. Thus, the divine intention for the church and specific ways to practice baptism, requirements for ordination, and the political form of church order coincide.[18] This means that the voice of God is heard not only in Scripture but in the formulations of church assemblies. To reject or disobey these practices and pieties is to reject or disobey what God himself requires. The splintering of Protestantism into hundreds of sects and denominations has done

17. See the Savoy Declaration of the Congregational Churches, 1658, Preface.

18. Therefore, the Formula of Concord can say that the errors it condemns as "false and heretical" and "inconsistent with the Word of God" are to be accepted only at hazard to eternal salvation (art. XII), and this includes errors of various Protestant groups on such specific matters as restricting baptism to adults, listening to sermons where Catholic masses are said, swearing oaths to magistrates and princes, and so on. The Westminster Confession of Faith (1647) speaks of decrees and determinations concerning the worship of God and the government of his church which "if consonant with the Word of God, are to be received with reverence and submission, not only for their agreement with the Word, but also for the power whereby they are made as being an ordinance of God, appointed thereinto in his Word" (chap. XXXI, 2). At the same time it adds that all such assemblies can err and should be a "help rather than a rule of faith or practice" (chap. XXXI, 3).

little to this absolutistic claim. Nor is it to the point to observe that ecumenically disposed churches now acknowledge valid plurality and even relativity at this level. We are describing the classical criteriology, not its qualification by modern social, historical, and theological attitudes.

Yet the church's identification of its own institutionalization with something divinely intended is only one way that Protestantism retained the identity principle in the third locus. The second way appears in the Protestant conviction, shared with Catholicism, that the church, gathered in official assemblies, could discern and declare the very communication of God. The condition of this discernment, of course, was the anchoring of its claims in Scripture. Thus, we have a qualified or quasi-doctrine of infallibility.[19] Councils can err, but they do not err *insofar as* they are obedient to Scripture.[20] It is a small step from this conviction to the view that the results of assemblies are (because they are scriptural) absolute, immutable, and inerrant. This is not a theoretical but a de facto claim for infallibility which came to preside over both Lutheran and reformed Christendom and which grounded the confidence by which they excommunicated the heterodox. Protestantism likewise saw the deviant believer (heretic) as one who violated not simply a historical but possibly errant and changeable expression of Christianity but a divinely communicated and required content. Because Protestantism extended divine–human identity to the structures and living voice of the church itself, it has, like Catholicism, retained the three-location structure of the way of authority and falls within the framework of the classical criteriology.

19. See Hans Küng's exposition of the Protestant version of the infallible or undefeatable church (*Infallible?*, p. 195).

20. "The Church does not err. It does not err as long as it rests upon the rock of Christ, and upon the foundation of the prophets and apostles." The Second Helvetic Confession, 1566. Quoted from A. C. Cochran, *Reformed Confessions of the Sixteenth Century* (Philadelphia: Westminster Press, 1966), chap. 17.

6

Theological Criticism
of the Classical Criteriology:
Levels of Facticity and Levels of
Internal Correspondence

The overall purpose of this volume is to offer a critique of theological judgment. *Critique* here means the constructive task of exposing and formulating the foundations of these sorts of judgments. We did not begin with the constructive task itself but with a detour into an archaeology of the classical criteriology. The purpose of the archaeology was to set the stage for a major theological criticism and theological decision. The theological criticism shall offer reasons that the classical criteriology and method are no longer viable. The theological decision is whether or not the classical criteriology is part of the foundation of theological judgments. *Criticism* in this chapter is a moment within the critique of theological judgment but is specifically directed at the problems which attend the classical criteriology. The criticisms offered here are radical in that they are directed not merely at discrete features of the classical theological method(s) which are self-evidently problematical but also at the presuppositional strata of the classical criteriology. The criticism, in other words, follows the archaeology. This means that it utilizes a fairly simple exercise of what phenomenologists call bracketing or epochē.[1] It is characteristic of much Christian theology to criticize and reformulate certain features of theological method with little attention to the underlying strata. Bracketing as a methodological operation means temporarily putting the presupposed validity of a set of claims into brackets, thus setting them temporarily out of action, for the purpose of an investigation to see whether and how such claims are justified. The archaeology of chapters 2 through 6 involved a kind of bracket-

---

1. See the author's *Ecclesial Man* (Philadelphia: Fortress Press, 1975), pp. 70 ff., for an exposition of the theological epochē.

ing, putting aside beliefs in order to uncover meanings. The purpose was descriptive. In this chapter we shall suspend the claims to the authority and truth of these strata in order to assess their validity. Thus, for example, we shall bracket even the presuppositions of the Scripture principle in order to assess them. Before proceeding with the criticism itself, we must consider the question of the extent to which bracketing and assessment (criticism) are valid. It is by means of this issue that the classical criteriology has insulated itself from assessment of its deeper presuppositional strata.

THE PROBLEM OF A THOROUGHGOING
INTERNALLY APPLIED CRITICISM

What is attempted here is a radical but at the same time internal, that is, theological, criticism. We intend to interrogate the classical criteriology by means of the faith it purports to express rather than by subjecting it to the symbolic universes of other determinate faiths and philosophies. It is just at this point that a serious dilemma threatens to undermine the critique from the start. The presupposition of that dilemma is expressed by a contemporary theologian using a line from Kierkegaard, "you cannot sew without a knot in the thread."[2] Medieval scholasticism's counterpart to this saying is its Aristotelian insistence that every science works from *principia*. We have something similar in mind in using the term *theological given*. Because human being is being-in-the-world, no human activity is absolutely its own self-reference. No discipline originates its own foundations. The dilemma arises as follows. Since the method of a discipline is made possible by its foundations, it seems impossible to criticize and assess the foundations themselves. This translates into a specific either-or. On one side, we draw on Apostles, Fathers, and Church for materials and the vantage point of criticism. The result is that the darts thrown at the classical criteriology are provided by that criteriology itself. The serpent bites its own tail. The other option is to ground the criticism in universal-rational criteria, thus violating the principle of positivity.[3]

2. Robert C. Johnson, *Authority in Protestant Theology* (Philadelphia: Westminster Press, 1959), p. 11.
3. As defined in *Ecclesial Man*, the principle of positivity expresses not only the correspondence between any science and its method but insists that such correspondence occurs at *determinate levels*. The generic fallacy which violates this principle thus uses universal or very general levels of evidence as criteria for realities or spheres of reality more determinate than those levels. See Farley, *Ecclesial Man*, pp. 57 ff.

The dilemma is the choice between remaining in the circle of the classical criteriology, thus presupposing its validity in order to engage in *theological* criticism, or adopting an external vantage point, thereby forfeiting the theological given and all theological determinacy.

I can only respond to this dilemma by acknowledging its seriousness. Every cognitive undertaking occurs in a situation of determinacy and has both a determinate referent or subject matter (even a priori sciences such as mathematics and logic are determinate though not concrete) and determinate criteria and spheres of evidence. Therefore, thoroughgoing criticism of foundations can never render problematic the total sphere of immediate evidence which founds its cognitive experiences. If that happened, nothing would remain as the subject of criticism. The determinate sphere of reality-givenness may be bracketed for the purpose of permitting that sphere of evidence to disclose itself. But assessing it could only occur by means of another sphere of evidence. Thoroughgoing *theological* self-criticism must occur within and from the determinacy of faith itself. If this is so, how can it be thoroughgoing and how far does the criticism reach? We would argue that criticism and assessment reach all the way back to the sphere of faith itself and at the same time make use of criteria of assessment which preserve faith's integrity. To explore this thesis, we pose the following two questions.

First, can thoroughgoing criticism of criteriology be directed at the so-called essence of Christianity? Admittedly, the expression *essence of Christianity* reflects the agenda of postclassical liberal theologies from Schleiermacher to the present.[4] Yet the attempt to grasp what is "true religion," true Christianity, is an ancient as well as modern undertaking.[5] Without specification, the expression is little more than potter's clay waiting to be shaped. Two alternative meanings especially render it ambiguous. On the one hand, the essence of Christianity can refer to what is a priori to Christianity, features (whether they are shared with other faiths or not) without which Christianity cannot be itself. These

4. The present work offers its own version of the essence of Christianity in chap. 9. An excellent recent treatment of the essence of Christianity with special emphasis on Troeltsch's contribution is Michael Pye's "Comparative Hermeneutics in Religion," in M. Pye and R. Morgan, eds., *The Cardinal Meaning* (The Hague: Paris, Mouton, 1973).

5. The fullest study in English of the essence-of-Christianity movement and literature is William A. Brown's *The Essence of Christianity* (New York: Charles Scribner's Sons, 1902). Brown begins his account with the early church and its depictions of the "Catholic faith."

would include features both distinctive of Christianity and shared with the religion of Israel and other faiths. On the other hand, the phrase can mean what historically has always characterized Christianity. This second meaning recalls Vincent of Lerins's dictum that the Catholic church should hold "that which has been believed everywhere, always, and by all."[6] In this case the essence of Christianity is simply what is historically universal to Christianity.

It is apparent that in this second sense universality (essence) is not a criterion or norm for assessment. In the Middle Ages it could be said that all Christians always and everywhere believed in a geographically located hell and in demonic interference in the daily affairs of human beings. This adds up to the historical fact that such beliefs were present at the time of Christianity's origin and nothing intervened subsequently to discredit them. This historical, de facto universality establishes neither the truth of beliefs nor even their status as *sine qua non* to Christianity. Overwhelming historical data inform us that human communities, including religious communities, adopt beliefs and practices which are nonfunctional, a posteriori, and even contradictory to their own principles and nature, which beliefs continue throughout the history of such religions and thus occur *ubique, semper*, and *ab omnibus*, and that human communities and religions are fallible. If so, the mere historical persistence of a practice or belief establishes neither its internal necessity to Christianity nor its truth. This means that criticism can be directed to even those features in the classical criteriology which have de facto universality, which have, in fact, attended the Christian movement from its beginnings. Accordingly, the mere universal historical persistence of the Scripture principle throughout Christian history does not make that principle a priori to this religious faith nor does it immunize it against assessment. This is not to say that the de facto universal features are necessarily arbitrary or unimportant. They may have played a crucial and positive role in the history of the religious community. But such a role does not place them beyond the reach of assessment.

Second, can criteria be directed at faith itself? The Augustinian slogan, "faith seeking understanding," is an ancient and perennial interpretation of theology working under the principle of positivity.

---

6. Henry Bettenson, ed., *Documents of the Christian Church* (London: Oxford University Press, 1943), p. 119.

But it lends itself to a variety of applications. Within the classical criteriology it functions to insulate the criteriology and the church's doctrines against the cold winds of criticism. The way of authority's version is "faith (the doctrinalized, assented-to truths of revelation deposited in Scripture, formulated in the church's dogmas, and guarded by the church's teaching office) seeks understanding." Yet faith cannot be simply identical with the doctrinal accumulations of centuries. Christian faith existed in human formulations (preaching, Gospels, letters, prayers) prior to the controversies which engendered christological and trinitarian dogmas. Furthermore, in its individual mode, faith is predogmatic in that it occurs as a personal response and corporate participation which may strive for cognitive expression but is not identical with it. Yet this predogmatic faith is never simply nonlinguistic, contentless feeling. Its origin is attended by interpretive (and thereby linguistic) responses. And these responses always occur in a complex of symbols and a determinate historical piety.[7] Many kinds of linguistic entities carry this predogmatic faith: metaphors, allegories, stories, images. In other words interpretation does not enter faith in some later "cognitive" moment, it is present from its inception.

Does this mean that faith's *understanding*, its theological doctrinalization, is a valid object of criticism while *predoctrinal* faith as that which seeks understanding is the untouchable pregiven criterion of assessment? The answer must be negative. The philosophers keep reminding us that human being is being-in-the-world. We would expect, then, that faithful human being occurs as a faithful being-in-the-world, which means that faith's linguistic expressions are faith's perpetual incarnation of itself into the situations and activities of the world. This being the case, faith's images, parables, and stories, illuminating though they may be, are neither immutable nor infallible expressions. Thus, when Israel grasps the divine being through the social and political metaphor of the monarch and his subjects, it is offering a linguistic interpretation of its experience of the divine influence. But we falsify both faith and the nature of its language when we entertain this metaphor as a global, metaphysical, and unchangeable expression of God's relation to the world. This meta-

7. Austin Farrer would prefer to say that the most fundamental mark of being is *activity*. *Faith and Reflection* (New York: New York University Press, 1967), pp. 114 ff.

phor, so pervasive in the religion of Israel, is not a divinely dictated communication but a human interpretation. It persists into future generations of the religious community not as a doctrinalized criterion but as a bearer of human insight. Because faith is also interpretation, struggling always to incarnate itself in the world and express itself in worldly terms, the expressions of faith are situational, historical, and relative. In this sense criticism confronts faith itself, that is, faith's attempt to interpretatively and linguistically incarnate itself.

Thoroughgoing criticism is therefore not restricted to the relativities of commentary or dogma as if the religious community's precommentary expressions of faith in the "period of revelation" were inerrant givens. Criticism applies thus to the presuppositions of faith, formed as they are in the process of interpretation. We recall that Israelite religion and Judaism supplied the classical criteriology with such presuppositions as the monarchical metaphor for God's relation to the world, the logic of triumph, salvation history, and the principle of identity. These contents obtain the status of absolute criteria only if they originate in a divine communication, intended as immutable truth, which is made available to the religious community. Only then can we claim the royal metaphor to be God's own self-proposed metaphor. At work in that view is the principle of identity, itself a candidate for thoroughgoing criticism.

Even as criticism reaches to basic metaphors which attend Israel's faith-interpretations, so it applies also to such apparently normative entities as the kerygma, the Gospel, and the apostolic teaching. These terms express in the Christian movement something to which it is subject, the reality which grounds and unifies its very existence. But realities occur as *interpreted*. The interpretation of the "Gospel" by its earliest extant Christian authors occurs in an apocalyptic and salvation history framework. Are we to conclude then that apocalyptic and salvation history are thereby established as absolute criteria because they functioned in early expressions of the Gospel? The "Gospel," like the Israelite wisdom or prophecy, reflects a faith attempting to express itself and drawing on available language and inherited interpretative frameworks to do so. And inevitable to the attempt are the relativities and fallibilities of human interpretative acts. Only a theory of divine intervention in the process of interpretation could guarantee infallibility. The church, extending the Judaic Scripture principle, elaborated such a theory, which elaboration is itself another historical-human act. We shall raise questions about the adequacy and appropriateness of this theory in the next section. We conclude that thoroughgoing criticism is obliged to direct itself at faith itself, at the faith which from the very first has attempted to interpret itself and which has appropriated available languages for that purpose.

Therefore, in what follows we shall not be bracketing (temporarily suspending) simply the validity of the self-doctrinalization of the classical criteriology and method. We shall place brackets (which thus suspends decision about the presupposed validity) around all four strata yielded by our archaeology. Accordingly, theological criticism is thoroughgoing not simply at the surface level of method but as pertaining to the presuppositions generated by the religious faith itself as it attempted to interpret itself to itself and to the world.

THE FIRST LEVEL OF CRITICISM: HISTORICAL ANALYSIS AND THE EXPOSURE OF FACTUAL INCOMPATIBILITIES

We begin the criticism at the surface stratum, traveling from there to selected features of the lower strata. This first level of criticism is widespread in nineteenth- and twentieth-century theologies informed by historical consciousness.[8] It would be more historically accurate to say that the modes of thinking that first uncovered problems in the classical criteriology began in the early Renaissance. Nicholas of Cusa was one of the first to question the genuineness of the Donation of Constantine, a document which had functioned to legitimate the institution of the papacy. Without in any sense offering a historical account, we simply note the effect of the new postmedieval sciences on the classical criteriology.[9] Evident especially are two major ways in

---

8. *Historical consciousness* is an elusive phrase. I am exploiting its elusiveness by using it fairly comprehensively. Hence, I mean something broader than simply commitment to historical method although it includes that. Historical consciousness includes the following: (1) It takes for granted the general marks of science: evidence, truth, inquiry, the correspondence of object and evidence. (2) Thus, it is antiobscurantist in posture, working from the results of the network of natural, social, and human sciences without absolutizing them. (3) It interprets human phenomena as occurring in a network of interacting biological, political, sociological strata of causality. At the same time many models of the nature of causality continue to guide types of enterprises within historical consciousness; thus "causality" need not mean something incompatible with human self-transcendence.

9. The literature is a vast one. A useful summary of it is John Herman Randall's *The Making of the Modern Mind* (Boston: Houghton Mifflin Company, 1940), especially books II and III. Emphasizing the new scientific world picture are E. A. Burtt's *Metaphysical Foundations of Modern Physical Science* (Garden City, N.Y.: Doubleday Anchor Books,

which the new scientific and historical modes of thought discredited much about classical theological method.

The most obvious and dramatic conflict between the classical criteriology and the new sciences occurs simply at the level of *matters of fact*—beliefs which had the status of facts in ancient and medieval Western thought and which overwhelming evidence simply obliterated. The conflict arose originally in a situation where the church was politically and culturally dominant. Therefore, instead of responding to the evidence submitted by such persons as Bruno and Galileo, the church dealt with the men themselves by way of suppression. Heretical human beings, not evidences, were the threat. But suppression was only a finger-in-the-dike strategy. When the dam burst, the church was faced with a vast new world of facts which simply could not be reconciled with the fact world of Scripture and the dogmas. The story is a familiar one. It includes the alteration of the age of the universe, the discrediting of Genesis 1 and 2 as literal historical accounts of world origins and human origins, philosophical anthropology, and the problem of soul-body dualism. Although the pressure was definitely on the church, ever fighting a losing battle on various fronts, we need not interpret the new sciences as offering a new immutability and new inerrancy. Rather, these sciences offered evidence sufficient to discredit certain fact claims of Scripture and dogma and, in doing so, discredited the axiom of leveling and the principle of identity. In the axiom of leveling, everything in Scripture is true in the sense in which it is presented. With science's discrediting of this principle the way was clear to question mythical-doctrinal secondary accounts of Scripture's origins and authority, the notions of verbal and plenary inspiration, and the dictation model of God's authorship of Scripture.

Our concern so far has been with the clash between the natural sciences and the locations of authority at the level of specific truths or facts. Actually, this clash only sounded the starting gun. Much more effective in demolishing the atomism and literalism of the way of authority were the new historiographies, the application of historical-critical methods to Scripture and eventually to the "historical" myths

1954); and Ian Barbour's *Issues in Science and Religion* (Englewood Cliffs, N.J.: Prentice-Hall, 1966), part one. Ernst Cassirer's *The Philosophy of the Enlightenment* (Princeton: Princeton University Press, 1951) is a brilliant study of the science, psychology, history, and religion in that period.

that underlay the doctrinal legitimation of dogma and papacy.[10] The origin of these methods can be found in the late medieval and Reformation figures. The enterprise proceeded on many fronts: textual (Levitas's [1538] demonstration that the Hebrew Bible's vowel points and accents were not original), authorship (the multiple authorship of the Pentateuch [Peyrerius, 1655], and the authorship of the Gospels and many Pauline letters), origin and context (the wealth of discoveries about the ancient Near Eastern roots of Israelite religion and the Hellenistic and sectarian Jewish roots of Christianity). Not only have many factual historical claims of the biblical materials been discredited by such investigations; the whole process of the origin of the biblical material is now grasped as a historical not a supernatural process.[11]

The effect of post-Renaissance science and history on the classical criteriology was more far-reaching than simply the emergence of irreconcilable factual claims. It is surely an oversimplification to say that post-Renaissance modes of thought offered a unified worldview which displaced the medieval synthesis. It is true that new understandings of the physical cosmos were propounded in the work of Kepler, Copernicus, Newton, and Einstein. But the term *worldview* suggests more than a portrait of the space-time universe. It is laden with connotations of value, reality, and knowledge. Thus the recent centuries of Western culture have seen many worldviews—comprehensive systems in which human being, politics, and nature are understood. At the same time, the accumulation of historical, natural, and social scientific discoveries has shaped all of these worldviews in a certain direction. As different as B. F. Skinner, J. P. Sartre, and A. N. Whitehead are, all would agree in rejecting the ancient ahistorical concept of a definitive culture, of events which are causal effects of a direct divine act, of an expression of knowledge which could claim

10. See Cassirer, *Philosophy of the Enlightenment,* chap. 5, for a brief but insightful description of the origins of Enlightenment historiography. Other works pertinent to the origin of the historical treatment of Scripture are G. Hornig, *Die Anfänge der historischenkritischen Theologie. Johann S. Semlers Schriftverständness und seine Stellung zu Luther* (Göttingen: Vandenhoeck & Ruprecht, 1961); and Peter H. Reill, *The German Enlightenment and the Rise of Historicism* (Berkeley: University of California Press, 1975).

11. An example of factual critique directed not at Scripture but at dogma, the Roman Catholic dogma of papal infallibility, is that of Hans Küng. Küng's fundamental although not total thesis is simply that the popes did and do make errors. See *Infallible? An Inquiry* (Garden City, N.Y.: Doubleday and Co., 1971).

inerrancy as an a priori principle. All of these persons would affirm the continuity of the human being with prehuman biological ancestors, the enormous variety of value systems present in different times and places of the world, the overall psychosomatic unity of the human individual. As I previously indicated, historical consciousness does not mean some particular philosophical understanding of causality, such as determinism; it is essentially the understanding of any entity, including the human being, as occurring in a very complex network of influences that operate without and even from within (e.g., body chemistry) that being. The entity may exercise some responsiveness to these influences and even transcend them in creative activity. Nevertheless, every entity occurs in an ever-changing situation and is itself, whatever the nature of its self-identity, an ever-changing situation. This view, assumed by all modern cognitive efforts from physics to history to contemporary philosophies, is the very heart of historical consciousness. All the data accumulated over the centuries lead in the direction of this general principle.[12]

It is just this general principle which is incompatible with, which has discredited, the mode of thought presupposed by the classical criteriology that places entities (human individuals, writings, institutions) outside the network of multiple influences. The middle axioms of atomistic authority, immutable formulations of truth, the predication of infallibility all contradict this most basic axiom of historical consciousness. Given that axiom, any single utterance of a human being not only has this dynamic network as its background but is pervaded by a multiplicity of biological, cultural, depth-sociological, and depth-psychological meaning-intentions. To predicate immutability and inerrancy to such an utterance (or individual, institution, or set of writings) requires either an extension of inerrancy to all the contents involved, which ultimately leads to ever-larger matrices of influence, or the location of some infallible and immutable aspect of the subject of the claim. Responding to these issues raised by historical consciousness, Christian theologians have more and more pursued the second course. Acceding to the general principle of historical consciousness,

12. The most ambitious and comprehensive synthesis of such data and exemplification of historical consciousness in the mode of speculative philosophy is the work of Alfred North Whitehead. A more recent example of an attempt to synthesize a multiplicity of disciplines and their perspectives into a unified view of human being is Ernst Becker's *The Structure of Evil* (New York: G. Braziller, 1968).

they acknowledge the complexities of the entity and its background in a myriad of environments. This sets for them the task of searching for the gold nugget somewhere in the network—the authoritative element in the dogma, the Scripture passage, or the papal declaration.

For instance, a historical relativity is granted to the *language* and the philosophical concepts used to formulate the dogma, and these are distinguished from the dogma itself which is inerrant. Or a similar relativity is granted to the authors, periods, customs of the religion of Israel, but the authoritative unit is located in the testimony of God's mighty acts or to selected theological themes. At this point, I can only say that these efforts are not so much digging for gold as peeling an onion. Most pathetic are those interpreters who finish peeling the onion, find no authoritative kernel there, and say, we really do not know what the inerrant core of the locations of identity is but we are sure it is there. The reasons for such empty talk are apparently certain a priori commitments. If Scripture is a divinely given location of God's communication, the inerrant aspect, the authoritative evidence, *must* be there a priori.

Once historical consciousness has a foot in the door, there can be no piece within a historically occurring entity which is an exception to its general principle, something which has successfully fended off all influences so as to be an immutable and inerrant expression. This does not mean that historical consciousness is incompatible with the notions of truth and knowledge. On the contrary, truth and knowledge are its very business. What it excludes are entities or aspects of entities so isolated from the processes of nature and history that they are pure, unambiguous instances of absolute truth.

It should be apparent that the Judaic model of authority, the Judaic Scripture principle, is unhistorical, violating as it does the general principle of historical consciousness. When measured by that principle, all the locations of divine–human identity (authority) are revealed as functioning in an unhistorical way. If historical consciousness discredits the middle axiom on which these vehicles of social persistence are based and by which they claim inerrancy, it abolishes these vehicles as authorities in the sense claimed by classical criteriology.

This, in fact, is what happened in the critical theologies of the past two centuries, but it happened in a half-way sense. Interpreters of the Christian faith perceived the incompatibilities created for the classical criteriology at the level of facts, and likewise perceived the effect of historical thinking on the interpretation of Scripture. But the typical response of liberal and postliberal theology was to view this as a hermeneutical issue. That is, the authority is itself intact and only the way it is interpreted presents a problem to theology. This half-way use of historical consciousness indicates why this first level of criticism is not thoroughgoing. What is subjected to criticism are selected middle axioms of the Scripture principle which are obviously incompatible with historical consciousness and its results. What is not bracketed for the purpose of the investigation is the way of authority itself and most of its underlying strata of presuppositions.

THE SECOND LEVEL OF CRITICISM: SOCIAL PHENOMENOLOGY AND THE EXPOSURE OF STRUCTURAL INCOMPATIBILITIES

We begin the second level of criticism by placing brackets around the way of authority itself. This means that we are not *presupposing* the way of authority as valid or invalid. We suspend the question of its validity in order to interrogate it and expose the foundations of its validity for assessment. The first level of criticism merely rejected certain senses in which Scripture and dogma were authoritative, thereby retaining the task of looking for acceptable senses. When theology stops at that level, it tends to become hermeneutics. We shall interrogate the locations of authorities themselves, focusing primarily on the Scripture principle.

A Historical Approach to the Problem

Posing the question in a historical way, we recall that the description of Christianity's appropriation of the Scripture principle included the fact that there was never a time in the Christian movement when the Scripture principle was absent or seriously questioned. The earliest Scriptures of the church were the Scriptures of Judaism, a record of the history and religion of Israel. Further, the church inherited not only Judaism's Scriptures but Judaism's presuppositions concerning the *meaning* of Scripture and its hermeneutical rules for its interpretation. And the church's earliest use of its Scriptures, the Jewish Scriptures, was in controversy with Judaism, for the purpose of showing that the new sect grown from the Jesus movement was the fulfillment of the story recorded in those writings. The whole business is completed when the church adds a collection of its own early writings to the Jewish Scriptures and proposes the new two-testament canon as Scripture in one sense of the Jewish Scripture principle.

At the same time it is clear that the church retained the Jewish Scripture and its accompanying hermeneutical practices only with difficulty. The so-called Old Testament was and was not an authority for belief and practice. The writings of early Christianity were highly regarded, even as "authorities" in the sense of the oldest available testimonies to early tradition. But granting authority to writings in that sense is a great deal different from claiming divine authorship, inspiration, and identity. The point to which this speaks is that the Christian movement represented a departure from as well as continuity with its Jewish matrix. Because of this departure, there was a point in its early history when it could have received the Jewish Scriptures into its cultus not as "sacred Scripture" but as something else. Likewise, its canonizing of its own early literature was a historical act which actualized one among several historical possibilities. We can understand and sympathize with the motives behind the appropriation of the Scripture principle in early Christianity. Some theologians who have repudiated that principle acknowledge that the church's refusal of Marcion's proposal to abandon the Jewish Scriptures resulted in deep and positive benefits to Christianity, helping it to retain continuity with the faith of Israel instead of dispersing into the pluralities of Hellenism.[13] We can thus admit the positive effects of the church's embracing of the Scripture principle. At the same time we note that such an acknowledgment not only does not amount to an argument for the Scripture principle but is destructive of it. For the grounds of that acknowledgment are historical, pragmatic, and sociological. The moment a religious community self-consciously justifies its sacred writings by these thought systems, it has abandoned the Scripture principle. Sacred Scripture is thereby abolished. The acknowledgment of the Christian movement's provisional, historical

13. Harnack argues that Christianity's embracing of the Old Testament helped prevent it from becoming a religion of the book by the very fact of the ambiguity of the Old Testament and the impossibility of using it consistently. *The Origin of the New Testament* (New York: Macmillan and Company, 1925), part II, 3. He likewise points to a number of benefits Christianity received in adopting the Scripture principle such as the creation of a mirror into which the church can look in any age, thus making continuing reformation possible, keeping alive the memory of its origins, and so on (part II, 7, 9). Gager stresses the role of a definitive collection in helping the church make a transition from the instability of a millenarian movement to an enduring institution (*Kingdom and Community: The Social World of Early Christianity* (Englewood Cliffs, N.J.: Prentice-Hall, 1975), chap. 5, B. 2.

wisdom in retaining *Scripture* as a vehicle of stability and duration is not a theological justification. Given the inherent problems of the Scripture principle, these historical-sociological observations do not offer a sufficient reason for Scripture to be a necessary element in Christianity's social persistence and in theology's criteriology.

Ideal Correspondence Between the Vehicle of Duration and the Immanent Essence of the Community

Less familiar than the problem of factual incompatibilities between the classical authorities and accumulated historical and scientific knowledge is an issue which social phenomenological analysis yields. "Social phenomenology" refers to the attempt to apprehend the ideal elements, structures, and interrelations within a social phenomenon.[14] It investigates some actual type of human sociality on the assumption that the very act of "meaning" that type, of "having it in mind," involves grasping its distinguishing essential features. Thus, to entertain in an act of imagination the picture of a squad of marine trainees and a rural Baptist congregation involves grasping features of each which distinguish it from the other and without which it would not be itself. In my own view, the basic stratum of a social group which bears these a priori features is the determinate intersubjectivity of the group, that is, the ways in which the members intend or mean each other not just in the universal intentions which grasp each other as human but in determinate intentions through which they are present to each other as fellow marines, fellow Baptists, fellow family members, and the like.[15] These distinctive and essential features of sociality are "ideal" because they both transcend and are immanent in the group. They are immanent in that the group's distinguishing specificity is not possible without them. They transcend the group in that any actual, historical human group has ways of diverging from its own constitutive features, by either the process of development into another kind of group or the process of self-alienation. However, the fact that a group exists in varying relation to its ideal essence does not

14. Farley, *Ecclesial Man,* part II, contains an exemplification of the method of social phenomenology. See the Appendix of the present work for a brief but comprehensive account of its major social categories.

15. See ibid., pp. 151 ff., for an account of the concept of determinate intersubjectivity.

disestablish such essences or idealities. If that were the case, the cointentions of all human groups would be exactly the same.

In addition to immanent ideal essences which endure in the intersubjectivity of a human group, there are features which logically attend that intersubjectivity but which may have never been historically actualized or even perceived by the group. In other words, the determinate intersubjectivity of a group has idealities that reach into many strata of its sociality such as its vehicles of duration, its social space, and its social time. The relation between the determinate intersubjectivity and these idealities is a logical one, one of correlation or correspondence. Since they are actual historical entities, human groups may or may not actualize these appropriate correlative idealities. In other words, human groups, like human individuals, can actualize themselves in ways which contradict their own immanent ideal essence. For example, given the kind of intersubjectivity which constitutes a familial group, there may be a corresponding social space which involves a place for nurturing the young, a "home" place in the sense of a protective and private environment. This correspondence does not necessitate the actualization of such a space in any specific family, which, like families in the entertainment world, may lack such home space.

I have pursued this concept of essences and correspondences occurring as immanent and ideal features of human groups because adequate assessment of the classical criteriology cannot avoid this deeper level of the relation between the way of authority and its ecclesial idealities. There are a great many levels and types of idealities that correspond to the intersubjectivity of a group. Central to this critique is the *social duration* of the group, thus the social space, the social time, and the vehicles through which the group obtains sufficient stability to endure.[16] This focus on social duration and its vehicles may seem arbitrary. The reason it is not is that in the Christian movement, what came to be regarded as the bearers of evidence, the authoritative deposits of truths available for proof by citation, were also the movement's vehicles of social duration. Scripture, dogma, and church institution were classical Christianity's authorities. They were also the entities through which it bridged the

---

16. See Appendix, below, "The Role of Unifying a Paradigm," for an exposition of the concept of vehicles of social duration.

generations and survived. This coincidence of written authority and vehicle of social persistence is the central feature of the Scripture principle wherever it occurs. Our concern goes beyond this social phenomenological observation. Does the vehicle of duration, sacred Scripture, correlate with or contradict the immanent, ideal essence of ecclesiality and the determinate intersubjectivity which attends it?

Sacred Scripture as a Vehicle of Duration in the Universal Faith-Community

The assessment now being undertaken is, in one sense, premature. Its argument would be clearer and more cogent if it followed the general morphology of social duration (Appendix) and the analysis of the ideal features of ecclesial duration (chapters 10–12). Yet our proposal of a theological criteriology occurs as an alternative to the way of authority, hence we proceed by means of an uncovering and critique of that way. We must acknowledge that the critique and the proposal are closely connected, each presupposing the other in certain respects.

We continued to note in the archaeology of the classical criteriology the important contributions of Judaism. We now offer a thesis. *The Scripture principle does not offer a vehicle of duration that corresponds ideally to ecclesial existence.* We begin by observing that there is no such problem for Judaism, that there *is* a correspondence between Judaism's immanent distinctive essence and Scripture as a mode of social persistence. The reason is as follows. Part of Judaism's determinate intersubjectivity comes from its heritage from the religion of Israel. This includes the pervasive themes of Israel's writings: a specific selected people with a specific cultural heritage (a language, territory, mode of government, cultural taboos and mores), faith in Yahweh in whose activity that people originated and persists, the Adamic myth of creation and alienation, Torah and covenant as specifying the relationship with Yahweh. Although Judaism retained all these features, its historical situation jeopardized or abolished their traditional social framework of the nation and its institutions of duration. Judaism then is a community perpetuating the faith of Israel in the insecure situation of what Weber calls a pariah people, who survive as a minority population in a larger, dominant, and alien society. This created a social space of a relatively closed community within some larger nation regarded as more or less alien. Its national and territorial element continued to function as a symbolic framework of self-identity, memory, and hope. Its social time, like that of the religion of Israel, had the character of salvation history—recollection and hope—but because of the enclosed social space, the present was always a provisional time, a time of maintenance until Zion could be restored. Thus arose the new institutions of maintenance by which the isolated and relatively powerless Jewish community could endure; the synagogue, the rabbinate, and the Scriptures. What founds and unifies those institutions is the commitment of Judaism to a method of enduring as the landless people of God, namely the study of and obedience to the Torah, applying it in such a way that it organizes and redeems individual and social life.

We have here the clue to the distinctive intersubjectivity of Judaism, the ways in which the Jew prereflectively constituted or meant his or her fellow Jews. Not only do Jews "mean" each other through the Adamic myth, the symbolic territorial and nationally oriented memory and hope inherited from the religion of Israel, they also intend each other through the centrality of Torah, especially Torah as *halakah*. Therefore, the written Torah, functioning as an instrument of the survival and social duration of the pariah people, is an essential correlate of this intersubjectivity. Sacred Scripture is God's communicated Torah for the regulation of the life of the people and as such is available as specific authoritation texts. In other words, the Judaic Scripture principle and its middle axioms fits closely with Judaism's very nature. The ideal correspondence between Scripture and the social outcast ethnic community is apparent.

In the Christian movement the correspondence between the vehicle of authority and the ideal essence of the faith community is anything but evident. Christianity's initial appropriation and extension of the Scripture principle is suggestive. The Scripture principle was present in the earliest period when the Christian movement was a sect of Judaism. The Christian community used the Jewish Scriptures in polemics against Judaism to prove itself the true Israel and the community of the Messiah. Later it self-consciously applied the features of Scripture to its own early literature, employing Jewish hermeneutical methods of interpretation as means of sifting and fixing the authentic tradition. These activities may have had a certain situational wisdom. The fact remains that the Christian movement appropriated the Scripture principle in the crisis of controversy and amidst the threat of disunity and dispersement. What it did not do, and, as far as I can tell, never has done, is to ask itself whether the Scripture principle is necessitated or even permitted by its own immanent essence, its own characteristic intersubjectivity, its own distinct social duration. That Scripture has been in a sociological sense a successful vehicle of social duration is without question. That it is a vehicle of *ecclesial* duration which corresponds properly to the ecclesial structure of social existence is not at all self-evident. Can the Scripture principle justify itself in the face of this question? We should not take the question to be merely a sociological one appealing to merely sociological criteria. We are, to be sure, making use of the sociological insight that a community's sacred writings function in and reflect its social duration. But it is a theological concern that insists on a correlation between a community's distinctive reality and its vehicles of social persistence.

We notice that Christianity, like Judaism, inherited certain features of the religion of Israel, and it is possible, even likely, that some of these features persist in the immanent essence of Christianity. We recall, however, that the Christian movement's actualization of Israel's incipient universalism resulted in an abandonment of all territorial and ethnic features as conditions of the divine, salvific presence. This meant that Christianity could begin as but could not remain a sect of Judaism in the sense of the retention of that central feature of Judaism, the obligation to be God's people in the form of an ethnic minority surviving under alien cultural conditions by means of *halakic* regulations. We remember at this point that Scripture "means" the divinely authored Torah given to the people of Yahweh (be they gathered in Zion or dispossessed of Zion) for their salvation, which means the ordering of all of life according to the divine will. Given this meaning, Scripture's other features follow: divine authorship, the time of revelation, atomistic authority. We offer two questions to guide our critical analysis of the Scripture principle. First, is sacred Scripture in this Judaic sense necessary to ecclesial duration? Second, is there an actual incompatibility between ecclesial existence and the social duration appropriate to it and the Judaic Scripture principle? Since a description of ecclesial duration occurs in a later chapter, the suggestions here anticipate and presuppose what is more fully pursued at that point.[17]

17. See chaps. 10–12.

I have argued that the Scripture principle is an appropriate solution to the problem of survival and social continuity of the Jewish community. To more clearly expose correspondence between Scripture and Jewish community, we recall the sociological ground of the principle. The community preserves its unity and cultural-religious distinctiveness through a system of *halakic* regulations that pertain to all of life. We have here an *ethnic* entity which preserves itself within and in contrast to every culture in which it exists by means of a comprehensive system of cultic, moral, and social regulations. Because of these two factors, specific ethnicity (Jewishness) and *halakah*, that which must be cited as source and authority for the regulations must be available in an atomistic or leveling way. The reason is that a specific practice (such as, what exactly are the "corners of the field" to be left to the poor) requires interpretation and commentary on specific literary units. This regulation-grounding function of Scripture and the consequent meaning of Scripture as a collection of authoritative texts requires that each text of Scripture originate in the will, knowledge, and intention of God. Thus, *halakic* regulations and ethnic reference correlates with atomistic or text hermeneutics and with Scripture as divinely and verbally inspired.

A glance at any stage of the Christian movement reveals that the Judaic solution to the problem of social survival and identity has been abandoned. That is, after the Gentile mission, the new Christian congregations were ethnically pluralistic and the maintaining of their unity and identity was not primarily by means of *halakic* regulations but by an experience of a salvation that was a foretaste of the completed salvation of the end-time. Characteristic of the new sect was not the "study of the Torah" but "hearing the message of salvation." Characteristic of the activities of the leaders of the new sect was testifying to the inauguration of the new age, which in their language meant preaching Jesus as the Messiah, as the Lord, and preaching the Gospel of salvation through faith in him. It would be incorrect to say that the new sect had no concern at all for Torah or community regulations. But Gospel not Torah characterized the group's self-identity and self-understanding.

Since the new sect as a universal community abandoned the attempt to formulate the conditions of salvation as participation in an ethnic community, this renders superfluous *halakic* regulations functioning to preserve ethnicity. If that is the case, there is no required set of writings whose function is to ground the regulations and no commentary in the sense of a perpetual device to mediate the units of authority to culture. In other words, atomistic, leveled authority of texts is superfluous for the new nonethnic and nonhalakic community. The actual use of the Jewish Scriptures in the early Christian movement confirms this. They were used not to regulate the Christian Gentile communities but to show that these communities were the inheritors of the ancient faith of Israel.

Further, the new sect did itself produce a literature within a generation of its beginning. Again, the actual early use of that literature confirms the thesis. It was not interpreted by means of the axioms and middle axioms of Scripture, construed as a collection of equally authoritative texts. It functioned in the genres, apparently intended by the authors themselves, of testimony to the events of the new age, descriptions of the historical person in whom the new age was inaugurated, and accounts of the local communities rising in the wake of the ministry and death of Jesus. The new sect had the character of a community experiencing and testifying to an individual and corporate salvation interpreted as a sign of the newly inaugurated epoch.

Correlative to that is not a collection of texts available for *halakic* regulation of the total life of the community but rather a literature which preserves the community's memory of the events and person in which the new age began. The genre of that literature is thus "testimony," "kerygma," "Gospel," narrative. This being the case, there should be little inclination on the part of that community to offer a rationale for that literature in theories of inspiration which would level each passage into a possible authority for citation. Such a literature of historical testimony would not be "Scripture." And it was not, in fact, viewed as Scripture until over a hundred years after the death of Jesus. These narratives of Christian origins need not be constituted or meant as supernaturally and verbally inspired. They need not displace evidence. They need not be inerrant. They need not function in the community in the mode of authoritative citation. They need not be construed as closing down the period of revelation, ending God's revealing activity. All this is the case because the set of correspondences which interrelate sacred Scripture with the mode of social duration in Judaism do not carry over to the ecclesial community. I conclude that early Christianity embraced the Scripture principle not by self-conscious attempts to discover the correlation between its own nature as a "Gospel" community and the literature present in it, but because of temporary apologetic tendencies impelled by crisis and controversy.

Christianity in fact did embrace the Judaic Scripture principle and with it the way of authority as the mode of understanding itself and grounding its interpretive judgments. In so doing, did the Christian movement take into itself an incompatible principle which contradicts its own nature? This seems to be the case. Essential to the Judaic Scripture principle is not merely the principle of identity but the claim that such identity is present atomistically in each saying and text. Thus the Scripture is authoritative (inerrant, trustworthy) on whatever the saying is about. This kind of distribution of authority is appropriate to legal documents which compile specific laws that can then be consulted as discrete entities. Authority distributed in atomistic units (texts) also pertains to collections of oracles where each saying can be considered apart from the others. But these legal and oracular types of authority are simply incompatible with a literature whose genre is testimony to a salvific epoch or narration of certain events. Such a literature can function to control unbridled mythical speculations on the salvific epoch. It can preside over the collective memory of the community so that its self-understanding continues to be informed by the historical transition which took place in the formation of the community. But a literature construed as an atomistic collection of authoritative texts but which is in genre narrative can only contradict the nature of a community whose continuity is experience of and testimony to the Gospel.

This contradiction between the Scripture principle and the ecclesial community appears in a second way. We recall the nonethnic, universal nature of the ecclesial community. Because of this universality, the knowledge and presence of God and the experience of the transition from sin to redemption, while always occurring within some cultural and ethnic sociality, should be capable of being experienced in any and every form of cultural determinacy except insofar as that determinacy has itself become a structure of evil. In principle there should be nothing contradictory between the presence of God and a culture in the first or the twentieth century, or between salvation and the Roman, Norman, Germanic, and Polynesian civilizations.

At this point we recall that Scripture presupposes a definitive period of revelation and that under the principle of identity and leveling, every unit of Scripture is true and authoritative. At the same time Scripture is a collection of writings which occur within historical contexts and are addressed to specific times and situations. The principle of identity thus renders not only the descriptions of these times absolutely trustworthy but the message and counsel of the authors absolutely and timelessly valid. Hence the taboos, laws, liturgies, beliefs, and social institutions of a specific historical group (Israel) stretched out over many historical periods and those of a multiethnic community in one historical period (early Christianity) are proposed as the very commands of God for every time and place and for every human community. To be sure, the very plurality of times and situations in Scripture itself prevents consistent systematizing. This has not prevented systematizing efforts by Christian interpreters. Even if these efforts to systematize an ancient collection were success-ful, the result would contradict the culturally pluralistic nature of the ecclesial community, fostering on its diversity a collection of writings which, in content, reflect various provincial communities and their times yet offered in the mode of atoms of authority. The inescapable result is to render the ideological-symbolic interpretative framework and concepts in vogue at specific historical times as timelessly and absolutely true and authoritative for human belief and imitation. The observation of a day of rest, the sabbath, by the Israelite community, becomes a universal command of God for all peoples of all times, transformed into Sunday in the Christian version. Detailed sexual ethics (on homosexuality, on masturbation) are given the status of commands of God for all historical times and places. Ancient patriar-chalism obtains the status of immutable, divine law.

The Scripture principle can be workable if one grants the desirabil-ity of a continuation of a single ethnic community which perpetually adopts Scripture's regulations to its situation. But once a religious community accepts the validity of cultural pluralism, it cannot model itself on Scripture under the principles of identity and leveling. This is why the Christian movement has always been a hybrid phenomenon. It embraces the Scripture principle in full, with each age claiming to model its communal and individual life on Scripture. This can be done only by ignoring most of the actual contents of Scripture or by so interpreting selective parts that Scripture appears to be the authority. But the enduring solution was to develop a postscriptural tradition and grant it the status of an extension of Scripture. Thus practices could arise, and with them whole branches of Christendom, which only vaguely resemble a repetition of the concrete communal life of the times and peoples recorded in Scripture. It appears then that a universal religious community cannot embrace the Judaic Scripture principle without contradicting its own nature.

The result of the early Christian rendering of its own earliest literature into the form of Scripture is a number of antinomies which seem to go unnoticed by many interpreters of Christianity but which may be responsible for confusions that continue to attend the use of Scripture by Christians. Some of these antinomies are the following.

1. If Scripture is a bipartite canon of old and new covenants, the latter fulfilling and in some sense replacing the former, then the historical relativity of the contents of Scripture is acknowledged. At the same time, all of Scripture is divinely given and atomistically authoritative; hence evidence for the truth of judgments and church practices is drawn from any unit of expression throughout the Old and New Testaments.

2. The meaning of Scripture as Torah is the basis for the *halakic* model which, in turn, is behind atomism and leveling. The church rejected the Scripture as Torah and the accompanying *halakic* usage but retained the atomistic understanding of the distribution of authority.

3. The act of setting a two-covenant Scripture implies that a continuous narrative is that which unifies Scripture. On the other hand, Scripture is not used as narrative in the classical criteriology but as an atomistic compilation of truths.

4. The primary feature of the early and continuing ecclesial community is an experience of salvation in universally available mode, thus without any particular ethnicity as its a priori condition. On the other hand, the New Testament is grasped as a deposit of revelation in the form of atomistic truths and under the Jewish theory of inspiration.

5. The literatures of the Old and New Testaments express the pluralities of times and situations and therefore of interpretations which enrich the testimony to the Gospel but which are not totally consistent with each other at the level of propositional truth. At the same time, under the Scripture principle the New Testament is cited as if each unit of expression were in itself a truth in a system of truth.

These examples may help illustrate the thesis I have been arguing in this section. The problem that attends this cornerstone of the classical criteriology is not simply a hermeneutical one, as expressed in this way: "We know from historical evidence that atomistic citation of Scripture is invalid so let us discover a more adequate set of rules by which to apply, interpret, believe in, and appropriate the texts of *Scripture*." The problem is the Scripture principle itself and its incompatibility with ecclesial existence.

7

Toward an Internal Critique
of the Classical Criteriology:
The Level of Religious Foundations

Chapter 6 offered a thoroughgoing critique of the classical criteriology which placed brackets around faith itself, the gospel itself, insofar
as faith always occurs in the form of specific interpretation and
interpretation is always both fallible and relative to the historical
vehicles it appropriates for its expression. We are now at this point,
the deepest sense in which Christian faith can be critical about itself.
The critique shall bracket (not presuppose) the validity of certain
elements which historical Christian faith has thought necessary to
itself, part of its immanent essence. However, this deepest level of
critique is still not external criticism whose framework is some life-
world or symbolic universe exterior to the faith-world of faith. The
critique remains an internal, that is, theological one. And this is
possible only if there are realities apprehended by faith which can
come to expression in a variety of ways and in degrees of clarity.

THE THIRD LEVEL OF CRITICISM: SCHEMATIC THEMES
FOUNDATIONAL TO HISTORICAL CHRISTIANITY'S
SELF-INTERPRETATION

To launch this criticism we return to the cornerstone of the classical
criteriology, the Scripture principle. I argued previously that the
Scripture principle was incompatible with the very nature of ecclesiality and that its retention results in antinomies and confusing ways of
grounding theological judgments.[1] Proponents of the classical criteriology could well reply as follows: "We grant that the Christian

---

1. See chap. 6, "Sacred Scripture as a Vehicle of Duration in the Universal Faith-
Community."

community is not unified by ethnic-*halakic* regulations. The Christian Scriptures are not a new Christian *halakah*. Nevertheless, Christianity requires a sacred Scripture because the testimony it makes to Jesus and the gospel must be a trustworthy one. If the testimony is simply turned over to human beings, it will be merely a human work: errant, false, legendary, and biased. If the gospel is to persist, therefore, God must do what is necessary to ensure that an authentic and not spurious version persists. Thus, even as God inspired the authors of the Jewish Scriptures, so God inspired the authors of the early Christian writings. The total Scripture, therefore, is like Christ himself, and like the church itself, a gift of God, to ensure certain knowledge of and continuity with Christ and the saving truths of the Gospel."

We recognize in this reply the two foundational strata of the classical criteriology, salvation history and the principle of identity, and behind both the monarchical metaphor of God's relation to the world. Expressed most generally, we have in such an argument the expression of the logic of triumph according to which God accomplishes what he sets out to accomplish, and thus makes sure that nothing along the way is a *decisive* interference. The church looks back from a certain stage along the way, the inaugurated kingdom, and from that vantage point designates what was necessary to get that far, namely, creation, covenant, incarnation, revelation deposited for perpetual availability and certainty (Scripture), dogma to interpret it, and teaching office to guard it. The more traditional expression of such triumphalism is salvation history. And we must acknowledge that the faith of Israel, Judaism, and Christianity all took for granted some version of that scheme. Salvation history is thus clearly an empirical universal, which can be characterized as an element of the empirical essence of Christianity.[2] At this point we are in something of a predicament. Salvation history is a comprehensive framework, not a single concept. It includes the monarchical metaphor of God's relation to the world, teleology, and specific divine interventions. The analysis and criticism of this framework is practically as comprehensive as the theological enterprise as such. In such a situation we can do little more than to provide some indications of the problems inherent in

2. See chap. 9, "Theological Portraiture and the Essence of Christianity," for the distinction between the "empirical essence of Christianity" (what in fact persisted in every historical period) and what constitutes ecclesiality.

salvation history. We cannot avoid such a cursory effort since salvation history is a cornerstone on which the house of authority rests.

The Problem of Salvation History

Salvation history is not a single concept subject to a simple and clear definition. Its original version arose with the faith of Israel. In that version its reference is not universal history but a salvific strand of events which manifests the planning, willing, and executing of God. The divine election of the people of God as a specific vehicle of God's purposes is one way to formulate it. It would not be accurate, however, to say that in the Israelite version God is present only in Israel's history and powerless and absent everywhere else. Further, the telos of this salvation history appears to concern the "nations." Thus, if the history of salvation is a specific chain of events which concern a particular geography and period of the world, its end is the worldwide reign of God. Granting these universalistic elements in Israel's version of salvation history, the focal reference remains the nation of Israel both as the elected means of salvation and as the world center and inheritor of salvation.

In *Ecclesial Man* I suggested that ecclesial existence is an abolishment of salvation history in the above sense because its universalism abolishes all national and ethnic conditions of salvation. Early Christian literature, reflecting such notions, retains salvation history but in a transformed way. After the decline of expectations of an immediate world end, there came (in Paul and Luke) a new salvation history scheme. It differentiated between the old epoch begun with Adam and symbolized by Moses and the new epoch of the church begun by Christ. The second epoch fulfills the first in that the reign of God, postponed in the sense of the end-time, now reaches out to the Gentiles who inherit Israel's election. Salvation history is still a strand of events within world history. Its story (for instance, as told in Peter's sermon in Acts 2) is the story of God and Israel, of the coming of the Messiah, the rise and spread of the church, and the final divinely effected conclusion. The Israelite and Christian versions share certain elements. Both assume the monarchical metaphor of God's relation to the world. God is the world king, and although he must deal with resistance and disobedience, he accomplishes what he wills to accomplish. The course of world history is the result of his volitional activity. A variable in the application of the metaphor is posed by the issue of determinism and historical contingency. Apocalyptic thought exemplifies a deterministic view with a qualification of God's kingship. World history as a whole occurs under the rule of the powers of evil. God's kingship is manifested in this period by permitting this and by a strand of salvific and preparatory events. But history ends with an exercise of God's sovereign kingship which overthrows the powers of evil and rectifies all wrongs. A more contingent view (infralapsarianism) acknowledges historical contingencies and God's responses to them but always affirms that God maneuvers what resists him toward a resolution which is his will for creation as a whole.

Essential to any salvation history view, however, is that God wills a definite end and accomplishes his will toward his creation. And this poses a dilemma of such serious magnitude as to discredit the salvation history framework in its Israelite and Christian versions. There are two key issues involved in this dilemma: determinism and indeterminism, and the scope of God's salvific work as universal or provincial.[3] If we assume that God's way of working is an exercise of deterministic causality, the outcome of his activity and the projects of his will coincide. Accordingly, the book of 2 Kings, the sinlessness of Jesus, the crucifixion, and the papacy are effects of God's causal agency, and they amount to no more and no less than what he willed. This causality is exercised either toward one selected strand of history, such as the history of Israel or a line of events within Israel's history, or it is exercised on all history. If the royal metaphor of God's relation to the world is retained (which it is in salvation history), then the first alternative involves a willful nonsalvific presence in most of human history. But if the royal metaphor is retained and the other alternative is chosen, namely, that the scope of God's will and action are universal, this means that all the horrors of human history have the same relation to God's causality as salvific events. Needless to say, both alternatives break up on the reefs of theodicy considerations, for they involve admitting either that God can but does not will to operate salvifically in all his creation or that he can and does determine all his creation and is thus the determiner of good and evil. Both alternatives retain the royal metaphor but abolish any meaningful affirmation of the goodness and love of God.

The other major issue gives up the insistence on God's determinative causality of what is other than himself. Its model is not causality but influence, and contingencies in world-process are acknowledged.

In this case, whether the *scope* of God's activity is only one strand of history or universal history, the events of human history including events identified as salvific have the status of mixtures of divine act and creaturely response. In this alternative the logic of triumph is dissolved. The church cannot look back from its actualized existence and claim that the book of 2 Timothy and the Council of Chalcedon are necessary events in an overall plan. It cannot claim that they are required by the coincidence of God's projected action and what actually occurs. For these arguments require the deterministic causal (and monarchical) framework of the first alternative. This second option thus avoids the theodicy problem. Its price is the abandonment of the salvation history framework.

To summarize, with the first alternative, salvation history, God's activity as heteronomous causality violates creaturely freedom and autonomy and therefore divine goodness and love are sacrificed. With the second alternative, these features are retained but salvation history goes. In my view there is really no choice. The images of God as love, the reality of human evil, and the reality of creaturely contingency and freedom are all part of the immanent essence of the ecclesial symbolic universe and the monarchical metaphor of God's relation to the world is not. The theodicy issue is thus a devastating problem for the salvation history framework and its elements, including the element of specific interventions. And the problem is not removed or even slightly reduced by theological rhetorical devices which, when faced with such matters, speak about the scandal of particularity, paradoxes, mysteries, or the freedom of God to do what he pleases. This latter "adolescent" notion of freedom is surely inadequate as an account of the freedom of God. For God's freedom, like all true freedom, is an expression of his being which means his character as goodness and love.

The Problem of the Principle of Identity

The principle of identity is the second foundation stone of the house of authority. My earlier description of it focused on the way the principle functioned to found cognitive or truth claims.[3] Actually, identity between divinely willed communication and humanly grasped truths or behavior has itself a basis in a prior divine-human

---

3. See chap. 4, "Theological Grounds for the Classical Catholic Institutionalization."

identity. This comes to light when we realize that the principle of identity is an outcome of what I have termed the logic of triumph, which includes both the monarchical model of God's relation to the world and the salvation history scheme. It may not, however, be evident that classical Christianity embraces the principle of identity.

Depictions of God's relation to the world in the faith of Israel and the Christian faith occur within the Adamic myth of God the world maker. Hence, God and the world are ontologically distinct from each other, and the most universal feature of the being of the world is its dependence on God.[4] Given this conviction, the principle of identity is excluded in the sense of an ontological identity between God and the world, ontological transformation of God into the world, or an identity of God's mode of experiencing (apprehending truth) and that of anything in the world. I have pursued this briefly in order to expose the primary way in which the monarchical model describes God's relation to the world, namely, that of causal efficacy. According to the Adamic myth God is the world author. According to the royal or monarchical metaphor God is the world governor. As the world governor God wills a telos for the world, is the source of the lawful (moral, ontological, logical) aspect of the world, and is active in the world to effect its processes toward its end. Salvation history exemplifies this causal effectual activity.

Such is the situation according to the logic of triumph and salvation history. And this expresses for us the first and most basic meaning of the principle of identity. In this foundational sense of causal efficacy, there is an identity between what God wills to happen and what does happen in the world, especially in history. The relation here is not causal in the sense of an external relation of cause and effect between two entities but is personally and teleologically causal. The phenomenon from which the model is taken is the individual self who imaginatively projects an ideal or wished-for outcome and who takes a successful course of action which effects that outcome.[5] In other

4. I would emphasize here that I am briefly describing elements in the Adamic myth, not theological refinements of it. It may, therefore, be valid to argue as process theology does that in some senses God is also dependent on the world. The dynamic element in the being of the world coupled with any doctrine of God's knowledge and relationality as active, responsive, and personal would imply such dependence.

5. In the classical Catholic and Protestant theologies the anthropomorphic, personalistic elements of the metaphor were rejected as literal descriptions of the *mode* of God's activity. The reason was a view of God's temporality as nonsequential. God's experience

words, the model is the agent self. According to the monarchical metaphor, the God-king projects specific events (or a total course of events) and, through successful causal efficacy, ensures their occurrence. Thus it can be said that Israel's victory in a certain battle (as well as certain defeats) was brought about by God. The meaning here is not that God joined the Israelite armies as simply another powerful warrior who helps but does not ensure victory. Rather, God is determinative of the event. The outcome may involve what appears to be a multiplicity of contingencies, but these contingencies are so dominated by the cosmic monarch that the outcome is sure. Thus there is identity between God's projected, ideal aim and the Israelite invasion of Palestine, the preservation of the infant Moses, the collection of the New Testament, the papacy, and so on.[6]

The identity between God's projected will and events in history is the presupposition of the divine–human identity laid claim to in the classical criteriology. The form of that claim varies. When it takes a primarily social and moral form as in prophetic, social criticism, individual and social ethics, church polity, and canon law, the identity is between a projected will of God in the sense of a commanded ideality and a human individual or social behavior and course of action. Thus there is claimed identity between God's will and the Crusades, the Inquisition, specific forms of ecclesiastical organization (congregational, episcopalian, presbyterian), a specific fund-raising campaign of a congregation, a genre of church music, and an individual's decision to be a minister (though rarely between God's will and such occupations as journalism, landscape architecture, or ac-

---

of the world is thus not one in which past, present, and future are really distinguishable. They all occur simultaneously in God, hence in the literal sense God does not "foreknow" the future. The result of this view is not the abandonment of the principle of identity between God's willing and actual events, but a revelation of the "will" to an eternal plan and election, rather than the more anthropomorphic view of God willing-actualizing in a sequential series.

6. I am aware that the principle of identity between divine will and specified events occurs in a literature and in a set of interpretations which indicate sensitivity to evidence against it or exceptions to it. There is a willingness, for instance, especially within apocalyptic views to acknowledge resistance to God's will, occurrences which anger God and frustrate God's will, and thus events which seem not to be units of the identity. Apocalyptic views attribute such to the provisional reign of power alien to God to be overcome in the time of God's final display of power and will. The outcome is ensured, thus the logic of victory and the monarchical metaphor are still operative. Yet history is a history of provisionally successful struggles against God. On the other end of the spectrum some Hebrew prophets appear to see all events, even rebellion against God, as the work of God.

counting). When it takes a primarily cognitive form, as we find it in the classical criteriology, the identity is between the determination of God to disclose a truth and the linguistically formulated interpretation of an individual or institution. Both forms presuppose God's causal efficacy, his successful actualization of his will in human and historical events.

It is evident that insofar as the principle of identity depends upon the logic of triumph and the monarchical metaphor as applied to an interpretation of history, it is discredited to the degree that the logic of triumph is discredited. In addition, there are difficulties that accrue to the principle of identity itself. Perhaps the most obvious thing to say about the principle of identity in both its causal-efficacy root meaning and its specific forms is that it is a literalized myth. I put it that way so as not to give the impression that I am opposed to present-day hermeneutic attempts to uncover illuminating strata and function of metaphor and myth. But in the classical criteriology the causal-efficacy of God and the principle of identity are not thought of as myths. For some theologians they may be regarded as analogies, but this refers to the fact that human understanding and language never grasp divine reality according to its own mode of being. Such a view is informed by a symbolic universe where the most literal, solid, and certain reality is the divine realm to which creation is an approximation. To say that God inspired the words of Luke writing the Acts of the Apostles, brought about the papacy, and revealed the dogma of the immaculate conception, and that God wills Sunday as a day of rest is to state examples of actual fact. The identity involved is an actual, literal identity. The analogy is due to the inaccessibility of human beings to the mode in which God exercises his causal efficacy.

Several things are involved in calling the principle of identity a myth. First, we are locating its roots in a very ancient pre-Christian, pre-Israelite mode of thought unified by a world picture in which there was constant intercourse between gods and human beings. This is not to suggest that there is no break at all in the faith of Israel with what Eliade describes as myth, where the fundamental problem is the renewal of the world itself through a cyclic restaging of the battle against chaos by drawing forth sacred power. The faith of Israel broke with myth in that sense, and the Adamic "myth" introduced an understanding of the unity, world-transcendence, and mode of presence of divine being which negated a plurality of deities, intercourse between human beings and deities, and a cultus which represents negotiations with the deities.[7]

Characteristic of the ancient religious view and perhaps of all religion, especially insofar as it remains folk religion, is a cosmological (mythical) understanding of God's relation to the world. This means simply that God is conceived as thinking, willing, reflecting, and accomplishing in the mode of an in-the-world being. Insofar as some events (or a course of events) are singled out as products of God's activity, this activity is interpreted as an intervention in the world process. Intervention is what the deities of various religions do, according to the myths. They leave their location and effect things in some human location. They participate in wars, stage catastrophes, prevent catastrophes, make appearances. It is this way of understanding God's relation to the world—namely, divine intervention—which the principle of identity takes over. The classical theology is therefore a mixture of an ancient mythical-literal view with a Hellenistic-philosophical and Hebrew view. The mixture is not a coherent one. The former mode of thought persists in all folk religions including contemporary Catholic and Protestant folk religion which would attribute the occurrence or lack of occurrence of specific events to specific actions of God: bouts of illness, accidents, death, promotions, increased church attendance on a specific day, and the like.

The above paragraph focused on that aspect of the principle of identity which draws forward into Christian interpretation ancient cosmological-mythical views of God's intercourse with the world, especially as a special salvation history involves a selective and interventional intercourse, and as specific claims of piety and belief ground themselves in a divine interventional causality. The emphasis is on the incompatability between such an ancient, "pagan," literalistic view and contemporary modes of thought informed by scientific and historical consciousness. I should add at this point that the selective interventional understanding of God's relation to events faces the same theodicy problem that attends the salvation-historical scheme. Human beings who are disposed toward ideal outcomes "selectively intervene" in their world about them because of the

---

7. For an eloquent exposition of the transformation of "religion" and the Israelite experience (or nonexperience) of God the Unnamed, see K. H. Miskotte, *When the Gods Are Silent* (New York: Harper & Row, 1967), pp. 120, 131.

limitations on both their will to good and their power and knowledge. It would be scandalous and intolerable if a children's cancer hospital had a cheap means of curing all of its cancer-ridden patients without complications but used it on only 10 percent of the patients and permitted the rest to die. Axiomatic in the Christian story is the unambiguous and unqualified goodness of God, the disposal of God toward the good of his creatures. It may be conceivable, as some world religions would have it, that the powers of good and evil are distributed within the world of gods. It is not conceivable that the God of the Adamic myth contains two opposing sets of dispositions, one good and one evil. If this is the case, God's "influence" on the world, assuming for the moment there is such an influence, may be variably efficacious. It cannot be "selective." Assuming the uniform goodness of God, his salvific presence may vary, taking many different forms. The form it cannot take is "selective intervention." If suffering and evil continue in the world, and it would seem they will continue due to certain structural elements built into any nondivine entity, it would not be because of divine selective intervention or nonintervention. This brings us to the second problem.

I have argued that the principle of identity in its causal-efficacy aspect is modeled after the human experience of an identity between a willed aim and an accomplished act, events, or state of affairs. What precisely is it which is identical in such an experience? It is surely not a state of affairs that is identically present or shared in two other states of affairs. The identity or common denominator between willed (intended, projected) aim and actuality is an identity of *meaning*. When something wished for is obtained, the meant entity of the wish remains a meant object in the accomplished occurrence. But is this then real identity? We can say so only at a very synthetic and global level. There are certain constitutive or essential elements of any meant or intended (wished-for) apple, and they are present in the synthetic act of intending an apple both in the act of wishing for it and in the act of buying and eating it. But beyond that synthetic level, identity falls apart. The meaning-act of simply imagining an apple occurs in a concrete psychological act, with the tones of that act reflecting a specific situation: the intensity of hunger, the association of the apple with something else, and so on. In the fulfillment of the wish (eating the apple) that specific situation is replaced by another, resulting in the alteration of these tones, nuances, and the like. This discrepancy is not simply one between essence and existence, as if existence were merely a solidification or actualization of an envisioned form. The discrepancy is promoted by the many factors that make up the dynamic nature of existence: anatomy, plurality, novelty, and so forth. All actualization is thus more complex than the human willed act which can envision only a tiny strand of the billions of events, aspects, and relations that comprise an actual thing. All actualization thus contains surprises for the willing person, at least if he or she is alert to them.

What happens when this model of human agency and action is employed to affirm an identity between divine willing and its actualization in history and nature? At this point we shall pass over the problems involved in assigning to the divine will the in-the-world, intentional structure of the agent self. We shall provisionally grant to the classical theology its voluntarism, its insistence that God does have aims, that God wills. What does it mean to say that there is identity between that will and an actualized, nondivine entity or happening? It depends, of course, on how God's relation to creation is interpreted. If we posit direct causal control of God over every event and process at whatever submolecular levels there are, even to the *res verae* themselves, whatever they are, then presumably what happens is literally what God wills. The trouble with this position is that it simply cannot be maintained without admitting that all freedom and self-initiation in creatures is illusory and that, given the actual content of history, God is an incompetent bungler or some sort of sadist. Identity in that sense carries a high theological price. A more tenable position is propounded by Austin Farrer who argues that autonomy is intrinsic to any real, creaturely entity distinguishable from God.[8] He means that all realities, be they the ultimate constituents of reality (if there are such things) or various levels or combinations of such constituents, from protons to cells to complex mammalian organisms, have self-survival propulsions and self-initiations and responses which serve them. When we connect this notion to the interrelational nature of all real things, their life in various kinds of environments, which environments, themselves, exist in other environments and in a total network of reciprocal influences, we discover an inevitable discrepancy be-

---

8. Austin Farer, *Love Almighty and Ills Unlimited* (Garden City, N.Y.: Doubleday and Co., 1961), pp. 50 ff.

tween what God wills and what occurs. For what occurs is partly the consequence of an unaccountable flow of events reaching from the past, a network which cannot simply be identical with what God directly causes, and partly the result of the contemporary autonomies, responses, and creativities of each level of the created being.

There are those who rest comfortably with the principle of identity even in the face of these considerations because of something they call God's provisional will. God's absolute will is thus acknowledged as being frustrated and no actualization in the world can be identical with it, but God can have a will in relation to all specific situations. I have no difficulty with such a distinction. But it offers little help to the classical criteriology. Translated into an example, we acknowledge that a sequence of historical moments, each event a compromise, leads to some outcome, some accumulated phenomenon: for example, Scripture or writings thought of as holy Scripture. Even if one acknowledges such Scripture as God's provisional will, this will not yield an identity on the basis of which the phenomenon can be an *authority* with predicates of infallibility and immutability. What we have instead is a historical entity emerging out of a series of struggles and compromises between God and the world. Whatever else one can do with this entity, one cannot assign that entity the a priori characteristics of truth, inerrancy, or immutability. Once God's *provisional* will is acknowledged, the claimed identity collapses.

In the light of these problems what would the identity be when affirmed between God and something not God? If we follow the human agency model and say it is the *meaning* object, this appears to be at least conceivable, if we forget for the moment the difficulties involved in such detailed anthropomorphism. That is, it seems possible that God wills a global state of affairs which comes to pass; for instance, a new historical existence is inaugurated. But in assigning the identity to a *meaning,* a kind of comprehensive vision, we have not headed off the enormous discrepancies that can and will occur between the willed aim and the actualized processes, given their authority, contextuality, and creativity. Thus even with this identity of meaning we would not be justified in assigning identity between God's will and the actualized occurrence in the new historical existence by saying God willed the destruction of Jerusalem in 70 c.e., or Paul's remarks about women, or the early Christian appropriation and extension of the Scripture principle. Such an admission would not yield the locations of identity claimed by the church. The only thing that would establish these and their proper use would be the actual demonstration of their necessary place in the new historical existence.

Thus, when we move from the founding causal efficacy moment of the principle to its moral and cognitive form, we discover even more formidable difficulties. We have concluded that the discrepancies between even God's envisioned aim and the autonomous network of the created world ground permit similarity not identity; hence identity cannot be applied to the thing itself. The alternative is to assign the identity to the meaning resident in both the willed aim and actualized aim. But how does one ever discover God's willed aim? The traditional answer is, it is deposited in a locus of authority, but that assumes the principle of identity. And how would one discover that there is identity between God's willed aim and a historical occurrence? The discovery of identical meaning between our willed and accomplished aims is possible because of our own direct access to both sides, to our wishing for the apple and the act of eating the apple. We have no such direct access to God's acts of willing and actualizing, if indeed we can speak that way of God at all. I conclude that the principle of identity, a basic foundation of the house of authority, cannot be retained, partly because it partakes of the same problems as the first foundation stone—salvation history and the monarchical metaphor—and partly because identity between the divine will and creation is either a synthesis of *meaning* which is inaccessible or an identity between detailed states of affairs which violates the autonomy of creatures.

THE COLLAPSE OF THE HOUSE OF AUTHORITY

The multilevel criticism offered in this chapter is in sum a critique of the Christian religion's early construction of the house of authority as its methodological home. As I earlier maintained, the church not only worked within this house; it subjected it to mythical, historical, and doctrinal rationalization, the final effect of which was to render the house an impregnable castle. Any single criticism was referred to some other room, and all were necessary, or else God's own sovereignty and victorious plan of salvation themselves would be in question. If we ask why Ezra's words are true, we are told they are a divine communication. If we ask how they are given that status, we are told that they occur in a permanent record of a divinely authored work, the canonical Scriptures. If we ask why this collection of human writings is to be regarded as divinely authored, we are told that the *act of canonizing* on the part of the church is divinely authored. If we ask why (how we know) this particular set of events in history is divinely authored, we are told that the church has declared it so and its declarations are divinely authored. If we ask how it is that the church's declarations are divinely authored, we are told that such are *necessary* to the certainty needed for salvation and its historical perpetuation. If we ask why (how we know) such "necessity" is actually operative and not just a logical ideality, we are referred to salvation history and the logic of triumph. If we ask why we are to regard the logic of triumph and its attendant notions as an unquestionable criterion, something which is both a priori to Christianity itself and true, we are told that the overall interpretative framework of Scripture, dogma, and the church has never questioned it. So the circle, a vicious one, is complete. The questioner has been referred from one room to another in the house of authority only to find himself or herself back in the original room.

I am thus not simply assuming but am attempting to show why the house of authority has collapsed. In spite of enormous efforts to keep the house propped up, what remains is a verbal house, occurring in both the rhetorical and the up-to-date language of church gatherings, writings, and even official declarations. And with the collapse of the house of authority has come the demise of the method(s) that presupposed it: the substitution of authority for evidence, the genre of citation, and the formalistic restriction of truth. Such a declaration is, in one sense, outrageously inaccurate. Only a superficial glance about the Christian world discloses the house of authority still standing and crammed full of both eager and reluctant occupants. They are many types. Most widespread is the persistence of Catholic and Protestant folk religion where religious realities are understood in literal and cosmological terms. These occupants are either untouched by historical consciousness or are so successful in compartmentalizing the psyche and areas of experience (like fundamentalist physicists) that the house of authority and whatever might count against it are kept on opposite poles of the psyche's planet, a virtual Arctic and Antarctica. And there are the theological occupants, some of whom recognize the radical results of the collapse of the house, the effect of an earthquake on faith's self-interpreted content, and who attempt to live in the house as antiquarians. The house of authority and Christianity are the same so they apologetically defend the house. So goes Catholic textbook theology and modern Protestant orthodoxy. Others of the theological occupants are full participants in historical consciousness and are fully knowledgeable about the uses and implications of critical methods. But they may not be as savvy as their conservative colleagues about the destructive effect these things have on the house of authority. Some have actually moved out but retain a verbal house of authority in their ways of talking about Scripture. They sound as if they were occupants. Others live in the house as renovators, thinking that what is needed is a bit of repair work, a new hermeneutical picture window in the living room, some new historical tiles on the roof. Such are the so-called Protestant and Catholic neoorthodox theologians.[9]

I have not mentioned another kind of occupant, the one for whom the house of authority is the house of God himself. It not only carries the predicates of God (absoluteness, certainty, purity, eternality); it communicates them to the occupant who then becomes certain, pure, eternal, and impregnable. The way of authority itself tends to evoke such a response for under the principle of identity it extends a divine act (of meaning, willing) to a nondivine event which is a multiplicity of historical-natural events. And this raises the question which has been present in the form of a mutual accusation between Protestants and Catholics, the accusation of idolatry. Our thesis is the obvious one— that the house of authority, like any created entity, can function as the ersatz god. History testifies that it has functioned in that way. It therefore attracts into its occupancy those (which can be any and every human being) who respond to the insecurity and anxiety, the fragility and threats of finitude, by securing themselves in an absolute system, institution, writing, or leadership. Because the meaning-acts involved in the way of authority intend the location of authorities as substitutes for a divine presence which is not ontologically identical with them, it may not be accurate to say that idolatry is a priori to the way of authority.

Yet, there is such a subtle difference between such acts, driven by the principle of identity, and the constitution of the idol, that the way of authority becomes transformed into the synthesis of a creaturely-historical and divine entity, the very definition of the idol. This is why the church has been willing to do and be so many terrible things in its own name and for its own defense. These include excommunication,

---

9. For a similar and fuller analysis of the spectrum of hermeneutical responses in contemporary theology, see Ray L. Hart, *Unfinished Man and the Imagination* (New York: Herder and Herder, 1968), pp. 29 ff.

persecution, and capital punishment of those who challenge the house or even elements connected with the house which seem to us today utterly trivial. We remember, however, that in the house of authority, because everything is bound up together, no challenge is trivial. The house of authority's self-defense has included the Inquisition and the legal persecution of those like Bruno and Scopes who affirmed realms of evidence which conflicted with the authority. Defenders of the church are happy to point out that such persecutions are not as bad as they seem given the historical context and worldview of the church at the time. Such challengers were regarded not as mere individual mavericks but as threats to a whole divinely authored system of salvation. Precisely! That is just the point. We have here the very heart of human evil as it rationalizes itself. Once a finite, historical complex is given divine status, all means are justified in protecting that complex.

More is at stake, therefore, than simply the collapse of an ancient and historical vehicle of the church's self-understanding. That vehicle, honored as divine, continues to be the occasion and framework for human pathology, sin, and grief. The way of authority hardened into the Protestant religion of the book and the Catholic religion of the institution. It continues to foster obscurantism, dualisms in the human self, superstition, sexism, reality denial, legalism as a unifying piety and mindset. Of course, we must acknowledge that the locations of identity (Scripture, dogma, church) have their greatness and therefore have exercised in every period of history humanizing influences on the interhuman struggle, pieties which have been sources of human strength, consolation, and even prophetic criticism. But the price now is too high. The time for Christian faith to look for another house in which to live, if it must have a house at all, is long overdue. Is there such a thing? To those who see the way of authority as a priori to Christianity itself, as part of its immanent and not simply empirical essence, the answer must be negative. Thus all alternatives to the house of authority lie, in that view, outside Christianity altogether, in the house of rational religion, the house of natural theology, the house of humanism. And this brings us to the constructive side of our critique, the exploration, though in no way completion, of another way. Involved in the exploration, hopefully, will be a disclosure that the way of authority is not a priori to the immanent essence of Christianity, at least in the sense of ecclesiality.

PART TWO

THEOLOGICAL CRITERIOLOGY OUTSIDE THE HOUSE OF AUTHORITY

8

The Structure
of Ecclesial Reflection

After our long detour into the house of authority, we now take up our constructive task. The detour was unavoidable. Too many theological enterprises appear to take place outside the house of authority when in fact they are living quite comfortably in one or more of its rooms. Failure to grasp the house of authority as a total structure inevitably results in a theological muddle. It is simply a fact that the very nature of theology undergoes serious alterations with the collapse of the house of authority. And the formulation of the possibility, character, criteria, and methods of theology is almost impossible as long as there is ambivalence about the nature and validity of the way of authority. The theologian can opt to live in the house of authority or away from it. But he or she cannot do both. And if theology abandons the house, it also abandons the foundational materials on which the house is constructed: salvation history, identity, canon, inspiration, sacred Scripture, infallibility, and the rest.

There are ways of pursuing theology outside the way of authority which appear to retain it because of the continued use of its language and categories. Thus, while Schleiermacher speaks of the "inspiration of scripture," in his hands the term has little to do with inspiration in the sense of the classical criteriology. Less misleading is a clean break. Only with this can we begin to see what theology is up against, what the problem of theological judgment is, when theology abandons the presuppositions and methods of the classical criteriology. The purpose of this first chapter of part 2 is to try to formulate the problem created for persons who would persist in the working of theology after the house of authority has been dismantled.

SETTING THE PROBLEM

We can formulate the problem of theology *post viam auctoritatis* in several ways. The first recalls that within the way of authority, what it means to undertake theology is relatively clear. This is not to ignore or downplay the vast multiplicity of styles, methods, and even controversies which have marked that pursuit. The point is that theology is a relatively clear matter insofar as one agrees on the things one does to settle its questions. Within the way of authority there is such agreement. For there are, in that way, agreed-upon deposits of authority which, when cited properly, settle a question of truth. Does God know all things? One can answer this question by proper appeal to an authority or by extending the implications of the authority. But with the passing of the way of authority, there are no *authorities* (divine–human identity in authoritative locations) in the sense that understanding and citing them is at the same time grasping and establishing the truth. If that is the case, how can theology ever settle anything? The severity of the problem is disclosed by the tendency among contemporary theologians to translate the theological enterprise into one where it *is* clear how matters are settled—historical description, literary criticism, hermeneutic interrogation, and universal ontology. Our question is, how can theology proceed to make true judgments and back them up if it cannot draw on the features and concepts of the way of authority?

A second and more specific way to formulate the problem begins from what seems to be a contradiction within my own overall approach. The two volumes of this prolegomenon constitute a distinction between the problem of reality apprehension and the problem of making judgments. In *Ecclesial Man* I described the matrix of faith's reality apprehensions as a depth intersubjectivity, an ecclesial social existence. Insight attends participation in that social existence. This distinction between concrete reality apprehension ("religious knowledge") and criteriology ("theological understanding") helps explain why the collapse of an ancient ecclesiastically constructed framework for the latter, the house of authority, does not necessarily involve the disappearance of faith. It also helps explain why theology, theological understanding, continues to be a possibility in the wake of the collapse of the house of authority. Note, however, that a determinate historical community (ecclesia) is affirmed as *the* mediating vehicle of religious insight. But is it not that very religious community which our critique of the way of authority has described as errant, fallible, and situational? Have we not said that some of its own most basic interpretive notions and institutions of duration are at best situational and at worst idolatrous? We seem to be saying that the community of faith is and is not the criterion for theological judgments; that we both relativize and yet regard as necessary ecclesial tradition.

This is a fair and useful question because it forces us to be very specific about the role the community of faith plays in the grounding of theological judgments. We have observed its indispensability in religious knowledge. The problem of a postauthority criteriology is to discover how the apprehensions that attend participation in ecclesial existence and that occur prior to theological understanding fund a reflection that is concerned with truth and that eventuates in understanding. This is just what this constructive proposal about theological judgment attempts to do.

We offer now a third and yet more radical formulation of the problem. Having distinguished the precriteriological matrix of *insight* from the phenomenon of *understanding*, we must avoid what is now a common but innocuous way of acknowledging the church's historicity. According to this approach, the Christian faith is self-evidently a changeless, doctrinal content. Acknowledged is the historical, linguistic, and philosophical relativity of the *expressions* of that content. This seemingly balanced approach to tradition and modernity proffers the following. "It is not necessary to *express* the *homoousion* in the *language* of the Council of Chalcedon." Distinguished are a changeless determinate content and changing historical expressions which carry interpretations, with little or no effect of the latter on the former.[1] The problem is that every determinate content, such as the *homoousion*, is an interpretation, a specific understanding. It is not separable from the criteriological framework which establishes it. Its "meaning" did

---

1. The present-day "neoorthodox" Catholic version of the kernel and husk metaphor is an acknowledged distinction between the unchanging and true content of the dogma and the human, historical vehicles in which the dogma finds expression. Lonergan, for instance, distinguishes between the explanatory technique at work in the concept of homoousious and the content and proposition present there. "The Dehellenization of Dogma," in Gregory Baum, *The Future of Belief Debate* (New York: Herder and Herder, 1967). See also Lonergan's *Method in Theology* (New York: Herder and Herder, 1972), p. 326. Similar distinctions are found in Karl Rahner and K. Lehman, *Kerygma and Dogma* (New York: Herder and Herder, 1969), pp. 92–93; Gregory Baum, *Faith and Doctrine: A Contemporary View* (New York: Newman Press, 1969), pp. 36–37.

not simply continue when it persisted in new interpretations since it itself is an interpretation. In short, this apparent acknowledgment of the situationality of dogma still retains an element of the way of authority, namely, that the criteria for theological judgments are the determinate dogmas of the church's past interpretations. It is a kernel and husk approach within the way of authority.

Needless to say, such a view shipwrecks on the self-evident axiom that content (doctrines, determinate beliefs) and method (criteriology, interpretive frameworks, selected categories) are correlative. There is no changeless content which generates a multiplicity of methods. Rather, we have on each side two determinacies, one of content and one of method. And changes in either side affect the other. This critique helps us formulate our problem in its most radical sense. If serious difficulties attend the classical criteriology, if the way of authority is discredited, this cannot but affect the doctrinal content of faith which the church has always affirmed as necessary to Christianity itself. The problem is, if content itself is relative, there seems to be no determinate given at all to which theological judgments are subject. This pushes any postauthority theological prolegomenon to distinguish between the theological given as a determinate dogma (the way of authority) and the theological given as something else. This means that part of the task of such a prolegomenon is to discover the determinate references of theological judgments without absolutizing and dehistorizing the situational and doctrinal accomplishments of the past. In other words, prolegomenon after the way of authority involves an alternative view of the very content of faith, not simply a formal, methodological framework. There are those, of course, who will see this more radical step as simply a new assertion of human autonomy. I can only reply that the way of authority, by absolutizing and dehistoricizing errant and situational accomplishments of the church, was an assertion of human autonomy. What more radical autonomy can there be than that present in the principle of identity where human accomplishments are passed off as the very intention and work of God?[2]

2. One way that this third formulation can be expressed is to speak of the vulnerability of tradition itself as a material norm. We are not speaking here of tradition in the formal sense of an apparatus of the church's continuity but of tradition as the identified *content* of that continuity. Our point is that this content occurs in connection with a history of human and historical interpretations, theological endeavors and

CRITERIA AS FIELDS OF EVIDENCE

It is clear that a postauthority criteriology cannot assume that theology remains what it always was and is simply moving to a new address. When theology moves outside the house of authority, its very nature is altered. This and the next section describe two of these alterations, the changed meaning of both criteria and the genre of theology. Viewed together, these alterations amount to yet another account of the problem of postauthority theology. We take up now the question of the nature of theological criteria.

The change in the nature of theological criteria will remain obscure unless we observe a frequently passed-over distinction.[3] We begin by noticing at a more general level the distinction between experience and a field of evidence. Our thesis is that experience itself does not function in any interpretative enterprise, cognitive or otherwise, as a field of evidence. The field of evidence is available through experience and the entities of that field are apprehended as existing entities through experience. But a field of evidence is more specific than "experience," even more specific than the kind of experience to which the field is presented. One would be correct in observing that sense experience attends an ornithologist's investigations. It would be quite inaccurate to say that sense experience is the ornithologist's field of evidence. I say this partly because a field of evidence is a bounded and selected region (cells, birds, antebellum American politics, and so on) and sense experience is at work in some way in most of the inquiries into such fields. But the basic reason is that sense experience coupled with other dimensions of experience functions to mediate but is not itself the field. Nor is sense experience the *method* of inquiry. The field of evidence for an ornithologist is established by the entity studied, birds and their environment. Thus, experience is not evidence for the claim that birds are territorial. The evidence is manifested and repeated territorial activity of the birds which repeated observation (experience) mediates. Evidence for judgments is thus the activity,

---

accomplishments. And since these depend on the presuppositions of the house of authority, they share the fate of that house. The crisis we are talking about then is nothing less than the crisis of the church's material norm, the church's accomplished tradition.

3. Experiential theologies especially tend to pass over this distinction, thus confusing experience with criteria.

manifestation, or behavior of the entity. Experience mediates but does not constitute that evidence.

A more complex example is offered by the relation of aesthetic experience to aesthetic criticism. It would be misleading to say that the literary critic's *criterion* (field of evidence) is aesthetic experience. Rather, what he or she refers to in order to justify the judgments made are the structure (and behavior) of the aesthetic object. Thus the qualities of a dance performance are assessed in terms of fluidity of motion, the manifest unity of bodily movement, and affective mood. Aesthetic experience mediates but is not itself these things.

Theologically this distinction is between the experiential world of faith and the criteria of theological judgments. It is not incorrect to say that theological judgments are grounded in experience. In a certain sense all judgments are. But as it stands, the statement is elusive, and it is utterly misleading if it is taken to mean that experience is that to which theology appeals to justify a judgment as true. The reason is the one just given. If theology is able to make true judgments at all, it must have some field of evidence to which it refers. That is, it must have some manifested activity, behavior, and structure disclosing itself through experience.

We can make the distinction yet more precise. Alfred Schutz appropriates William James's term *paramount reality* to express the immediacy and primacy of the "world of everyday life."[4] Paramount reality in this sense is not simply the world of sense objects but a social and cultural world of values, intersubjective expectations, and the social past and future, which is the immediate, taken-for-granted environment of every human being. I cite the James-Schutz term in order to make use of it in this distinction. Ecclesial existence is always a social, communal existence, and, as I argued previously, it occupies a faith-world of its own.[5] This faith-world is the paramount reality to which experience or the experiential aspect of faith refers. I shall not pursue the complex problem of the relation of the faith-world to the "world of everyday life." The point is that faith occurs in a world or environment in which certain realities come to light, specific mutual intentionalities occur between human beings, and a special symbolic

4. Alfred Schutz, *Collected Papers* (The Hague: Nijhoff, 1967), vol. I, pp. 341 ff.
5. Schutz prefers to call this a "finite province of meaning" (ibid., p. 345).

universe accompanies these activities. All this I have argued in *Ecclesial Man.* I am now going a step farther.

Believers do not live in the faith-world in such a way that they have the same relation to all the elements of that world. Contents of the faith-world include the religious community, the fellow believer, the stranger, the vehicles of duration, the transcendent, anthropological structures, the past and the future, and so forth. Obviously these are not all present in the same way. Rather, there is something paramount in the faith-world itself, something which grounds it, unifies it, influences it, and which is the primary reference of faith. The way to express that something in the language of the house of authority is to say, God is *the* authority behind all penultimate authorities. I would prefer to avoid such language since its meaning remains dominated by the monarchical metaphor of God and the world and the logic of triumph. Yet it is clear that faith's primary act is an act toward God, not self-analysis, not an acceptance of the authority of the church, and not theological understanding. This act toward God is a multidimensional one. It involves worship, repentance, trust, and belief. This act does occur in a specific context, the breaking of the power of human evil, hence, the act toward God occurs as a response to the Adamic-Gospel story. Such, in brief, is faith's experiential dimension.

Because the primary act of that experience is toward God, faith is a response to something not at its disposal, the experience which not only characterizes but unifies and dominates faith has to do, paradoxically perhaps, with something that is not *immediate* to any cognition, formal or internal, something that is not an object of faith's environment, something that is not a mystery but *the* mystery. And this leads us to our thesis. *The faith-experience and its central paramount reality is not available as a field of evidence, as a criterion.* We have two reasons for making this claim. The first is the general relation between experience and fields of evidence. The faith-experience qua experience is not itself a field of evidence but mediates fields of evidence. Second, the paramount unifying reference of faith is a mystery, a transcendence not at the disposal of method, and therefore is inaccessible as a field of evidence. "God" in other words, is not a theological criterion.

Faith therefore exists in a faith-world. There is a paramount reality which is its primary referent. It does have an experiential dimension (although its primary referent is not the "object" of that experience).

177

So we are left with this question: If authorities (locations of divine–human identity) are not theology's criteria, and if experience itself is not its criterion, what is left? We have already tipped our hand as to the altered meaning of criterion outside the house of authority. Within the way of authority the criteria were the cited authorities and these functioned as substitutes for evidence. In postauthority theology criteria are themselves fields of evidence. For theology to subject itself to criteria, to consult criteria to support judgments, means simply that it consults appropriate fields of evidence.[6] Thus to say that there are theological criteria means that there are accessible fields of evidence pertinent to theological judgments. Theological criteriology means, then, the description of those fields and how they operate. Before proposing what those fields are, I would first take up the question of the nature or genre of theology itself.

THEOLOGY AS REFLECTIVE INQUIRY

The collapse of the house of authority alters not only the meaning of criteria but the genre of theology itself. According to the way of authority, the genre of classical theology is explication or citation, and this is especially apparent as the way a claim is established as true. Such a view of theology assumes that the theological given (the authoritative criterion) is an infallible doctrinalization. Classical theology acknowledged in various senses the limitations of human understanding in the apprehending of divine things. But such limitations pertained to the analogical mode of apprehension and expression. To be apprehended was a divinely disclosed, comprehensive world-plan, a sequence centering in the incarnation and culminating in the last judgment and in a dual eschatology.[7] And this content was regarded as occurring at the level of cognitive propositional certainty. It was

6. Note that the definition of criterion as a *field* of evidence distinguishes the criterion from the evidence itself. Thus, the criterion for a historical judgment is a field of evidence, the recoverable past. The actual evidence for the historical judgment is the data gathered from this. Evidence itself exists as specific reference, not just a general field. Evidence that Druids practiced sorcery occurs as specific archaeological data, not just as a field.

7. A clear example of a work offering just such a scheme is the unfinished work by Jonathan Edwards, *A History of the Work of Redemption*. Nor is this work an exception in its chronology. In sixteenth-century Protestant theologies "world history" coincided with history as offered in the Old Testament and history which had occurred since. Furthermore, the arrangement of the loci of doctrines in Protestant dogmatics tended to be a salvation history arrangement beginning with creation and ending with the eschaton.

premethodological, and it therefore set the task of theology as an explication of that world-plan, which could mean deriving implications from it, discovering coherences between its elements, and relating it to a general rational scheme. Citation was sufficient to establish the truth of the doctrinalized given. Understanding occurred as the result of a formal application of reason to that content.[8]

One feature of this classical view can be retained. It is correct to say that theology has a given and furthermore some sort of preunderstanding, insight, or apprehension is part of that given. If this were not the case, theology would be perpetually chasing its own tail. This simply means that theological judgments do not fund themselves. On the other hand, the classical view that the theological given occurs in the form of doctrinalization, dogmas which are correlative to faith itself, affirms past *theological* accomplishments as authoritative criteria. In our view the patristic doctrine of the trinity is the *product* of theological work and thus retains the features of fallibility and situationality which attend all theological work. Patristic theological work occurred in an appropriated criteriology, the way of authority, which seems now to be unusable. It too had a theological given which was not simply itself. Thus by regarding the results of patristic theology as an authority, the church transformed its own past theological work from a human to a divine accomplishment.

If this feature of the way of authority is rejected, the theological given as an authoritative doctrinalization, if "authorities" are displaced by fields of evidence as theological criteria, then the genre of theology can no longer be citation-explication. For in a critical and historical approach, the doctrinal scheme ceases to have the status of a premethodological given. Rather than further specification of divine communication driven by the logic of triumph, the classical doctrinal scheme is grasped with the help of historical methods as an eclectic synthesis of a plurality of movements in the ancient world: Jewish apocalypticism reappearing in the form of individualistic dual des-

---

8. A consistent Protestant version of this view of the citation character of theology is the result of the Protestant principle of *sola Scriptura* and its suspicion of philosophy. Thus, in forms of Protestant theology where discovery of internal coherence among the givens of Scripture (systematizing) is dropped, theology is regarded as exegesis and "biblical theology." Any movement beyond this is superfluous. Needless to say, this view presupposes the way of authority as intact. The place where such a notion is dominant is not so much the formal writings of Protestant systematic theologians but the Protestant ministry and cultus.

179

tiny, Hellenistic views of the nature of truth, the monarchical meta-phor of divine being, and so on. If this synthesis is rejected in the sense of a theological given, an absolute criterion, then theology cannot mean simply explicating that synthesis or scheme regarded as the extension, culmination, and systematization of Scripture. If the Judaic Scripture principle is repudiated, if the Bible is not simply the deposit of doctrines whose truth is ensured by their very presence in that collection, theology cannot mean simply the explication of Scripture. Instead of working from explicit linguistic units that have obtained (by a supernatural activity) the status of truth, theology will be working toward this goal. Its pregiven reference will not be the former theological accomplishments of Paul or Irenaeus or a church council but the fields of evidence which attend ecclesial, social existence. Formulation will not be behind theological work as its presupposition but ahead of it as its goal and accomplishment. And this means that the *genre* of theology will not be citation but inquiry. Inquiry as the genre of theological work is the correlate of criteria in the sense of fields of evidence. Instead of explicating authorities, theology becomes an interrogation of appropriate fields of evidence.

We should not permit the term *inquiry* to mislead us. That is, we need not grasp inquiry by means of a model taken from natural or social sciences. There are as many kinds of inquiry as there are fields of evidence. The term itself suggests that understanding is a process of some sort, not an instantaneous cognition or assent, and that the process goes from a pregiven situation marked both by reality-apprehensions and confusions to formulation. Because of the com-plexity of theology's matrix and reference, that which it brings to formulation will require a multiplicity of inquiries. Such, however, are always contributory and penultimate to theology itself. For the kind of inquiry which occurs when theology comes to formulation has the character not of research but of reflection. This is the case because only in a reflective activity can the contributions of the several disciplines which consult the fields of evidence come to formulated synthesis. For this reason we are persuaded that the genre of theology outside the way of authority should be reflective inquiry.

Theological Judgment and Theological Reflection

The collapse of the house of authority is not simply a hidden historical phenomenon uncovered by an occasional scholar-pedant. It is a widespread cultural occurrence which has evoked response from most branches of Christendom and from most types of theology. Even fundamentalism is one such response.[9] Another response has become increasingly familiar. "The way of authority is dead. Its assignment of infallibility to its authorities and certainty to its interpreters is discredited. Theology must learn its lesson and never again try to distort faith and the Christian faith by way of a correspondence theory of truth, by units of reflection called propositions, by being preoccupied with evidence and judgments—in other words, by trying to be a science." Such a response is an unfortunate one. Most specific versions of it are simply ambiguous. That is, it is not often clear what those who reject a correspondence theory of truth—subject-object modes of thought, propositions—are up to. Are these repudiations based on the conviction that there is no subject matter at all to which theology is addressed and therefore all uses of language that suggest a content which transcends the subject are misleading, or do they serve the more modest conviction that the realities in question resist these traditional modes of apprehension and formulation and require other ones?[10] The ambiguity reduces to these two major programmatic alternatives: a thoroughgoing subjectivizing of theology's references and a linguistic therapeutic which would uncover the correlation between these references and their modes of availability.

We begin the section with this issue as a prelude to the main thesis. The demise of the classical criteriology does not release the theologian from the task and responsibility of making judgments. Judgments are involved, obviously, in the very repudiation of the correspondence theory of truth, propositions, and the like. Although judgments can occur in many different literary forms and styles, even disguised, they nevertheless attend every critical-cognitive and reality-oriented enterprise. The initial stage of this exploration argued that the symbols, stories, and myths of the ecclesial community carry insights that attend the breaking of the power of evil and the occurrence of

9. See Sydney E. Ahlstrom, *A Religious History of the American People* (New Haven: Yale University Press, 1972), pp. 709, 811–812; Martin E. Marty, *Righteous Empire: The Protestant Experience in America* (New York: Dial Press, 1970), p. 218.

10. There appears to be some issue at stake between the author and Gordon D. Kaufman on this point. See Kaufman's *An Essay on Theological Method* (Missoula: Scholars Press, 1975), p. 38, n. 2. Whether there is actually an issue will depend on whether and in what sense Kaufman is identifying objectivism with simply subject matter or with certain specific modalities of presence and thought.

redemption. There is something, therefore, about human possibilities and actualities, something about the way the world is, to be discerned and interpreted. And where there is interpretation, there can be distorted, shallow, and contradictory interpretation. Interpretation involves judgments even if the *form* of the interpretation is not an easily identifiable assertory sentence.

Judgments, in other words, occur in both authority theology and postauthority theology. But the nature of theological judgments varies depending on the genre of theology. If theology is citation or explication (or logical derivations therefrom), judgments have the character of citation or conclusions from citations. On the other hand if criteria are fields of evidences and the genre of theology is reflective inquiry, judgments are correlated with evidence and have the character of evidential claims. They are then the telos of the process of reflective inquiry. In both cases they are attempts to bring reality to expression and formulation. But in postauthority theology this "bringing to formulation" might be understood in the sense of correspondence views of truth or in the more recent disclosure theories.[11] It is likely that theology's references and fields of evidence are sufficiently multiple to permit if not even require both approaches.

Why do we correlate judgment and evidence? This question pushes us to consider briefly the character of true judgments. A true judgment brings reality to formulation under two levels of criteria— one formal and universal, the other determinate and specific. The formal and universal criteria are the conditions without which the judgment cannot be true. Thus, an analytic judgment cannot be self-contradictory and be true. The determinate criteria are the specific evidences which fulfill (or block) what was cognitively intended. Thus in the process of reflective inquiry one intends, means, projects as the case that sin arises as one type of response to the fragility of human existence. The true judgment occurs as a fulfillment of that intention made possible by some sort of evidence, thus calling for an interrogation of a field of evidence.

We have before us, therefore, two key correlative notions proposed

---

11. For criticisms of the correspondence theory of truth and attempts to replace it or supplement it, see Leslie Dewart, *The Future of Belief* (New York: Herder and Herder, 1966), pp. 91 ff. See also William Reiser, *What Calls Forth Heresy?* (Nashville: Vanderbilt University, diss., 1977), pp. 142–159.

as descriptions of postauthority theology. They are criteria or fields of evidence and inquiry eventuating in judgments. The central task of a postauthority theological criteriology is to discover the fields of evidence which are appropriate to the bringing to formulation of precriteriological realities which attend participation in the ecclesial community. At this point we should, at the risk of repetition, introduce a cautionary consideration. *Theology, that is, ecclesial reflective inquiry, does not itself determine or originate the realities that attend the ecclesial community.* Theology does not found these realities but is founded by them. Thus, a theological failure is a failure to bring such realities to expression in the mode of understanding. The failure can never have the status of disestablishing those realities. What can be disestablished are interpretations of the realities by the ecclesial community and reality-assertions which are extensions of those interpretations.

This brings us to a provisional definition of theology. Theology is the attempt to bring pretheological, apprehended realities to formulations intended as true by interrogating the fields of evidence pertinent to those realities. Requiring as they do the interrogation of fields of evidence, theological judgments are correlative with evidence. As a concern with formulation which expresses a truth-intention, theology is a reflection oriented toward making judgments. This definition is highly formal and, as it stands, traditional. We have already reviewed why postauthority theology transforms criteria from authorities to fields of evidence. Our task now is to understand what is involved in the transformation of theology itself from judgments as citations of authorities to judgments as truth-intending expressions of realities. And this pushes us to set forth in outline form the general structure of ecclesial reflection; for it is this structure which is determinative of what is taken up in the chapters that follow.

The Dimensions of Ecclesial Reflection

Understanding by its very nature occurs as a truth-intention. The "intention" part simply calls to mind that human being orients itself toward realities through a multiplicity of meaning-acts which themselves may be informed by different premeaning concerns. Resounding in my ears are the sounds of contemporary jazz music. The quality of my experience may be quasi-conscious enjoyment when the music is background to something else on which I am concentrating, such as reading a book. It may be direct, immediate enjoyment which displaces all other activities and makes them secondary. It may not be aesthetic enjoyment at all but an intellectual act which attends to the music because of an interest in the engineering quality of the recording. Or it may be an intellectual act that tries to locate the music in the history of jazz or attends closely to the development of the improvisation. Before me is a global phenomenon, the Christian religion. I can simply enter into its cultus in an uncritical, prereflective participation. I can synthesize it in an intellectual act of categorizing it as a psychological device, a legitimation of economic interests, and so on. I can attempt to describe the continuities and discontinuities in its historical development. I can attempt to uncover manifest realities which attend its symbolic universe. *Meaning*-intentions are inevitable to the determinate apprehension of any entity and are present in all the above examples. *Truth*-intentions are particular kinds of meaning-acts in which we attempt to understand what is before us.

It is just at this point that understanding and truth-intentions become a multiplicity. At what may be the most primitive level, the entity can be investigated simply through the distinction of reality and fiction. Assuming the entity is something before me as *meant,* does it have the minimum features of existence? Fictions, of course, are "real" in a fictional sense and therefore can be parts of a given life-world. But the very category of fictional entities suggests the distinction we are making here. At a second level an entity can be investigated simply as to its nature: its genesis, development, structure, essence, immanent interrelations. Thus historians, anthropologists, sociologists, and psychologists bring truth-intentions to the study of religions, attempting to understand their nature and function in a particular scheme of reference. At a third level we can investigate an entity which itself is marked by truth-intentions, which lays a claim on the interpreter. Marxism, transactional analysis, biochemistry, and theology all set claims before the understanding. At this level one directs truth-intentions at the truth-intentions of the entity and tries to determine their adequacy. In all these levels of truth-intention some field of evidence is interrogated as the way of fulfilling the intention.

At this point we return to the question of theological reflection. It would be misleading if we described ecclesial reflection so as to suggest there is an indifference to truth in the prereflective situation where the paramount realities appear. Truth-intentions can be evoked by any manifestation of reality. In such a manifestation there is something that is there, that is differentiable, that is not simply a screen on which the subject projects itself, that evokes linguistic expressions, and that does not permit simply every possible expression. Thus, faith as it occurs in ecclesial existence and is expressive of a modification in the direction of redemption is not simply indifferent to the question of the status of the realities which attend that modification. Faith, as a truth-intention in itself, is not indifferent to whether or not its paramount reality is fictional. Faith itself, in other words, is characterized by truth-intentions in the primitive sense. At this level, however, the truth-intention is not so much a focused reflection aimed at understanding as a concomitant of other acts such as prayer, worship, proclamation, and cultural criticism. With theological reflection, faith's truth-intention arises into a self-conscious and focused act. Understanding moves beyond mere reality-intentions to concern with the propriety, accuracy, adequacy of the linguistic, interpretive vehicles in which the realities are carried. Faith may intend the reality (truth) of the death of Jesus, functioning in some way in the modification toward redemption. Theological understanding is concerned with the adequacy and propriety of a forensic formulation of that function.

These observations should not obscure the plurality of truth-intentions. Many types of questioning are immanent in a disposal toward truth. Does it truly disclose itself? Are its expressions internally consistent? Is it consistent with other factualities? Does it exemplify universal ontological structures? Such questions occur in ecclesial reflection not as determinants of the nature of ecclesial reflection but as determined *by* the structure of ecclesial reflection. And this we must set forth, at least in outline, in order to indicate what fields of evidence and what types of judgment mark the program of that reflection.[12]

12. One of the few works in contemporary theological method that thematizes the structure of theological reflection is Friedrich Mildenberger, *Theorie der Theologie enzyklopädie als Methodenlehre* (Stuttgart: Calwer, 1972), chap. 2. Like the one presented here Mildenberger offers a threefold analysis of the *Stufen* (stages) of theological reflection. Furthermore, Mildenberger's dogmatic-normative and historico-critical are counterparts to the first two dimensions of this analysis. On the other hand, his empirical-critical reflection does not seem to be reflection moving to situationality so

Ecclesial reflection is a directional or progressive reflection and it has a dialectical character about it. The realities which occur prereflectively in the setting or matrix of theology (ecclesial existence) determine its first dimension.[13] As I have previously argued, the paramount reality is something experienced, but it is not available as such as a field of evidence. Rather, that paramount reality is garbed in a historical determinacy, ecclesiality. Ecclesiality refers to an actual historical community pervaded by a dominant story, the Adamic-Gospel story, and having a distinctive sociality, such as space, time, duration, and vehicles of duration. Accordingly, this historical existence in and through which the paramount reality appears and is experienced has a normative or criteriological character insofar as it expresses that through which the human being is modified toward redemption. Prompted by truth-intentions toward that paramount reality prior to reflection, theology's first move toward understanding is an interrogation of the historically clothed vehicle, ecclesiality itself. The question which occurs in this initial moment is simply: What is ecclesiality? Or, to put it in a criteriological way: Is that which we are assessing (a doctrine, practice, claim) ecclesial?

This first dimension can occur at greater or lesser distances from the ecclesiality depicted, depending on the extent to which ecclesial existence is objectified. On one end of the spectrum, historical consciousness and method interrogates ecclesiality. The search for the "essence of Christianity" as a moment in theology exemplifies this interrogation.[14] I am proposing two main fields of evidence or ways of approaching ecclesiality as a field of evidence: the ecclesial symbolic

much as toward practical theology. If this is the case, Mildenberger's three stages are close to the Schleiermacherian encyclopedic structure of philosophical, historical, and practical theology.

13. It is difficult to find usable language to express the units of the structure of theological reflection. I have used *dimensions,* and, at times, *moments.* We are after something not unlike Kierkegaard's *stages.* The problem is to do justice to the dialectical character of reflection and the fact that some enterprises do presuppose others, without positing three separated methodological inquiries occurring in isolation from each other.

14. This dimension of theological reflection is analyzed in more detail under the metaphor of theological portraiture in chap. 9. The "essence of Christianity" as a historical-theological enterprise is inadequate as a synonym for theology as such. In this sense criticisms of this essentially nineteenth-century movement of liberal theology are valid. However, as one dimension of theological work, the historical effort to grasp Christianity in its distinctive, enduring, and dynamic respects is unavoidable to any postauthority theology.

universe, which I am calling with the help of some of Ricoeur's investigations, the Adamic-Gospel story, and the depth social structure constitutive of ecclesial existence.[15] At the other end of the spectrum, at the least distance from the paramount reality, are descriptions of ecclesial existence from the confessional standpoint of a specific branch of Christendom. Here the faith-community consults in a confessional way its own corporate experience and determinacy. This is not so much an approach exclusive of historical method as confession giving motive and unity to historical description.[16] Whatever the place in this spectrum, we have here one moment of inquiry. It has an essentially historical character even if informed by confessional intentions. It is never "merely historical" because as a dimension of ecclesial reflection it grasps that which it describes (the Adam-Gospel story) as an expression of experienced, normative realities.

The second dimension of ecclesial reflection introduces fields of evidence that are wider than ecclesial existence. Why ecclesial reflection goes on to this dimension is only superficially expressed in the correct observation that in the Christian faith the status of the world as a whole is positive and real rather than negative and fictional. According to this observation, ecclesiality is a world-affirming faith because of its view of God as the world author, thus it cannot settle with obscurantist dualisms which dismiss natural and human sciences as fictions. Because this is the case, ecclesial reflection quite properly subjects what is before it, even the determinate descriptions of ecclesial existence, to formal, rational criteria of internal consistency, to external consistency with other realms of factuality, and to considerations raised by universal ontological accounts of being and knowledge. Ecclesial existence resists being translated without remainder into these wider fields of evidence but it cannot avoid being related to them. Yet these considerations do not formulate that which propels ecclesial reflection from the historical-confessional description of ecclesiality to a wider, one might say, universal field of evidence. If

15. In what follows I want to argue that the social structure itself is a clue to more specific fields of evidence for describing the Adamic-Gospel mythos and their employment.

16. Illustrative of a confessional approach is the account or portrayal of Christian faith which one finds as the historical dimension occurring throughout the work of Karl Barth. Illustrative of the more phenomenological-historical approach would be accounts of Christianity or aspects thereof in the work of Harnack and Troeltsch.

truth-intention stops simply with the description of a determinate historical existence, we have a symbolic universe and social existence valid only as a provincial occurrence. This provincial validity might seem at first sight sufficient since reality is always historical and therefore reality and normativeness might characterize any social-historical entity: the great religions of the world, types of human culture, types of political organization. I have no quarrel with this. But the truth-intention which ecclesial existence has about itself goes beyond simply a provincially valid truth. Evil and redemption as motifs in the Adam-Gospel story are intended as being in some way universal. And this is what propels ecclesial reflection to a second step, not just because of general world affirmation, but because the realities are experienced as themselves *universal* realities. That is, they have to do with human being as such, not simply with a certain race, nation, epoch, or subculture.

We cannot go any farther at this point without stopping to notice the ambiguity in the term *universal*. Universal can be a correlative term to science as such, and thus will mean what *any* inquirer following such and such methods will discover. Second, it can mean that which all determinacy presupposes, that without which being cannot be, knowledge cannot be, the human self cannot be. Such is the generic universality of formal analytic disciplines (logic, mathematics) and ontological schemes. Third, universality may mean simply what is universally present, even if it is not present as an a priori or generic item, or is not grasped through a universally accessible instrument of cognition. In this sense sin is universal. At the same time it may not be constitutive of human being, or accessible through general, scientific analyses. We shall call this universality *existential* or *determinate univer-sality*. The human experience of itself and its situation is the mode in which this universality is present. And it is universality in this sense with which the second dimension of ecclesial reflection is concerned. Thus the second dimension of reflection proposes to the first dimen-sion (ecclesial existence) the question, is this item of ecclesial existence a determinate universal? The methods of pursuing this second dimension of reflection are many. One may attempt a depiction of generic universality followed by an exploration of how ecclesial existence corresponds thereto. Such is the correlation theology of Paul Tillich. Or one may attempt to discover in a single reflective act the existential universal element formulated in the Adamic-Gospel story. Such is the way of hermeneutical theology as typified in the work of Paul Ricoeur.

The third dimension of ecclesial reflection is a move back to determinacy—not the determinacy of a social historical existence with which the reflection started, but the concreteness of individual and social, contemporary situations. This dimension brings forward and draws upon the first two dimensions, the symbolic universe of ecclesiality and the determinate universal dimension resident therein. But the focus of the third reflection is on specific autobiographical, political, and cultural situations taking form in the present. When successful, this dimension of reflection uncovers reality dimensions of these situations by means of the postures set by the first two dimensions. Thus the idolatrous foundations of a particular system of social oppression and the possibilities of liberation may be uncovered. Although it may sound like it, this third dimension is not really discovering how ecclesial existence in its universality is "relevant" to the present. Such a formulation tends to make the present the criterion, and perhaps in the old sense even an authority, and then sifts the contents of faith for adaptive possibilities. Needless to say, the very structure of ecclesial reflection is thereby lost. In the sense of a field of evidence, the present situation may be a criterion in this third dimension. All this means is that it forms a field of manifesting realities which the theologian interrogates, attempting by the retention of the first two dimensions as criteria to insightfully grasp the problematics and possibilities of the situation.

Hopefully, the cogency of this account of ecclesial reflection will be clearer in the following chapters which offer analyses of at least the first two dimensions. At this point we shall simply say that if ecclesial reflection stopped with the first dimension, its orientation toward ecclesial reality might be a truth-intending one but only of a very provincial sort. Ecclesial realities would be grasped as Israel's truth or Christianity's truth or the denomination's truth or my truth, but not as the truth for human being. If the reflection stopped with the second dimension, truth would have a universal intention and universal field of evidence, but the total reference of Christian faith would be to a continuity, perhaps even immutability, which becomes repeated and translated in every generation. Its reflection would remain imprisoned in the past or in the universal with no way to move to the present, and thus unable to follow the novelties of nature and history.[17] We may recognize that there are global counterparts of these three moments of reflection in the form of types and branches of theology. Historical and biblical inquiries describe the first; philosophical and systematic theologies describe the second; and practical theology, including liberation theology, black theology, theologies of various disciplines such as literature or psychology, describe the third. Insofar as any of these enterprises restricts the meaning of theology, ecclesial reflection, to its own discipline or agenda, it has lost touch with the very structure of ecclesial reflection. We are familiar with this phenomenon, with those who reduce theology to a biblical theology or to liberation theology. The problem with the former is its historicism and provincialism. One kind of hermeneutic theology sees theology *as* hermeneutics and thus identifies theology with the first dimension of reflection. This is because of its formulation of the theological task as understanding or interpretation of ancient texts. In this view "theology" occurs in connection with a hermeneutical enterprise directed to the texts or sources of the past. "Theology" means the (existential) understanding which attends the historical-hermeneutical investigation of the texts of a religious faith. I find no difficulty with such enterprises as such. However, that restriction of theological reflection is clearly one more symptom of the refusal to entertain the question of truth for theological matters.

The problem with the restriction of theology to the second dimension, having to do with the existential or determinate universal, is that the question of ecclesiality is obscured. When that happens theology becomes increasingly inclined to discover its contents in generic universals. It courts and weds ontology. Furthermore, this restriction cuts theological reflection off from the specific and from the future. Denied its historical matrix and its contemporary function, theology

17. The restriction of theology to the historical and the normative (truth-oriented) dimensions is the very thing liberation theologies are repudiating. Theology so restricted ignores its own situationality and unwittingly becomes itself an instrument of an oppressive system. The "liberation of theology" refers then to the introduction of what is called here the third dimension of theological reflection. See, for example, Juan Segundo, *The Liberation of Theology*, trans. J. Drury (Maryknoll: Orbis Books, 1976). It is not always clear, however, that liberation theologians have retained the full structure of theological reflection. Some tend to so locate theology in its situationality that either the question of truth is obscured or the truth of faith is identified with its liberating power.

becomes speculative and academic in the pejorative sense. The problem with the limitation of theology to the third dimension, the leap directly from the symbolic universe of the first dimension into some situational present, is that it presupposes but does not establish the universality of that symbolic universe.

Theological reflection should not, however, be turned over to a mere aggregate of special disciplines. If that were the case, there would be no ecclesial reflection at all but only autonomous cognitive enterprises in the sense of fields of scholarly investigation. It seems apparent that ecclesiality itself makes possible, in fact, makes obligatory, a reflective orientation which goes beyond simply ecclesial prereflective participation. This reflection has a telos, a goal, and that is the transformative illumination of everyday social and individual life. There is nothing distinctive about this in itself. The human reflective interpretation of everyday life is a characteristic of the way we get along in the world. The first two dimensions, ecclesiality rising into universality, offer new possibilities of interpretation, discernment, and orientation. Ecclesial reflection therefore can be a concomitant of the Christian life, not simply an esoteric discipline. It can also be the long-term, rigorous pursuit which Schleiermacher attached to one part of the leadership of the church. In both cases the structure of the reflection is the same insofar as it is a postauthority activity. It is a bringing to formulation of prereflective realities apprehended in the intersubjective participation in ecclesial existence by means of the interrogation of ecclesial, universal, and concrete fields of evidence.

The remainder of this investigation will not attempt an account of all three dimensions of ecclesial reflection. Our focus shall be on the first two dimensions, ecclesial existence and determinate universals. We shall follow reflection toward fields of evidence up to the point where the transition back to concreteness is made. Because of this restriction, the primary task before us is to discern how the prereflective realities of ecclesiality determine the fields of evidence consulted by historical method. At this point our focus shall be on the immanent social structure of ecclesiality itself and on its symbolic universe, described as the Adamic-Gospel story. Second, we shall follow the reflective act into its universal orientation and explore how ecclesiality and universality can coexist without contradicting the principle of positivity, the principle which prevents all translations of determinacy into generic terms.

191

In the chapters that follow, a number of themes are taken up which may strike the reader at best as oddities in a work on theological criteriology. The literature of theological prolegomena leads one to expect chapters on Scripture, tradition, dogma, authority, faith and reason, verification, and experience. Instead the reader is offered inquiries into social duration, ecclesial duration, theological portraiture, and determinate universals. Some brief account of what guides these investigations and requires such concepts is in order.

Two theses are especially important in determining the overall approach of these investigations. The first is that what has traditionally been conceived of as authorities are vehicles of the generation-bridging duration of the ecclesial community, and the function and nature of these vehicles is correlative (although the correlation does not necessarily obtain historical actualization) with the essence, telos, social space, and social time of that community. Hence, the use and function of the writings which testify to the origin of ecclesial existence should be determined by the very structure of ecclesial duration. This is why there are inquiries into social duration in general, ecclesial duration, and the vehicular norm. The second thesis offers a distinction between the material (phenomenal, historical) description of Christianity as a historical reality and the making of theological judgments. Theological judgments refer the phenomenal-historical subject matters obtained in the description or portrait of ecclesial historical existence to the intuitional grasp of reality and its coherent formulation. Insofar as these contents are intended as "real" and "true," they are intended as having some universal status. What this universal status is and how it differs from simply the generic universality of ontology is the very center of the inquiry. Needless to say, the collapse of the house of authority prevents that which can be historically established about Christianity from being normative. In the light of this distinction, inquiries are offered into both the material norm (see the first dimension of reflection) and the universal norm, which is the end and focus of the entire investigation.

9

Theological Portraiture

The passing of the house of authority is acknowledged by most modern theologies. On the other hand, Protestant and Catholic neoorthodox theologies (Barth, Rahner), emphasizing as they do the discrediting of liberal theologies, combine that acknowledgment with certain features rescued from the old criteriology. The issue between the nineteenth- and twentieth-century liberal theologies which tried to rise phoenixlike out of the ashes of the conflagrated house of authority and the neoorthodox theologies is misunderstood if it is cast as the issue of natural theology. What they contend over is rather the status of tradition in the church and its theology. "Tradition" here refers to theology's comprehensive, material reference, that religious determinacy which makes theology's setting and symbol system a specific historic faith and not just general ontology. We have seen that one feature of the house of authority was the identification of revelation with some deposit of tradition (the Bible, the post-Bible dogma). Theology's genre thus became exposition of that authoritative deposit, that is, exposition of tradition. Tradition, the material reference of theology, with all its periods and varieties, existed for theology in the mode of authority. Needless to say, tradition in this sense is imperiled by the demise of authority. The problem this leaves the church and its theology is how to theologize without tradition. The solution offered by the liberal theologies, schooled as they were from Semler on in historical method, was to offer in the place of authoritative tradition (authoritative Bible, authoritative dogma) a historically arrived at "Christianity." Theology thus migrated from What does the

Bible say? to What is Christianity?[1] Since there was an intention of truth and value directed to "Christianity," the question was a *theological* one, and yet the primary methodological commitment of the liberal theologies was to *historical* method. Historical method would yield the real, undogmatic Jesus of history, his teachings disentangled from later dogma. Historical method would yield the very essence of "Christianity." Thus theology moves from exposition of authority to exposition of history. And it was not difficult for the so-called neoorthodox theologians to see what in fact Troeltsch had already also discerned. If historical method discredits the house of authority by exposing the historical and therefore relative character of its contents (of biblical books, church councils, the canonical principle, the magisterium), the price it pays is simply the relativization of everything. There may be a historical faith called Christianity, but it has no essence or core or residue which, eluding relativizing, offers a material theological given. Theology is left with "Christianity," a historian's entity, not the faith once delivered. On what basis could anyone ever think of this now relativized plurality of historical data as having anything to do with truth or reality? So much was clearly seen by the neoorthodox theologians and their response was to quickly reincorporate, without appearing to repudiate historical consciousness, elements from the way of authority.

Thus is posed the problem of tradition for theological method. What happens to theology's material contentful reference, the symbolically rich and determinate past, when the way of authority disappears? Is tradition, that comprehensive flow of heritage through the panoramic ebb and flow of traditions, a possible reference of a *critical* theological reflection? If we say no, we translate theology totally out of its churchly matrix, out of its religious determinacy, into the world of universal ontology. If we say yes, we appear to require the

---

1. One can see from this statement the conviction that the "essence of Christianity" theologies were more than simply a brief flurry of polemics occasioned by Adolf Harnack's *Das Wesen des Christentums* of 1901. The term *Christianity* or some equivalent is an ancient term used, for instance, by Ignatius (*Christianismos*) and also in the Middle Ages (*christianitas*). See Rolf Schäfer, "Welchem Sinn hat es, nach einem Wesen des Christentums zu suchen?" *Zeitschrift für Theologie und Kirche* (April 1969), pp. 330 ff. Yet the question of Christianity in these periods was not the sort of question occurring in the Enlightenment and after in which a distinction is fostered between the traditional but discredited vessel and a discerned, valid core or essence. Nor was it the history-of-religions question which asked after the distinctive shape and contours of this religious faith as it is distinguished from other religious faiths.

apparatus of authority to keep tradition intact. The present chapter takes up this dilemma. It maintains that tradition, the material, historical reference of theology, does occur as a valid criterion (field of evidence) for theological reflection but is insufficient in itself as a sole criterion. It searches for an alternative beyond both the liberal view of theology as historical description of "Christianity" and the neoorthodox retention of this or that room in the house of authority.

How then can theological reflection retain tradition, the historically determinate reference of theology, without the way of authority and without relativism? In the structure of theological reflection the first dimension is, in fact, this material reference. After all, in contrast to philosophy, theology is a determinate religious faith attempting to understand itself, bringing its prereflectively apprehended "realities" into a reflective mode which grasps their interior structure and interrelationships as well as worldly situations illumined by them. Tradition, then, is the matrix and setting, the symbolic universe, the bearer of the content of theology. Our task is to understand how it can be also a criterion and field of evidence.

THE CONCEPT OF THEOLOGICAL PORTRAITURE

We begin by recalling the situation in which theological work takes place. Granting that such a situation is inevitably contemporary and biographical, it is *theological* only as its reflection works from the theological given, that set of realities presented and appresented in conjunction with ecclesial redemptive existence. Theological reflection is not a move from nothing to something, from total ignorance and confusion to light and understanding. Its ground and given includes apprehensions concomitant with ecclesiality. Furthermore, these apprehensions occur in the determinate intersubjectivity, the reciprocal meaning-acts which structure the ecclesial community, thus they occur linguistically in connection with a specific set of symbols, stories, and myths. Reflection begins, therefore, already disposed by prereflective insights, and, we might say, by tradition. *In brief, some view of ecclesiality is already at work in theology's prereflective situation.*

What shall we call this already given and determinate material reference which is partly the church's presupposition and matrix and partly the consequence of its interpretive theological task? To call it dogma would imply that the primary way ecclesiality is present in and to redemptive existence is through units of relatively precise, discrete, and official churchly affirmations. Yet we would also distort the matter if we described it as simply a vague feeling of well-being, an experience of freedom, and the like. Here we search for a metaphor, and the metaphor we propose is that of a picture, less a photograph than an impressionistic painting. When the human being is shaped in redemptive existence, participating thus in the determinacy, the social world, of that existence, some picture of that existence forms. Like a picture, it does have discrete, identifiable elements: hope, messiah, ecclesial community, evil, the eternal. Like a picture, these elements are not simply numerically present, merely listed like items on a shopping list. They exist in some sort of relationship to each other. One might say they form a landscape. These relations are not simply created by interpretation, for the elements are given originally as being related to each other. Like all metaphors, this one has its limitation and the most serious one is that it does not indicate the temporal mode in which the "picture" occurs. A picture, even a painting, brings reality to a stop. In fact the "picture" which attends the ecclesial human being is in perpetual change, being reformed as the individual's worldly and ecclesial discernments and experiences occur.[2] The step we have taken here is to state that the *givenness and material references of ecclesiality which precede and ground ecclesial reflection occur as a picture of ecclesial existence.*[3]

We now take another step. We begin with a not unfamiliar distinction between "having something in view" and the secondary act which represents what we have in view. For example, the farm I used to visit as a child continues with me in memory. I have a certain picture of it. But it would involve a second sort of act if I attempted in a novel or a painting to reproduce that picture. I could do it simply from memory. But I could also revisit it, consult records, or discuss it with my relatives, so that the farm reproduced in the painting would be quite different because of added detail from the memory-picture I carry with me. Retaining our visual metaphor, we call that which is

2. Such change is highly relative to the type of piety, the cultural epoch, and the branch of Christendom in question. Presumably the way the "picture" of ecclesiality attends medieval piety would be a more stable one than that of contemporary liberal Catholicism. No such variations add up, however, to a picture utterly unchanging and unchangeable.

3. It should be clear that the presence of a "picture" is not unique to ecclesial existence. Something of the sort would occur in the prereflective situation of any determinate, religious faith.

produced by this second act a portrait, and the act of reproducing it a *portraiture*. And, in fact, this is what we are proposing as the way tradition, the material, historical reference of theology, enters into the first dimension of theological reflection. Because some picture of ecclesiality attends the transition to redemptive existence, *portraiture*, the deliberate enterprise of describing ecclesial existence is not the creation of the picture. The move from picture to portrait is the move from the prereflective to the reflective, from faith to at least one moment and type of understanding. Because the portraiture is an activity of understanding, it connotes a process of building up by inquiry of various sorts a portrait of ecclesiality as a type of historical existence. Needless to say, as a portrait is formed, one's picture of ecclesiality is affected, even as it is affected when no portrait is attempted and one's interpretative cues are taken from portraits of human being offered by the natural, social, and human sciences.

THE THEOLOGICAL CHARACTER OF THEOLOGICAL PORTRAITURE

We begin our specific description of theological portraiture with a question. What kind of enterprise are we talking about? Clearly, it does not coincide exactly with any one specific discipline of inquiry. What prevents this coincidence is both its theological and its multidisciplinary character.

Giving it a theological coloring are its setting as a dimension of theological reflection, the "picture" of ecclesial existence already present, the normative character of its results, and its overall object. We have already discussed its relation to the "picture" of ecclesial existence, and we shall take up the question of normativeness at the end of the chapter. What then is the object (portrait) of theological portraiture? Only global, comprehensive, and unifying terms can express it. That which is being drawn, redrawn, and ever more filled out is a portrait of that total corporate historical phenomenon, ecclesial existence. Because it is the comprehensive phenomenon, the portrait does not coincide with simply its founding ("apostolic") period, nor any other single period, nor with one among the several types of Christendom. Yet "total corporate historical existence" can be construed in several different ways. Looked at in one way, the only thing that is total is simply a historical time span filled in with innumerable events and details. In one sense this does describe what is being portrayed. Yet that which theological reflection would discern when it turns to its material-historical reference is not simply an aggregate of details but a unified corporate existence. But because this particular corporate existence has to do with a redemption which itself is only partially experienced and actualized, the description of that existence has an ideal and eschatological aspect. Hence, the summary terms associated with that existence (kingdom of God, the Christian faith, the gospel, the new being, ecclesia) are not exhausted in their empirical-historical referents but express an ideal-eschatological dimension. The portraying, the painting of the portrait of ecclesial existence, is therefore a depiction of an actual corporate existence and its transempirical telos and ideality. In brief, that which gradually comes into view in the theological portraiture is ecclesiality.

We can express the unity sought by theological portraiture in several ways. Historically, portraiture attempts to grasp ecclesiality as an "axial existence" (Jaspers, Cobb), the culmination of a long-term, cultural-historical process in which a *type* of corporate, human existence emerges. Linguistically (hermeneutically) portraiture attempts to grasp the comprehensive total mythos or story which is the setting for primary stories. Insofar as every religious faith presents a vision of the relation of human beings in their fragility, misery, and evil to the sacred, giving some account of the activity of the sacred toward those things, theological portraiture has the character of theodicy. In this comprehensive sense the Adamic myth is a theodicy even as the Gospel is a theodicy. Drawing the portrait is thus discerning ecclesial existence as a theodicy.[4]

Needless to say, while this attempt to grasp both the real and ideal unity of ecclesiality involves many specific scholarly enterprises, portraiture itself is not simply a collection of sciences. A comprehensive study of the role of Fulda in the beginnings of Christianity in Germany may contribute in its own way to the portrait, but this scholarly investigation plus thousands of other such studies would not, taken together, comprise a portrait of ecclesiality. Portraiture, we recall, is a dimension of *theological* reflection. Some grasp of the material-historical reference of ecclesiality in its unity, *as ecclesiality*, must attend any theological work. Thus, anyone doing it must

---

4. *Theodicy* as used here should not be taken in the narrow and rationalistic sense of a set of arguments which address or "solve" the problem of God and evil. It is rather the attempt to discern how the symbolic universe of the religious faith "makes sense of," addresses, alleviates the human experience of chaos, misery, mortality, and evil.

participate in this transition from picture to portrait and cannot remain at the atomistic level of specific historical depictions.

In the history of the church and theology there is a very ancient way of understanding the material-historical reference of theology. This is the Jewish concept of tradition. Like most ancient yet persisting notions, it drags behind it a long train of controversies, connotations, and meaning-strata which make it impossible to appropriate without critical refinement. Used in one way, tradition can simply be a shorthand for the house of authority, a way in which classical Christianity understood its own duration, occurring thus through a network of correlative authoritative entities: Scripture, dogma, the church. In this sense tradition is the flow of Christian reality through historical time, definitively formulated in Scripture and dogma and presided over by the church.

Rejecting this classical notion, tied up as it is with the house of authority, we propose instead a view associated with Möhler, Blondel, and others. We have accepted the essentially Catholic view not only that redemptive existence is a corporate existence occurring through participation in the ecclesial community but that faith's cognitive dimension is founded in that participation and therefore theology's given and ground begins there. Furthermore, that which gives theological reflection its determinacy, shape, contents, and symbolic reference is the persistence of ecclesial corporate reality out of the past. The problem with the house of authority version of these "catholic" insights is that relative-historical (fallible) institutions and their products are given a priori, necessary status to ecclesiality's existence and duration. It is our conviction that tradition (*paradosis*) in the sense of persisting ecclesial existence is found primarily in the depth sociality, the determinate intersubjectivity of the community.[5] Upper strata of the community reflect its survival and maintenance-oriented struggles, and at that level occur controversies, dogmatic formulations, schisms, and institutionalizations. Here occur traditions, to draw on Congar's well-known distinction.[6] Yet the focus of theological portraiture is less on details than on contours, interrelationships, unity—in brief, on ecclesiality—and one finds ecclesiality in the depth

---

5. *Determinate intersubjectivity* refers to the specifically ecclesial mutual intentions or ways of meaning through which participants in ecclesial reality are present to each other.

6. See Yves Congar, *Tradition and Traditions* (New York: Macmillan Company, 1967), pp. 283 ff.

sociality of the community. Insofar as this is the case, we can say that theological portraiture is a theology of tradition. It is that moment in theology where tradition informs theology, not as a house of authority, but as the duration of the ecclesial stratum of the faith community's past.

THEOLOGICAL PORTRAITURE AND THE ESSENCE OF CHRISTIANITY

I have described theological portraiture as *one* thing and not many things. The discernment of a total, corporate historical existence as ecclesial existence is that one thing, and this gives the portraiture its theological character. At the same time theological portraiture is unavoidably the result of many things, many kinds of inquiry. The reason this is the case is simply that its subject matter, whatever else it is, is a historical phenomenon. As a historical phenomenon it embraces originating events, a continuing history through a variety of periods and places, a vast and many-sided literature, the many aspects usually present in complex corporate entities (political, educational, aesthetic, cultic, polemical, economic), a symbolic universe, and so on. The portraiture is thus drawn not instantaneously from a vision of ecclesial existence but is built up gradually out of a multiplicity of inquiries. This does not mean that the portraitist as an individual engages in all these studies. For the most part these inquiries occur not in an individual but in the community as a whole. We would say with Schleiermacher at this point that theology is typically a phenomenon of the religious community and it is dispersed into many activities of that community as it attempts to understand itself.[7] In this sense we could say that the faith-community not only has a *picture* of itself

7. The essential ambiguity of the term *theology* is herein manifest. The ambiguity goes back to the two meanings now in use. As it emerged from the Middle Ages into the Reformation and post-Reformation theologies, it referred to a *habitus* of human being whose genre could be wisdom or prudence and which habit could have but not be identical with a cognitive element or knowledge. Something like this is meant in the work *Theologia Germanica*. See especially Johannes Wallmann, *Der Theologiebegriff bei Johann Gerhard und Georg Calixt* (Tübingen: J. C. B. Mohr [Paul Siebeck], 1961), chap. 1, sec. A. This usage clearly reflects the monastic line of the Middle Ages and it continues in Luther and also in the Spener school. On the other hand, the Thomist line and medieval school theology saw theology as a science and, with certain qualifications, having the marks of a science. This set the stage for the late-eighteenth-and-nineteenth-century encyclopedic movement in which theology came to be an inclusive term for a number of "sciences" or disciplines pertinent to studies for ministry or priesthood. Theology here means an aggregate of scholarly approaches or methods and cognitive enterprises: historical, philosophical, practical.

which persists through social time but that it is perpetually drawing its own portrait and drawing on past portraits as it does so. Most of the actual inquiry that goes into portraiture is present as something the individual theologian makes use of but does not engage in. Even when the theologian engages in a discrete inquiry, such as the eschatology of Moravian pietism, this is not itself the portrait of ecclesiality of theological reflection. At best it joins a variety of other inquiries in building up the portrait.

Proposed here is replacement of the way-of-authority use of tradition with another way of dealing with faith's corporate, historical aspect, namely, a *historical* attempt to form a portrait of ecclesiality. This replacement, in fact, began with the entrance of historical consciousness and methods into theology since the Enlightenment. Reflecting this are biblical criticism, the search for the historical Jesus, the search for the essence of Christianity, the new hermeneutic, the death of God proclamation, and so on. Needless to say, the entrance of historical thinking into theology was not simply a transition from an older discredited enterprise into a new successful one. The story of the embracing of history by theology is not a success story.[8] Insofar as one reviews this story as a multiplicity of specific investigations on the part of a plethora of historical disciplines (archaeology, linguistics, textual criticism, semiotics, period studies, biographies, histories of concepts), its accomplishments are impressive. But when we ask how these data, these methods, contribute to or function in theological reflection, how they assist in making theological judgments, we find that historical consciousness has created a world of new problems.

Setting aside most of the above-mentioned historical enterprises, we concentrate on that nineteenth-century movement which promised to replace the way of authority as a way of pursuing theology, namely, the attempt to answer theological questions by setting forth the *essence of Christianity*.[9] There is, we should acknowledge, a sense in which this

8. The literature documenting the entrance of historical consciousness and methods into theology is vast. See F. C. Baur, "The Epochs of Church Historiography," in *Ferdinand Christian Baur on the Writing of Church History,* ed. and trans. by Peter C. Hodgson (New York: Oxford University Press, 1968); G. Ebeling, *The Study of Theology,* trans. D. Priebe (Philadelphia: Fortress Press, 1978), chap. 6; and F. J. Foakes-Jackson, *A History of Church History* (Cambridge: Heffer and Sons, 1939).

9. The notion of a "portrait" of Christianity obviously has some similarity to the expression especially associated with Harnack, the essence of Christianity. This concept of a portrait of ecclesiality is clearly indebted to the essence of Christianity theologies and continues their concern. I am, however, avoiding the expression *essence of Christianity* for two reasons. First, a fundamental ambiguity attends its usage in the

question is posed in the classical theological tradition, in the framework of the way of authority. There is in that view a revealed, unchanging deposit of divine truth, its unit of expression being dogma. The first effect of historical consciousness on this view was in the form of the problem of the *development of dogma*.[10] The problem was the reconciliation of unchanging dogmas as the units of divine truth with the fact that new dogmas did in fact arise in history. How can the unit which carries the immutable Christian truth have a history? And the attempt to solve this problem has itself a history, most of which falls within the Catholic theologies and within the house of authority.

The attempt to fathom the essence of Christianity steps outside the boundaries established by the house of authority altogether. Instead of asking how the authoritative deposits of revelation contain and disclose divine truth, it poses the historical question of the nature of Christianity.[11] This approach, subtly pervading some theological programs (such as Schleiermacher) and thematized in explicit controversy in others (such as Harnack), did reflect the attempt to substitute historical inquiry for the appeal to authority. Many if not most of the criticisms of Harnack's *Das Wesen des Christentums* (1900), including

essence-of-Christianity theologies. For an account of this ambiguity, see Troeltsch's essay, "What Does the 'Essence of Christianity' Mean?" translated in Robert Morgan and Michael Pye, *Ernst Troeltsch: Writings on Theology and Religion* (London: Duckworth, 1977). The term can refer to something primarily *historically* retrieved or *theologically* proposed. As the former it refers to whatever the historian might discern as *distinctive* of Christianity. As the latter it refers to that which survives all critical assessment and is the end product of theological assessment, something experienced and proclaimed as salvific, real, true, and so on. Both senses can occur in the famous kernel-and-husk metaphor of Harnack. The second reason is that it expresses something in or about Christianity as a historical religion which, when the historian discovers it, is utterly normative. Theology thus is historically reduced to what I have described as its first dimension, and the whole step or dimension of truth is avoided. However, the real intention of some version of this phrase and literature is retained in the concept of theological portraiture.

10. Two fairly recent histories of the literature of the development of dogma issue are J. H. Walgrave, *Unfolding Revelation: The Nature of Doctrinal Development* (Philadelphia: Westminster Press, 1972), and Owen Chadwick, *From Bossuet to Newman* (Cambridge: Cambridge University Press, 1957). Maurice Wiles's *The Making of Christian Doctrine* (Cambridge: Cambridge University Press, 1967) focuses on the patristic period. In addition, see Georg Soll, *Dogma und Dogmenentwicklung* (Freiburg: Herder, 1971).

11. Thus the theological effort moves from being characterized as *dogmatic* theology (the setting forth of definitive units of divine truth) to the term probably used first by Spener, *Glaubenslehre*, a term whose essential ambiguity is rooted in the double meaning of the term *Glauben* or faith, which refers both to individual-personal faith and to *the* faith of the religious community or Christianity. Schleiermacher's usage includes both subjective and historical poles and their attending methods.

Loisy's famous *The Gospel and the Church,* were in my opinion misrepresentations of the work. On the other hand Harnack's work, as Troeltsch's penetrating analysis shows, participates in the fundamental ambiguity of the essence-of-Christianity movement.[12] And this ambiguity posed a paralyzing dilemma for anyone who regarded the total task of theology as captured in the historical question, What is Christianity? We have here an intellectual enterprise whose only method and therefore type of evidence is *historical,* but whose motivation and expectation is *theological.* "Essence of Christianity" is therefore both whatever historical method procures about Christianity and whatever is fundamental and indispensable to faith. A dilemma rises from this double-sidedness. One side of the dilemma rests on the commitment to historical method. The issue turns on what "essential" means within historical method. Let us grant that the historian is looking for something "necessary" to the historical phenomenon without which it would not be itself. How will the historian establish this necessary feature? The historian at this point can search for what is universally present in every presentation of Christianity. But this yields something merely factually or contingently universal since any historical entity may in the next phase of its development abandon any given feature unless that feature is formally necessary to any historical entity as such. The historian can search for what is *unique* to Christianity, what is not shared with other comprehensive types of religious faith. But this changes as the religion develops, and it becomes ever more pluralistic. What is unique is different in content in primitive Christianity, in medieval Catholicism, and in sixteenth-century Protestantism. Because of the capacity of the "unique" to develop into something else, it becomes increasingly difficult for the historian to label it "necessary" to Christianity. The result of the historian's search for the necessary is therefore a historical and mutable entity. There may be historically plausible reasons for regarding some things as more enduring, more characteristic and differentiating, than others. But when the historian offers any of these to the believer as theological criteria for the religious community's self-understanding or proclamation, their relativity is only too manifest.

This brings us to the other side of the dilemma. If the search for "Christianity" or an essence of Christianity is without qualification a

---

12. See Morgan and Pye, *Ernst Troeltsch.*

theological endeavor, this means an act of understanding which arises out of the faith-situation, an already given disposition toward something meant as reality, norm, or truth. "Christianity" in this sense cannot mean simply what happens to persist over generations or what happens to arise as unique in period after period. It is that which necessarily conditions and attends salvation. The problem in a nutshell posed by postclassical What-is-Christianity theology is the search for something self-evidently normative at the level of faith and its attending realities by means of relativizing, historical method.

I shall not seek a solution to this problem since there is no solution. The historian's attempt to describe "Christianity" can never itself *be* theology. Theological portraiture, while it is not synonymous with the totality of theological reflection, is a stepchild of the essence-of-Christianity movement. I have already indicated what gives it its theological character. It remains now to describe its historical character.

One of the problems with the essence-of-Christianity movement even as a historical enterprise was the metaphor associated with it, namely, the differentiation of a kernel within a husk.[13] The metaphor of a portrait, on the other hand, has some distinct advantages. There is no "essence" of Christianity which, once found, is an a priori criterion for theological reflection. That is, there is no "essence" of historically discerned content which coincides with faith's normative realities. Nor is there an unchanging essence distinguished from a changing husk. What is portrayed is something historical and therefore in process. Thus the portraiture is itself a constantly changing enterprise. It resembles an artist constantly redoing a portrait and even offering new portraits of a child who is growing up. We need not

---

13. Kernel and husk is the well-known metaphor proposed by Harnack. However, he also uses another metaphor which is less known but more adequate, that of the tree with its roots and branches. The passage goes, "Just as we cannot obtain a complete knowledge of a tree without regarding not only its root and its stem but also its bark, its branches, and the way in which it blooms, so we cannot form any right estimate of the Christian religion unless we take our stand upon a comprehensive induction that shall cover all the facts of its history." *What Is Christianity?*, trans. T. B. Saunders (New York: G. P. Putnam's Sons, 1912), p. 11. The interpretation and criticism of Harnack has for the most part focused on the kernel-and-husk metaphor, accusing him of restricting the essence of Christianity to three themes connected with the teachings of Jesus, something he explicitly denies (pp. 10–11). I am convinced that the kernel-and-husk metaphor does not really express Harnack's own view of the essence of Christianity, which is not simply an ancient immutable idea located in the teachings of Jesus but a total, developing historical phenomenon.

conclude from this metaphor, however, that the process of change in the history of Christianity is necessarily one of maturation. Further, the focus of the portrait is not on essence, a kernel in a husk. Yet the portrait does try to capture the unity, the interrelation of features. The result, if successful—the face staring out of the portrait—is ecclesiality.

HISTORICAL CLUES TO ECCLESIAL EXISTENCE

At this point some distinctions are called for. *Christianity* is the most comprehensive term available for the historical phenomenon of the Christian religion. It is a parallel term to Judaism, Hinduism, and the like. *Ecclesiality* or ecclesial existence is not the "essence" of that larger entity but is the same historical phenomenon viewed as a *type* of historical existence. As a comprehensive type, ecclesiality is only in part actualized in Christianity, and therefore it has an ideal, teleological aspect. *Church* or Christian church is a comprehensive term for the social and institutional carrier of Christianity. *Ecclesia* or ecclesial community is the church or some aspect thereof insofar as it carries ecclesiality. It, too, is a partly actual, partly ideal and teleological notion. The study of Christianity can be thought of as a historical study using historical methods to depict persons, periods, literatures, institutions, and so on. It thus names a plurality of efforts, most of which are not concerned with the ecclesial dimension of Christianity. Thus we have treatments of Christianity in Gibbon, Toynbee, Latourette, Schaff, Marx, and others.

We make these distinctions in order to say that the focus of theological portraiture is not Christianity but ecclesiality. It may use the results of historical studies of Christianity, but the face that emerges from its effort is a type of corporate existence. Theological portraiture then is a historical effort, but its object is not the total phenomenon of Christianity. That being the case, what does it do other than draw the multiplicity of church historical studies to obtain the portrait? If ecclesiality does have an actualized historical aspect which coincides in some fashion with Christianity, we can expect it to disclose itself, to be accessible to inquiry. But where does inquiry look for ecclesiality? The gathering of historical data will not necessarily yield the portrait. We propose at this point three regions which stand out as places where ecclesiality comes into view. They are, the original transition from older types of corporate existence to the new type;

ecclesiality's overall mythos and primary symbols; and its depth sociality which functions as a continuity in development. In other words, portraiture involves inquiry into the origin of ecclesiality, depth linguistics, and depth social structures. The present work does not purport to be an effort of portraiture, hence these three dimensions of portraiture are not thematized systematically. However, chapters 10 and 12 explore questions of method and ecclesial origins, and chapter 11 offers some suggestions about ecclesiality's depth sociality. The remainder of the present chapter will take up the problem of origin and development of ecclesiality in relation to theological portraiture.

The Historical Origins of Ecclesial Existence

A proposal to study the origins of ecclesial existence must surely appear, especially to the believer, as an exercise in hubris. For insofar as ecclesial existence attributes itself to divine activity, its origin resides in mystery and resists historical explanation. Although I would be prone to reject traditional interventionist models of understanding divine activity, I have no desire to dispute this claim. The mystery of origins actually pertains to all creatures. Let us acknowledge that there are dimensions of all creaturely and historical occurrences which elude and limit our understanding. The business of historical inquiry is that of relative not absolute origins. And theological portraiture attempts to grasp the relative origin of ecclesial existence in the sense of describing the event(s) and person(s) to whose causal efficacy the new kind of historical existence owes its being.

Why does the portraiture of ecclesial existence involve an account of historical origins at all? Part of the answer is suggested by the general structure of social duration, the elements which constitute the perduring of any complex society.[14] It is the case that most societies maintain their continuity, their tradition by collective memory of the events, mythical and historical, of their origin. Further, the content of these originating events and symbols is not something alien to the society but has some relation to that society's distinguishing historical existence. Hence, this distinctiveness can be maintained in part at least by means of the recollection of those events. Without going so far as to

14. See the Appendix, "The Role of Remembered Origins in Social Duration," on the general structure of social duration for an elaboration of this brief analysis of the role of remembered origin in a society's persistence.

say that there is an a priori relation between the society's origin and its way of enduring, we would point out that ecclesial existence does have a recallable origin, and institutionalized recollection has always played some function in the ecclesial community's self-interpretation and social duration. Hence, any portrait of what ecclesiality is would be seriously remiss if it ignored this interrelation between ecclesiality's social maintenance and its originating events.

Yet there is a more specific reason for the study of the originating events as a part of theological portraiture. To give an account of it we need to explore why the originating events are *normative* events. After all, it is conceivable that a given society has accessible, recollective events of origin which have no normative status. Normativeness does not seem to be an a priori feature of a society's originating events. Why then is the event which initiates the ecclesial community normative? First, we recall what sort of thing ecclesiality is—a corporate, historical mode of human being undergoing redemption under universal conditions. Second, this means that that which creates this mode of human being is a set of historical events effecting a transition in history whose outcome is a specific type of redemptive community. Furthermore, the experience of redemption in the ecclesial sense occurs by participation in this historically originated universalized community.[15] And this being the case, the participant in the ecclesial community unavoidably "means" (constitutes) these originative events in an act which acknowledges dependence on them and celebrates their decisive significance. In more traditional language, the believer experiences redemption mediated through the ecclesial community (its tradition, proclamation, sacraments, symbolic content, intersubjectivity), and honors that which is responsible for that community. Insofar as the participant attributes this universalized redemptive existence to an activity of God, he or she honors God. Insofar as the historical transition to ecclesiality is attributed to the activity, teachings, and tragic victory of Jesus of Nazareth, that same relation of dependence and praise is given to him. Thus the originating event, including the ministry of Jesus, its effects within a small circle of followers, and the Gentile mission, are normative to the extent that their outcome is a mode of human corporate existence which offers

15. I am postponing a discussion of the complex question of the senses in which redemption is available outside the ecclesial community, the question which Rahner has posed in his concept of the "anonymous Christian."

universally accessible redemption. And this is the specific reason that a portrait of ecclesial existence includes a study of the originating events.

Because ecclesiality is the outcome of a historical transition and because human evil is a perpetual possibility and actuality, the effect of that transition is never absolutely procured. The transition thus is never completed or perfected. However, because it is a historical event, it is not something which is simply repeated or perennial. Ecclesial existence, therefore, perpetually requires that which effected and enabled that transition, hence it always attempts to subject itself to the event (or person) of origin. Any portrait of ecclesial existence is inevitably a portrait of that subjecting. The originating events are not simply past events offering themselves to antiquarian curiosity. They are the events which effected a new condition of redemptive existence; thus their content is, ever after, the content of what ecclesial existence requires to remain a distinctive historical type.

These considerations speak to the general question of why theological portraiture includes depiction of the originating events of ecclesiality. They do not tell us what would be involved in that depiction and why. We have acknowledged the genre of theological portraiture as *historical* inquiry. That being the case, one could easily turn the question of origins into an utterly dispersed endeavor, a multiplicity of inquiries into the details of primitive Christianity. With this problem in mind, we take up a second question. What is it about the historical study of ecclesial origins that gives it a theological character and locates it in theological portraiture and theological reflection? In general, the theological study of the origin of ecclesiality is guided by a conviction of its normative character. Yet a more specific answer is called for. The events from which ecclesial existence comes forth are not just isolated, accidental occurrences. There are certain requisites for any new historical mode of existence to endure beyond its initial generation. Even if we are persuaded that the decisive impetus to ecclesiality was provided by the activity of Jesus of Nazareth, the transition from the actions and prophetic vision of an individual to a community able to survive over generations in an alien and complex world is by no means an inevitable or guaranteed occurrence. Major accomplishments are required. It is focus on the originating vision and the corporate accomplishments of the primitive community which prevents the study of ecclesial origins from yielding a mere multiplicity of historical data. Without pretending to be exhaustive, I propose two prominent tasks which attend the study of ecclesial origins for the sake of theological portraiture.

First, the historian-theologian will attempt to grasp that to which the proclamation of the ecclesial community has attributed its existence. Because the community attributes the possibility of redemption to something which occasioned the historical transition to ecclesiality, that something persists in the community not just as an ancient piece of information but as something celebrated and proclaimed as the redemption-effecting event or person. Proclaimed in this way is Jesus of Nazareth. Proclaimed as the redemption-effecting person, he is thus set forth in the language of Jewish messianism and apocalypticism, as Messiah, Son of man, Lord, and so on. And this sets one of the tasks, perhaps the central one, of origins-oriented theological portraiture. It inquires into the ministry of that figure with special attention to the qualities of the figure that initiated a sequence of events the end of which is universalized redemptive existence.

Yet it is difficult historically to simply isolate the ministry of Jesus from its impact, its effect on those immediate to Jesus, and its outcome in a new community in which Jesus the proclaimer of the kingdom becomes also the proclaimed. Thus the enterprise of describing Jesus includes not only Jesus' own activity and teaching insofar as they are accessible but also the response to that activity and the historical effect thereof. The ministry of Jesus and the rise of the early Christian community expresses the general aim of this inquiry into ecclesial origins.

Second, even if a messiah figure had such an impact as to bring into existence a gathering of followers resulting in a new sect of Judaism, this does not show how it was that this new sect survived and maintained itself over generations. To endure over time, the new sect had to solve certain problems, equipping itself with generation-bridging features such as a sedimented language of new primary symbols and new forms of institutionalization.

The new sect could not endure as new without capturing the vision of universal redemptive existence in language. To use the terminology of recent linguistic studies, a new story had to be fashioned. We might also say that a new symbolism or universe of symbols was required, in order to differentiate the new proclamation both from the synagogal tradition and from Hellenistic religious syncretism. The event, the person of Jesus, had to be given a linguistic vehicle suitable for continued proclamation. This process and vision began, no doubt, in the ministry and teachings of Jesus himself. But most of the work was the accomplishment of authors whose writings the church eventually gathered into the collection now called the New Testament. The study of that literature is, of course, a study of a variety of interpretations, a plurality of languages. Furthermore, it is the study of language and symbols which are largely appropriated from adjacent Jewish and Hellenistic religious groups. Like all language, it is time-bound and culturally originated. At the same time it is a language of proclamation, the first instance of the ecclesial community attempting to subject itself to and measure itself by its originating person and event. The narratives, theologies, parables, and images of this initial linguistic deposit, which the new ecclesial existence is, struggle for expression. In addition to the language formed in the new community, the originating event involves the forging of a new institutionality, a concrete community with leaders, cultic practices, and education. Hence, this second task, the study of the community emerging from the nucleus figure, includes also a grasp of its initial social structure.[16]

To summarize, the study of ecclesial origins occurring within the portraiture of ecclesiality includes at least these two tasks: the historical description of the proclaimed figure, Jesus of Nazareth, and the historical account of the rise of the new community incarnated in a new language and a new sociality.

Christian Tradition in Historical Change

To restrict theological portraiture to an account of ecclesial origins is to presuppose that these origins are an exhaustive source and norm, that ecclesial existence obtained final and definitive form in the period of origins. This, of course, is the inclination of theology governed by the Scripture principle. Ecclesial existence is viewed as an unchanging identity persisting through subsequent historical times. Such a view in the end loses ecclesial existence as a historical notion since any global *type* of historical existence cannot avoid historical change, participating as it does in the network of historical occurrences and influences. The price paid for escaping that network is high. It means the

16. See Congar, *Tradition and Traditions,* chap. 1.

reduction of ecclesiality to some sort of ontological entity which without self-contradiction can have the feature of immutability. Ours is another route. Given the historical character of ecclesial existence, the task of depicting it cannot be limited to an inquiry into origins. The alternative, however, is not simply the relativities of change, as if a type of existence obtained actuality in the period of origin only to be immediately dispersed into the multiplicities characteristic of historical phenomena. Thus theological portraiture involves the attempt to discern ecclesial existence as something which itself has a history, something which, as a type, represents a continuity amidst change. We ask, then, in what sense is ecclesiality subject to historical change? More precisely, can a *type* of historical existence develop?[17] We have already offered a general affirmative answer in the assertion that all historical entities are subject to change. Comprehensive historical societies and movements (communism, Buddhism, Native American "nations") occur in specific and changing historical situations. As they respond to the challenges of those situations, they actualize some possibilities and not others. Adaptive development is thus inevitable to enduring corporate historical existences. At the same time, a historical movement may or may not develop in the "logical" direction indicated by its type, toward its own proper entelechy or telos. When it does we have an entelechaic development, an actualization of possibilities which accord with the type. It is just this sort of possible development that grounds the historical attempt to fill out the picture of the type in question.

We are now ready to deal with the question set up by this analysis. What is the function or role of the study of historical change and development in theological portraiture? We have tried to describe the study of origins as offering clues to ecclesiality. Does the study of the subsequent history of Christianity provide other clues? Does the face of ecclesiality take on more detail from the study of the history of Christianity? The answer is surely affirmative. The reason is as follows. We have already tried to establish that a type of historical existence is not simply self-identical, utterly coincident with every actualization that takes place in connection with it. In other words a

17. It should be clarified that "development" is not being used here to mean progress but rather complexification over time. In this neutral sense even a demonic social structure might be said to "develop," to have a history.

certain ideality and teleology presides over comprehensive types of existence. Thus from the very beginning, participation in ecclesiality could react to this or that possible development critically, arguing that such departed from the paradosis handed down, the Gospel, or from the "apostolic faith." In the controversy over the law Paul pressed the logic of ecclesiality in a certain direction, arguing that the ethnic dimension of law (Torah) was not essential for the realization of redemption. We have here not only theological insight obtaining a literary expression, but the community itself taking on certain features. What happens, then, is that certain individuals, periods, and movements in the history of Christianity discern within their own newly originated historical situation something about ecclesiality not previously actualized.

I am not suggesting that the history of Christianity is simply teleology, the history of a gradual, inevitable actualization of ecclesial existence toward its telos. We must acknowledge that the salvation history framework of the house of authority was also a framework of the church's self-understanding. Hence, it was easy for the church, citing a priori reasons, to assign the status of divine origin to whatever developed. Insofar as such a notion of a priori progress is an unacceptable version of God's relation to history (the royal metaphor), the view of traditioning and change as necessarily teleological realization is discredited. This does not discredit, however, the ideal-teleological dimension of ecclesial existence nor the possibility of occasional historical actualizations of that dimension. The point here is that the grasping of such realizations fills out the portrait of ecclesiality far beyond simply the study of origins.

Are we not involved in a circle? That is, must we not already know what ecclesiality is before we can identify something in history as an actualization of its immanent logic? Such language reflects a rationalistic hermeneutic. In fact, theological portraiture is not so much an applying of clear criteria worked out in advance as it is the gradual discernment of a historical type emerging out of a rather vast field of evidence. This pushes us to be more specific about what it means to do portraiture from such a field of data. We have already said that the study of origins provides some clues. And we have further indicated that portraiture also draws on postorigins developments. But what prevents the portraiture from being at the mercy of the multiplicity of data? Will the portrait emerge from the consultation of a million details? Here we identify two other regions of clues, language and depth sociality.[18]

That a historical enterprise must work with language is self-evident. But the problem of discerning ecclesial existence is not so easily solved, for language can conceal as well as reveal. The cosmological and mythical language of popular religion or the tightly argued connections of a theological system may simply disguise ecclesiality. After all, what does one learn about ecclesiality as a type of historical existence from the popular religious picture of graves opening and the dead meeting Jesus in the sky or from the scholastic distinction between preservation and consursus in the providence of God. Such things may in fact be pertinent for discerning ecclesiality, given certain kinds of explorations. But that is just the point. The clues to ecclesiality lie more at the deep levels of symbols and images than at the levels of religious language, which serve everyday communication or theological understanding. Language presents itself to theological portraiture as a multistrata phenomenon. If a community of faith is in fact a distinctive type of historical existence and has been successful in perpetuating itself over generations, language is functioning in that perpetuation. In other words the type has found some linguistic expression. The level of this expression is the enduring symbol (Tillich), the comprehensive myth (Ricoeur), or the story (Dunne). In short, theological portraiture attempts to grasp the symbolic universe present in Christianity, and as that universe is mapped ecclesiality comes more into view.[19]

The other region which points to ecclesiality is *depth sociality*. We thereby distinguish the fundamental intersubjective structures of the religious community from their various attending social strata such as institutionality and everyday, actual personal interactions. The most fundamental intersubjective structure is made up of the *meanings* which attend those reciprocal intentions that are determinative of the community's distinctive sociality. If a sociality or community is of a certain type (and every sociality is), that type would be most manifest at this level. The level is obtained only in an inquiry which asks, What are the meanings or meaning-acts which occur between the human

18. These regions are described in Edward Farley, *Ecclesial Man* (Philadelphia: Fortress Press, 1975), chaps. 5 and 7.

19. The semiotic work of the structuralist movement is an example of this moment of theological portraiture.

beings of this community, without which they are related to the community as strangers? Obviously there is close correlation between a community's depth sociality and its symbolic universe. The depth sociality is composed of mutually intended meanings, and these meanings are always linguistically carried. Thus every new type of historical existence generates a new symbolic universe correlative with its depth sociality.

Conclusion

We have in theological portraiture a dimension of reflection which is both theological and historical in character. The task of portraiture as a *historical* endeavor is primarily the interrogation of a vast and complex historical phenomenon (Christianity) as to its type of corporate existence, and it does this by focusing on origins, on depth sociality, and on its symbolic universe. Because of the depth levels of the interrogation, we could also describe theological portraiture as an *archaeological hermeneutic.* Portraiture is a hermeneutic not simply because it has to do with the written texts of ecclesial existence but because the structures and continuities of ecclesia find their most explicit expression in perduring symbols and unifying myths. Hermeneutics, in this broad sense of understanding a corporate existence through a discernment of its mythos, is the overall enterprise to which the many specific historical studies contribute. Further, ecclesial corporate existence has some features analogous to the human self.[20] Like the human self it occurs in layers or strata, some of which are on the surface presenting vast amounts of data for the investigator (such as papal documents) and others beneath the surface (such as human mutual intentions, corporate space and time).[21] Portraiture of ecclesia will involve, therefore, not just linear tracking of the periods of ecclesial history but the uncovering of various strata and relating them to each other.

It should not be necessary to point out that theological portraiture names or describes a constitutive dimension of theological reflection, not a methodological novelty only now being proposed. Theology

20. See the Appendix, "The Elements of Social Duration," for a discussion of the social self metaphor.

21. The archaeological inquiry of part 1 of this work is an example of this sort of archaeology. See also chapters 11 and 12 of part 2 for the attempt to discern the community's corporate space, time, and mode of social duration.

from early Christianity (Paul, John) to the present has always operated from the given of ecclesial existence and therefore has devoted
great efforts to characterizing, interpreting, and understanding the
faith once delivered.[22] I have stressed how different this effort is when
carried out within the house of authority and the Scripture principle
from the method of theohistorical inquiry. But portraiture of some
sort is going on in both. One might say that most of the efforts of
theology in the broadest sense of that word concern the portrait,
efforts such as textual and interpretative work on the literature of the
Old and New Testaments, patristic studies, Reformation studies. Even
high scholasticism occurred on an educational base which included
years of biblical studies.[23] Looked at in another way, portraiture as I
am describing it replaces the method of authority. Furthermore, it
also replaces or goes beyond that type of historical work where the
overall reference is "Christianity," an aggregate of data, and whose
method is the assembling of information or the tracing of causal
sequences.

One final question. Is the result of theological portraiture, the
portrait, in any sense a norm in its own right? The issue presses on us
some fine distinctions. In a nontheological sense we could say that all
three dimensions of theological reflection have norms, that is, fields of
evidence, with which they work. In that sense the portraying of
ecclesial existence *has* norms, fields of evidence such as depth sociality.
But is the portrait itself a norm for theology in the redefined sense of
a field of evidence? On the one hand we would resist any answer to
the question that would simply identify theological reflection with the
portraiture, a tendency of both essence-of-Christianity theologies and
hermeneutical theologies. Even though portraiture is driven by theological motivations, its method is primarily historical and what it yields
is a historical entity, ecclesial existence. This historical entity is
complex, is in process, and is relative to the dialectic of interrogation

22. Different branches of Christendom have arisen in connection with new insights,
new visions of ecclesiality or some aspect of ecclesiality. Thus the Protestant Reformation occurred as a new way of relating institutionality and redemption. The Lutheran
branch of the Reformation could eventually distinguish the formal principle (Scripture)
and material principle of theology (justification by faith). The description and interpretation of this material principle closely resembles what I am calling theological
portraiture.
23. Charles Briggs, *The History of the Study of Theology* (New York: Charles Scribner's
Sons, 1916), vol. II.

necessary to building up the picture. In other words, portraying is not yet "judging as true" nor the grounding of such judgments. For these reasons we resist saying that whatever is established as ecclesial by theological portraiture is true a priori, able to function as a premise in a true judgment.

On the other hand we recall that what originates the portraiture in the first place and what makes it theological is ecclesial existence already given as redemptive. Prior to the portrait and guiding it are intentions, meanings, ways of being related to it which grasp it as reality. Thus to the believer the portrait being filled out is a portrait of reality. To the extent that this is the case, the portrait of ecclesiality is not merely one among many types of historical existence but one whose redemptive realities are manifest. This gives the portrait a certain status, if not that of a norm, at least that of an indispensable source for the second and third dimensions of theological reflection. If the portrait itself does not constitute or settle the question of the truth of judgments about ecclesial existence, at least it offers that which lays claim to truth. The most it can be as a criterion (field of evidence) is as that now clarified mode of historical existence which dominates, informs, and supplies the content to those subsequent dimensions of theological reflection that explore both truth and praxis.

At the same time we must acknowledge that in the community, as it understands itself, as it attempts to be and perpetuate ecclesiality, the portrait of that historical existence functions as normative in the sense that the community's immanent inclination is to avoid lines of development, actions, and institutions that contradict ecclesiality and to pursue lines that promise to actualize it. The portrait has always been a norm for piety. But theological reflection is not piety, working as it does from a critical distance toward what piety takes for granted.

10

Ecclesial Duration:
The Problem of Space and Time

Chapter 9 described the first dimension of theological reflection by means of the metaphor of portrait painting. There is, accordingly, something (ecclesial existence) to be described. Furthermore, that which is portrayed must in some way be available. The possibility of theological portraiture suggests that not only was there a historical phenomenon, ecclesial existence, but it somehow remains available, accessible to those who would portray it. Now one could say that in some sense pre-Hellenistic Minoan civilization is, through crumbled and covered ruins, accessible. But theological portraiture is both a theological and historical enterprise. It is historical because ecclesial existence is a historical phenomenon with historical origins and development. It is theological because ecclesial existence is a *contemporaneous*, living, corporate reality which to some degree continues to occur. The availability of ecclesiality for portraiture is both its presence in the form of past tradition and continued presence, its traditioning. In other words, that which makes ecclesiality available is its generation-bridging duration over time. Somehow in the period of its origins it obtained a form that enabled it to endure as a social type of existence. Thus, as an extension of the description of theological portraiture, I shall in this and the following two chapters attempt an account of the social duration of ecclesial existence.[1] Theologically

1. It would be not inaccurate to describe such an account in the phrases, the contemporaneity of Christ, the *Christus presens*. But what is offered here is in no way a full account insofar as this requires an explicit theology of salvation and a Christology. Recent works on the presence of Christ include Tom W. Boyd, *Contemporaneity and the Presence of Christ* (Nashville: Vanderbilt University, diss., 1973); Hans Frei, *The Identity*

expressed, our task is the delineation of tradition and traditioning. The present chapter will focus on the strange kind of social space and social time which attends ecclesiality. Chapter 12 thematizes the actual structure of ecclesial process and its specific elements (sedimentations, vehicles, activities). Hopefully the result will indicate the criteria or fields of evidence available to theological portraiture and how it is that such fields of evidence have formed.[2]

This and the next chapter investigate how ecclesiality as a social corporate existence offers itself to theological portraiture, how it rises into fields of evidence which can be drawn on in theological reflection's first dimension. Since the fields of evidence coincide with the places where ecclesiality, an actual-ideal phenomenon, shows itself, and since it shows itself only because it has obtained some form which can endure through social time, what we are looking at are the elements of ecclesial social duration. Accordingly, ecclesial duration, its structure and elements, is not only one aspect of what is portrayed in theological portraiture but the clue to the proper fields of evidence as such. For example, it will be self-evident to those who work in the house of authority and presuppose the Scripture principle that holy Scripture is the criterion (authority) for statements about the distinctive social perpetuation of Christian faith. But such a procedure has things backwards. A set of writings meant as an authority does not determine a community of faith's proper duration. Rather, the duration proper to that *kind* of faith and social existence determines how writings function in that community. Social duration, the bridging of the generations by a historical social existence, occurs in part as the group procures its identity and continuity by "remembering" its past. Since this occurs through specific vehicles (writings, institutions) and activities, it is not surprising that the written vehicle in which the authoritative past, the tradition, is embodied, would function as an entity in the "memory," the duration, of the community.

It may be that the writings which contain interpretations of ecclesiality's originating events play some proper role in the portraiture of

---

of Jesus Christ (Philadelphia: Fortress Press, 1975); Dietrich Ritschl, *Memory and Hope: An Inquiry into the Presence of Christ* (New York: Macmillan Company, 1967); and Howard Harrod, "Christ as Predecessor and Contemporary," *The Journal of the American Academy of Religion,* 44, no. 2 (1976).

2. The three chapters draw on categories and concepts proposed in the description of the general structure of social duration (Appendix). Hence, it would be helpful although not necessary to consult the Appendix in the course of reading these chapters.

ecclesial existence. However, the ecclesial community cannot discover that role by simply imitating another faith community (such as Judaism) or by arbitrary assignment. Rather the nature and function of written deposits of tradition are determined by the nature and structure of the social duration of the community. This is the basis for the statement that the structure of ecclesial duration contains the clues to the fields of evidence proper to its portraiture. The problem of discerning the structure of ecclesial duration is not, therefore, solved by citing the New Testament collection. Rather it involves the discernment of the main elements at work in ecclesial social time and discovering a set of ideal interrelations and correspondences between them.

For this reason the method and subject matter of the investigation do not coincide with any single discrete discipline. This alone may discredit the attempt in the eyes of some. Negatively stated, what makes the inquiry somewhat elusive is that it is neither a straightforward historical or empirical description of past or present actuality nor a speculation on a mere possibility. Positively stated, what places this inquiry into an unusual genre is that which makes any *theological* inquiry unusual. The realities with which theology concerns itself are never merely actualized, fulfilled, or complete. They are mixtures of historical realization and ideality.[3] These are the two referents or dimensions of the symbol, kingdom of God. Ecclesial existence, a term to describe a determinate kind of historical being, is both a historical phenomenon with a historical origin and development, with actual social structures, literatures, epochs, and the like, and a not-yet-realized telos for human existence—an ideality if you will. Accordingly, the duration of ecclesial existence is an ideality which occurs in conjunction with a historical actualization. Ecclesial duration is not,

3. One way of expressing the element of ideality in theological work is to appropriate what Paul Ricoeur calls *poetics. Freedom and Nature: The Voluntary and the Involuntary*, trans. E. V. Kohak (Evanston: Northwestern University Press, 1966), p. 31; *The Symbolism of Evil*, trans. E. Buchanan (Boston: Beacon Press, 1969), pp. 13-14. The term may not have exactly the same meaning in the two works cited. In the former, poetics refers to a "spirituality of the will," a consideration of the will's freedom empowered and conditioned by the transcendent; hence it is a stage of consideration which goes beyond both phenomenological (eidetic) description of the constitutive structures of the will and an empirics which reviews the will's finitude and enslavement. The latter, drawing especially on Bachelard's poetics of space and poetics of reverie, sets poetics in the hermeneutic task, hence, a stage of recovery of symbols which displays the symbol in its nascent state when it is "a welling up of language."

therefore, simply the general structure of social duration (Appendix) translated into the history of Christianity. It is the duration implicit in, the ideal correlation of, the determinate and distinctive historical entity, ecclesial existence. In other words, the actual historical phenomenon, ecclesial existence, contains implicitly its own ideal telos. This is why the description of ecclesial space, time, and duration is not a straightforward empirical description of actualities but includes the uncovering of teleological ideal elements resident in the actual.

What is involved in this uncovering and description? Our study of the general structure of social duration discloses that social duration is closely bound up with social space and time. The ecclesial community is a distinctive and determinate intersubjective structure, and this establishes its distinctive social space and time. Hence, our first task will be to discern in at least a beginning way ecclesial space and time. Furthermore, the ecclesial community is initiated and maintained by a distinctive, originating event or set of events, interpreted as the epoch-fulfilling arrival of the Messiah. How that event is remembered and even perpetuated and how it generates generation-bridging sedimentations constitute the essential features of ecclesial duration. This depiction of ecclesial duration thus begins with an account of the originating and normative event and moves from that to the space–time continuum created by that event.[4]

Before moving to our exploration, we note that *ecclesial* duration, the perpetuation of ecclesial existence, tends for certain specific reasons to elude description. As we have noted, the emergence of the ecclesial community was in part a break with Israel and Judaism. Expressed as a transition from Torah to Gospel, from Israel to the kingdom of God, this break involved an abandonment of what Max Weber called the pariah community and the Judaic institutions of social perpetuation: synagogue, Torah, rabbinate. The new commu-

---

4. *Originating event* is used here much in the way John Knox uses the term event. It is not simply identical with the biographical events of Jesus of Nazareth since it includes a network of events involving the origination of the ecclesial community. Yet the effect of Jesus of Nazareth is surely the nucleus of this event. See John Knox, *On the Meaning of Christ* (Richmond: John Knox Press, 1947), for an analysis which untangles this complex event. Event in this sense is a series of historical happenings in a limited period of time whose interrelations had produced some discernible unified historical outcome. The Norman invasion of England is an event in this sense. Since the event accumulates from the past and disperses into the future, it has no absolute beginning or ending. Nevertheless, it may have a dominant period with a relatively identifiable beginning and end.

nity (ecclesia) of the new age experienced salvation under universalized conditions and therefore understood itself as a community able to coexist and permeate any human society whatsoever. In short, ecclesia means a *universalized* redemptive existence. But the very universalization which marked its origin set for it a severe problem for its social survival. How can a *universalized* redemptive community possess any distinctive kind of duration? The generation-bridging duration of a provincialized form of redemptive existence (a tribe, nation, racial conglomerate, ethnic group) has no such problem since the duration of the provincial community is at the same time the duration of the religion. But a universalized ecclesial existence has no built-in provincial community which is necessary to the redemption to which it testifies. There is no ecclesial human language, no ecclesial political structure, no ecclesial jurisprudence. The most obvious solution to this problem is simply to point out that ecclesial existence attaches itself remora-like to any and all forms of human society and endures through those forms. And yet that is simply not sufficient to describe how *ecclesial* redemptive existence is perpetuated. For that which is perpetuated includes the originating universalizing event, the ecclesial community (and its intersubjectivity), and the experienced and proclaimed salvation. The adoption of a specific society's language, customs, and institutions might account for the assimilation and eventual disappearance of ecclesiality into that society, not its perpetuation. Beyond this adaptation to the plurality of human society, ecclesial existence must find some way to retain its specific memory, its symbolic universe, its testimony. And discerning this universalistic yet determinate traditioning is a more difficult task than discerning the social duration of provincial religious communities.

This and the next chapters set forth ecclesial duration. In this chapter we look at the general structure of that duration. In the following chapter we take up the question of the vehicles correlative to that duration. These chapters draw on the account of the *general* structure of social duration (Appendix) but can be read apart from that account.

THE NORMATIVE EVENT

The general structure of social duration (Appendix) manifests close correlations between a community's space and time, its vehicles of duration, and the *kind* of origin it has and the way it remembers that

origin. These correlations are clearly exemplified in ecclesial existence. The origin of ecclesial existence and the literature of origins
have dominated and unified the self-understanding of the ecclesial
community from the beginning. Such expressions as the kingdom of
God, promise and fulfillment, the new aeon, Jesus the Christ, the
resurrection of Jesus, and the apostolic faith all refer to the event of
origin. It is clear that a decisive feature of ecclesial duration is the
remembering and celebrating of the originating event(s). The two
great Christian festivals, Christmas and Easter, are such celebrations.
Hence, any description of the way ecclesial existence endures would
be seriously inadequate if it omitted the way in which the originating
(normative) event functions in the community's perpetuity.

The self-interpretation of the ecclesial community has, like that of
the Israelite community, a historical character. That is, it grasps
conditions of its continued existence, its perpetuation, as bound up
with the memory and celebration of an originating and normative
historical event. In the case of the ecclesial community, it is an event
unified and founded in a historical person. Granting that the community *interprets* itself in this historical way, is there a correlation between
the very nature of ecclesiality and an originative, normative event? Is
the continued reference to that founding event an accident of history,
something whose absence would have little effect on ecclesiality, or is
the memory of that event somehow a condition of ecclesiality's
continuing duration? Our attempt is to understand why ecclesiality
refers to a founding event which continues to function as normative.[5]

It would be accurate but insufficient to say that every determinate,
historical movement has a beginning, a period of origins in the sense
of a transition from the preceding historical period and situation to
the new movement. That transition and all the subevents that it
comprises mark the "originating events" of any historical movement.
Even if this is the case, many historical movements can and do endure
without much attention to their historical genesis. So we must look
farther.

At this point we recall what ecclesiality is—a corporate, universalized redemptive existence. Although it does involve human individ-

5. Normative is used here to mean an occurrence or disclosure of reality or truth by
which ever-new historical periods of a community measure themselves, thereby
establishing both the continuing identity and ideality of the community.

uals, ecclesiality itself is a corporate existence, a community with its own distinctive intersubjectivity, a distinctive kind of coinherence of selves in each other.[6] As a *redemptive* existence, ecclesiality connotes some breaking of the hold of evil on the individual and social human self, an experience and interpretation of evil initially formulated by the faith of Israel and continuing as a substructure of ecclesiality. As a *universalized* existence, ecclesiality coincides with no discernible form of human sociality (a nation, race, ethnic group); thus none of these can have the status of an exclusive condition of redemption. These features of ecclesial existence disclose the nature of the originating event necessary to ecclesiality. It has to be an event whose outcome was a corporate existence, a community, and the nature of the event as a historical transition has to be one of universalization. The founding event is that set of subevents and persons whose telos and outcome was the creation of a universalized, redemptive existence.

This shows us the character of the event which effects ecclesial existence; it does not as yet indicate why the continuing duration of ecclesiality requires that event. To take this second step we need to first understand why and in what sense the originating event is normative for ecclesiality and what is involved in the apprehension of that normativeness. That the event was normative even for the generation living in the transition to ecclesiality goes without saying. Life in the ecclesial community means a participation in redemptive existence. This means an experienced transition from sin to redemption, an actual alteration (though not perfecting) of human being. Furthermore, this redemptive change can occur regardless of one's determinate cultural and provincial socialization. In short the individual is not disqualified from redemptive existence because he or she lacks membership in some designated provincial community. Because of this redemptive dimension, life in ecclesiality is a *reality* experience, an actualization of redemptive possibilities and world relationships. Furthermore, this salvific participation in a community of redemption depends on an actual historical universalization of redemption. These

---

6. This task of portraying ecclesiality as a historical task is exemplified in the kind of "ideal" history offered by the English novelist and lay theologian, Charles Williams, whose account of ecclesial existence is one of a distinctive kind of interpersonal coinherence. See *The Descent of the Dove: A History of the Holy Spirit in the Church* (New York: Meridian Books, 1956), pp. 234 ff.

two things, redemptive transformation and historical actuality, establish the originating event as normative for any participant in ecclesiality. "Normative" here does not mean "authoritative" as in the house of authority. It means that the continuing ecclesial community must retain the character (universalized, redemptive) of that which the originating event established. The originating event as "normative" means that it is definitive for the self-interpretation of subsequent historical expressions of the same type of corporate existence. And this presupposes that this specific historical event was necessary to the universally available, redemptive reality which the community continually attempts to appropriate.

What is involved in the apprehension of this normativeness? It is evident that the event cannot be even discerned as an event if that which is grasped is simply the innumerable details of a historical time. It is necessary to have a synthesizing act of meaning that grasps some interrelation between Jesus' activities, teachings, death, and certain events which succeeded his death. For such interrelations to come to light, *the* ideal *telos*, that for which these events are significant, must be discerned. In addition, the decisive, unifying thing that procures that telos must be identified. In the language of those contemporary to the event, the telos was identified as the kingdom of God, the new aeon, the faith. The decisive cause was the activity and person of Jesus of Nazareth.

Such was the discernment, gradually dawning on those experiencing this new historical type of redemptive existence. But discernment does not occur without language. And the significant accomplishment of the so-called apostolic period was the clothing of the normative event in a language.[7] The term for that language as it functioned to testify to that event is *kerygma*. The term for the message of that testimony is *gospel*. Thus even as the originating event is normative for participants in ecclesiality, *gospel*, its linguistic carrier, is likewise normative. Because of the discerned telos of the event, the gospel was and remains the good news of the kingdom of God.[8] Because of the discerned central and founding precipitant of that telos, the content of the gospel was the good news of Jesus the Christ. These normative

7. For a description of this step see Karl Rahner, *Inspiration in the Bible* (New York: Herder and Herder, 1966), p. 51.

8. See chap. 1, "The Kergyma of the New Testament Period," for a summary of *gospel*.

expressions show that identifying this event as the normative event for the ecclesial community is a synthetic meaning-act whose origin is the experience of salvation. Gospel thus refers in part to an experiential matrix or setting in the ecclesial community. In addition, it refers to an event (historical personage and so on), an occurrence whose effect was to make redemptive existence universally available.[9]

We return to the question, How does this normative event function in the continuing duration of ecclesial existence? Every community endures in part through its remembering, its retention of the past. In the case of ecclesial existence, what endures is that which was obtained in the normative event, namely, universalized redemptive existence. In other words the transition from provincial to universalized redemption cannot be simply a remembered past event but a perpetually maintained situation. In this sense the originating event must be ever-contemporaneous with ecclesiality. The originating event describes what ecclesiality must always continue to be. Or, to use the symbolic language of gospel and kerygma, ecclesial duration involves not simply the past Jesus but the present Christ. That is, it requires a continuing, ever-present universalizing power. It is for this reason that the ecclesial community continues to "proclaim the gospel" and subject itself in its self-interpretation to its originating event. To fail to do so would quickly result in the transition of ecclesiality into a merely individualistic religion of salvation and likely one inclined to new provincialisms. These observations have not covered the specific ways in which the normative event effects ecclesial duration, only the claim that it does so function. How it functions is the question of how that event effects a distinctive ecclesial space-time continuum and its sedimentations, to which themes we now turn.

ECCLESIAL SPACE AND TIME

The analysis of the structure of social duration (Appendix) includes a brief account of the space-time horizons of human experience. It further proposes that the lived-space and lived-time of individual experience coupled with the cointendings which structure the interrelationships of individuals are presupposed in the space, time, and

---

9. Gospel is functioning, therefore, as a dominant paradigm for the community's self-interpretation and its continuing duration. See Appendix, "The Contribution of the Individual," for an account of the function of a dominant paradigm in social duration.

duration of a society. More specifically, when individuals intend each other under a common paradigm as sharing the same originating event, past, value-structure, and responsibilities, the "here" and "there" of each individual's space are broadened to include the "here" and "there" of the others. The biographical time of the individual's past and future is broadened to mean *our* past and future. For this reason one can rightly speak of a society's space and time generated out of the society's dominant paradigm and determinate intersubjectivity. Furthermore, even as the individual's space and time are actually a continuum of experience, so a society's space and time are correlative aspects of that continuum.[10]

The Genesis of Ecclesial Space and Time

In order to apprehend the genesis of ecclesial space and time, we must introduce some additional considerations about the ways in which human beings are spatial and temporal. In the analysis of social duration (Appendix), we deal with space and time as "neutral," one might say, benign features of human being-in-the-world. However, when phenomenological brackets are removed, and we view the human being as a concrete, existing, biological-historical being struggling constantly for survival, meaning, and well-being, lived-space and lived-time take on the thickness and color of history. We find the human being not only *in fact* living in a particular time or epoch and a particular place, but *needing* to do so.[11] Experiencing as such would not be possible apart from the familiar and accumulated standpoint purchased by living over time in a determinate place. What we call human consciousness could never be formed in a situation of perpetual, momentary space and time. The feature of being historically placed is a correlate of self-transcending embodiment, the human way of being finite.[12]

At the same time historical human being as experienced, inter-

10. Calvin Schrag analyzes space and time as "lived coordinates of experience." *Experiences and Being: Prolegomena to a Future Ontology* (Evanston: Northwestern University Press, 1969), pp. 66 ff.

11. Tom W. Boyd distinguishes between space and place (*Contemporaneity and the Presence of Christ*, p. 246).

12. See Gaston Bachelard's *The Poetics of Space* (Boston: Beacon Press, 1976), for a specific description of this historical spatiality, the human need and appreciation for familiar spaces bound to earth, the dwelling, and its spaces.

preted, and symbolically translated in the faith of Israel and Christianity is radically alienated from its own envisioned well-being. Human being's way of being-in-the-world is not only structurally fragile and anxious but includes a response to that fragility which attributes to worldly entities the capacity to remove the fragility and to overcome the chaos ever lurking at the edge of human space and time. The resulting alienation (sin) alters the human being's way of being finite and pervades and distorts the human need for continuity, permanence, and protection. It invades, accordingly, the human need for and way of having space and time. Thus the familiar comes to mean that which ultimately secures—the eternal. Relations to one's space and time of appreciation, loyalty, and celebration undergo subtle transformation into absolutizing acts. Home, tribe, nation, school become the center of the universe not in the benign, ontological sense established by human embodiment but in the destructive sense of unqualified loyalties.

It was necessary to offer this brief description of how sin affects human lived-space and lived-time because the redemption testified to in the ecclesial community presupposes it. For redemption means a modification of the way of being human in the mode of sin, and that modification concerns absolutizing, alienated ways of being spatial and temporal. Ecclesial space-time therefore is not simply the distinctive space-time of the ecclesial congregation as a face-to-face group. Rather it is a space-time continuum generated first of all by the effect of redemption on alienated, absolutized space and time. This effect does not mean the elimination of the human need for and appreciation of provincial, determinate places and times, but rather the way of meaning and having them as securers against chaos and its ciphers.

That which replaces sin in its individual and corporate forms and its absolutized spaces and times is a new historical being, a distinctive kind of sociality determined by the way human beings "mean" or cointend each other.[13] These cointentions or specific ways that human beings mean each other as human and as ecclesial include both a theological substructure obtained from and shared with the faith of Israel and what we have called the gospel. The theological substructure embraces the Adamic story, a comprehensive interpretation of

13. See Farley, *Ecclesial Man*, chaps. 6 and 7, for an account of ecclesial cointentions.

the human problem as sin against the background of God, the world maker, and a meaningful and good though dependent creation. The effects of sin are the proneness of human beings to violate each other in various ways, implying not only that violation is improper but that human beings essentially exist in a network of mutual positive and negative obligations. In short, Torah is an element in the substructure appropriated from Israel by the ecclesial community.

With gospel the sin-redemption cointentions (and their symbols) of this substructure undergo universalization and certain of its undeveloped aspects are drawn out, such as Torah-transcending cointentions. The universalization means that conditions of actualizing redemption require no specifiable form of provincial human sociality. Thus human beings in the ecclesial community intend or "mean" each other as part of an open community which potentially includes all human beings who can retain their cultural-ethnic-social determinacies and yet experience the breaking of the power of sin. With such universalization Torah is retained but transformed. Universalization fosters a distinction between the necessary but highly plural, and ever-changing codes that regulate the space and duration of ethnic-national societies (such as the statutes of law of a metropolitan area) and the expressions of mutual human obligation that are anchored in certain essential requirements for being human.[14] This distinction transforms Torah from the legal-cultic code regulating the religious-national or religious-ethnic community to the universal structure of human obligation.[15]

In addition, gospel includes a Torah-transcending element. We have observed that Torah changes when the religious community undergoes universalization, when the ethnic-national framework is relativized as the medium and condition of God's presence. But with the breaking of the power of sin universalization occurs at yet another

14. This distinction is not meant to suggest that the two are not related. Ideally, the regulatory laws of a society should express in specific historical situations the universal structure of human being with its need for protection against various kinds of violations.

15. The traditional Christian distinction between the Ten Commandments and the detailed regulations of the Pentateuch suggests this distinction between the Commandments as absolute and the detailed regulations as relative. Yet this solution to the problem of Torah will not do. Insofar as the materials of the Ten Commandments are correlative to the ethnic-national community's accomplishments and requirements, they, too, are relativized and have provincial elements.

level, that of the mode of human being-in-the-world. On the negative side, redemption means the reduction of the need and inclination of the human being to secure itself, to obtain the foundation of its own meaning and telos by absolutizing attachments to worldly entities valued as the eternal. It is clear that anxiety, fear, and enmity of various sorts attend this self-world relation since that entity which the human being regards as the eternal exists in a perilous, worldly environment and thus is as relative and vulnerable as the human being itself. Relating to worldly entities in these anxious modes of guardianship and protection, the human being is not free toward them.

On the positive side, redemption alters the idolatrous way of being-in-the-world. The world and its contents are grasped as not-the-eternal and dependent-on-the-eternal. Replacing enmity and fear are wonder, awe, and concern toward worldly entities, an empathetic, emotive appreciation of them, as part of the network of created being. Universalism is involved here because all worldly entities (persons, nations, possessions, nature, beautiful objects) are relativized and at the same time are manifest and available in their value, usefulness, importance, and beauty. Insofar as such a redemption has been operative, it effects a singular kind of cointentionality between human beings. They "mean" each other not simply through the story and symbols of redemption, but as sharing the new being-in-the-world, as beings who universally have the world in empathetic wonder, awe, and concern (that is, in agape).[16] Gospel thus is not simply a universalizing alteration of Torah but a transcending of Torah as *agape*.

The originating event is simply that which effected both the universalization of this Torah community (the altering of the nature of Torah), and the redemptive existence in the sense of the new focus. Its initiating center is clearly the message, ministry, death, and renewed presence of Jesus of Nazareth. Yet as the event effecting a transition to a new kind of historical-corporate existence, it also includes the transition of Jesus' accomplishment into kerygma and ecclesial community. This event effects the cointentions of the univer-

---

16. I have elaborated what is here only a capsule in an account of both evil and redemption as modes of being-in-the-world in an essay, "Psychopathology and Human Evil: Toward a Theory of Differentiation," in R. Bruzina and B. Wilshire, eds., *Crosscurrents in Phenomenology* (The Hague: Nijhoff, 1978).

salized and Torah-transcending community, and these generate the space-time continuum of ecclesial existence.[17]

The Structure of Ecclesial Space and Time

Ecclesial space and time is not an unambiguous expression. It would surely be misunderstood if it were regarded as a direct parallel to the determinate social space and time of a provincial community, for instance, urban space or Navaho space-time. The phrase suggests both a spatial and temporal mode of being-in-the-world correlative to redemptive existence and the space-time continuum which attends the ecclesial community. Furthermore, the community's space-time is dependent on but not identical with the lived-space and lived-time which attends the individual's transition to redemption. We have argued previously that while ecclesial existence is a corporate, inter-subjective reality, it cannot be interpreted as a mere collectivity. For the community is comprised of individuals whose very singularity and freedom is enhanced in the transition from sin to redemption. Accordingly, we distinguish between the *individual's* lived-space and lived-time that attends that transition and the ecclesial *community's* space-time continuum. The concern of this inquiry is with the latter, but it seems apparent that the community's space-time structure finds interiorization in the individual, thus effecting a distinctive spatial and temporal being-in-the-world. The relationship between the individual's altered lived-space and time and the community's space and time is a reciprocal one. The community's determinate intersubjectivity, its "social self," mediates a new and self-shaping reality to the individual. The individual's experience of a deabsolutized lived-space and time contributes to the cointentionalities of the community. This occurs as a new way of having or meaning the world. In other words, the being-in-the-world of *individual* redemptive existence involves a new sense of world or cosmos. This new sense of world becomes determinate in the way the individuals "mean" each other in the faith-community,

17. I would not suggest that this Torah-transcending element is in no way present in the faith of Israel and Judaism. The motif of creation, the psalmist celebration and praise of it and of steadfast love, the elements of mercy all suggest it. But once the ethnic-national element underwent actual universalization, changing the nature of Torah itself, the stage was set for a new focus, making agapaic existence central in the community's experience and self-understanding. And that is the reality witnessed to by the Gospel.

thereby creating a distinctive way in which community is spatial and temporal. Thus the ecclesial way of being-in-the-world transforms the space and time of individual existence but at the same time is translated into an ecclesial intersubjectivity and symbolic universe. The following analysis begins with an account of the individual dimension and then moves to consider the very strange space and time of the ecclesial community.

The Effect of Redemption on the Space and Time of Individual Existence

The distinctiveness of the space and time of ecclesial being-in-the-world comes to light as the effect of redemption on the structure of evil or sin. In turn, this structure of evil or sin can be better clarified, at least in its way of having the world, by contrasting it to the presin creaturely relation to the world.[18] I have elaborated elsewhere what I can only summarize here, that human being in its self-transcending autonomy resists chaos as its ultimate, most comprehensive environment and strives for cosmos. Human being resists threats to its being, both in the form of that which would torment or end its organic life and that which would heteronomously dispose of its being. Conversely, it strives for whatever entity, environment, or state of affairs that could secure its being against such things.[19] At the same time human being is not simply universality, nor is its eros for cosmos a striving for translation into universality. The reason is that human being is an individual, embodied existence, the finite center of a world grasped through perspectival activities such as perception. Its past is not the universal past but something available in a memory which

18. This statement calls for several clarifications. First, the "pre" does not refer to a chronological period but an ontological priority, expounding the Adamic myth's notion that evil is not ontologically a priori to human being. Second, while some theologians (such as Karl Barth) would question such language as "pre-sin creaturely structure" or at least would insist we have no access to it, I offer the following. Human being has no actual experience of human structure outside the situation and network of evil. Nevertheless, its essentially human traits (will, feeling, rationality, embodiment, and so on) are not thereby annihilated but present themselves and their essential features for our comprehension. In other words, we can grasp certain things about time-consciousness, finite limitation, and linguisticality which are not simply characteristics or effects of sin.

19. This notion of an eros (striving) for cosmos is obviously part of a well-known family of theological motifs: absolute dependence (Scheiermacher), ultimate concern (Tillich), openness to being (Rahner).

gathers up the experiences and activities of an individual existence. It is this specific embodied being, I myself, which would overcome the challenges to its life, its embodied self. Its enjoyment of being does not occur in the anonymous space and time of anywhere, everywhere, anytime, everytime, but rather in the specificity of a place and time. This means—and this is the critical step—that its striving for cosmos is at the same time a striving for the sanction of this specificity of its being. Human beings not only occupy the world as an embodied center of that world, a center which is extended into the culturally centered world of family, groups, tribes, and nations. They desire the sanction of that center. The possibility that their embodied being, located in a specific place, with its specific language, terrain, and customs is something illegitimate, invalid, or guilty is unthinkable.

What happens to this eros or striving structure of the human being under the impact of evil? We cannot attempt anything like a full account of human sin, but we can briefly indicate how sin effects this presin, space-time structure.[20]

The situation of sin is the situation of physical, psychological, and ontological insecurity. The human being may strive for cosmos, but its actual situation is ambiguous, a mixture of cosmos and chaos. It may strive for life free from pain, disease, and oppression, for certainty about its own origin and destiny, for the cosmic validation of its most specific enterprises. But it lives in a situation where such things are given ambiguously at best. Refusing this ambiguity, human being "finds" the cosmos it is looking for by means of a strange, fabricated act of meaning in which something in or about the ambiguous world itself is assigned that role. It would be a mistake to see the setting or situation of sin, the ambiguity of the life-world, as the "cause" of sin. Augustine, Kierkegaard, and Berdyaev are right in concluding that sin is uncaused, born in meontic freedom—born, we might say, as a human response to its own insecurity. Nurtured in insecurity, sin's motivation is to secure, to anchor human being in a cosmos projected by itself, a creation of its own act of meaning or intentionality.

With sin comes a way of meaning the world and being-in-the-world.

---

20. A brief exposition of sin was attempted in Farley, *Ecclesial Man,* chap. 6, sec. B. A fuller description is found in the above-mentioned article, "Psychopathology and Human Evil." It should be evident that the view there presented, with some refinements, is in the line of Reinhold Niebuhr's anthropology and theology of sin.

The materials offered to sin, the field on which it plays is the specificity of space and time which the human being strives to validate as part of its presin creaturely situation. Specific times and places become candidates for another kind of act. Specificity refers here to the physical, cultural, and symbolic environs of the embodied self and therefore to provincial spaces and their times. This means family space, the space of the home, the tribal, urban, neighborhood, or national space. The correlative time of such spaces is that strand of time which is that particular family's background or the history of that particular nation. In the presin creaturely situation human being (or so we now speculate) simply wants its specific spaces-times to be validated in the cosmos before the eternal. But with sin, the reduction of the eternal to the worldly entity, the provincial space and time becomes not just *a* "here" with its past and future, but the one and only here. And the relation between that here and other heres is a relation between an absolutely valid here and the invalid theres (spaces and times) elsewhere. In the framework of sin *my* family, neighborhood, business, race, school, and nation are all able to remove the limitation, ambiguity, and peril of life itself. And yet sin creates a strange paradox of acceptance and rejection of specificities, the heres, of the surrounding world. The here, meaning the larger sphere of one's own family, nation, and so on, is accepted as absolute. Thus the contrast between it and the spheres of what is not one's own is between what is of final and unqualified value and what is not. Because what is not "my own" may offer a threat to my spheres or spaces, it is meant as a potential enemy.

How does sin affect the *temporal* dimension that accompanies the here, the provincial space of everyday life? Even as sin's way of having personal space is as the one and only space, *the* securing, chaos-removing space, so the time correlated with that provincial space is grasped as the one and only time—what for my nation has been, what it will be. Insofar as one's here is meant as *the* one and only here over against the enemy's there, the origin of that here is the one and only origin, and the tradition perpetuating that origin, the story of that provincial space, is that to which I am absolutely subject. The future of that space (and entity) is one's very destiny, the one and only future, so that everything increasingly becomes legitimated which protects the here, the entity in the provincial space, against threatening possibilities.[21] The future then must be guaranteed. Hence, sin involves an act of meaning that freezes and fixes both past and future.[22] The frozen past thus functions as an absolute norm. Yet the past as such is too multiple and too self-contradictory to function as a norm and, therefore, must be synthesized into a single, self-consistent entity from which present existence takes its cue. The future correlated with such a past is not a sphere of novelty or real possibility but a sphere of maintenance of the past, the past reproducing itself. The present thus is meant as simply the point between past and future where the maintenance occurs, it is not a moving, living present. When this constitution of past and future as servants of an absolutized provincial space obtains corporate expression, we have institutions and their symbol systems glorifying the past and a mere maintenance-oriented future, for instance, the institutions of totalitarianism.[23]

We are ready now to consider how redemption affects space and time altered by sin. Redemption effects a new human being, a new mode of being-in-the-world, because the presence of the eternal ends the refusal or denial of anxious and insecure existence and brings to an end the search for a mundane remover of chaos. This has two

21. A contradiction may be discerned at this point in the meaning of absolutized, provincial space. If the absolutizing act grants to that space the power to secure, to remove all threats, how could there be anxiety about the effect of the future in it? What is disclosed here is in fact the ambiguity and paradoxicality of the idol toward which one levels expectations of salvation, of the removal of anxiety, and at the same time *increased* anxieties to the degree that the idol's historical nature, finitude, and vulnerability are (secretly) sensed. Hence a double intentionality occurs toward the idol in which the idol is the final source of one's protection and also an object of one's protecting activities. It is this double act which structures and defines the absolutizing of finite and provincial space or entities within it.

22. We call attention to the difference between this description of how sin affects human temporality from existentialist views in which time-consciousness *of the individual*, that is, the individual's biographical past and future, is the primary focus. One version of this describes the individual's death-anxiety as the occasion of activities which would relieve that anxiety by freezing the self into the past and closing off future possibilities. According to the interpretation offered above, absolutizing typically bypasses the individual as a way of having the *world*. Some region of the world is the primary occasion of its self-securing activities, and what is frozen is not so much the individual's past as the past of the provincial space with which the individual's self and destiny are bound.

23. The interpretation of sin's effect on human temporality as producing a fixed past is well known in Bultmann as he made use of Heidegger's *Being and Time*. See Bultmann's *Essays Philosophical and Theological*, trans. J. C. G. Greis (London: SCM Press, 1955), p. 81. But the systematic relation between human being's altered temporality and altered spatiality is not so apparent in that literature.

decisive influences on human spatiality or, more specifically, on the human way of living in or having provincial spaces. First, one's own *here* or provincial space receives validation, not as an idol, a one and only here exclusive of all alien spaces, but as one among other heres all grounded in the creative power of the eternal. This removes or reduces the meaning of other or alien spaces as enemy spaces a priori. This validation confirms the primacy which is natural, to finite, living beings. Hence, the pleasures and loyalties evoked from one's specific natural and social environment are neither evil nor tragic. Yet in the presence of the eternal the human being means or intends the other in his or her alien primacy and alien provincial space as being also valid. One cannot assign the other's alien space the ontological primacy of one's own space, but its primacy *for the other* is acknowledged. Cosmos then becomes a totality term for a plurality of spaces with their times, all of which are essentially valid as expressions of the eternal's creative power.[24]

The second effect is simply an inevitable accompaniment of the first. Because redemption establishes a plurality of valid alien provincial spaces along with the valid primary space, it deabsolutizes one's own provincial spaces. This means that those spaces (with the institutions associated with them) are no longer meant as one's ultimate securers, as removers of chaos. It also means that one's former absolutized space is now grasped as one among others. Provincial space is one's own only as something adjacent to, tied in with, the alien provincial spaces outside one's experience. The nation is one's own but in an act which cointends other nations as valid.[25] Needless to say, the temporal dimensions of these provincial spaces undergo the same alteration under the impact of redemption. That is, the times correla-

24. I hope it is clear that *provincial space* is a more comprehensive term than simply geographical territories. Such spaces also refer to the many cultural spaces which attend human experience: the space of dwelling, the concert hall, the football stadium, the classroom. Further, the nature of such spaces is not solely due to their physical measurements but also to intentionalities and expectations brought to them. An architect may experience most of his or her provincial spaces in aesthetic and functional ways, and hence may experience the same location, a cathedral, for instance, in a different way from a worshiper.

25. Even when an alien space for good or bad reasons becomes an enemy in the sense of an economic or military threat to one's own primary provincial space, the result is not a return to an absolutizing of space. In other words, conflict between spaces does not necessarily arise out of an absolutizing of space even though the relation between conflict and the absolutizing of space is very close.

tive with primary and alien spaces are both validated and deabsolutized.[26]

The Ecclesial Community: Ecclesial Time for the Sake
of Everyday Space

We recall at this point that the goal of this particular inquiry is to
describe "ecclesial space and time." So far we have considered the
alteration of space and time under the impact of redemption on
individual existence. We anticipate that the individual's deabsolutized
way of being-in-the-world founds a corporate space-time which we
are calling "ecclesial space and time." And yet such a step at this point
is premature if not disastrous. For here we must make a rigorous
effort to let ecclesiality be manifest without determining the outcome
by presuppositions in our question. Must the inquiry presuppose that
there is an ecclesial corporate space and time? We recall that the
ecclesial community is a determinate community which, like all
communities, is characterized by a specific intersubjectivity, language,
and institutionality. That being the case, is the "ecclesial space" we are
about to depict simply the specific, provincial space of our actual,
historical community, a counterpart to the provincial spaces of a
nation, a school, or a factory? We can discern in this designation
something contradictory to the very nature of ecclesiality. For the
more the ecclesial community itself becomes a provincial space and
time, an *alternative* to the provincial spaces and times of the everyday
world, the more it loses its ecclesial character. Historically speaking,
ecclesiality came into being as a universalizing event which prevented
any specific cultural or ethnic heritage from being an a priori

26. We shall avoid, however, confusing this relativizing of space and time with the
cultural relativity characteristic of modernity. Relativity is now a pervasive social feature
of the contemporary, literate Western world partly because of the pluralism of value-
worlds fostered by mass media and partly because of modern historical social and
scientific consciousness. Yet something quite different is at work here. Modern cultural
relativity, not being the result of deabsolutized lived-space and time, is not a simulta-
neous acknowledgment of the validity of the other provincial space together with the
valued centrality and primacy of one's own space. The validity of the other culture,
created as it is simply by the fact of the other's presence, is a value-oriented validity;
hence all cultures including one's own are leveled. The result is the paradox characteristic of modernity of alienation from one's own culture and tradition, the incapacity to
participate in and affirm real social determinacy, and the easy absolutizing of one's own
society. Modernity tends to be a mode of life increasingly bereft of the past, of valued
tradition, and increasingly attracted to fanatical social movements.

condition of the redeeming presence of the eternal. We are ready now to state our thesis in three propositions.

1. There is a certain spatiality and temporality in the reciprocal cointentions of individuals in the ecclesial community and their linguistic expressions.

2. Insofar as the ecclesial community is a historical community that persists over generations, it will at any given period have *some* space-time character, but the only unity it has which could be called ecclesial has to do not with provincial space but with time, a way of having past and future.

3. There is no provincial space which could be called "ecclesial," but there is a corporate time which is ordered toward redemptive life in the "secular" provincial spaces of everyday life.

First, it is evident that space and time have some thematization in the ecclesial community. At this level one could use historical method to study the space-time symbolism of the religion of Israel. Much of this symbolism persists in the ecclesial community, for instance, the salvation history framework with its symbols of creation and eschaton and messiah. Insofar as we have permitted New Testament literature or New Testament theology to delimit the inquiry, we might be tempted to identify ecclesial space and time with the treatment of those motifs in that literature. Clearly what we have in that literature, the Scripture principle aside, is a community's self-interpretation, pluralized into many situations and authorships. We have, in other words, Mark's or Paul's *interpretation* of time. To what does that interpretation pertain or what does it bring to expression? At the surface level the expressions seem to be an account of the originating messianic event in the "objective" framework of apocalyptic or salva-tion history or both. In short, they seem to be *about* time writ large, about the saving events in the framework of world historical process as such. Beneath the surface, that which is being expressed is the new cointentionality characteristic of the ecclesial community and there-with the deabsolutizing and relativizing of provincial space and time. There is, in other words, linguistically expressed space and time in the formative literature of Christianity but a depth hermeneutics is required to get at it. And what it expresses is not the experience of a *provincial* space-time of the ecclesial community but the space and time which attend the new redemptive being-in-the-world.

Second, because the ecclesial existence is located in an actual historical community, it cannot avoid having features of provincial space and time. When human beings gather in a face-to-face community, a place of gathering is involved and its nature is relative to the kind and purpose of the gathering. If the group persists over generations, whatever marks the identity of the group must be transmitted from one generation to the next. No group can endure without some institutionality, that is, without some fixing of its identity in tradition and without transmitting vehicles of tradition. Because the ecclesial community is at some levels a face-to-face community which gathers for certain purposes and because it does persist over generations, it has a social space and time. In other words, various provincial spaces and times are inevitable to ecclesiality as a plurality of historical communities. Are these provincial spaces and times "ecclesial space and time"? Here we note the following: there is no single provincial space and time which marks the gathered, empirical community but a multiplicity of spaces and times. The variation is historical with many different types of religious communities arising, enduring for a while, and disappearing—early monasticism, enthusiasts, persecuted underground cells, Christian ghettos, Western denominations, Third World versions of the latter, and so on. And in the present period the variation continues in the form of major branches of Christendom with their subgroups. What determines the provincial space and time of these gathered communities is itself multiple. It includes the degree to which the group appropriates the provincial space and time of its time and culture, the degree to which the group is surviving in a crisis period, the economic level of the group, and so on. Thus there is a space and time characteristic of Eastern Orthodox Catholicism, medieval Christendom (in which the basilica plays not a small role in setting both the space of gathering and the means of duration), a mission outpost in the South Pacific, a revivalist sect. Our conclusion is that while provincial spaces and times do attend the gathered ecclesial community, they occur as the specific spaces and times of a specific religious and cultural situation. These specific provincial spaces and times may have their own validity and appropriateness, but they are not "ecclesial" space and time in the sense of something indispensable to the ecclesial mode of corporate existence. At best they are *church* spaces and times, or *religious* spaces and times.

Third, our general conclusion and the real thesis we want to argue is that *there is no provincial space which can be called ecclesial. On the other hand, the ecclesial community is marked by a time which rises from the cointentions of redeemed individual existence into corporate memory. Its function, however, is to disestablish any provincial ecclesial space as the absolute condition of redemptive being-in-the-world.*

Such is our thesis, a tight knot which needs unraveling. Let us begin with the fundamental reason that there is not and cannot be a provincial ecclesial space. The first two theses simply stated that a kind of space and time attended the being-in-the-world of redemptive existence and various kinds of provincial spaces and times attend the gathered ecclesial communities. To set forth the reason there can be no ecclesial provincial space is to also describe what ecclesial existence's relationship is to the provincial spaces of the everyday world, that is, family space, national space, and so on. To do this we must take a look at the time of the ecclesial community.

We have already treated the motif of time in the setting of the effect of sin on human temporality and its alteration by redemption. What is before us now is the temporality of the ecclesial community. Insofar as any community endures at all, it has a temporal dimension. We have resisted identifying the specific modes of duration that attend different periods and types of churches with ecclesial time. If there is an ecclesial time at all, it will be something which attends the way ecclesial existence is perpetuated under the influence of its normative event. If there is an ecclesial corporate memory, remembering with an ecclesial character, it should be a remembering in which the normative event and its central figure continues to effect that transition.[27] At this point we recall the content of that transition. It meant, first, a redemptive breaking of the power of evil and thus a certain new way of having the world, including living in provincial space; and, second, the occurrence of redemption in the framework of universality apart from any cultural-ethnic heritage as indispensable to the presence of the eternal. Already certain things are suggested about ways of having the past which contradict ecclesiality. If sin generates a relation to the past which freezes it into an absolute norm (because the past is meant as

---

27. Even as there is a distinction between *retention* (an element in time-consciousness as such) and *remembering* (a deliberate act) in individual consciousness, there likewise seems to be such a distinction in the social self. The essay on social duration (Appendix) makes this distinction by discussing the temporality of individuals and the social "remembering" of its origins by way of sedimentations.

239

the one and only past of an absolutized provincial space), then "remembering Jesus Christ" cannot mean the attempt to repeat his life, teachings, or ministry, to imitate them, to subject present situations and alternatives to content discerned historically as his situation and decisions. Such a remembering would only foster the "idolatry of the second person." Nor can the person, the nucleus of the originating event, be remembered simply for himself, as in hero worship, since that would ignore what makes him memorable, namely his central role in the transition of ecclesiality.

What then is ecclesial corporate remembering? Let us recall that redemption disestablishes absolutized provincial space and time and establishes one's validity, one's own and the other's *here*. This means that the orientation of the ecclesial community, the goal and telos of its proclamation, is not its own provincial space but the now-validated provincial spaces ("secular" spaces) of its participants. Ecclesial memory is for the sake of redemption, and redemption is not the forming of a "religious" space alongside or in competition with other spaces but a new way of being in the provincial spaces and times of the everyday world. Ecclesial remembering, the perpetuation of the originating event, cannot without self-destructive contradiction, create an ecclesial space. It is simply the occasion for the redemption of the human spaces and times of any and every human culture and period. This is the reason that great plurality of provincial spaces and times in the history of the church is a valid phenomenon and no one of them is ecclesial space.

In our account of the temporality which attends redemption at the existential-individual level, we observed that redemption affected both the past and the future. The deabsolutizing of provincial spaces and their contents inevitably alters the frozen past and its correlative future as an envisioned maintenance and protection of that past. So far, in our move to the level of ecclesiality, we have focused on one temporal dimension, the past, and argued that a corporate remembering of the normative event was a central feature of ecclesial time. The question is, does ecclesial time have any kind of distinctive futurity? We anticipate an affirmative answer both because of the general principle of the interrelation of past and future and because in individual redemption deabsolutizing the frozen past affects the individual's way of being toward the future. We would expect the ecclesial celebrative retention of the normative event to effect a distinctive corporate futurity. This is the case because the redemption of provincial spaces involves more than simply uncovering their idolatrous structures. In redemption those spaces discover their own valid and legitimate foundation and content, and this in turn indicates new worlds of possibilities for those spaces which absolutizing had closed off. In ecclesial existence redemptive possibilities attend the worst of times. The future then presides over the corporate community neither as a fated apocalypse of victorious evil nor a fated progress toward utopia. It is not a fated progress since the discerned possibilities are dialectically bound up with ever-new appearances of evil. It is not a fated victory of evil because of the experienced presence of the transcendent in the process of redemption. This strange futurity is not utterly unnoticed in the community's self-interpretations. In the literature of ecclesial origins, it obtained primary symbolism as the impending kingdom of God. And it obtained doctrinalization in salvation history theologies, which, because of their logic of divine victory and their royal metaphor of divine activity, collapsed the dialectic into a fated conclusion and even a fated salvific direction of time.

Ecclesiality then is a redemptive way of being-in-the-world not through a determinate religious space but in everyday lived-spaces and times.[28] Further, insofar as the presence of the eternal is at work in this alteration, the conditions of that presence can never be limited to any one historical or ethnic tradition. The telos of the whole apparatus of tradition and transmission is everyday space and time, not a bounded space of ecclesia. Thus the cointentions between individuals in the ecclesial community are not ecclesial insofar as they are simply mutual ways of meaning within a provincial religious space, the space of "fellow Christians." These cointentions have an ecclesial character only to the degree that they refer to each other's alterations in their provincial everyday spaces. To be more specific, the ecclesial human being "remembers Jesus Christ" not to be churchly but to be a member of a nation in a certain way. We repeat our thesis. For these reasons there is no ecclesial provincial space, but there is an ecclesial corporate time, namely, a memory structure which functions to deabsolutize and revalidate one's own provincial spaces and times.

28. This feature of ecclesial time as ordered toward the redemption of everyday space and life in the everyday world, including its very structures, would be a presupposition, though unthematized, of current theologies of liberation.

11

Ecclesial Duration:
Structure and Institution

The task of this and the preceding chapters is to describe the conditions through which ecclesiality continues through social time and is thus available to theological portraiture. Having cursorily discussed ecclesiality's strange "secular" space and its temporality ordered toward such, we move now to the more specific problem of its generation-bridging duration. Describing this duration requires more than simply listing features of elements of tradition. Ecclesial social existence displays its duration and process in the form of an apparent paradox. We can best express this paradox by recalling that all social duration is determinate: that is, it occurs in and through special historical and cultural vehicles, through a specific language, institutionality, ritual activities, social leadership, and so on. For example, the social duration of Judaism involves specific carriers of that social existence over time; the deposit of the divine Torah in sacred writings, the authoritative commentary on such writings, the commentators (rabbis), the synagogue. Ecclesial existence is a historical existence. Its sociality will likewise persist in specific bearers. Yet have we not said that a central feature of ecclesiality is its refusal to make any specific culture the a priori condition of salvation? Ecclesiality relativizes and appropriates any and all determinate, historical cultural networks. Therefore, we have a universal community whose modes and vehicles of duration must be nonuniversal. And this sets our task of discerning how ecclesial social existence can eschew identification with any specific provinciality and at the same time have specific cultural vehicles that carry it across the generations.

A second problem which makes the task difficult is the deep

rootedness of the way of authority. Most residents of contemporary Christendom have been shaped by branches of Christianity that regard the house of authority as a priori to "Christian faith," or, in our language here, to ecclesiality. Hence, most modern theologies, Catholic and Protestant, are mixtures of elements of the house of authority and elements of postauthority modernity: for instance, canon of Scripture and new hermeneutic. To avoid such a mixture, we remind ourselves of the interpretation of ecclesial duration assumed by the house of authority. The house of authority bypasses ecclesiality's strange combination of universality and determinacy and grasps the church as primarily a community of *revelation* which endures by means of *deposits* of revelation: holy Scripture, dogmas, the guardian institution. The original and definitive deposit is subjected to continuing commentary which transforms it into a systematized body of doctrine. Many of these developments are rendered more or less inevitable by the initial interpretative act of assigning primacy to revelation. In contrast, we see ecclesial existence as the redemptive presence of the transcendent which transforms any and all provincial spaces. The problem is to discern the duration which attends that kind of redemptive community.

Sociologism names a third way our investigation could quickly go astray. Sociologism tends to permit general sociological features of Christianity to determine the problem of duration. My own use of general phenomenology of social duration may resemble such an approach. However, the central character of ecclesial duration would surely be missed if we restricted ourselves to an analysis of the vehicles and features of duration. This approach implies that the preservation of the past is the fundamental problem and focus of ecclesial duration. The paradigm question becomes, How can ecclesiality maintain its identity and continuity by guarding the traditional past? Such an approach misses the very thing that makes it *ecclesial* duration. For ecclesial existence means the redemptive transformation of various provincial spaces. If there are events in which ecclesial existence originated, their unifying feature is their capacity to contribute to the transition to a new mode of redemptive existence. Remembering the events, therefore, will not be for the sake of the events themselves—an antiquarian interest in the past—but for the sake of redemption. In other words, the past functions in the ecclesial community as a way in which redemption occurs in the present. Ecclesial duration and the bridging of generations is at the same time the occurrence of redemption in ever-new situations, the deabsolutizing and validation of ever-new provincial spaces. This is why the grasp of ecclesial duration coincides with the theological theme of the presence of Christ. Thus the overriding question of the inquiry which is now underway is, How does redemption occur?[1]

THE DIPOLAR STRUCTURE OF ECCLESIAL PROCESS

We propose the following order of inquiry into ecclesial duration as the redemptive permeation of ever-new and strange spaces and situations. I shall first attempt a description of the general character of ecclesial duration as a redemptive process. I shall then set forth the vehicles (the sedimentations and activities) in which ecclesiality persists over time. Together, these studies should be at least a beginning picture of how and why ecclesiality is available for portraiture as well as a beginning of the portrait itself.

I have already argued that to understand ecclesial duration is to understand how redemption occurs. Therefore, we begin with that question. Since sin and redemption have an individual-existential dimension, an individual dimension of the question is not utterly meaningless. Yet ecclesiality itself is a social historical existence, and the way individual redemption occurs has to do with the individual's participation in that corporate reality. We shall thus bypass this individualistic dimension and look at redemption as a corporate occurrence. We have already looked briefly at the content of that occurrence. Socially speaking, redemption means the alteration of some provincial social space away from its self-absolutization and toward a new validation of itself and the world. Pressed further this involves both a desacralization as it understands its origin, nature, and destiny, and a resacralization as it understands its own relative being as nevertheless proper (justified, accepted, and valid). To be sure, this is a highly formal description and any more specific account would involve the work of portraiture itself, the bases and features of which are now under consideration.

What this brings us to is one pole of the structure of ecclesial process, that of *transformation*. In ecclesial process something endures, is continuous, and something is transformed so that the new is

---

1. Needless to say, I am only posing a limited aspect of this question, the role of tradition in redemption, and thus am setting aside most of the material issues: the divine activity, Christology, pneumatology, belief-ful response, and so on.

perpetually occurring. Of course, all process involves the new in some way, and our task is to grasp what this means in ecclesial process. The reason for the new should be transparent from the nature of ecclesiality as such. Transformation occurs and the new arrives precisely because ecclesiality is a *redemptive* existence. What it redeems is whatever specific form of historical existence is receptive to it. I have labeled this with the comprehensive term *provincial space.* I have argued previously that ecclesiality does not stand for a provincial space formed alongside ordinary cultural spaces as the haven of redeemed individuals. It does not form such a space just because ecclesiality *means* the redemptive transformation of corrupted social being. Since historical, social being is a vast multiplicity of ever-changing "spaces"—that is, social networks with some determinate, symbolic bounding—whatever transforms those spaces must itself adapt to and create the new. Ecclesial redemption thus has a truly historical character: "historical" in the sense that it occurs as the historical occurs, in the network of reciprocal interrelations and interactions.

Transformation, however, is only one pole of ecclesial process. If there were only this pole, nothing would differentiate how this transformation is redemptive. The process would simply coincide with the general character of all process. Ecclesial redemptive presence and duration, besides involving the new, also refers to a continuity which bridges time. Here we are referred not to the transforming (the adaptive, innovative), but to that through which the transforming occurs, the traditioned, the remembered.[2] One way to describe this pole of historical givenness, the tradition, is by recalling the analogy of a community with the human self. In this case, the analogical element is the "ideality" of that self as it retentionally accumulates its past. Yet there is in a human community something analogous to retentionality. For even as a human self accumulates its past by a selective activity governed by interest and value, so the past of a community persists into the present by a similar bounding and selecting. The question of how this occurs in the ecclesial community pushes us to consider the way in which the content of redemptive

2. The distinction is between tradition as a content and as a living process. The latter is sometimes termed *traditio viva,* and also *traditio activa.* Deneffe's language is *traditio constitutiva* and *traditio continuativa.* See Yves Congar, *Tradition and Traditions* (New York: Macmillan Company, 1967), pp. 189–221.

existence along with its paradigm and symbols achieves sedimentations, both institutional and linguistic. This we shall take up in the next section. What we would emphasize now is that the retention of the past in the ecclesial community is not simply a matter of maintenance. The house of authority, because it isolated the tradition pole from the transformational pole, understood continuity and tradition in just that way, as something to be preserved. When these poles are held together, the retention of the community is ordered toward redemptive transformation. The function of retained tradition is thus the deabsolutizing and validating of provincial space.[3]

How does this occur, the retention of tradition in order to transform? When a provincial space, for instance, the space attending one's own nation, is absolutized, it is constituted (meant, intended) in a double-level act which grasps it both as that nation and at the same time as something absolute. The participant in his or her very existence is that intentionality, that way of being-in-the-world toward the nation. One's "world" includes having the nation in that way. Redemption therefore must involve a new way of having it, meaning it, which frees one for a multiplicity of relations and activities in that provincial space. What happens when the tradition is retained by the community, the paradigm of redemption and its operative symbols? The nation is experienced through a paradigm, symbolism, and intentionality different from the language and institutionality of absolutization. This indicates that the community's relation to the retained tradition is not for its own sake. It does not bring forward the tradition in order to imitate it, conform to it, or believe in it. Faith in the sense of ecclesial existence is rather a faith through the tradition, a believing through it, a seeing through it, into the provincial space and into the situation in its problematic and possibility. This is one difference between ecclesiality and religions where tradition itself is the object of faith. The corporate retention (tradition) functions more as the lens through which contemporaneity is experienced, in which realities and dimensions hitherto not grasped come into view. The metaphor here is visual, but we use it to stand for experience as a whole. Tradition persists in the ecclesial community as something through which the ever-changing situations of the world are experienced.

3. The third dimension of theological reflection focuses on just this process, attempting to uncover in this or that region of contemporaneity dimensions of evil or possibilities of salvation.

Even though tradition is not ecclesiality's object of faith, neither is it a mere multiplicity of ever-changing and easily dispensable referents. It has some self-identity, procured by the normative event which generated ecclesial existence and by the renewal of ecclesiality in different historical periods. The self-identity of ecclesial existence is not so much a cluster of ideas as a genre of historical being, and it has obtained expression in a sedimented liguistic deposit. This we want to treat in the next chapter. The continuity of ecclesial existence is that self-identity as it transforms various provincial spaces and thereafter obtains *solidification* of the new, transformed space. Accordingly, theological portraiture does not paint a single, timeless genre of historical existence but rather an enduring, temporal corporate existence ever accumulating new solidifications of transformed provincial spaces.[4]

THE CELEBRATION OF THE NORMATIVE EVENT

In our preoccupation with the most general and formal features of ecclesial process, we have set aside what may be the most characteristic feature of all. Granting that the tradition is one pole of that process, persisting into the present as that through which contemporary provincial spaces are uncovered, interpreted, and transformed, in what kind of act is tradition remembered? To say that it is remembered in order to be utilized in the present would surely be misleading. We recall at this point our discussion of the normative nature of ecclesiality's originating events. Ecclesial existence is a historical entity brought into being through certain past events. The believer does not experience redemption (the new redeemed provincial space) by direct, individual contact with those events but by participation in the communities shaped by those events. The actual, present-day ecclesial community, therefore, does not have a neutral and merely historical relation to those events which effected the universal community or redemption. It remembers the originative events in a special focusing act of value, a remembering which has the character of honoring and celebrating. If the originating events are normative for the commu-

---

4. I distinguish, therefore, between the *sedimentations* of ecclesial existence in which the genre of this historical existence presents its contours in the form of a dominant paradigm, symbol, originating event, and *solidifications* of this perpetually changing community as it obtains ever-new historical forms, such as medieval Roman Catholicism, the American black church, and so forth.

nity in this sense, then they are remembered in the mode of celebration. The term *normative* as used here does not mean authoritative, the community's attempt to make all subsequent events and empirical religious communities repetitions or limitations of the original one. The general polar structure of ecclesial process and the lens function of tradition prevent this.

Retention is thus a celebrative retention, and this means that the tradition, the gathered past, is not retained simply in the sense of a comprehensive collection of details. It is not "church history." What the church celebrates, at least as it concerns the past, is the occurrence of the universal redemptive community. In the traditional language, it celebrates the coming of the Messiah. In the language of the Fourth Gospel and of Nicene Christianity it celebrates the enfleshment of the Word.[5] Tradition, of course, is more inclusive than the originating event which formed ecclesial existence. To celebrate this event is at the same time to celebrate the continued (and future possible) redemption of provincial spaces insofar as that has occurred. The main point is that the event (person) responsible for the new universal community is what gives tradition and the past the status of something to be celebrated.

We are now ready to press the question in more detail. What makes the (celebrated) past available? It is one thing to say that originative events occurred in the past whose retention could play an indispensable role in subsequent redemptive transformations. It is another thing to say that these events are in fact accessible to the present. What must happen to make them accessible? Two major things must occur for those events of the historical transition to ecclesial existence to survive the generations. First, they must obtain sufficient *linguistic sedimentation* so that they can be remembered, celebrated, and taught in the activities of the ongoing community. Second they must find *vehicles* in the form of institutions which function as frameworks of social persistence across the generations. The understanding of ecclesial duration is, therefore, not only a grasping of its formal bipolar structure and its celebrative retentionality but also of its sedimentations and vehicles. This chapter looks at the institutional vehicles while the next chapter takes up the question of sedimentation into language.

5. This is not meant to be a description of celebration and its contents. Such a description would have to deal with the future and hope as a dimension of celebration.

INSTITUTIONAL VEHICLES OF ECCLESIAL PROCESS

I proposed in the previous section that two items were necessary to render the celebrated past available in ecclesial process: a linguistic sedimentation of the new corporate existence into an enduring symbolism and story, and institutional vehicles. All social process involves institutions. In fact, the central function of institutionalization is to qualify a social entity to endure through time.[6] Ecclesial process is no exception. That process cannot, therefore, be reduced simply to a social process dominated by a linguistic, symbolic tradition and its literary deposits. Such a view makes ecclesial process into the history of Scripture interpretation (the Protestant version) or the history of authoritative tradition (the Catholic version).[7] The bases for the institutional aspect of ecclesial process reflect but are not reducible to the sociological elements of social duration. I reemphasize the theological nature of this account. *Ecclesial process* is an ambiguous term insofar as it can be taken in a strictly sociological sense to mean simply the persistence through time of a specific, historical religion or religious community. I am using it as an ideal-historical term for the ecclesial community's persistence through time as the occurrence of redemption. While the faith of Israel exemplifies one historical form of redemption, ecclesiality refers to a universalization of redemption which pervades, judges, and transforms ever-new secular spaces. The closest traditional symbol to ecclesial process is, accordingly, the kingdom of God.

Ecclesial process is a theological term, and there is a theological reason for its institutional aspect. I have argued elsewhere that the individual and community are redemptively transformed by the alteration of intersubjectivity, by participation in a new, distinctive, intersubjectivity or corporate consciousness.[8] If ecclesial process concerns "how redemption occurs," if it occurs intersubjectively, then redemption requires whatever is necessary to the social persistence of that (ecclesial) intersubjectivity. It would be misleading to say that

6. For the role of institutionalization in social duration, see Edward Farley, *Ecclesial Man* (Philadelphia: Fortress Press, 1975), pp. 98 ff., and also the Appendix, "Vehicles as Sedimentations."

7. Ebeling's essay, "Church History Is the History of the Exposition of Scripture," comes close to the biblicist identification of ecclesial process with linguistic sedimentation and its interpretation. See Gerhard Ebeling, *The Word of God and Tradition*, trans. S. H. Hooke (Philadelphia: Fortress Press, 1964), chap. 1.

8. Farley, *Ecclesial Man*, chaps. 7 and 8.

redemption occurs by direct participation in institutions, in the social network of organizations, leaders, and the like. Yet the distinctive social intersubjectivity of ecclesial existence requires much to endure. Hence, ecclesial process includes institutionality.

Not only is institutionality required for the social persistence of intersubjectivity, the matrix of redemption, it is also required by the linguistic sedimentation which informs that matrix and which connects every present with the normative event of universalization. Linguistic sedimentations (symbols, stories, myths, basic metaphors, doctrines) do not function simply by themselves. They do not endure as dead entities but in living interpretation. In other words, linguistic sedimentations themselves have a social matrix in which they survive and function, and that matrix includes the characteristic activities of the living community and the social structures necessary for these activities. Hence, in Judaism the sedimented tradition endures by means of an oral and written literature, a continued interpretation of that literature in the community, and social structures such as the rabbinate and the synagogue. And characteristic activities and social structures are entities of institutionality.

Institutionality is thus an aspect of ecclesial process. But it is one thing to acknowledge the necessity of *some* institutionality in a community's duration and another to discover whether *any* institutionality will do or whether there are features of institutionality which that type of social historical existence requires. Not only do linguistic sedimentations require institutions as their matrix of social persistence, they also require a correspondence between themselves and the *kind* of institutions present. That which establishes this correspondence in ecclesial existence is redemptive process.

An absolutistic account of this correspondence attends the ecclesiology of the house of authority. Church activities and structures, whether derived from Scripture or ancient church tradition, are grasped as divinely and for-all-time originated. According to the house of authority, there is one divinely established institutionality. Our problem is to discern the appropriate forms of institutionality that correspond to the nature and structure of ecclesial process without giving them absolute, nonhistorical status. I shall explore the matter through the somewhat arbitrary distinction between the characteristic, persisting *activities* of the ecclesial community and the *social structures* which those activities presuppose.

The Activities of Ecclesial Institutionality

Institutions are not simply structures or relatively stable relations between groups, strata, and so on, but living activities. Activities, in fact, are the most visible as well as the most essential aspect of institutions since they are the institution as it lives and functions. The real essence and purpose of an institution is more apparent in its activities than in its elements and structures. The living activities of a law court tell more about that institution than its presupposed structures. So when we turn to the institutional aspect of ecclesial process, we find ourselves looking first at a set of activities characteristic of a redemptive process. These activities share certain features. First, they are directed toward the actual ecclesial community (church) and away from the community to various environments near and distant. This feature simply reflects the structure of ecclesial process as the impending kingdom of God, a moving horizon between present, determinate life and future possibilities. Second, the activities, ideally considered, reflect the general structure of ecclesial process as a celebrative remembering. In brief, they reflect tradition, the sedimentation of both faith and the normative event. Therefore, the imagery and paradigm of ecclesial existence, its mythos of redemption, is present in all the activities. The direct referent of these activities is not the remembered tradition itself as an object of belief, since what occurs is a seeing of present realities and situations through the tradition.

Third, the most distinctive feature of these activities is their function as *universalizing* activities. The normative event itself is a universalizing historical transition. The universal element refers both to the negative fact that no specific human cultural entity (language, land, nation, sex, epoch) is an indispensable condition for the redemptive presence of God and to the positive fact that redemption applies potentially to *all* the environments or life-worlds in which human beings have their being. The activities of ecclesial institutionality carry forward tradition in order to open up ever-new environments of both individuals and communities. Since the universalization works from the imagery and paradigm of redemption, it is addressed to both corruption and redemptive possibilities and has, therefore, both iconoclastic and transformative elements.[9] Needless to say, insofar as

9. Specific historical expressions of the universalizing impetus of the concrete, religious community, the church, are established religion, the missionary movement,

any of the activities of ecclesial institutionality lacks any of these features, it loses its ecclesial character.

Three types of activities are constitutive of ecclesial process. The following are not so much specific activities as principles and general types of activities. These activities are proclamation, sacrament, and care, or *proclamatory* activities (preaching, teaching, writing), *sacramental* activities (communion, baptism, marriage, confirmation), and *caring* activities (political liberation, individual welfare).

Proclamation is distinguished as a type of activity because it is primarily a linguistic and interpretative undertaking. The proclamation principle is that redemptive transformation of ever-new spaces of environments occurs, in part at least, through interpretation of those spaces (life-worlds) with the imagery and paradigm of ecclesiality. And this is a peculiarly complex interpretative act, more complex than simply addressing and interpreting ancient texts. It is neither making present reality conform to past realities, as in the way of authority, nor making past realities and texts relevant to the present, as in modernism. The imagery and paradigm of ecclesial existence are rather hermeneutical instruments which help open up both the corruptions and redemptive possibilities of present environments. Proclamation, then, has the double orientation of interpreting the received tradition as it carries ecclesial existence and interpreting present reality by means of that. Because ecclesial existence is partly a *historical* existence with a nucleus figure at the center of the transition to that existence, proclamation is the proclamation of Jesus as the Christ. Because of the *ideal* and eschatological character of ecclesial existence, having to do with redemptive possibilities in the present, proclamation sets forth the impending kingdom of God. Like theological protraiture, proclamation is both a historical and an ideal enterprise. Ecclesial process occurs through a perpetual, living activity of prophetic interpretation which looks through received paradigms of salvation at the ever-new spaces in which human beings find themselves both collectively and individually. And, to repeat, proclamation embraces a number of specific activities: editorial, theological, homiletical, pedagogical.

Sacramental activity is distinguished as a type of activity because it is primarily a bodily symbolic act of incorporation. The sacramental

---

and revivalism. Each expression universalizes in its own way, showing a refusal to conceive redemption in utterly parochial terms. At the same time, all three examples are corruptions of universalizing insofar as they all universalize not simply redemption but the cultural and provincial bearers of redemption.

principle is that salvific transformation occurs through a bodily and visible incorporation both into a distinctive corporate intersubjectivity and into new secular environments. The proclamation principle is the principle that insights and perceptions attend redemption. The sacramental principle expresses a dramatic activity, a bodily acting out which synthesizes the remembered tradition and the present. Instead of attempting a full theology of sacramental activity, I shall simply indicate what appear to be that activity's major elements and the end toward which they are ordered. All sacramental activities have, it appears, the three elements of body, community, and divine presence. The function of these elements is clear, however, only in the light of the essential purpose of the activity, which is to incorporate the participants into what is essentially a social space. Reflecting the bipolar structure of ecclesial process, the participants are incorporated both into the determinate ecclesial community as a distinctive historical existence and intersubjectivity and into transcommunity secular spaces. There are, accordingly, two fundamental types of sacramental activities: those that incorporate into the ecclesial community (baptism, communion) and those that incorporate into some worldly region (marriage, blessings and prayers of various sorts, dedications, and so on).[10]

As to the former, sacramental activities of the community, the key to their function is that salvific transformation begins through participation in the distinctive intersubjectivity of the ecclesial community. While proclamation brings the imagery and paradigm, the linguistic aspect of that intersubjectivity, to consciousness, that which it evokes is primarily insight. In sacramental activity the community's intersubjective intentions are given visible, bodily expression. For example, in communion the structure of loyalty and commitment, the intentions of the community members toward each other, the transcendent, and the world are all acted out. These intentions vary, of course, from one type of sacramental activity to another.

As to the transcommunity sacramental activities, the key to their function is the salvific transformation of lived-space or environment.

10. Note that what is under discussion are sacramental activities, not sacraments in the sense of a finite number of divinely established and commanded acts. A full theology of sacramental activity may want to distinguish between the many sacramental activities possible and actual and certain specified "official" sacraments. This distinction would be acceptable here only if the specified sacraments were not simply defined by the method of authority.

Proclamation's interpretative acts offer insightfulness into the corruptions and possibilities of that space. In sacramental activity the community exercises a visible, corporate validation of that space as a possible space in which redemption can occur. Accordingly, when the community applies sacramental action to marriage, it is not only granting corporate validation to one of the ways human beings live in the world but is actively incorporating the participants into the marital environment, relation, and newly constituted interpersonal space.

It should be clearer now why sacramental incorporation has the above-mentioned elements. Because it is an act of incorporation into and by the community, the symbolic act requires visibility; hence it has a bodily element. Because incorporation presupposes the possibilities of redemption in the space or environment involved, and because divine presence is at work in the effecting of redemption, sacramental activity refers to (without "causing") divine presence. Because redemption is a matter of restructuring the self (consciousness, being, person) through participation in a distinctive intersubjectivity, it is effected by acts which make visible the reciprocal intentions of the community. Thus the bodily, symbolic act of baptism is a focal point between the intentions of the individual and those of the community. This act is one way in which the community's intentions are expressed toward the individual. Therefore, through response to that expression, the individual is drawn into the community's intersubjectivity. This participative luring goes beyond simply the receptive interpretation and insight evoked by proclamation.[11]

If proclamation is primarily an interpretative activity and sacrament primarily an incorporative one, *care* is primarily a change-oriented activity. The care principle is that salvific transformation involves the actual effecting of human well-being and an alteration of the conditions which assault that well-being. It is the creation myth, the validation of creaturely being as such under the transcendent, which removes all bounds of care. In principle, care is as wide in scope as creation itself. Hence, the care which attends ecclesial institutionality is not of *human* creation alone, or of some human beings and not others, or of some aspects (the spiritual) and not others (the bodily,

---

11. Some sacramental activities have *repetition* as an essential characteristic and some do not. To grasp why this is the case would require an exploration of the purpose of the specific activity in question. In other words, incorporation lends itself to both once-for-all and repetitive-ritual activities.

the social). Thus we find in the historical and empirical religious community very widespread enterprises of care which include medicine, education, mental health, prison reform, and social liberation. On the other hand, it would be misleading to see the caring activity of ecclesial institutionality as simply ordered toward creaturely well-being without a guiding paradigm. Although ecclesial caring is ordered toward the needs, suffering, and oppressions of human beings, its paradigm of redemption offers a specific account of the human problematic, human evil, the human need for redemption. And although vulnerability and suffering are inevitable to human organic and historical life, they are experienced in a historical setting and network pervaded by human evil. Therefore, behind much of human suffering, the suffering which is not simply the exploitation of a finitely vulnerable, organic, and self-transcending being, is injustice and oppression. Because of its paradigm of evil and redemption, the care of ecclesial institutionality is not identical with the distribution of care by government and social agencies. Ecclesial caring is informed by an attempted penetration of suffering as symptom to the matrices and causes of suffering in injustice and oppression. Those who are now arguing that oppressions of various sorts are not simply a single item in a series of human problems but *the one* background of human problems, including overpopulation, war, ecological crisis, and individual mental health are persuasive. If this is the case, the care of ecclesial institutionality, dispersed as it is and ought to be, has the primary characteristic of liberation. For ecclesial care works from a paradigm of redemption which identifies the human problem as a social and individual idolatrous bondage which pervades the very structure of human history and historicity.

Even as there are many specific sacramental and proclamatory activities, so there are many activities of care. These activities tend to fall under two models, the one personal, the other political. The personal model of care has dominated the pietistic tradition, and it continues in various forms of "psychological" care in the pastoral psychology movement. When secularized in thoroughgoing fashion, it becomes therapeutic care. The political model has been present in most of the history of the Catholic church as well as in contemporary movements of social gospel and liberation theology. The extent to which the ecclesial community exercises care toward possible regions of need varies with the historical situation. In modern times governments, corporations, and unions have appropriated many areas of care, minus, of course, the ecclesial paradigm of redemption. Such variations aside, the impetus toward care is an immanent feature of ecclesial existence and a constitutive way in which ecclesial process is institutionalized into an activity.

Proclamation, sacraments, and care are the types of activities through which ecclesial existence occurs historically through time. They mark the distinctive way ecclesial existence endures, at least as a set of activities or undertakings. As such, they are fundamental to ecclesial existence. I repeat that they are *types* of activities, not specific activities. The way of authority not only has identified certain specific activities with "Christianity"—finite numbers of divinely established sacraments, for instance—but has regarded these activities as established once and for all in the Scriptures (the biblicist version) or by the church (the Catholic version). Thus the accomplishments of a specific historical situation are regarded as immutable and absolute. An alternative approach affirms certain types of activities as characteristic of ecclesial process and yet acknowledges their relativity to historical situations. Furthermore, these types of activities have different expressions and different emphases in different epochs of the actual, historical community and in different branches of Christendom. Criteria for these emphases and expressions arise out of the threefold structure and the interrelation of the activities. And this poses for us the question of how the three types of activities are related to each other.

These activities are related to each other by common matrix, by supplementation, and by mutual pervasion. Their *common matrix* is ecclesial process itself. This means that all three reflect the double orientation toward tradition and futurity, determinate community and worldly environments. And it especially means that each one is in its own way an instrument of universalization without which the activity loses its ecclesial character entirely. They *supplement* each other because each one has its special contribution to make to the others in ecclesial process. Since proclamation presides over remembered, celebrated tradition and its paradigm of redemption, it offers both focused interpretation needed to prevent care from being simply dispersed philanthropy and insights into the world spaces presupposed by care. Without care itself the other two activities take on both a quietistic and a legitimating character. That is, proclamation and sacramental activities become religiousness in the Marxist sense of parasitic living off of the structure of oppression. Sacramental activities supplement the other two by mediating them, occurring as they do both in the concrete community and in provincial space in the mode of bodily visibility. They render the insights of proclamation corporately visible. Care in its uniquely ecclesial sense, informed by the redemptive paradigm, is that toward which the other two are ordered, the goal and telos of the activities. The three *pervade* each other because each one has qualities of the other two. There is something both sacramental and caring about the specific activities of proclamation; something proclamatory and sacramental about the ecclesial way of caring; something caring and proclamatory about all sacramental activities.

The Structures of Ecclesial Institutionality

A summary may be the best way into our discussion of the structural aspect of institutionality. The ecclesial community as ecclesial lives on an ever-moving horizon of spaces or environments in the primary mode of care. This care, while pertaining in principle to all human needs and sufferings, occurs under a particular paradigm of redemption made insightfully present in proclamation and bodily present in sacraments. It should be evident at this point that the ecclesial community is not simply a set of activities. Even though characteristic activities do express a community's institutionality and therefore evoke one way of describing its social duration, they themselves require locations in the community, enduring environments which hold them in being and prompt their continuance. The activity of firefighting is characteristic of a fire department, but that activity itself requires certain continuous entities such as fire fighters, role differentiations within the group (chief, driver), equipment, funding, support from community institutions. These items which give location and stabilization to the institution's activities, enabling them to be repeated, are what I am designating as the structural aspect of institutionality. Even though activities presuppose institutional structures as their matrix and location, they nevertheless are more primary than structures as bearers of an institution's distinctiveness. This is because an institution is a functional entity and its distinctive functions occur in its characteristic activities.

What follows is clearly not a full theology or even an adequate phenomenology of ecclesial institutional structures. There is simply an indication of some of the structural aspects required by the activities. Hence, the description omits many of the structural aspects of interest to the sociologist, structures pertinent to institutional maintenance such as bureaucracy, capital, family, and the like. Again, the route of inquiry is from ecclesia's distinctive activities to their accompanying structural environment.

The inquiry into ecclesial institutional structures does face one distinctive and formidable problem. The problem is created by the bipolar structure of ecclesial process. This means that the ecclesial community must be able to function in a radical iconoclasm toward every environment, space, and historical entity to which it relates. It also means that, prompted by its universalizing impetus, it must be able to pervade and redemptively modify any human, historical environment.[12] If that is the case, can there be any structures of ecclesial institutionality at all? For to function in this iconoclastic, transformative way, the ecclesial community must appropriate a great variety of institutionalizations, as in fact, the history of the actual community shows. But it can have no institutions that are necessary to its being. The problem is, how can there be social structures which function both to locate the activities and bear the tradition and yet retain the built-in relativity necessary to ecclesial process? Is ecclesial institutionality simply a pan-institutionality? The approach of the house of authority to this problem is clear. There are, it maintains, definitive, for-all-time institutions. These are established by the authorities (Scripture, tradition, church). Thus the way is cleared to claim that specific institutions (the papacy, congregational polity, revivals), are a priori to Christian faith as such. Outside the house of authority, such claims lose their cogency, and the inquiry must be made on other grounds. In this case, the other grounds are simply whether or not the activities of ecclesial institutionality require characteristic social structures.

The Paradoxical Character of Ecclesial Structures

The most general feature of the structural aspect of ecclesial institutionality is paradoxicality.[13] We shall not explore what appears

---

12. This would not mean "Christianize." It would not necessarily involve the alteration of a secular space into a religious space, or even the alteration of another religious space, such as Judaism, to Christian religious space.

13. This term had widespread usage in the European and American neo-Reformation theologies of the 1930s through 1950s. See H. Schröer, *Die Denkform der*

to be the ultimate ground of the paradoxical character of ecclesial existence in the relation of transcendence to creaturely being and the expression of this in the impingement of the kingdom of God. The penultimate basis of the paradoxicality of ecclesial institutions is ecclesial existence itself as something which occurs in a determinate historical mode with determinate tradition, imagery, and paradigm for the sake of every cultural time and provincial space. It is for this reason that ecclesial institutional *structures* occur in paradoxical form. In this sense the problem of discerning or discovering structural aspects behind the institutional activities is not so much solved as illuminated in paradox. I offer three examples of paradox as a feature of ecclesial structures.

The first is the paradoxicality which attends the way in which the ecclesial community as a cultural determinacy is related to its contemporary period and environment. The elements of the paradox are the *separateness* and *entangledness* of the community with the environing world. On the one hand, the ecclesial community cannot become a differentiated subculture in its time and place in the sense of a distinct ethnic, racial, or cultural grouping with an "ecclesial" language, government, and economy. The empirical community may, of course, develop in this way in certain periods, but insofar as it does, it loses its ecclesial character. Ecclesial existence (and the kingdom of God) names a way in which the spaces of any culture become open to a redemptively transforming power. Even if the paradigm of that redemption is borne by a socially visible community, the community's visibility cannot be procured by cultural differentiations of language, custom, and the like. The ecclesial community in its determinacy is a distinctive intersubjectivity and shared interpretative paradigm. At the same time it shares with the specific culture the historical time, situation, economy, political structure, and language. Yet the ecclesial community requires distance, separateness, independence from the dominant culture in order to exercise a proclamatory function. It

---

Paradoxalität als theologisches Problem (Göttingen: Vandenhoeck and Ruprecht, 1960), for a study of paradox as a theme in Kierkegaard and major contemporary theologians. Another term that could serve almost as well is dialectic. Well known in philosophical (Plato, Hegel) and social-critical (Marx) analyses, dialectic has a distinctive meaning as an expression of ecclesial existence. Since the term is more fittingly used of a *process* (of being, thought, history), it would be useful if what was under consideration was ecclesial process. Because structure is our concern here, it seems more accurate to speak of paradoxical elements in a structure than the "dialectic" of a structure.

cannot be utterly identified with king, parliament, congress, party, or corporation and at the same time exercise its iconoclastic and universalizing function.[14]

A second example of paradoxicality describes the relation between those who are foci of proclamation and the empirical religious community. The proclaimer, be he or she prophet, minister, editor, writer, book publisher, or priest, requires both a *dependence* and *independence* in relation to the empirical community. The dependence is required because proclamation is not an activity external to the community but intrinsic to it and to its process and institutionality. The proclamatory voice is the community's voice. The proclaimer's very access to the criteria of proclamation is by way of the imagery and paradigm present in the community's memory. At the same time proclamation subjects the empirical community itself to iconoclasm and transformative possibilities. And this requires sufficient independence to survive the community's resistance to the proclaimer. The proclaimer thus has a paradoxically dependent-independent relation to the empirical community.

The third paradox describes the way in which ecclesial existence obtains expression as a visible society, an empirical religious community. It goes without saying that any empirical religious community has at least some degree of unity. The house of authority manifests a number of different ways in which that unity is understood: doctrinal, hierarchical, experiential, enthusiastic. The paradox here is between the ecclesial community as a *unified* and as a *pluralistic* community. The traditioning of the community, its function as bearer of celebrative memory, requires whatever unity that traditioning requires. At the same time the situationality of ecclesial existence, its existence on an ever-moving horizon of new times and spaces, means that proclamatory, sacramental, and caring activities are correlative and adaptive. Furthermore, ecclesiality's possible pervasion of any space and time means that the empirical religious community is actually composed of a great number of communities in the sense of different cultures and subcultures. This paradox of unity and plurality inevitably attends the

---

14. It was thus appropriate that the Holy See was a determinate power yet distinguished from the Roman Empire. The more it became structurally bound up with the empire, the more its voice was the empire's voice, the more this paradox was diminished. The doctrine of the Two Swords was one historical expression of an aspect of this paradox.

way in which ecclesial existence attends an actual religious community.

The history of the empirical, religious community (churches, branches of Christendom) is the history of the emergence of many different institutions: monastic, papal, revivalistic, cultic, legal, and educational. Many of these have actually been "successful" institutions of the churches' survival. However, this history is not a history of ecclesial existence in the ideal-historical sense. That is to say, the paradoxicality of institutional structures is frequently compromised on one or the other side of the paradox. So culturally entwined are contemporary churches in civil religion and therapeutic culture that it is difficult to imagine them engaging in caring activity based on a radical cultural iconoclasm. So separate were some utopian communities (Shakers, Amish) that a pervasion of spaces beyond their own parochial social space is almost unimaginable. Yet insofar as the empirical community has not become simply a subculture but has retained its universal culture horizon and insofar as it has tolerated iconoclastic proclamation within its boundaries, it has retained something of ecclesial paradoxicality.

Selected Structures

The term *ecclesial institutionality* suggests something more specific, more concrete, than the ideal-historical term *ecclesial existence*. It describes some empirical-historical manifestation of ecclesial existence in a determinate community, a visible society. The way to dealing with this term is through the general structure of ecclesial process and the activities which attend that process. That being the case, we look for structural or enduring features that these activities require in the society in which they occur.

The most important requirement of these activities, that without which they cannot exist at all, is a community of a distinctive type. It must be able to exist in any time and space, in any culture or historical period, and in this it is like the synagogue. But its mode of existence cannot be that of a cultural subgroup within a larger cultural space. This is because what unifies and distinguishes the community is nothing cultural at all but a universalized and universalizable paradigm of redemption. The community must then be determinate enough to have a social memory, a tradition in which the paradigm survives. But its cultural actuality—its language, aesthetics, organizations, and participants—is nothing else than the people of the provincial time, space, and culture of the day.

Presupposing this distinctive sort of community, I would offer the following three features which appear to be necessary to the purpose of that community and to the activities through which it endures through time. The first feature is that of a *distinctive leadership*. All religious communities have, it seems, leaderships appropriate to the community and its faith-world: shamans, priests, gurus, monks, rabbis, saints. Do the activities of ecclesial process call for a distinctive leadership? It seems so. The reason comes forth when we remember that one element in the redemptive transformation of lived-space is "seeing through" the received imagery and paradigm to the situation. And this does not occur by the mere persistence of the past through dead or uninterpreted tradition. It happens in the event of living interpretation which both portrays and revivifies the paradigm of salvation and thereby interprets the present. Furthermore, the paradigm of salvation is less a set of facts to be enumerated and applied as a mystery to be penetrated, wondered at, and lived. Living interpretation and the activity of proclamation calls for masters of the tradition whose interpretative work occurs at the juncture of past and present. The paradigm in question is complex enough, profound enough, and mysterious enough to perpetually elude exhaustive articulation. Insofar as ecclesial process involves this insightful interpretation, an element in that process is a leadership of this sort.[15]

The same holds for the sacramental and caring activities. Activities of this kind are not accomplished by a community without distribution of roles and expertise. Furthermore, insofar as the leadership functions in the universalization of ecclesial existence, it is giving contemporary reality to the normative event in which universalization began to occur. If "apostle" refers to a proclaimer and participant of that event, it is plausible to say that the leadership of the ecclesial community should be "apostolic." That is, it should be subject to the normative event of universalizing and should function in the continued universalization of ecclesial process. By making apostolicity a matter of succession, ordination, and office, the house of authority did

15. The first of the theological encyclopedic works to make the church's leadership in the guidance of the church the very telos of theological study was Friedrich Schleiermacher's *Brief Outline of the Study of Theology*, trans. T. Tice (Atlanta: John Knox Press, 1977). See sec. 5 through 25.

achieve a certain stability of leadership but at the same time risked the reduction of apostolic leadership to ritualistic and bureaucratic functionaries of institutional process, thus obscuring the parallel between the ancient and continuing leadership of the community.

A second feature of the religious community is that which grounds it as a real, human community, namely, face-to-face relationships. The activities of ecclesial institutionality presuppose a face-to-face community not simply for the self-evident reason that caring and sacramental activities require such relationships but because all the activities presuppose the determinate ecclesial intersubjective structure of intentionality. This means human beings in community "mean" (intend) each other through the elements of the corporate paradigm, with the result that each self is intersubjectively shaped by distinctive reciprocal intentions.[16] This intersubjectivity becomes actual and concretely historical in a face-to-face community. And all three types of activities of the community (proclamatory, sacramental, and caring) presuppose that intersubjectivity. The community's very impetus to universalize redemption through those activities is prompted by the faith-world of that intersubjectivity. If there is no such face-to-face community incarnating a distinctive intersubjectivity, what we have is simply the plurality of provincial communities in human culture subject to the competing paradigms of reality under which life occurs. Instead, ecclesial existence transists through units of parochial or face-to-face communities existing before the horizon of the impending kingdom of God, and transcending the parochialism of their culture's space toward the larger spaces and communities of the world.

We are verging already on the third feature of ecclesial structure. If the face-to-face communities (congregations) in an ideal-historical sense transcend themselves toward universality, toward all human spaces and cultures in their corruptions, oppressions, and redemptive possibilities, and if these communities transcend *from* a determinate salvific paradigm, then some kind of unity is present in both their foundation and their entelechaic goal. The catholic or universal element resident in the determinate paradigm and intersubjectivity participates and merges with the universal concern of care and proclamation.

Sensing this unity is one thing; formulating it is quite another. It is

16. See Farley, *Ecclesial Man*, pp. 93 ff., 114 ff., and chap. 7.

easy to say in a negative vein that the unity is not simply a cultural unity, that at the point of cultural content (languages, styles, customs, aesthetics, hymnodies, pieties) pluralism is natural to the ecclesial community. It is also easy to say that unity in some sense accrues to any corporate historical type of existence, in this case, ecclesial existence. And it is the unity of a type of ideal-historical existence which theological portraiture attempts to discern and set forth. More difficult is the question of unity at the level of institutional structure. Does the structure of the ecclesial institution manifest a unity? The terms of the question itself presuppose a positive answer. If there *are* such structures, some unity is present. The specific problem is how such unity can endure given the proper and valid plurality of the empirical religious community. The best description can do is to formulate the nature of the unity without specifying the vehicles which may produce it, for there is no specific social structure which can in advance and by its function guarantee the unity of the empirical community without distortion. This in fact is the very essence of the approach to institutional unity in the house of authority. The institutional unity is identified with organizational structures, entities, and processes.

Instead of proposing vehicles of unity, I would prefer to say that the ecclesial community is less than itself when it is simply a plurality of dispersed and autonomous communities, each attempting to be subject to the normative event. I have stressed that the salvation paradigm not only creates reciprocal intentions between individuals in a face-to-face community but intentions toward the stranger and toward ever-new cultural spaces. However, it would be a misreading of the matter to restrict the corporate intentionalities of the community to intercongregational intentionalities or congregation-to-stranger intentionalities. For on the horizon of the intersubjectivity of a face-to-face congregation is ecclesial existence as a total, corporate, historical reality. This reality is the larger matrix of the sedimented tradition of ecclesia in the form of faith, kerygma, and interpretation. These deposits and expressions of the paradigm of salvation do not refer the individual or congregation simply to other individuals or some other congregation but to the community's corporate past, present, and future.[17] And because one aspect of the paradigm of

17. I am suggesting that there is in the structure of the social world of the ecclesial community a determinate version of what Alfred Schutz calls consociates, contempo-

redemption describes a dialectic of continuing corruptibility in the empirical religious community, and because ecclesial contemporaries are intended in their own way as existing from the normative event, it is appropriate for individuals and congregations to constantly test themselves in the face of the larger community. There are specific versions of this "subjection" of the congregation to the larger corporate reality in the house of authority. My only point here is that the larger reality is intentionally present to congregations and individuals and that the total absence of institutional relations between congregations distorts the unity proper to the ecclesial community. Formulations of unity more specific than this concern the community's situatedness in the times and places of history and culture.

---

raries, predecessors, and successors. The community in direct, face-to-face relationships is composed of consociates (*Mitmenschen*). Present intentionally in the living ecclesial community are also contemporaries (*Nebenmenschen*), living persons of the same ideal-historical type. See Schutz, *The Phenomenology of the Social World* (Evanston: Northwestern University Press, 1967), pp. 143–44.

12

Ecclesial Duration:
Tradition and Sedimentation

The description of ecclesial duration continues to be our task. To use Gadamer's language, we are describing ecclesiality's distinctive traditioning.[1] So far, we have set forth only the general structure of this generation-bridging process and its institutional carriers. Prominent in this account is the normative event in which ecclesiality originated and which continues to be celebrated and proclaimed. Yet that event persists beyond itself clothed in a language which itself was gathered into the literature that gave initial accounts of the event, the literature of Jesus of Nazareth. And this literature is closely bound up with the religious heritage which the event presupposes and draws into itself, the writings of Israel. Furthermore, the postorigins history of the ecclesial community also has a literature in which are sedimented prominent moments of the community's interpretations. Because these literatures have to do with the normative event, reflecting its sedimentation for the purpose of survival and duration, they continue to function in continuing ecclesial process. Thus the description of that process must investigate the function of the literatures of Israel, of kerygma, and the doctrinal tradition. And if theological portraiture includes the discernment of ecclesial process, then these literatures function in some way in that portraiture. It is just these functions that we must now explore.

THE VEHICLES OF ECCLESIAL PROCESS: THE KERYGMA

If the normative event is to *persist* in the community as normative, presiding over the community's self-identity and its salvific pervasion

1. Hans-Georg Gadamer, *Truth and Method* (New York: Seabury Press, 1975).

267

of cultural space and time, three requirements must be met. (1) The event must find linguistic expression. It must be linguistically incarnated. (2) That language must be further clothed or located in a vehicle that will enable it to persist from generation to generation. (3) That language and vehicle must obtain or be granted some sort of normative character. These three requirements set for us our task of understanding the function of the literature of ecclesial origins in ecclesial duration.

The Oral and Written Kerygma: Linguistic Embodiment and Literary Deposit

If we begin our account of the sedimentation into language of the events which originated ecclesial existence with a look at the language the community has always used to interpret those events, we discover immediately that it is christological language. The clue to the significance of these events is a historical figure, Jesus of Nazareth. The life and ministry of Jesus of Nazareth is not, to be sure, so comprehensive as to embrace all the events that mark the historic transition to ecclesiality. Nevertheless, this historical figure is the decisive nucleus of that transition. What he initiated and what happened to him was the catalytic agent of the event. The only historical picture of this origin of ecclesiality available so depicts it. For this reason, there is in the events themselves a paradigm in the form of a historical figure. Thus it is not the case that the first step of the event's discovery of a language was the direct creation of images, symbols, or paradigms. Of course, the event always had a linguistic element even if that linguistic element was initially the inherited language of Israel, Judaism, and Hellenistic culture. But that which propels the impulse toward a new imagery is the historical figure and the occurrences which mark his story. He himself was the paradigm about whom a circle of followers gathered and whose story they continued to tell after his death. In other words, the events of origin arising as they did from the life and ministry of this figure, already had a kind of unity and paradigm coincident with the figure.

When we say that the figure was himself a paradigm of some sort for his immediate followers, we are not talking about something utterly without language. Of course, a language was present, the language of the inherited faith of Israel, of the varieties of Judaism and other religious movements. This language was employed and, it appears, transformed by the paradigmatic figure himself. And yet this exacerbates rather than reduces the problem. If Jesus of Nazareth was paradigmatic to the events comprising his ministry and flowing from it, if something new (ecclesiality) was beginning to make its appearance in that ministry, it could not be contained in the given language of the tradition. "You have heard it said to the men of old . . . but I say to you." So the new was launched by Jesus himself, and with it the need for a linguistic embodiment. The initial problem of this search was finding a language in which to remember, celebrate, and testify to the paradigmatic figure himself. We are familiar with the result, the early appropriation of the language of Jewish messianism (Messiah) and the language of Jewish apocalyptic (kingdom of God, resurrection) as the language for that figure. The titles applied to Jesus with their respective interpretations which rise from different regions and periods of early Christianity are part of the story of this search.[2] With such languages come frameworks in which Jesus is interpreted and his role in the new age is explored. The outcome of this whole stage is that the paradigmatic figure, Jesus of Nazareth, obtains linguistic expression beyond simply the language of the tradition. Even when traditional language and language frameworks are employed, they take on new meanings insofar as ecclesial existence is beginning to appear in the new intersubjectivity of the universal community of redemption.

We have said that the figure himself was a paradigm for his early followers and that they sought a language in which to entitle that living paradigm. But that is only part of the story. The primary character of the presence of that figure, the character of the experience of the followers, was redemptive. But this does not mean simply that persons experience salvation by means of an individual relationship to him. The experience was one of being in a new age inaugurated somehow through his activity. Redemption was available in a different mode. Jesus and his immediate followers formulate this, so it seems, without making Jesus himself the decisive occasion of this new reality, and see the new availability of redemption as a relativization and criticism of the religious piety and cultus of the day. It was Paul and the Gentile mission in which the logic of the new availability was

2. See Ferdinand Hahn, *The Titles of Jesus in Christology*, trans. Knight and Ogg (New York: World Publishing Co., 1969); and Reginald Fuller, *The Foundations of New Testament Christology* (New York: Charles Scribner's Sons, 1965).

spelled out, namely, redemption is available on other terms than the heritage of Israel. In short, it is available universally. The new time now comes to mean that, and Jesus as the paradigmatic figure is the occasion of that new availability of redemption. This is the setting for the creation of a paradigm which is not simply the paradigmatic figure himself but is *about* that figure. Its form was an announcement that Jesus of Nazareth has made available for all who hear and believe salvation from sin. The paradigm was, in content, largely the faith of Israel. It presupposed the Adamic myth's account of the human problem, the transcendent creator God, the universality and radicality of human sin, the essential goodness of the world. But it transposed this myth from its location in the Israelite heritage to the world community. In other words, a decisive step in the reduction of the original events to language was the unifying, interpretative act in which the many things that were happening find a paradigm. Because Jesus, a historical figure, was central to the events, he was central to the paradigm. The paradigm was, in fact, a paradigm of Jesus. Its nucleus form as the "apostolic kerygma," the gospel, was an announcement that, through certain things Jesus did and underwent, salvation was now available to all. In this expanded form the paradigm was the "story of Jesus."

A third feature of this discovery of a language in which the transition to ecclesial existence could be embodied was the broader forging of a new religious symbolism available to help the new community understand itself, interrelate its inherited tradition with the new situation, and incorporate traditional human, cultic, and moral issues into the entelechy of ecclesial existence.[3] Bringing to expression the new paradigm (the gospel) is one part of this undertaking, but the task itself is broader than the paradigm. How does one talk about the new community or its congregations? The term *synagogue* will not do. What does one call its leaders? In what language are its ordinances, rituals, and beliefs to be expressed? How is the ancient tradition of Israel including the Torah commanded in the Scriptures to be interpreted? How is the traditional symbolism related

3. This new symbolism is not simply exclusive of the framework and mythos of Judaism. Much of it occurred in the form of an anti-Judaism polemic which, in order to be heard, appropriated distinctive notions of Judaism: messianism, apocalypticism, synagogal types of congregations, and so on.

to the new age and new community: God, people of God, salvation, Torah, covenant? We shall make no attempt to repeat an account which is now familiar to students of early Christianity.[4] Our point is that the task for forging a language for ecclesial process is more extensive than the paradigm itself. If we find ourselves perplexed by the great variety of language in the literature of early Christianity, we should keep in mind the enormity and complexity of this task. Four requisites attended this task of a new symbolic embodiment of the event of ecclesial origin. What was needed was a language (symbolism) stable enough to endure beyond a few years and expressive enough of the new reality to function in the continued remembering and celebrating of the community. Further, the symbolism had to be comprehensive enough in relation to fundamental areas of human life to orient them toward the many dimensions of provincial space. Third, it had to prevent the new reality from being reduced to the ancient tradition and at the same time retain the language and paradigms of that tradition which were, in fact, part of the new reality. Finally, it had to differentiate itself from the world of its day so as not to be amalgamated with it and yet have enough relation to the world to transform its provincial spaces.

We would miss the mark if we formulated the relation between the events and the linguistic embodiment as merely chronological, the events preceding the language. Rather, one dimension of the events of transition to ecclesial existence is just this linguistic accomplishment, this forging of an old-new symbolism. The result was a historical accomplishment. That is, the resulting symbolism was taken largely from existing symbolism (the Messiah, Scripture, apocalypse, redemption, sin, priest, church). It met a historical need. It was relative to the times. It carried no guaranteed a priori truth value. (That status was conferred on it by the house of authority.) It was more or less successful in expressing the reality and entelechy of ecclesiality. Yet to a certain degree this language, this new symbolic universe, did meet all the above requisites, and through it the ecclesial

4. See Helmut Koester and James Robinson, *Trajectories Through Early Christianity* (Philadelphia: Fortress Press, 1971), chap. 6; Harnack's *The Expansion of Christianity in the First Three Centuries* (New York: G. P. Putnam's Sons, 1904). Volume I is especially good in raising historical questions of just this sort. See also Joh. Weiss, *The History of Primitive Christianity* (New York: Wilson-Erickson, 1937), book I.

community was equipped to endure, remember, celebrate, and proclaim.

The first step in the preparation of the normative event for an enduring function in ecclesial process is its linguistic embodiment, its rise into an oral kerygma. This was accomplished as part of the origin of ecclesiality. The paradigmatic figure, the saving event, the transition to the universal community did find expression in a unifying paradigm, the gospel. But linguistic expression is not necessarily written expression. And we must ask whether the oral kerygma is a sufficient vehicle in which the normative event can endure over generations. The distinction proposed in this question is between reduction to a symbolism expressive of the community's experience of the new reality and the further location of that symbolism in writing, a second sedimentation, the "apostolic paratheke."[5] Without an institutional activity of verbal memorizing of that tradition or a written deposit, there is little chance for the paradigm and symbolic universe to survive the changes of a historical community. Thus, we note a second accomplishment of the original community, the creation of a written account of the events of ecclesial origin, and thereby a generation-bridging literature which could exercise some control on the celebrative remembering of the community.

The Normative Status of the Kerygma Collection

Acknowledging the fact of this literature which attended and recorded ecclesial origins, our task and problem is to understand the function of that literature in ecclesial process. We put the issue this way to show that the question is an open one. The community early on did arrive at a way of understanding that literature, namely, by accepting the framework and presuppositions of the Jewish Scripture principle. In part 1 we offered an account of the presuppositional strata of this principle (chapters 3 and 4) and argued that this principle is not only no longer viable but is contradictory to ecclesiality (chapters 7 and 8). Our task, therefore, is to understand the nature and role of these writings outside the framework of the Scripture principle. I hope this position is clear and unambiguous. If the

5. For the concept of *paratheke,* see Josef Geiselmann, *The Meaning of Tradition* (London: Burns and Oates, 1956), p. 12.

framework and presuppositions of the house of authority are not in operation, these writings cannot be regarded as "holy Scripture." That is, they cannot be differentiated from other writings as having their origin in a special divine act of inspiration which gives all their parts (passages, texts) the a priori quality of truth and authority.

We put the matter as clearly and bluntly as possible because it is our conviction that much of the confusion that attends modern theology is a result of ambiguity and vacillation on this point, symptomized in antinomies that attend the commitment to historical-critical methods *and* the Scripture principle. A number of unsolvable problems have occupied theologians as a result. One unsolvable problem attends the long and fruitless search for a new locus of authority *in* Scripture. This search acknowledges the discreditation of the old model of plenary inspiration and the a priori authority of all biblical passages. It looks for some *residual* authority, some nucleus in Scripture where a priori truth, the truth to which the church is subject, makes its last stand. Proposed are salvation history, revelatory events, a canon within the canon composed of Jesus Christ, justifying faith, and the like. The problem is simply that there is no such residue once the presuppositions of the Scripture principle are undercut.

A second unsolvable problem appears in the attempts to confirm the early church's criteria for canonical books of the New Testament. Any consistent version of Scripture must insist that what does and does not comprise Scripture be absolutely given. The two major criteria in the early church both contained historical judgments which compromised such absoluteness. They were the judgments that these and only these works offered the content of the apostolic faith and that they dated from an apostle or an apostle's disciple. The historical element in these judgments could quickly be obscured in the church's theology of its own teaching office as guided by the Spirit. Thus the absolute bounding of the canonical list finds its basis in the absoluteness of the magisterium. But contemporary theology with its commitment to the principle of historical evidence faces a much sharper version of this dilemma. In the determination of a book as having "apostolic content," theology cannot combine an unambiguous, divinely given criterion (gospel) with a historically determined one (Gospel). In the determination of a book as an apostolic autograph or near autograph it cannot combine relative uncertainty about dating which attends all historical evidence with the certainty required of a *divinely* given list.

A third problem is that modern theology attempts to put together some sort of christocentrism or christocentric piety with historical consciousness, making the former subject to a historically constructed Jesus, the historical Jesus. Hence a whole literature arises which seems to suggest that the historically offered Jesus is an indispensable condition for faith. Theologians are thus in the position of seeming to be disinterested in history and its studies of Jesus (Kierkegaard, the early Brunner) or of basing faith on the outcome of scholarly enterprise, surely an unsolvable problem. These problems created by mixing elements of the way of authority and historical consciousness are unresolvable.

Not only must the normative event find appropriate linguistic expression and a literary deposit which can continue to present that event to subsequent generations. The normative character of the event must find its way into the language and the writings. *Normative* here means definitive for the self-interpretation of subsequent expressions of the same type of historical existence. That is, the subsequent historical communities define themselves not simply in reference to their provincial, contemporaneous settings to some other historical sociality but by their historical, corporate type, for example, ecclesiality. The reason that self-definition by reference to the normative event is appropriate is twofold. First, if participation in ecclesiality is redemptive, this means that realities attend this participation which have to do with human good and insight into the way things are. Second, the way these realities occur is through tradition, that is, through the participation of a present, actual community in a historical-corporate existence enduring from the past. If this is the case, the linguistic sedimentation of that event, the expression and interpretation of that event in language and symbol as an immanent aspect of the event itself, also retains a normative character. That is, the new paradigm, the story of Jesus, and the primary symbols are referred to in this definitive act. The celebration and remembering of the event of transition cannot avoid the linguistic incarnation of the event, its embodiment into language. As sedimentations of ecclesial existence these symbols are not just expressions of historical contingencies external to ecclesiality (such as the journeys of Paul) but have obtained a form enabling them to persist over generations and function as definitive for future communities of the same type. The *written* accomplishment, the writings in which the originating event is described, thus retains the normative character of the *linguistic* accomplishment.

Writings do not in themselves have an intrinsic durability. They do not function simply by being writings as vehicles of social duration. But we recall that the sedimentation of language (the paradigm, symbols, story of Jesus and the community) itself has a durability. While the occasions in which it functioned were ephemeral, such things as church controversies, incidents of persecution, journeys, and missions, the paradigm and symbols attending such things did express in varying degrees the new historical existence and therefore had the character of sedimentations able to inform more than one generation. This is why the written literature obtained by this language is itself not simply occasional and emphemeral but takes on the character of a literature of tradition, a deposit of ecclesial origins able to function in the celebrative remembering of the continuing community. Accordingly, the normativeness of the event and language is transferred to the literature. We should repeat here what we said about the relation between the event and the language. It would be a mistake to think of the relation between the sedimented language and the written vehicle as simply chronological. Although the literature did in some sense follow the oral preaching and teaching of the community, it is also true to say that much of the language and paradigm first occurred in the written communications. Hence, the event of transition to ecclesial existence includes the sedimentation into both language and the literature which initially recorded that transition.

But admitting a normative character to the literature of the transition to ecclesiality is not yet specifying what that normativeness is. At this point it would be very easy to permit the Scripture principle to take over. Since the Scripture principle specifies the normativeness through the principle of divine–human identity and its legal model of how divine authority is distributed through the passages, the genre of that literature is either that of a divinely given Torah for a people in a specific cultural-historical situation (the Judaic version) or the divinely given "true religion" or "revealed truths" (the early Christian version). The issue of normativeness is partly that of the *genre* of the literature of ecclesial origins. If the genre is neither Torah nor revealed truths, what is it? A generation of historical studies of this literature confirms what theological analysis must conclude. The genre of the literature of ecclesial origins is *kerygma*. We say this first of all not on literary but theological grounds and we mean it not as a literary but a theological claim. To establish this we simply recall what unifies the literature. The literature (Gospels, epistles, histories, stylized compositions) was not commissioned by any one group for any one purpose. The particular authors had no common assignment such as to record the "truths" being disclosed to them by God. The situations of the writing of this literature are occasional. The literature as a whole has no "purpose" in the sense of something imposed by a single mind, and one must fall back on the Scripture principle and divine authorship to obtain such a purpose. What then can its unity be if it is the literature of ecclesial origins functioning in the subsequent celebrative remembering of the ecclesial community? It cannot be Torah since ecclesiality as a universal redemptive existence has no single historical-cultural people for whom the customs and practices of this literature would be forever valid. Ecclesial existence permeates the multitude of provincial spaces and offers no single Torah for them all. It is not "revealed truths" able to find and found systems of dogma, since this presupposes the Scripture principle. The only unity intrinsic to these occasional writings is something all the authors have in common. They all write their occasional pieces under the conviction that, as they would put it, "Messiah has appeared," offering redemption in a new form and inaugurating a new epoch. There are, of course, variations in the literature as to what this means. Some works and passages reflect the period when the new epoch was thought to be the end-time. Some realize more than others the new universal nature of ecclesial existence.

There is, then, a literature that attended the transition to ecclesial existence which records, even if the purpose of the author was specific and occasional, various moments of the transition from the perspective of belief-ful participation in the transition. This literature, written from faith, records the events of ecclesial origin. For this reason it has the character of kerygma. In the literary sense most of the pieces are not literally recorded sermons. But the viewpoint of the writings, the admonitions, disputes, and narratives, is proclamatory. That is, even when a polemical criticism is offered, as in Paul writing to the church at Galatia or in the first letter of John, the standpoint behind the polemic is the above-mentioned conviction. The criterion is the newly forged paradigm, the story of Jesus, the gospel, the *paradosis*.

What then should this literature be called? Because it is not a mere multiplicity and has some unity since it is the vehicle recording the first linguistic sedimentation of the originating event, it can properly be unified in a period of time. Clearly, however, the term *New Testament*, burdened as it is with connotations of the Scripture principle and one of its founding axioms, salvation history, will not do.[6] We propose that the entitling of this literature follow the precedent of Judaism, which, by calling the Scriptures Torah, suggested the unifying genre and function of the writings.[7] We propose, therefore, the term *Kerygma* as the name for this literature of ecclesial origins. Realizing that the term connotes originally and primarily a living message voiced in an actual situation, we differentiate between kerygma and the Kerygma, that is, the literature of ecclesial origins.

The genre of kerygma suggests the ground for the normative function of this literature, the attestation to the originating events of ecclesial existence. What then is the normative function itself? It is suggested by the bipolar structure of ecclesial process and contemporary presence. We have argued that tradition accumulating from the past is not itself an object of faith but is that through which faith grasps, experiences, and interprets its contemporary world. Thereby is provincial space transformed. The most general thing we can say about the normative function of the literary vehicle of tradition is that it assists in this "seeing through." This is unavoidable if we acknowledge that the original historical transition ever after presides over the ecclesial community's interpretation of itself as a type of historical existence, that this transition obtained sedimentation into language

6. It is clear that a virtual Newtonian revolution of piety and tradition would have to occur for contemporary branches of Christendom to even entertain the question. But then it is my conviction that contemporary branches of Christendom have at best a highly tenuous relation to ecclesial existence. We recall at this point that our exploration is of an ideal-actual entity, ecclesiality, and that the branches of Christendom, representing as they do a multiplicity of historical actualizations which contradict ecclesiality, are not normative for the inquiry.

7. Some grasp of whole literatures as types or genres is at work in the liturgical tradition of the Christian churches as they incorporate into the liturgy readings from Prophets, Gospels, and Epistles.

and paradigm, and that this language obtained a literary vehicle. The normative character of the events themselves follows this development into this literature. These events can be celebratively remembered because they have found stable units of social memory. The Kerygma, that is, the literature of ecclesial origins, bridges generations by making available to each new generation the originative dimension of tradition. This is why this literature properly exercises some control over the community's perennial inclination to render its provincial spaces autonomous. Ideally, the community celebrates the originating events and their paradigm and symbols not primarily as a frozen and authoritative past to be reproduced or imitated but as an opening onto the world.

I do not mean to propose here a perspectivism in the sense that theology, natural science, poetry, and the like are simply different ways of interpreting the same set of finite events and realities. That would miss the whole point. Realities appearing in provincial spaces are perpetually forthcoming and whole sets of them (dimensions) are missed because of being in the world in determinate ways. Ecclesial existence with its paradigm is a way of being in the world that opens up realities such as the structure of evil and the possibility of redemption. The ecclesial paradigm and Adamic myth may well uncover dimensions of contemporary reality not accessible to a gnostic myth. This does not exclude the possibility that the gnostic (or Hindu, Freudian, Marxist, tragic) mythos may function similarly toward another set of realities. We must stress, however, that what it is that is seen through is not the vehicle, the literature itself, but the sedimented language and paradigm, the gospel, the paradigmatic figure, Jesus of Nazareth. The literature's normative function as ordered toward "seeing through" is strictly that of the bearer of these sedimentations. In summary we have proposed two functions of the literature in ecclesial process. The first, based on its character of being a deposit of descriptions of the originating and normative event, is its function as a definitive reference to ecclesiality's subsequent self-interpretations. The second, based on its being a written expression of the sedimentation of the normative paradigm into language, is its function as a lens which, when "seen through," opens up and judges provincial spaces.

An unavoidable issue in any theology of the Kerygma (writings) is the question of how that literature is determined. Formulated within the house of authority, that issue is one of determining the list of canonical writings. This sets the stage for the dispute between Catholics, who acknowledge that this was the work of the church in the forming of tradition and therefore can identify the church's criteria of selection and elimination, and Protestants, who insist that the real canon preceded such a self-conscious ecclesiastical process.[8] The Catholic position is self-consistent but vulnerable to the discreditation of the traditional criteria on historical grounds, while the Protestant position is simply incoherent insofar as it assigns infallible authority to canonical writings—the work of tradition and church—and fallibility to tradition and church. Our problem is a different one. How can the written works which attended and attested the originating events of ecclesiality be identified? I shall not engage here in the task itself, although it is a task to be taken up anew. The nature of this literature displays three rather clear criteria. If this literature records the historical formation of ecclesial existence written in the genre of kerygma, each work identified as a part of the Kerygma should have three features. First, it should be a work from within some part or movement of the community, thus having the characteristic of a witness, attestation. This criterion would exclude many writings which fall within this period and which are pertinent to the study of the origins of ecclesiality, works of Hellenistic and Roman authors and works of various Jewish religious movements such as the Qumran sect or Alexandrian Judaism. Study of such writings contributes to the historical understanding of the origin of ecclesial existence and also to the interpretation of the writings in the Kerygma. But the writings of Cicero, Qumran, Philo, and the like are not sedimentations into paradigm and symbols of the new reality and have little or no function as vehicles of ecclesial process.

Second, each work should with some integrity function as a historical account of the forming of ecclesial existence. This need not mean that the writing in question has historical recording as its self-conscious purpose, or that writings with such a purpose (for example, Luke–Acts) need be taken at face value. Paul's letter to the Galatians

---

8. There is no longer a Protestant consensus on this point. Protestant theologians are divided between those who, like Barth, take the traditional view that the real canon preceded ecclesial process and those who, like Marxsen, frankly acknowledge that the canon is the work of the church. See Willi Marxsen, *The New Testament as the Church's Book*, trans. J. E. Mignard (Philadelphia: Fortress Press, 1972), chap. 1.

and the controversy over the law is part of the growing realization by the early community of its new universal framework, hence it is pertinent as such an account. The book of Acts, problematic as it is historically, nevertheless gives a picture of one way in which the church was beginning to understand itself. This criterion would exclude utterly fantastic works which seem to be minimally controlled by attendance to historical accounts and have the character of legend-making, such as certain works in the New Testament apocrypha. Although these works may contribute to the study of ecclesial origins, they offer little to the subsequent celebrative remembering.

A third criterion attends the fact that this literature does have to do with the *originating* event, the event and period of origins. Although it is inevitable as a criterion, "originating event" is anything but precise. This criterion is not so much a clear historical given to be appealed to as the product of historical and theological work. A historical approach will try to distinguish the event and period of origins from its successors, differentiating between the period in which the religious movement is creating institutions of survival and the period which presupposes such institutions. A theological approach will try to differentiate the period of origin from its successors by discerning when the transition to the new corporate existence has been accomplished. Because Jesus of Nazareth both in his actual ministry and in his role in the earliest paradigm of salvation is the nucleus of the event, the period of origins would include his life and ministry. However, the transition to the new existence has clearly not been accomplished at the time of the close of the ministry of Jesus. What still had to happen was the formulation of the kerygma in which Jesus himself becomes the proclaimed paradigmatic figure and the creation of an actual community which manifests the features of ecclesiality. Imprecise as it is, there comes a time when the community's *primary* problem is no longer generating a new paradigm and mythos but rather existing with its new sedimented "myth" in a new provincial space. There is, of course, no single year or even decade in which that shift can be pinpointed. But one should be able to identify writings that fall primarily into one or the other situation. We are obviously talking not about a list with an absolute character but about a group of writings which share these unifying features that fall roughly within this period and fulfill these criteria. If some writings (Clement of Rome, Ignatius) are included as fulfilling the criteria by some communities and are not by others, the principle of the Kerygma is not thereby violated. Its very nature includes the variability of accounts of writings which comprise it.

Acknowledging that there is a written vehicle operative in theological reflection, the Kerygma, are we now reopening the doors to the Scripture principle? The principle can easily be clandestinely restored by a type of question dreaded by both believer and theologian. How do we know that the events of Jesus of Nazareth and their paradigm and symbols have obtained authentic expression in these writings? In order to protect certainty at that point must we not reintroduce salvation history and say that God does what is necessary to ensure the continued availability of his redemptive activity, and therefore God guarantees the adequacy of these writings by his inspiring activity? Although we do not want to interpret these matters so as to exclude a priori the divine activity, we resist any special appeal to that activity as the basis for the Kerygma's authenticity. We answer this question simply by saying that no such certainty is given. What we have instead is historical plausibility that these writings contain a record of these events and their linguistic expression. Formulating the matter as we have, we are not in the position of being threatened by historical uncertainties about the authenticity of this or that saying of Jesus, of this or that incident of his life, of the early or late date of the Gospel of John. Such matters have importance for the total historical enterprise of gaining a picture of ecclesial origins, but the question of the availability of ecclesial origins and their paradigm and symbols does not hang on them.[9]

THE VEHICLES OF ECCLESIAL PROCESS: THE WRITINGS OF ISRAEL'S FAITH

We have tried to indicate why the literature of ecclesial origins, the Kerygma, has a normative character for the ecclesial community. We must acknowledge, however, that in reality historical Christianity has subjected itself in varying ways to another literature, the two together

9. The proposal of this section may not be as untraditional as it sounds. It is true that by the time of Irenaeus certain writings from the first and early second century were viewed as Scripture. But for a hundred years early Christianity used these writings in other ways, as accounts of Jesus and the gospel. The function of apostolicity as a criterion for these writings is a step away from the more formal criterion of "inspiration." Apostolicity at least suggests concern for writings approximate in time to the central historical figure of the events, and thus the content of the Christian kerygma is at work in that criterion.

comprising the Christian Scriptures or the Bible. Does theological reflection, which occurs outside the Scripture principle, abandon that other literature as irrelevant to the portraiture of ecclesial existence? So rises the "problem of the Old Testament." The problem exists for modern theology and the modern church in varying degrees. The more the axioms of the way of authority are admitted (the "high" view of Scripture), especially in the Reformation form of eschewing allegorical method, the sharper the problem becomes, since it involves applying the features of divine–human identity, leveling, and infallibility to the literature of Israel's faith while at the same time insisting that revelation in Christ is the norm. Thus are generated the various forms of Christianizing the literature of Israel. When historical modes of interpretation are accepted, thus abolishing the axioms of the Scripture principle, this problem is lessened, but new anomalies are introduced. Retaining both historical methods and the two-testament canon, the theologian tries to discover anew the "authority" of the "Old Testament." Thus are generated various ingenious hermeneutics of the Old Testament which locate and interpret an authoritative and revelatory nucleus within it (the acts of God, witness to the situation of human being). Both traditional and modern approaches have views attending them which swing from a high view of that literature to Marcionite and quasi-Marcionite views in which the Old Testament is a kind of shadowy anticipation of the true religion.[10] Two general dilemmas preside over this discussion. The first is the dilemma of the demise of the Scripture principle under historical methods and the retention of it in the bipartite canon and subsequent formulations of Old Testament authority within the canonical principle. The second is the dilemma created by the primacy of Jesus of Nazareth as the paradigm of faith. Given that primacy, the Old Testament is either treated in its own right, in which case one type of faith and historical existence (ecclesiality) is subjected to another (Israel), or it is subordinated to Christian faith, in which case it is not treated in its own right.

The first dilemma we shall eliminate at the beginning with our repudiation of the Scripture principle. The second dilemma survives that repudiation and presents itself as a problem to be resolved. We

10. For an excellent typology and account of the major Christian positions on the authority of the Old Testament, see John Bright, *The Authority of the Old Testament* (Nashville: Abingdon Press, 1967), chap. 1.

shall not hereafter speak of the "Old Testament," a term which not only suggests the bipartite canon but a *heilsgeschlichtlich* way of relating the two collections. Instead, we shall speak of the writings of Israel's faith.

We must first consider briefly what unifies this highly diverse literature. One of the most important contributions of a generation of "Old Testament" studies concerns this issue. The consensus of these studies is that the several collections within this literature give us a narrative or story of Israel and this narrative is told from the standpoint of a theology of history as the story of God's redemptive-judging activity.[11] We have here general features similar to those of the Kerygma, that is, a literature which altogether offers a historical picture of an actual community of people over time and written from within the faith of that community. This need not mean that "history" itself is a central or even self-consciously offered notion for the authors. Rather, what happens to that community in the past and present is of sufficient importance for the literature to remember and record. The "Old Testament," then, is a collection of writings in which various stages of the tradition of Israel find expression, the totality of which gives us a narrative of Israel's history from the viewpoint of Israelite faith.

The faith of Israel, "Hebraic existence" to use John Cobb's phrase, does not come to expression simply in a cluster of unrelated symbols.[12] There is an overarching paradigm of divine presence which unites such themes as Yahweh, the one and only Lord of creation and history, the people of Yahweh, the land, covenant, and Torah. This paradigm of divine presence and activity is a salvation history narrative. The paradigm thus expresses a particular *modality* of divine presence, a specific way of understanding how the divine activity effects redemption. The setting of that modality is a specific, historical, landed people, and the modality itself is the divine presence by way of historical activity. Thus the institutions (temple, priesthood), activities (annual recitals, sacrifices), and symbols (promised land)

---

11. For summary accounts of these studies see several of the essays (Hesse, Westermann) in Claus Westermann's *Essays on Old Testament Hermeneutics,* trans. J. Mays (Richmond: John Knox Press, 1963). See also Alan Richardson's essay in B. W. Anderson, ed., *The Old Testament and the Christian Faith* (New York: Harper & Row, 1963). This is likewise John Bright's approach; see ibid., chap. 3.

12. For a brief summary of these symbols see Chapter 1, "The Faith of Israel."

depend for their essential meaning on this territorial and landed modality. On the other hand, there is a substratum of the primary symbolic language of Israel whose essential meaning does not depend on that modality and which can exist apart from the paradigm of a redemptive, national divine activity. I have in mind the trans-territorial references created by Yahwism itself and the symbolism of the one creator God and the Adamic myth depicting a universal and radical loss of innocence. Thus is created a substratum in the symbolism of the faith of Israel which portrays the human problem as such and not just the historical situation of a single territorial people. And it does so in the primary symbols of the transcendent, creation, evil, and redemption. In short, a comprehensive mythos of redemption is present as a substratum of the paradigm of Israel's faith and its symbolism. The faith of Israel is a *theological*-historical term for Israel's response and relation to God set in a specific interpretation of the human problem (sin) and hope. We distinguish Israel's faith from the *religion* of Israel, that totality of practices, institutions, beliefs, and whatever paradigm weaves them into a family resemblance which attends Israel from its unrecoverable origins to the rise of Judaism.

Our inquiry into ecclesiality's relation to the faith of Israel will develop in two steps: a fundamental thesis concerning the relation between ecclesial existence and the faith of Israel and, on the basis of that, a thesis concerning the place of the literature of Israel's faith in theology.

Ecclesia and the Faith of Israel

Considering now the question of ecclesia's relation to this faith and its paradigm, we can say that the ecclesial community has always understood itself in continuity with Israel. The traditional interpretation has related the two by means of a salvation history scheme: a beginning and a promise declared in Israel and a fulfillment in the new Israel; law anticipating and obtaining fulfillment in gospel. Needless to say, this interpretation occurs in tension with the traditional desire to regard both testaments of the one Scripture as fully authoritative, a tension between the subordination and the authority of the "Old Testament." A rather pale version of the traditional view is the more contemporary-historical attempt to retain or justify the "Old Testament" by claiming that without it the "New Testament" can scarcely be understood. Consequently, the religion of Israel as the historical context of the Christian movement is indispensable. This resembles the traditional view by subordinating the "Old Testament" but weakens it by restricting the relation between the ecclesial community and the faith of Israel to the situation of an interpreter trying to understand the "New Testament." Furthermore, the syncretistic plurality of the historical context of the ecclesial movement nominates other candidates necessary for the historical understanding of the New Testament, obscuring the special relation ecclesia might have to the faith of Israel.

We begin by stating the thesis. *The faith of Israel is immanent in and constitutive of ecclesiality.* The emphasis, of course, is on the word *faith*. Israel and its religion is past. Its faith, in the sense of a historical type of response to God and vision of human problem and hope, is not. Israel's faith persists in both ecclesiality and Judaism, each of which has a different relation to the landed modality of divine presence in the religion of Israel. Needless to say, if Israel's faith is constitutive of ecclesial existence, the relation of ecclesia to that faith cannot be simply the fulfillment and replacement of a past, subordinate faith. It cannot be simply the relation of remembering a faith now past.

The thesis as stated not only needs to be established; it seems at first sight to contradict our continuing claim that ecclesia is essentially a universalized form of redemptive existence arising in an event of transition *from* Israelite religion. It is just this event of transition that shows why the faith of Israel is immanent in ecclesiability. We have described ecclesial process as occurring through an evaluative, corporate memory of the events of its origin, which means the events (and their nucleus figure, Jesus of Nazareth) through which a transition to a new form of historical existence occurred. In the language of social analysis, this transition involves a new social modality of divine presence, not a new faith.

But what was being accomplished in these events was a new modality of divine salvific presence, different from both the territorial modality of Israel and the quasi-universal pariah community of Judaism. To be sure, the new modality involved "faith in Jesus Christ," not as a substitute for Israel's faith, but as a new universal availability of divine presence. In making this point we are not committing ourselves to such a static view of history that new motifs are rendered impossible. Hence, it may well be that the Christian movement as it developed in the first century had unique features even in relating to the faith of Israel. This could mean the emphasis on some things and not others (grace, eschatology), reformulations of the tradition (the nature of the Messiah), even new motifs (agape as the central concern of the life of the community). After acknowledging this we would quickly add that uniqueness in this sense characterized the ages and epochs of the religion of Israel itself, and it continued to do so after the first century in the history of Christianity. These sorts of changes, "developments," and re-formations in the period of Christian origins no more amount to a new, "fulfilled" faith than the changes subsequent to that period in Christianity itself.

In other words, the response and relation to God, the world maker, which carries with it both the sense of sin and the hope of redemption, is the faith of Israel which is also the faith of ecclesiality. Ecclesial faith, because of the new universal paradigm of divine presence, and because of other new, transformed motifs, may be historically distinguishable from the faith of Israel. Yet it is not a faith replacing the faith of Israel.[13] One way of expressing the continuance of the faith of Israel in ecclesiality is to speak of certain "constants" between the two faiths. Two major ways of understanding these constants present themselves. The more traditional one is that of a salvation history scheme where one story of God's activity covers both faiths but relates them to each other by promise and fulfillment. The second way speaks of the faith of Israel as a theological substructure of New Testament writings.[14] The view offered here retains elements of both these understandings. While the salvation history scheme is not utilized, it does maintain that the faith of Israel has a certain entelechy toward a universalized modality of divine presence. And it maintains that Israel's faith does persist as faith in God, the world maker, and in a certain vision of the human problem and hope.

If ecclesial existence *is* or has within itself the faith of Israel, then what is celebratively remembered in ecclesial process is not merely the

13. Insofar as we try to argue that Israel's faith is immanent in ecclesiality on the grounds of social and historical process, the case is greatly weakened. For while it is true that the ecclesial community did accomplish its linguistic sedimentations of the events of transition by drawing on the sedimentations (imagery, stories, mythos) of Israel, it is just as true that Judaism and Hellenistic religious syncretism also contributed such sedimentations. Such an approach obscures the distinction between a faith's unifying "myth" concerning the human problematic and hope and the multiplicity of models and metaphors through which this comes to expression from age to age.

14. See C. H. Dodd, *According to the Scriptures* (New York: Charles Scribner's Sons, 1953).

events of transition to the new modality but that which persisted into that modality. Ecclesial process as a remembering process is both a celebration of the event of transition (of Jesus the Christ) and a remembering of the story of God, human being, and evil and hope which is the faith of Israel. Of course, such a sociology of knowledge observation does not amount to a justification of that story. It is only as that remembering in fact opens human beings to realities that it is truly grounded. And since the faith of Israel is located in the religion of Israel and has permanent expression in a literature, we can expect that literature to play some role as one of the vehicles of ecclesial process, that is, in the education, liturgy, and proclamation of the empirical community.

Having said that the faith of Israel is constitutive of ecclesiality and therefore of the literature of the origins of ecclesiality, it is surprising that the faith of Israel is not very apparent in that literature. In other words, the Kerygma is not a very explicit or elaborate expression of what we are calling the faith of Israel. In addition, the authors of the Kerygma viewed the writings of Israel's religion as Scripture. And yet the faith of Israel obtains only an oblique and indirect expression in the Kerygma. The reason for this is that the direct focus of these authors was on the new modality of redemption and its figure, Jesus of Nazareth. The situation of that focus was the critical situation of a minority religious community establishing its own identity in contrast to its competitors within its own tradition (Judaism) and outside (Hellenistic Roman religions). The character and tone of this litera-ture then is both the proclamation of the new modality of redemption and polemics against its competitors. The content of this literature is, accordingly, the newly born *paradosis* about Jesus and his followers and specific controversies and issues of the new religious communities in their settings. Most of the conceptuality of the imagery in which the tradition is formed and expressed is taken from Judaism and Helle-nistic faiths. In such a struggle the new religious community assumed its continuity with Israel and attempted to prove its superiority to Judaism. Although such a polemic might be expected, it created the Christian tendency to subordinate the faith of Israel to itself, and it obscured and played down the way in which the faith of Israel is constitutive of ecclesiality itself. One might say that the authors of the Kerygma were looking through but not thematizing the imagery of this faith in their own situation and its issues.

If the faith of Israel has only indirect and unfocused expression in the literature of ecclesial origins, it has direct and explicit expression in the literature of the traditions of Israel. For this reason the literature of Christian origins is not simply a replacement, a substitute Scripture, for the literature of the traditions of Israel, nor is it a higher version of something more primitive, less adequate, or anticipatory. With respect to many motifs immanent in ecclesiality, the Kerygma is itself a primitive, inadequate expression compared with the fuller, more profound treatments found in the literature of Israel. Thus, for instance, we find in that literature treatments of sin, idolatry, creation, wisdom, worship, justice.[15] We are not suggesting that these motifs are the only ones in this literature pertinent to the ecclesial community. Remembering and interpreting the faith of Israel which is also its own faith is partly a historical task, not a selection of authoritative items. Our point is simply that the Kerygma, concerned as it is to record and testify to the events of ecclesial origin, is not the deepest or most adequate written sedimentation of the faith of Israel. Hence, the early Christian propensity to retain the writings of Israel was an authentic one, born of ecclesiality itself.

The Function of the Writings of Israel in Theology

So far we have argued that the faith of Israel is immanent in ecclesial existence. This implies that ecclesial process involves a historical reference not only to the events of ecclesial origin but to the faith of Israel as a historical entity. Ecclesia's understanding of itself involves therefore understanding of the faith of Israel. We have depicted the historical, descriptive aspect of theology by means of the metaphor of a portraiture of ecclesial existence. Clearly, such a portraiture would include not only the events of ecclesial origin and their sedimentation into language but the faith of Israel. If the faith of Israel is constitutive of ecclesiality, theological portraiture will inevitably include the faith of Israel. And since the historical locus of that faith is the religion of Israel, and that which makes it available is the literature of the traditions of Israel, that literature will play some role in the portraying of ecclesial existence.

15. K. H. Miskotte, *When the Gods Are Silent* (New York: Harper & Row, 1967). Miskotte speaks of a surplus in the Old Testament, themes treated in much fuller ways than in the New Testament and unreplaceable by the new (part 2, chap. 3).

The basis for the importance of this literature for theology is the function of the literature in ecclesial process. We recall that the past plays a role in the continuity or self-identity of a religious community in process and that the continuity is partly retained by means of the linguistic and imagic sedimentation of tradition, as it concerns both the community's originating events and its unifying imagery. A major vehicle of that sedimentation is the written deposits of tradition, and these become the specific carriers of corporate memory along with liturgical, cultic, and institutional practices and structures. We add here that the imagery of Israel's faith functions in ecclesial process as that which is "seen through" into reality, and this *seeing through* attends the modification toward redemption. If the faith of Israel is immanent in ecclesial existence, then the *writings* of Israel will function as bearers of corporate memory. If a portrait of ecclesiality must include the faith of Israel, then it must work with the literature in which the tradition (imagery, stories, events, persons) of that faith became sedimented.

Such observations raise but do not solve a difficult problem for theological portraiture. Generally, it is the same problem that attends portraiture in general and it concerns the ambiguity of a portraiture as both a historical and a theological venture. Portraiture attempts to portray a real, corporate, historical existence. At the same time it portrays it in its ideal and entelechaic aspects, which may include features yet unrealized. Hence, the universal character of ecclesial existence has some historical realization and yet is perpetually compromised. The faith of Israel shares in this ambiguity, referring to a real, historical existence, and at the same time an ideality. Yet an even more severe problem attends any attempted portrayal of the faith of Israel. For the locus of that faith is the religion of Israel whose pervasive paradigm for divine presence is territorial and national. And this paradigm sets the dominant framework and pervades most of the imagery of the faith of Israel. The most basic metaphors and concepts (covenant, people of God, Torah, day of the Lord) occur in the meaning-horizon of that paradigm. How can these be incorporated into a portrait of ecclesial existence which has broken with that paradigm and modality of divine presence? Such is the hermeneutical problem of the use of the literature of the traditions of Israel in theological portraiture.

We begin by repeating that a theological hermeneutic operating outside the Scripture principle is not going to gather motifs from the writings of Israel as a mere assemblage to be added to motifs obtained from other sources. The endeavor is a portraiture and what is portrayed is ecclesial existence, which means a universalized modality of divine salvific presence. The faith of Israel is part of this portraiture only as it can occur in this universalized mode. We have previously observed the implicit universal character of that faith itself. And this sets the major structure of any ecclesial hermeneutic enterprise using the literature of Israel. That structure is the distinction already made between Israel's (implicitly universal) faith and its territorial-national paradigm of divine presence. So is set the hermeneutic task of grasping the faith of Israel by disengaging it from its landed-national paradigm of the religion of Israel. When theological portraiture turns to these writings, it is dealing with some themes and imagery of ecclesial existence developed much more explicitly than in the Kerygma. But it deals with them by peeling off the territorial-national modality of divine presence as their meaning-horizon and exploring their potential universal reference. This does not mean that theological portraiture selects out of the writings of Israel's traditions only passages or images with explicit universal references, for example, the universalistic statement of Amos that the Lord brought the Philistines from Caphtor and the Assyrians from Kir. It rather probes imagery, even nationally related imagery such as covenant and Torah, for its own potentially universal layers of meaning. It can do this only because there is in fact a nonterritorial meaning-horizon in Israel, established by its worship and following of the one creator God.

What do we mean by the "literature of the traditions of Israel"? Are we restoring the canon of the Old Testament which dropped from the picture with the collapse of the house of authority? The answer is negative. Canon is established by the concept of inspired origin and the concept of a period of revelation which ends with the death of the last prophet. Any literature that brings to expression the faith of Israel is pertinent for theological portraiture, and this could include the Apocrypha and Pseudepigrapha. It could also include the literature of Judaism. Judaic literature would present the portraitist with a different hermeneutical problem, since Judaism established a quite different modality of divine presence from both Israel and ecclesiality. The problem would be to discern the universal faith present in Judaism within its quasi-landed solution of the problem of identity and survival. That is, the solution of the pariah people and its institutions.

To summarize, insofar as the literature of the traditions of Israel is a locus and expression of the faith of Israel, it is not a subordinate or inferior source of theological portraiture of ecclesiality. It offers rather an imagery not duplicated or replaced by the Kerygma to be probed under the universalistic hermeneutic which attends ecclesiality. The use of these writings then is not a search for predictions that are later fulfilled, or the linking of a series of divine acts into one story, or the intensification of the sense of sin and predicament as propaedeutic to gospel, or the establishment of doctrines by authoritative citation. It is portraying ecclesial existence as a faith which is at the same time the faith of Israel.

THE VEHICLES OF ECCLESIAL PROCESS: INTERPRETATION

We have under consideration a corporate historical existence which has built into its own historical process sedimented expressions of an ancient faith (Israel) and of events of its own origin and transition. But it would distort both historical factuality and the nature of ecclesiality if we left the matter there, giving the impression of a community living directly off of ancient events and literatures regardless of its historical distance from them and regardless of its own subsequent history. In fact, the ecclesial community accumulates, remembers, and lives from events, pieties, theologies, and political structures, all originating in its postorigins period. This is as true for the biblicist or Protestant form of that community as for the tradition-oriented Catholic forms. In short, the writings of the faith of Israel and the Kerygma do not exhaust the sedimentations that persist and constitute ecclesial existence and that theological portraiture must have reference to. I shall explore this thesis in three issues. These are (1) the living interpretation which attends ecclesial process as a redemptive transformation of contemporary social space; (2) the sedimentation of this living interpretation into Interpretation, a vehicle of ecclesial duration and self-identity; and (3) the role of past, sedimented Interpretation in theological portraiture.

Living Interpretation

I recall that ecclesial process (ideally portrayed) is essentially a redemptive transformation, a deabsolutizing and revalidation of the provincial spaces of human experience. It is not so much a process within a culturally isolated community as a process in which a determinate, corporate faith negotiates its cultural environment. That which effects this transformation, described at least from below, is a set of activities in the community directed toward those spaces: controversy, proclamation, polemic, myth-making, all occurring in traditional (preaching, teaching, liturgy) or nontraditional (community organizing, political strategies) forms. All these activities have the character of "seeing through" the received symbolic universe of ecclesial existence at the provincial spaces and discerning in them both their structures of evil and their possibilities of redemption. In other words, redemptive transformation in ecclesial process occurs in connection with living interpretation. The actual religious community may engage in all sorts of political, social, and psychological activities, but these activities have an ecclesial character only if an interpretative act attends them which relates the symbolic universe of redemptive existence and contemporaneous provincial spaces. The phrase *seeing through* means that the symbolic universe of ecclesial existence so resides in the shaped consciousness of the individual and the "social self" of the community that it is not so much looked *at,* or believed *in,* as believed *through.* It is more a lens than an object, more a hermeneutical horizon of experience than the direct referent of experience. For instance, when the events and nucleus figure of ecclesial origin persist in the community's celebrative remembering, when one sees *through* them to one's familial or national spaces, these spaces are grasped as available for divine redemptive presence. Hence, the primary task of the interpretation which attends all ecclesial activities is not the interpretation of ecclesiality itself, as if it were a fixed content; it is the interpretation through ecclesiality of contemporaneity.[16] Ecclesiality itself is both a faith and a (universal) modality of redemption, and both are presupposed by the act of interpretation which discerns redemptive possibilities in the world at hand. This is why ecclesiality itself is more a horizon than direct object of interpretation.

16. It should be clear that living interpretation is synonymous with the third dimension of theological reflection (chap. 8, "The Dimensions of Ecclesial Reflection"). It is that toward which the other dimensions of theology have their telos. It is true that ecclesiality is given direct attention in the first two dimensions. The point here is that the presence of sedimented expressions of ecclesiality transcend such second-order inquiries in the discernments in which provincial spaces of culture and society were transformed.

Interpretation as a living activity of the community of faith participates in and reflects the general fallibilities of human beings and the network of evil under whose pervasive influence history occurs. Hence, the community's interpretation as a concrete activity may have the character of idolatry, superstition, oppression, or creative innovation. On the other hand, when interpretation has an ecclesial character, it is a discernment of realities of evil and possibilities of redemption. In other words, disclosure takes place. Because the interpretation occurs in a specific time and place and addresses itself to personal and cultural spaces, what is disclosed is specific, concrete, and involves realities of that time and place. On the other hand the content, scope, and reality reference of these disclosures may not be limited to their provincial setting. I say this not because the disclosure might by accident have more universal references but because of the very nature of ecclesial faith. For there are universal references in the symbolic universe through which the provincial space is experienced and interpreted. The sacred, for instance, is not a specific correlative entity of a provincial space, nor is human evil simply the actions discovered in a particular time and place. Hence, the interpretative act of deabsolutizing a provincial space, in addition to discerning the particularities therein, may also discern realities far more perdurable than the situation in question. That is, the paradigm and symbolic universe of ecclesial existence pertaining to divine being and human being are not complete, exhaustive visions. The lens itself arose in historical discernments, and it can be filled out in further disclosures. We are saying, then, that a double disclosure may occur for living interpretation. First, the "seeing through" may turn up situational realities of evil and redemption. Second, wider and even universal aspects of those realities may contribute to the lens itself, to the insight into the very structure of redemptive existence. Thus, insight into ecclesiality itself may occur and become part of the symbolic scheme of ecclesiality.

Of critical importance in understanding the character of living interpretation is the unavoidable presence in the question of truth. It is tempting to leave the matter as it is, with a community drawing on its received tradition to help alter its present life-world. But this perpetual interplay of remembering and transforming is at the same time a matter of truth because faith requires discernments about what is actually the case concerning the bondages and possibilities of its provincial spaces. Redemption would be impossible on any other terms. Further, the transformation called for presupposes what is in fact the case about the human condition, its world-historical situation, its ultimate, divine context. The universal dimension of interpretation described above presupposes the reality and therefore the responsibility for truthful testimony to ecclesial existence and the elements of its appresented horizon. It is because the discernments and disclosures that can attend interpretation have to do with truth that interpretation can achieve a sedimentation pertinent to future living interpretation. To this theme we now turn.

Sedimented Interpretation

In our general account of social duration, we described social process as occurring through innovation and solidification (Appendix A). These two features occur in ecclesial process in the dipolar form of redemptive transformation of provincial spaces and the traditioned. Living interpretation as discernment tends to become sedimented into tradition: oral, written, and institutional. And the more global and epochal the discernment, pertaining to the ecclesial community as a whole, the more the sedimentation will reach the depth social structures, the intersubjectivity, of the community. Furthermore, the forms of sedimentation are both institutional and linguistic. Interpretation itself is linguistic, and its discernments are expressed in stories, myths, concepts, propositions, images, and the like. And these linguistic sedimentations can become part of the symbolic universe of the community, part of that which is carried forward into new epochs, available to their living interpretation.

I find two reasons for this sedimenting process of living interpretation, one general and sociological, the other specifically ecclesial. The general ontology of a community's self-identity and social process discloses that self-identity is not simply formed directly from events of its origin. No community can seal itself off from the shaping, influencing effect of its own history. This does not mean that all events, persons, writings, and practices are equal in influence. Structurally prominent in social accumulations, in what endures in a community, are historical crises and their resolutions. The expressions of the community's situations of survival set the decisive turning points, the signposts throughout its past which it remembers and through which it understands itself. In Judaism crises and their communal responses would be, for instance, the fall of Jerusalem (70 C.E.), pogroms, and the holocaust. What Judaism is as a shaped corporate self-identity and a self-understanding is expressed not simply in the formative events of Judaism, but also in these subsequent crisis events. In Catholicism the gnostic crisis, the split between Eastern and Western churches, the papacy, the monastic movement, the Protestant rift, and counterreformation are all fundamental to what Catholicism is and to its self-understanding.

However, such events and their linguistic expressions would have little shaping effect unless they achieved permanent enough form to survive over generations. In other words, they need to achieve social sedimentation in the corporate community. Part of this sedimentation is the community's assigning of a certain significance to the event or resolution, a meaning for the accomplishment as of enduring significance. This acknowledgment may occur in some official and community-wide way (as at Nicea or Vatican II) or very gradually and at the level of the *sensus fidelium* (such as the Marian piety). This assignment of significance is a prerequisite to the sedimentation of the event into some enduring form. And the vehicles of sedimentation are many: liturgical practices, hymnodies, creeds, "classic" works by individuals, conciliar declarations, confession. Because these sedimentations are the community continuing to *interpret* itself and its situation through its remembered interpretations of the past, we designate them as Interpretation. Living interpretation then becomes sedimented in ways which comprise the self-identity of the community because of the inevitable accumulation of significant events in history in a historical community. So goes the more general and social account.

The second reason that sedimentation occurs in the ecclesial community goes beyond the rather neutral and sociological observation of social accumulations. Ecclesial process itself involves references to sedimented interpretation. It would be misleading to describe sedimented tradition as simply the past impinging on the present as a burden or idol, as if escape from the present were a priori to the use of the past. Such usage no doubt happens insofar as the actual community reflects the universal network of evil and thus experiences redemption in dialectic with continuing sin. Rather, sedimented interpretation itself contributes to the redemptive transformation going on in the ecclesial process. We recall that living interpretation has an intrinsic reality reference. It is at least attuned, even if not always successfully, to potential disclosures of aspects of specific situations which have transsituational significances. Living interpretation is oriented toward truth and reality, and these things are not always merely occasional but can pertain to the deeper condition of human being and its ultimate setting. In other words, the faith of Israel plus the new, ecclesial modality of divine presence do not exhaust all possible disclosures. Disclosures can and do attend the ongoing history of the ecclesial community. Acknowledgment of this does not mean commitment to a salvation history or a progressivist view of history. We are not saying that every new historical period of the ecclesial community inevitably carries new disclosures which are then sedimented for future living interpretation. We are saying that ecclesial process has an *interpretive* element, that the act of interpretation may be disclosive, and that the disclosure may obtain sedimentation. Insofar as these disclosures transcend merely occasional or situational truth, their sedimentations quite properly function in the future living interpretation of the community as Tradition or Interpretation.

In summary, that which is linguistically sedimented in the ecclesial community is the faith (of Israel) immanent in the kerygma, the kerygma concerning Jesus and the kingdom of God (that is, the events of transition to the ecclesial modality of divine presence), and the universally significant disclosive events and responses thereto in the subsequent history of the community.

Interpretation and Theological Portraiture

We have described as a dimension of ecclesial process a truth-oriented living interpretation which becomes sedimented into the church's memory and self-identity. We now take another step to say that this sedimented Interpretation is a major source of theological portraiture. Portraiture, we recall, is an ideal-historical description of ecclesial existence in its various historical incarnations. Because ecclesiality is a mode of corporate, historical existence, it can never be identified with any one historical manifestation, period, or branch. Accordingly, ecclesiality is not simply the ecclesial community in its period of origins, or even the community's historical totality from a designated period in the past to the present. It is my conviction that types of historical existences, simply because they are types, have their own distinctive unities, entelechies appropriate to them. By entelechy I mean an impetus or tendency present in a specific entity or historical type toward some strands of historic possibilities rather than others.[17] A community whose symbolic universe is unified by the hope and expectation of nirvana may tend to actualize institutions that promote individual, meditative practices rather than collective world transformation. The determinate intersubjectivity of the community with its symbolic expression will be that which presses or lures the community toward one entelechaic development and not another.

Some cautions are in order at this point. It would be a mistake to think of entelechy as a fated process of actualization. Communities can and do contradict their own proper entelechy. For instance, the ecclesial community's retention of the Judaic Scripture principle and of patriarchalism as well as its modern appropriation of civil religion all contradict its universalizing features. Also to be avoided is the view that a community's entelechy is an ahistorical structure fixed at the time of origin. Entelechy, itself a historical impetus, may be altered with the alteration of the historical community. In other words entelechy as a historical concept is only analogous to the sort of entelechies that may be operative in the development of preprogrammed organic entities. Finally, we should avoid formulating the actualization of a community toward its entelechy in a purely naturalistic framework. A theological account of that actualization could not avoid the themes of providence and divine salvific activity. The only point I am making here is that this activity is not simply an external imposition or causality but makes use of a community's immanent entelechy insofar as that entelechy is redemptively originated.

I propose this metaphor of entelechy simply to say that there are strands of future possibilities which "fulfill," confirm, and manifest historical types more adequately than others. If ecclesiality means a

17. The Greek term *entelecheia* was probably coined by Aristotle. In addition to his somewhat obscure use of it as a principle of the natural body, it means in general the internal specifying principle that actively directs an entity to its specific good or end. Leibniz uses the term more or less synonomously with monad, and as a way of describing the self-sufficiency of the monad as source of its own actions (*Monadology*, 1717, nos. 18–19). In the biologically oriented vitalistic philosophy of Hans Driesch the term reappeared as a whole-making factor in nature. See Driesch's *The Science and Philosophy of the Organism*, 2 vols. (New York: AMS Press, 1908). There are counterparts to the concept (although not using the term) in the works of Bergson, Whitehead, and Teilhard de Chardin.

universal modality of divine salvific presence, there are historical possibilities which contradict this and others which help realize it. This is why ecclesiality is not a mere structure or self-identity but an ever-unfinished historical corporate existence. Further, some of its historical developments contradict others which actualize its entelechy. And this founds an important operative concept of theological portraiture. Ecclesial existence stretched over a vast period of time by way of its entelechy manifests developments that actualize ecclesiality and no portrait of ecclesiality that omitted them would be adequate. If it were not possible to grasp entelechaic developments, the historical depiction of ecclesiality would be merely an unweighted offering of innumerable historical details. It would be "church history" in the modern sense of the word.

Theological portraiture attends not only to ecclesial existence as it was at the time of its transition to a new universal modality of redemption, but to its subsequent crises, responses, and their sedimentations which I have called Interpretation. Because it is a historical enterprise, portraiture cannot avoid historical study of the total, historical entity of Christianity in its various periods, branches, and dimensions, including its institutions, crises, polity, ethics, piety, saints, and so forth. But as a normative enterprise, operating already with *some* apprehension of ecclesiality and attempting to draw a fuller portrait, it must view these things under entelechaic considerations. In other words portraiture examines sedimented Interpretation of the past in its potentially disclosive aspects. A more theological way of expressing this is simply to say that portraiture sets forth the history of the presence of Christ in the ecclesial community. It neither grants Interpretation a priori authority or truth status nor repudiates it as if error were an a priori quality. The process of sedimenting the church's remembering into generation-bridging vehicles has already prepared the ground for portraiture by rendering past living interpretation into gradations of importance and reality. Most of the concrete past of the actual community does not survive at all in a remembered way. What does survive, such as the decision at Nicea and the writings of Luther, does so because of achieved significance in the community. It is just these vehicles of past living interpretation with which portraiture works. Portraiture, therefore, has a *theological* character in that its primary interest is past interpretation sedimented into vehicles of Interpretation of the community. It looks through and past the myriad of historical details to sedimented Interpretation in its attempt to paint and repaint the portrait of this ongoing historical existence.

A brief summary is in order. Our account of ecclesial duration has stressed three features. The first is the structure of the process itself, occurring as it does under the tutelage of a normative event and comprising a perpetual pervading and transforming of provincial spaces for the purpose of redemption. The second feature concerns the way in which the normative event as well as subsequent disclosive events obtain a form in which they continue to be available for the community's celebrative remembering. This sedimenting of language has a threefold form of faith (of Israel), Kerygma, and Interpretation. Finally, characteristic activities of proclamation, sacramental incorporation, and caring make use of the sedimented tradition in the process or traditioning itself.

13

The Form of Theological Truth: The Ecclesial Universal

THE PROBLEM OF TRUTH IN THEOLOGY

The preceding chapters on ecclesial duration have all concerned the first moment of theological reflection, that moment in which *ecclesiality* comes into view as historical matters are sifted and portrayed. Using the recent terminology, we can say that the first moment is primarily hermeneutical. This fairly narrow use of the term is a more accurate one, in my view, than the totalistic usage which identifies hermeneutic with theology as such. According to this discrete meaning the primary product of hermeneutical inquiry is historical (or historical-existential) understanding. That which is yielded by the hermeneutic probing of texts, language, symbols, and social structures is ecclesiality as a historical entity. However, theological reflection is not exhausted in the hermeneutic task, in the ideal-historical portrayal of ecclesial existence. Theological reflection and theological portraiture are not identical. That which propels portraiture beyond itself to a second moment of theological reflection is the question of truth.

At the same time it would surely be misleading to so distinguish the two dimensions of reflection as to suggest that theological portraiture is indifferent to truth. Concern for truth, born in faith itself, is a feature of theology as such and, therefore, is unavoidably present throughout all its dimensions although in ways distinctive of each one. Why is it that the concern for truth is a feature of theology?

It should be clear that the question of truth is not something imposed on the ecclesial community from without by an alien invader. Accordingly, the concern for truth in the ecclesial community cannot be described as simply early Christianity's flirtation with and marriage

301

to Hellenism, philosophy, and gnosis. All religious faiths have truth intentions in the sense of reality intentions.[1] All religious faiths claim to experience or apprehend how the world is, be that at the point of the structures of the (non)self as in Hinduism and Buddhism, the social and moral structure of human being in Judaism, or the interrelation between the sacred and regions of nature in Native American religion.[2] This general reality orientation of religion appears in ecclesiality as a feature of faith itself. If faith has to do with *realities,* and if its language is reality bearing, this suggests that truth-intention is immanent in faith itself. Faith is not content to "mean" the items of its world as simply lies, delusions, or even fictions. And the language of faith is not simply the bearer of delusions. We are not saying that, in fact, faith can never be deluded but are portraying its ideal immanent nature. Faith thus experiences and apprehends the world in one way and not another. Faith experiences in its own peculiar mode "the way things are." And this is the primary ground for the truth question being unavoidable in theology and why every dimension of theological reflection occurs under the propulsion of the question of truth.

Yet, truth intentions are not restricted to faith's prereflective orientation. They become explicit in faith's reflection (theology) and its dimensions. There is a sense, therefore, in which the first dimension, theological portraiture, is concerned with the question of truth. If the aim of this dimension is to portray ecclesial existence, then there can be no mere indifference to evidence, inaccuracy, and triviality. Theological portraiture cannot settle for lies, delusions, and fictions. Thus the portraitist attempts to grasp the primary symbol in both its immanent structure and against its own proper environment. The portraitist considers ecclesiality both synchronically as a developing

1. I would go farther, reflecting a philosophical tradition as old as Plato and Aristotle, and say that human being itself is disposed toward truth. This disposal need not mean self-conscious intellection but rather that reality intentions attend all human beings and with them the desire for a coincidence between what is meant and spoken and what is so. William Christian, *Meaning and Truth of Religion* (Princeton: Princeton University Press, 1964), sees proposals of religion, things put forward for acceptance, as essentially involving among other things proposals for belief and therefore truth-claims. See chap. 2.

2. Christian's account of religious discourse includes what he calls a basic proposal made by a religion about its subject having the formal structure of F is true of M. For example, the self is annihilated in nirvana. This is his way of saying that religions make claims as to how the world is. Ibid., chap. 2.

thing and diachronically as a universe of expressed realities. Within portraiture a second level of hermeneutics may work to uncover the reality references of the primary symbols, thus bringing to light the truth intentions and truth claims of prophets, apostles, and church fathers. Given the existential and theological posture of the portraitist, these symbols and claims may actually disclose some connection or analogy between present situations and the reality-intentions of the world of the text.

And yet truth-intentions resident in faith itself and in the portrayal of ecclesial existence do not express the central and decisive way in which truth is a theological obligation. In faith, truth occurs in the mode of transforming realities and the disclosures that attend those transformations. In the initial dimension, theological portraiture, there is concern that the portrait be a good one. And yet human being lives on a spectrum of understanding in which manifest realities may be poorly or well understood, in which judgments may or may not be made, and if made, may or may not be grounded. In fact ecclesial corporate existence has never occurred apart from interpretative judgments—about the transcendent, about Jesus of Nazareth, about ultimate destiny, about human evil. To acknowledge truth-intentions in the ecclesial and belief-ful community is not, therefore, to settle the status of the community's past and present interpretations and judgments. And this should clarify the distinction emerging here between the total mythos of the ecclesial community with its primary symbols, images, metaphors, and the like, and judgments about these things. The community may intend as reality-bearing the image of Jesus as the Christ, but this does not settle one way or another the claim that the second person of the triune being of God is incarnate in Jesus. And although that interpretative judgment may find its way into the portraiture of ecclesial existence, the portrayal itself does not settle its "truth." What this move from truth-intending reality and from theological portraiture to theological judgment actually means remains to be described. The point now is simply that reality-manifesting and portraiture (the first moment of theological reflection) do not exhaust the theological task.

It is not surprising that the ecclesial community has always had a reflective stratum, offering interpretations and assessments in the face of ever-new cultural situations. Throughout most of its history, however, interpretation has occurred in conjunction with the building of the house of authority, which, as we previously argued, seriously restricted the sense in which truth could be taken up. Since truth was an a priori feature of the authoritative documents which served as both the bearers and the criteria of truth, the only remaining task was to synthesize authorities into modes of coherence or to relate their contents to wider philosophical and cosmic schemes.[3]

What then is the problem and task of truth when the way of authority is not presupposed? It is one thing to say that truth intentions attend faith, the ecclesial community, and theological portraiture; it is another thing to specify how the question of truth transcends these things. Yet as soon as one attempts to formulate the question, the various competing philosophical theories of truth raise their ugly heads. I shall not attempt the metatheological task of assessing and adjudicating these theories.[4] I must confess that the major theories seem to be not so much mutually exclusive interpretations of the same phenomenon as illuminations of aspects of a phenomenon; thus, they disclose the unity of truth, the relation between that unity and reality, the conditions in which that relation is fulfilled, and the criteria of the fulfilling. My own inclination is to retain two fundamental features of truth proffered by these theories. The first discloses truth as a predicate of judgments, hence, the possibility of true and false judgments. That which gives a judgment this predicate is the degree to which the judgment expresses "how the world is." The second feature of truth indicates what in fact must happen for "how the world is" to obtain a judgmental expression, namely, a reality disclosure. These two features may help explain why language about truth is equivocal. Thus the problem of truth is at one time the problem of how reality comes forth, occurs, is manifest—in short, the problem of grounding, of evidence, warrants, and verification. At another time the problem of truth is the problem of

---

3. Chap. 5, "The Formal Role of the Question of Truth."

4. A more traditional typology of major theories is threefold: correspondence, coherence, and pragmatic or operational theories. I would assign the recent performative theories (Strawson) to the category of operational theories. The phenomenological movement has contributed a fourth major theory, begun by Husserl and elaborated into a major option by Heidegger. It could be called the disclosure theory or approach to truth. Its focus is not so much on the *bearer* of truth (the statement, language) and thus on truth as a relation as on the *essence* of truth and the region of its occurrence. See Martin Heidegger, "On the Essence of Truth," in D. F. Krell, ed., *Martin Heidegger: Basic Writings* (New York: Harper & Row, 1976).

types of statements, their qualities, references, and relations. When we shift the scene to theology, the first sense of truth turns out to be the problem of reality. What grounds theological claims as true and how does this grounding occur? The conventional theological approach to the problem of truth or grounding in this sense is the thematization of revelation. In the second sense, it is the problem of criteria, that is, how the ground is present in fields of evidence which function in the making of theological judgments.[5]

What is involved in the move from reality manifestation to the making of a judgment? I shall not at this point set forth a detailed account of judgment itself.[6] I simply call attention to four general features of judgment which persist in modified form in theological judgment. The first is the reference of the judgment to reality, to "how the world is," to what is the case. This reference can be to how the world is in fact or in structure. Because of the element of structure, some theological judgments are a priori in character. Second, because of this reference to something as itself, to something as such, judgments have a universal character. This does not mean that the reference itself is to something global or worldwide. Negatively expressed, it means that the reference is not simply correlative to a single apprehending subject. Its *as such* character makes it available in principle. In short, the references of true judgments have an intersubjective availability.[7]

Furthermore, however fleeting, however historically relative these references are, their intersubjective availability gives them a nonrelative aspect. Once something really is or occurs, the world is permanently modified. Its real thereness or actuality is what qualifies it as deposited data in future world happenings and in world process. This is the temporal dimension of the as-such character of the references of true judgments.

5. In the scheme followed here, *Ecclesial Man* struggled with the problem of truth in the first sense, the sense of grounding. The present work is addressing the problem of making judgments, or, we might say, how the reality-manifesting grounding rises into the judgment.

6. For such an account see Bernard Lonergan, *Verbum: Word and Idea in Aquinas* (Notre Dame: University of Notre Dame Press, 1967), pp. 59 ff., and *Insight: A Study in Human Understanding* (New York: Philosophical Library, 1957), chap. 9. See also Christian, *Meaning and Truth in Religion,* chap. 7.

7. See Edmund Husserl, *The Crisis of European Sciences and Transcendental Phenomenology,* trans D. Carr (Evanston: Northwestern University Press, 1970), sec. 47.

Third, all true judgments make a claim, thus implying the appropriateness of evidence. Reasons-for are an immanent meaning stratum of true judgments. The fields of evidence that supply reasons for, for instance, numbers, the historical past, or human behavior set the *criteria* for the judgment. Hence, the third feature of judgment is the presence as part of the judgment's proper environment of criteria.

Finally, the judgment is not born ex nihilo but represents a transition or moment in the cognitive process. The transition is from meaning-oriented insight or apprehension of the reference to understanding.[8] Understanding itself divides into a number of modalities depending on the types of references to which it is ordered. In general, transition is to self-possessed, self-conscious insight, to a claim with evidence, expressed in appropriate forms of discourse. In the historical community of faith this transition is represented in the transition to doctrine and is a process of doctrinalization.

In summary, the judgment refers to "how the world is," in its as-such or universal availability, in the form of a claim-with-its-criteria, and in discourse which expresses the transition to self-conscious understanding. This is why the question of truth in theology is not reducible to simply the question of whether realities appear and how they do so. Granting that they do, that faith and theology address in some sense "how the world is," there is still the question concerning how we can make judgments about these manifesting realities.

The problem now calls for refinement and focus. I have already argued that in one sense the truth question is the question of founding realities. As such, truth as disclosure is pretheological, prereflective, occurring in the apprehensions of faith and its corporate matrix. But given the transition to theological reflection with its three dimensions of portraiture, truth discernment, and praxis discernment, are we saying that only the second dimension is concerned with truth? On the contrary, each of the dimensions of reflection is concerned with truth. Portraiture or the hermeneutic moment attempts an ideal-historical picture of ecclesial existence. Its portrayal is subject to principles of

---

8. See Lonergan, *Insight*, p. 279. Lonergan identifies three levels of cognitive process. He sees judgment as moving beyond the mere grasping of data and its meaning to a grounding of a claim in sufficient evidence. This resembles his exposition (in *Verbum*) of Thomas's distinction between definition, which discloses the intelligibility of the phantasm, and the judgment. The well-known Hegelian version of this distinction is the route from *Vorstellung* to *Begriff*.

evidence, clarity, and other marks of truth. What it yields is an ideal-historical picture. But the portrayal does not exhaust reflection. Ideal-historical claims that a certain historical existence has this and that feature do not amount to claims that those features express the way things really are. Theological reflection which stops with portraiture is inevitably trapped in historicism, since the pretheological reality intentions of faith push theology beyond the first dimension to a dimension of reflective judgment which takes under consideration ecclesiality's claim to be an account of human being, world, and transcendence.

For example, theological portraiture may discover that for ecclesial existence the human problematic is understood as sin. Even if one grants that this particular historical community not only understood itself by means of this category but that behind that self-understanding is a primary symbol of sin which brought to expression an actual experience, the status of that symbol and experience remain determinate and provincial. If sin pertains only to the world-historical experience of Hebraism, Judaism, and Christianity, it remains culturally provincial. The second dimension of reflection goes beyond this provincial reference. It asks whether the primary symbol, sin, expresses anything about how the human world, as such, is.[9]

The problem emerges as soon as reflection begins to move beyond portraiture. This move is prompted by ecclesial existence itself which understands itself as both determinate *and* universal. Its mythos and primary symbols place the human being in its global setting, its setting in being. The mythos itself is a total theodicy, interrelating the transcendent, human being, and world in a drama of evil and redemption. Portraiture can set forth this universality as an intended reference of the historical community. It cannot uncover its actual universality. The second dimension of reflection with which we are now concerned, the transition to judgment, does attempt to translate the phenomenal universality which attends the determinate ecclesial existence into a claim-with-evidence. But there seem to be only two

---

9. The truth question occurs in all three dimensions of theological reflection. We are not pursuing the third dimension in this study to any great extent, that moment when the human being (individual or corporate) reflects out of and toward his or her own situationality. Here the truth question goes beyond simply the issue of the reality of a comprehensive mythos and its components (the second dimension) to the uncovering of the realities of that situationality.

alternative ways this can be done. The first option is to relate the claimed universality to a universal-rational structure, thus making it appear that the way the world is requires the mythos or some aspect thereof. This is obviously the way of natural theology. And it reflects the formal uses of truth which attended the way of authority. The second option is to view generic-ontological structures as the real content of the primary symbols of ecclesial existence. This second way of indicating ecclesiality's universal content has as its framework the well-known philosophical ontologies of Plato, Aristotle, Whitehead, Heidegger, and so on. In this alternative the determinate metaphors of redemption find universality by a translation into the vision of the immutable Good, or creativity, or authentic existence. Hence, ecclesial existence is, in content and in depth, ontology.

These two unhappy alternatives pose for us the unique and complex question of truth in theology. It is the impasse between two strategies: leaving ecclesial existence in its provinciality without any universal import, and thus without relevance to human being and history beyond its provincial boundaries, or translating it into the universality of general ontology, thus making its mythos and determinacy superfluous. It is just this paradox of determinacy and seemingly generic universality which poses the question of truth in its deepest sense. Formally, the problem is to understand how ecclesial realities can become subject to judgment. Specifically, this involves understanding how the intrinsic and apparent universality of ecclesiality can be uncovered without violating its determinacy. To express the problem in yet a different way, if ontology's universal references are such matters as *res verae* (Whitehead), existentials of *Dasein* (Heidegger), or transcendentals (Aquinas), what are the references of theological reflection that are differentiated from such things?

THE STRANGE UNIVERSALITY OF THEOLOGICAL TRUTH

It is clear that ecclesial reflection has a determinate and historical matrix. It occurs within and from realities which appear (occur) in attachment to a specific type of human intersubjectivity. Its mythos and symbolic universe is historical and determinate. At the same time, it is clear that the realities so apprehended are given some sort of universal status. Although they do have, as the third moment of reflection discovers, concrete and occasional actualization, they also seem to be perdurable and generalized. In some sense, they give expression to how the world is, to how human being is, and as such they are universal. Yet the term *universal* without clarification is simply an invitation to equivocation. Its fundamental ambiguity is due to its function as a term for a priori or essential features of a type of being (reason as a universal trait) and as a term for predicates or qualities of particulars (blueness, roundness). Our concern here is with the former sense, but that does not eliminate the ambiguities of the term. For different levels of being with their respective sciences offer different senses of universality: a formal or apophantic universality of logical systems and "laws," a factual universality in the sense that a persisting fact of the world is available to science as such (such as the sun-centered solar system), or a metaphysical universality characterizing that which is (such as temporality, situationality). Do such refinements give us the universality which attends the references and realities of ecclesial reflection?

It appears they do not. The universality which characterizes the references of ecclesial reflection is not one among several identifiable types of universality. The Christian mythos, with its elements, is not related to the various universalities cited above as a subcategory of one of them. It is not, accordingly, an instance of generic ontology. For this reason we should never ignore the cautionary and sometimes strident warnings that sound forth from the tradition in theology represented by Tertullian through Pascal to Barth. Why is this the case? The traditional grounds for claiming the uniqueness of the categorical world of theology tend to be epistemological. Their central concern is the availability or nonavailability of matters of faith, the access or nonaccess to these matters. The access to such matters is revelation, which makes possible "revealed theology" in contrast to reason and "natural theology." With this starting point one can say that the access is correlative to the objects given in the access. Therefore, theology is preoccupied with a unique realm or type of objects. Or, more specifically, the disciplines which inquire into the universalities of various sorts—sciences, history, ontology—lack access to the faith-world and therefore to whatever universalities it holds. While I do not want to dispute this primarily negative reason for the uniqueness of theology's references, I want to ground that uniqueness not in the unique *route* to the references (faith, revelation) but in the references themselves. The universalities that attend ecclesial existence are unique simply because they are not ontologically identical with *res verae,* cosmological matters of fact, and human existentials.

How can we describe the universalities of ecclesial reflection? There does not seem to be a category or term at hand in ordinary language which expresses the linguistic references that ecclesial reflection uncovers and formulates. Clearly that reflection inherits from the prereflective matrix and from portraiture the symbolic universe of ecclesial existence and therefore a set of primary symbols. And although these symbols may be intended or meant by faith to have universal import, their universality is not necessarily visible or apparent. This is the task of the second dimension of theological reflection, to expose and formulate the inherited linguistic bearers of the Christian mythos *in their universal character or reference.* Theological judgments, then, have to do not simply with primary symbols as such but with ecclesial universals. The reflective task is not just to translate symbol and metaphor into concept and proposition. Such an account passes over that unique entity with which theological judgment has to do, the determinate universal.[10]

This chapter attempts to give some account of this unique entity without which the nature of theological judgment and the question of truth will remain obscure. Because the ecclesial universal is unique and not a member of a more general class, the method cannot be to describe some general class and then see how the references and realities exemplify it. The task is, from the beginning, a theological one. I shall attempt this description in two steps, the first describing the universal's grounds of uniqueness in its participation in the faith-world of ecclesial existence. The focus of this first step is on the interior structure of the ecclesial universal. The second step describes the sense in which the universal is made mundane and propelled into contemporary life-worlds.

THE THREE DIMENSIONS OF THE ECCLESIAL UNIVERSAL

I recall that the ecclesial universal participates in and reflects the faith-world, and this is the main reason for its uniqueness. We would therefore expect that what bestows uniqueness, even strangeness, on

10. While the notion of the determinate universal may have some relation to Hegel's concrete universal, it should not be interpreted by means of the latter. On Hegel's distinction between generic and concrete universals, see J. N. Findlay, *Hegel: A Re-examination* (New York: Collier Books, 1958), pp. 227–29.

the universal is not a single feature or relation but a combination of relations. The ecclesial universal's unique structure is due in part to its multiple dimensions and references.[11] From these faith-world relations or dimensions the universal obtains both its determinancy and its universality. The faith-world itself is historically determinate with a historically determinate mythos. At the same time its own reference and horizon are universal. Because of this participation in the faith-world, ecclesial universals all have the following three features or dimensions: ecclesiality's global reference, the human problematic of sin and the reality of redemption, and the transcendent. "Participation in the faith-world" suggests some sort of unified context of ecclesial universals. This is apparent in the prereflective and pretheological apprehensions of faith. These apprehensions are not disposed toward a discrete set of entities like items on a store counter. Not only do faith's realities occur in a social and intersubjective matrix which mediates them, they occur in and under one reality. "The purity of heart is to will one thing." Thus the language in which such comes forth occurs in a symbolic universe which has a certain unity and structure, a meaning network in the sense that the meaning of one symbol is tied up with others.

Accordingly, all ecclesial universals refer to the totality or unity represented by the faith-world of which they are a part. Yet there is a deeper sense in which they have a global reference. The world itself, being in the most comprehensive sense, is an ever-present dimension of the ecclesial universal. The reason for this lies partly in what is now being called fundamental theology and which concerns the transcendental foundations of sin and redemption.[12] The way of human being

11. The multiple dimensions, references, and the complex structure of a theological assertion are very much manifest in Schleiermacher's notion of a twofold value (function) of dogmatic assertions (scientific, ecclesiastical) and also in his analysis of three types of references: human states, divine attributes and acts, and world. See *The Christian Faith*, trans. H. R. Macintosh and J. S. Stewart (Philadelphia: Fortress Press, 1976), sec. 17 and sec. 30.

12. I am using transcendental here in the Husserlian not the Kantian sense. Thus it does not mean the apperceived structure of the subject which grounds cognitive possibilities in relation to an object, thus creating the distinction between the object-present-through-my-structures and object-in-itself. Rather, transcendental refers to the distinction between realities (entities, contents) grasped in the everyday, "naive" natural attitude, and realities grasped in their noetic-noematic presence. Transcendental in the Husserlian sense is therefore a being-in-the-world notion because the presenting, noematic side is retained. For a more extensive exposition of this point, see the author's "Phenomenological Theology and the Problem of Metaphysics," in *Man and World*, 12, no. 4 (1979).

as being-in-the-world is in self-transcending world openness which thus experiences being in the mode of insecurity and anxiety. Attending this anxiety and insecurity is an ever-present resistance to whatever would violate the existence and autonomy, self-determination, and meaning of the human being, and a striving or eros for a world-environment or being that would secure these things.[13] It is this fundamental structure of human being-in-the-world which is behind the reflective response to suffering and tragedy in which occur questions of the nature of reality and transcendence. It is just this structure—the resistance to violation, the striving for cosmos rather than chaos, the reflection on world meaning—which makes the human being able to be in the world in the mode of sin and, likewise, to be subject to redemptive possibilities. Needless to say, the structure is not itself an explanation of the actuality of either sin or redemption. Given this structure, there is a *world* reference in both sin and redemption. In other words, the responses that these symbols describe are responses not simply to discrete events or aspects of the world but to the issue of what the total world environment is. The faith-world is determinate therefore as a historical, linguistic world, but the total world environment is what is at stake in its overall reference. In short, the faith-world is structured by a theodicy, and the reference of this theodicy is to reality as such, world as such, and being as such.

We take up now the second dimension of ecclesial universals. Recent treatments of "religious language" stress very much the existential and faith matrix of that language, the sense in which this language is not everyday-world objectifying language but the personal language of experience and commitment.[14] This now popular thesis is both illuminating and somewhat formal. It is insightful but very general to say that theological truth about how the world is is not properly expressed by information-oriented or ontological inquiries but rather personal and autobiographical experience. Less formal and more reflective of the faith-world, theological truth addresses human

13. See Edward Farley, *Ecclesial Man* (Philadelphia: Fortress Press, 1975), pp. 128–33, for an elaboration of this theme.

14. A few recent theologians who have especially uncovered the personal dimension of religious discourse are the following: Paul Van Buren, "On Doing Theology," in *Theological Explorations* (New York: Macmillan Company, 1968); David Burrell, *Exercises in Religious Understanding* (Notre Dame: University of Notre Dame Press, 1974); and Sallie McFague (TeSelle), *Speaking in Parables* (Philadelphia: Fortress Press, 1975).

questioning from the bent world, a history where interhuman violation is already there, an intersubjectivity already tarnished with
idolatrous intentions. Already we begin to see why the ecclesial
universal is not identical with a generic ontological feature or even an
existential feature. Sin, the symbolic term for this distorted, historical
matrix of experience, is experienced not as something ontologically a
priori or indispensable to (part of the constitutive meaning of) the
human being but as a violation, an interruption, a taint. If it is an
existential, it is an unhuman or antihuman existential, without genuine ontological status. Further, sin is experienced not as something
which appears and disappears with acts of choice but as something
which has already disposed the human intersubjective world, a
preceding social reality. Further yet, sin's already-thereness is experienced not in the mode of a culturally transmitted historical contingency, such as a human custom. Rather, how the (human) world is, is
experienced as sin. We can see then that sin is not meant as a universal
on the grounds of a priori insight into human being nor hypothesized
as an empirical universal on inductive grounds. It arises as a symbolic
expression because the human historical world is never experienced in
any other way than as already modified by this violation.

What does this have to do with the ecclesial universal? The question
calls for another step. The corporate existence which is the matrix of
the faith-world is a redemptive existence. As a Gospel, a proclamation,
a prophetism, its theme is primarily redemption and only secondarily
sin. There is correlative relation between redemption and sin. The
possibilities represented by redemption are not exact correlates of the
disruptions of sin, but nevertheless the experience of how the world is
as sin creates the initial meanings of redemption.[15] Given the correlation, the following should be clear. Sin does not describe either an
empirical or contingent universal (such as a widespread custom) or an
ontological universal but a unique inhuman existential, and redemption retains the same uniqueness. Redemption and redemptive possibilities refer neither to contingent, cultural possibilities nor to a return
to generic ontological features. As it is addressed to how the (human)

15. It is just as true to say that the experience of how the world is as redemptively
possible and actual creates the meanings of sin. This is a more appropriate expression
when ecclesial existence itself is described. The present exploration of the uniqueness of
the ecclesial universal is responsible for beginning with the experience of sin.

world is as sin, redemption concerns how the (human) world is and can be in contrast to sin. Thus the universals which arise in connection with the language of salvation are marked by the uniqueness of sin as a nonontological universal. Or, more accurately, insofar as *all* of the affirmations of theology have to do with the faith-world and therefore with sin and redemption, they will reflect this unique quality of being both universal, pertaining to the human being as such, and yet nongeneric-ontological. Accordingly, the language of redemption—forgiveness, peace, love, justice, reconciliation, and the like—is not simply interchangeable with the language of a philosophical anthropology and ethics—virtue, authentic existence, health, happiness.[16] Hence, the ecclesial universals of Christology, ecclesiology, theological ethics, and so on elude generic universality for this strange universality in sin and redemption.

I begin description of the third dimension of ecclesial universals with a straightforward affirmation. All ecclesial universals and therefore all theological judgments refer to the transcendent. The transcendent is a qualifier of, though not necessarily the direct content and theme of, all ecclesial universals. Some ecclesial universals do thematize the transcendent as God, yet all of them are indirectly "God-talk." The reason for this permeation of the transcendent into all ecclesial universals eludes direct formulation. It can be indicated, suggested, at the surface level, by discovering the transcendent as thematically present at every stage of faith's situation. The transcendent is present as a meant and striven-for reality in the resistances of the human being to death and violation. It is present in the act and structure of sin in the guise of a false transcendent, the false promise of the worldly entity made absolute. It is present in the experience and structure of redemption as the only presence capable of securing human being without violating its proper autonomy. Because of this thematic pervasion, all those linguistic units which persist from the prereflective faith-world and are discerned in their universal import refer to the transcendent.

---

16. This is not to say that the two are simply unrelated or dualistically present in the concrete human being. The redemptive pervasion of and transformation of generic-ontological human traits, the modification of nature by grace, is both possibility and desirability for ecclesial existence. But acknowledging this possibility does not mean that the ecclesial universal is identical with the generic universal.

And yet this *thematic* reference to the transcendent is only an externally perceived basis or reason. The apprehensions of faith are discernments, strange though they be, of how the world is. But we must keep reminding ourselves that the context of these discernments and of the theological reflection which they fund is not simply a persisting structure but an ever-moving horizon of redemptive activity which I have described as ecclesial process. Active and present in that process is the transcendent, and this is the deeper reason that the transcendent pervades all ecclesial universals. The universals are the forms in which ecclesial realities are present to the understanding and they give an account from within the social matrix of ecclesial process of how the world is in actuality and possibility.

The way in which the transcendent affects and qualifies ecclesial universals is even more elusive. Negatively expressed, the transcendent reference means that no ecclesial universal is an utterly literal, transparent, and direct expression.[17] It is, therefore, a misunderstanding to think that the problem of metaphor and analogy arises in theology only in the particular doctrinal locus on God. Because of the pervasive reference to the transcendent, every theological judgment has a certain opaqueness, or better, mystery. This is why the symbol of sin cannot be subsumed under moral evil, vice, and the like. As an ecclesial universal this act too is strange and mysterious, since it involves a transference and exchange between striving for the transcendent and the worldly environment. Because the transcendent is transcendent, it resists and eludes in its own special sense, encapsulation into language, and that gives all ecclesial universals their character of mystery.

These three features or dimensions disclose in part why the ecclesial universal is not exchangeable with other types of universals. These references all occur in the determinate symbolic world of ecclesial

17. There are those who would argue that there are no such expressions, that all reality language is inevitably metaphorical, since the density, complexity, and concreteness of reality can never be fully incarnated in words and expressions. Granting this point, I would nevertheless distinguish between language which expresses realities immediately and straightforwardly present to experience, language with ostensive experiential referents, and language which uses such referents to express realities that do not and perhaps cannot occur in ostensive manifestations. Pertinent here is Ricoeur's philosophy of metaphor which stresses the tension, the built-in ambiguity, the double reference to the literal and the new. See, for instance, "The Metaphorical Process," *Semeia* (Missoula: Scholar's Press, 1975), vol. 4.

existence but are directed beyond that world to the world as such as a problem and as an environment of redemption. They do purport to say how the world is, but they function this way only as they retain their distinctive references, not by translation into other modes of universality. To summarize, the ecclesial universal receives its strange universality partly from its global reference to the world environment as such, partly from the strange universality of sin which is a historical but not ontological or eidetic a priori, and partly from its reference to the mystery of the transcendent. This should make it clear that it is not simply the availability or nonavailability of contents which bestows uniqueness on these universals. It is not as if faith and theology are speaking about generic universals which have become universally inaccessible. Rather, the vision of ecclesial existence about how the world is simply evades and transcends the empirical and generic universals of both the sciences and ontology.

THE ECCLESIAL UNIVERSAL AS A DOCTRINALIZATION

If we left the matter as formulated above, it would still not be clear how the move from portraiture to judgment is a taking up of the question of truth in a new and special way. The three dimensions described previously indicate the distinctiveness of the ecclesial universal, but all three dimensions also characterize the primary symbols with which portraiture itself has to do. We recall our distinction between the idea-historical question of the nature of ecclesial existence and the question of truth. The transition to this question involves at least three minimal features: questioning through the symbol to grasp how the world is which is in some sense generalizable. I have proposed that this step to judgment is correlated with ecclesial universals whose universality is of a unique kind.

There is, however, a rather widespread approach to these matters which if followed would prevent the ecclesial universal from ever coming into view, keeping it buried in the symbol. This is the view that the *unit* with which faith and theology have to do in various stages of reflection is self-identical throughout these stages. The Hegelian view that sees theology as rendering the symbolic (metaphorical) contents of faith into a new form, the concept or proposition, is widespread. This approach tends to divide the theological community between those who think symbols and metaphors cannot be translated, for whom this enterprise is self-defeating, and those who think they can be. Behind this view is the hidden assumption that the concept or proposition as a translated entity is the result or product of theological work. The bearer of reality is the symbol and the proposition as a predicative form permits cognitive grasp of that symbol.

What this approach passes over is that each step of reflection (beliefful apprehension, historical portraits, understanding, prophetic insight) have correlative (noematic) referents. If this is the case, the symbol does not undergo translation into something else as a result of a reflective activity. Rather, the symbol is only one of several bearers or units of reality disclosure. To clarify this we return to the question of reality. If the symbol does bring to expression realities, how the world is, it is inevitable that these realities are linked in some way with the world structure and therefore with the universalities discerned in science, history, and ontology. But it is also the very nature of the symbol to hide this linkage. For example, if sin is a reality, it will be connected in some way with what human beings actually are and do, with the structure of the self and the structure of the community. But the symbol, sin, will not yield these connections because as a linguistic unit, it is correlative with the social process of a community. To function as symbol in that process, the symbol must be dominated by imagery (metaphors) and therefore must resist bringing to visibility its many discrete reality relations. Furthermore, the central function of that imagery is for the sake of the community's self-identity and duration and for the sake of redemptive transformation. Because of this primary function, the reality relations immanent in the symbol are obscured as the community uses the symbol in its activities of social duration.

Therefore, the exposure of the linkage of the symbol with world-structure requires a unit other than the symbol. The act in which this linkage becomes self-consciously possessed is understanding. The discrete activity of possessing it is the theological judgment. The unit correlative to this act and activity is the ecclesial universal. Viewed as a linguistic entity the ecclesial universal, like the symbol, is a human work, occurring historically in connection with a human community. On the other hand, also like the symbol, it has a prelinguistic counterpart that is not merely the product of reflection but is there to be discerned by reflection. For instance, if sin permeates the social involuntary, the structures of human institutions, then the way in which sin functions in social oppression, or the way the institutions function in the duration and causal efficacy of sin is something there to be discerned, not simply rendered into a new form of symbol by human reflection.

To pursue another example, the symbol God may include within it the image of world maker or creator. The truth of the image will not emerge in the postportraiture sense until the link between that image and world structure is discerned. If, in fact, world structure is something like the account given in process thought, a flow of events involving the prehension of eternal objects, the truth of the image of the world maker does not come forth until the function of God in that process is somehow discerned. Again, this is not simply rendering a symbol into a concept but discerning the link between symbolic content and world structure. And the unit which is so discerned is the ecclesial universal.

The ecclesial universal then is not an utterly occasional, momentary unit of meaning or truth. It has a historical character partly because world structure is continually evolving, epochal, and relative, and partly because the enterprises which discern world structures reflect human historicity. Yet because of the degree of generality and the duration of both symbolic contents and world structure, the units of their linkage do not come and go every instant. Hence, to grasp the sense in which sin pervades social realities is to grasp a perdurable feature of sin. It is because ecclesial universals have this generalized and perdurable character that they function in the *third* dimension of reflection in which the interpreter "looks through" them at contemporary situations and uncovers how the world now is and is occurring.

It may be clear by now that the term *ecclesial universal* is in some way parallel to what has traditionally been called doctrine. And the community's reflective discernment of the linkage between its symbols and world structures is a doctrinalization. Doctrinalization is not simply conceptualization, that is, translation into conceptual form; rather it is discernment of and expression of the connection between symbolic content and world structures. Such world structures occur over the whole spectrum of how the world is, from generic ontology to specific facticity. Thus, judgments which interrelate God and actual entities, sin and the structure of *Dasein* as care, or divine activity and the apparent randomness of molecular behavior, all exemplify doctrinalization. Doctrine, then, the ecclesial universal, is the unit both discerned and formulated, in the second dimension of theological reflection, the dimension of understanding and judgment. It is not translation of symbols *into* categories of world structure but a grasp of symbols in their world structural (human structural, historical structural, and so on) aspects.

14

The Making of Theological
Judgments

Up until now my preoccupation with the truth question in theology
has concentrated on the unit in which truth is self-consciously
grasped. This unit, the ecclesial universal, discloses the as-such and
transprovincial references of theological language. The next question
follows naturally. How is the ecclesial universal identified, discerned?
The question may be a misleading one. The ecclesial universal has the
character both of givenness and nongivenness. Because it does
express a real linkage between the primary symbol and world structures, it is a given and not simply the invention of the theologian. Yet
as a linguistic unit—a predication, for instance—it is something to be
formulated. We begin then with the already-thereness, the givenness
of the ecclesial universal.

Ecclesial universals are already there and in some sense precede
theological judgment as something to be discerned in two very
different modes, prereflective and reflective. They are present
prereflectively in the faith-world as the bearers of faith's apprehensions. It is the case that in this form their linguistic expression is not
that of a concept but of a primary symbol. To be sure, a primary
symbol (God, creation, sin, cross) may have universal references and
relations, but its linkage with world structures may not be explicit.
This linkage must accrue to primary symbols or they cannot function
in ecclesial process in such a way as to salvifically transform any and all
human social spaces. If there is no relation between the primary
symbol's references and how the world really is in both general

321

structure and discreteness, there is no way the symbol can be an agent of transformation except in the most accidental and arbitrary sense. But to repeat, faith's participation in the faith-world and the transformation of spaces and times may be an *intention* of relation to world structures, but this does not mean that the relation is visible and explicitly grasped. For this reason ecclesial universals (that aspect of primary symbols which expresses a connection with world structures) are present prereflectively in the faith-world, functioning as world-transforming agents, and in this sense they are given, already there to be discerned. And this prereflective presence is what grounds the possibility of their discernment in theological reflection. It is in this prereflective givenness that the general references toward which all ecclesial universals are ordered (the transcendent, world-totality, and sin-salvation) are discerned. Hence, these references are not the *result* of reflection but that which reflection inherits from the faith-world.

Yet the discernment of these universals is not simply an automatic product of acquaintance with the primary symbols of the faith-world. There is a second way in which ecclesial universals are already there to be discerned by theological judgment and this thereness is the result of the first dimension of reflection, theological portraiture. This calls for a more detailed formulation of theological portraiture as an initial and founding dimension of theological reflection. The first dimension, we recall, presents ecclesiality as both an actual corporate-historical existence and an ideality and entelechy toward possibilities beyond its past actualizations. What is uncovered then is not simply a collection of historical details, or even a series of historical epochs, but the unifying contours of a type of corporate existence. And while these contours do find institutional expression, ecclesiality itself names a corporate-historical existence with a specific mythos and symbolic universe. Thus the portrayal of ecclesiality is centrally though not exclusively a portrayal of a mythos. Its method is ideal-historical and what it portrays is a historical entity. At the same time, as a dimension of theological reflection which works within the faith-world, it intends the mythos and its elements as reality bearing and world trans-forming.

In other words, in theological portraiture the primary symbols that attend ecclesial process and salvific transformation are discerned at a historical reflective level. In portraiture they occur as units in the self's journey toward understanding. And this is a necessary condition for identifying the ecclesial universal. For in portraiture the primary symbols of ecclesiality are not only grasped in their overall symbolic setting, the mythos, and their interrelation to each other, but in their universal references as well. In other words, the three dimensions spoken of earlier come to light as the result of the ideal historical work of portraiture. This is not yet to relate these symbols to world structures, to grasp them in their explicit connections with such, but it is to uncover them as constitutive of ecclesiality which prepares the way for the discernments of the theological judgment. Accordingly, the universal references of the primary symbols may be uncovered by portraiture, but the formulation of these references remains determinate and provincial. For the question of portraiture is the determinate and historical question of what ecclesial existence is.

How does portraiture proceed in order to discern the mythos and symbolic universe of ecclesial existence? This question raises the set of issues which in the house of authority are virtually synonymous with theological method, namely, the function of the great collections that preserve the corporate memory of the ecclesial community. Chapter 12 described the nature of these literatures by way of their role in ecclesial process: the literatures of the faith of Israel, the Kerygma, and Interpretation. We now ask what is the proper use of these literatures in theological reflection? Because the more general issue is how portraiture retrieves candidates for ecclesial universals, the major thesis about these literatures is implied. The following two assertions summarize that thesis. First, at the prereflective, pretheological level of ecclesial process itself, these three literatures have proper functions of preserving the historical reality of ecclesial existence. In them the strange universality of ecclesiality, the structure and content of faith, the periods and branches of the empirical community, and the doctrinalizations of that community obtain linguistic expression and generation-bridging deposits. As these literatures function (ideally speaking) in liturgy, hymnody, teaching, and proclamation, the symbolic universe of ecclesial existence is carried forward as a continuing occasion of salvific transformation. Of course, this is an account of the function of these literatures at the level of ideality. The specific historical package in which this occurred was the house of authority according to which these literatures came to mean "authorities."

Second, while these literatures can and do have some function in all three dimensions of theological reflection, their central and decisive function occurs in the first dimension in theological portraiture. The reason is that it is in these literatures that the symbolic universe of ecclesial existence achieves its most comprehensive and enduring expression. These literatures make available ecclesial existence as a historical entity.

Because these literatures have a paramount place in portraiture, portraiture is the hermeneutic dimension of theological reflection. However, a cautionary remark is called for. The primary tendency of contemporary theological hermeneutics is to try to understand the usage and function of these literatures without portraiture at all. The theologian is depicted as working on these literatures conceived as collections of *texts* and attempting to evoke from them their reality references. Hence, the hermeneutic rules become rules for this evocation, this extracting from the text an enduring existential reference, a word of the text addressed to the individual interpreter.[1] If they are not construed as units of authority, the texts of these literatures can quite properly function for individuals in the everyday life situation of worship, piety, and prayer simply because at least some texts are "classic" expressions of primary symbols. In these situations the believer is tempted to construe the text as an a priori unit of truth if the portrait of ecclesial existence is in no way present as a third party besides the individual and text. But when we move to theological reflection, portraiture becomes that toward which texts are oriented. For ecclesial existence is what unifies these literatures and comes to expression in them. Because of this unity, these literatures are not simply aggregates of discrete units (texts). They concern each other as resources for portrayal. This is why any hermeneutic that omits portraiture and poses rules for the interpreter-text relation has retained vestiges of the house of authority. For it is the middle axioms of authority that justify seeing those literatures as collections of discrete and relevant texts. I would

---

1. Not only does the "new hermeneutic" of European theology fall within this approach but the recent hermeneutic writings of Paul Ricoeur remain in this framework. This may well be due to the influence of the new hermeneutic on Ricoeur's journey "from existential to the philosophy of language." *Philosophy Today*, 17, no. 2/4, pp. 88–97. In this article Ricoeur cites post-Bultmannian theologies as one of four major landmarks on this journey (p. 94). Ricoeur's individualistic orientation is apparent when he describes the individual submitting himself and his illusions to the world of the text. See "Philosophical Hermeneutics and Theological Hermeneutics," in *The Center for Hermeneutic Studies in Hellenistic and Modern Culture*, 17th Colloquy (Berkeley, 1975), p. 19. Such an individualistic and nonhistorical framework makes Ricoeur's hermeneutical program still a variation on "Cartesian" and romantic hermeneutics rather than an alternative.

contend that when the house of authority goes, what remains for theological reflection are not discrete texts with rules for their interpretation but literatures pertinent to the portrayal of ecclesial existence. Nor is this simply the historicism of the essence-of-Christianity movement, since ecclesial existence is already present prereflectively as the matrix of salvific transformation, and therefore reality- and faith-intentions attend the portrayal from the beginning.

These considerations indicate the real importance of portraiture and why it calls for a reflection beyond itself. The portrait shows forth primary symbols and their interrelations in a universal mythos. It brings into the foreground candidates for ecclesial universals. Discerning ecclesial universals, therefore, is not merely a speculative enterprise. As a historical task it is not an attempt to locate these universals in specific texts, terms, or happenings. How then does one go about locating in these literatures the candidates for ecclesial universals? The question is misunderstood if we assume that this activity is a creation out of nothing. There are hermeneutical clues operative in theological portraiture which prevent it from being at the mercy of ten thousand historical details. First, if ecclesial existence is in any way the prereflective matrix of theology, this means that in some sense salvific transformation of spaces and times continues to occur, and therefore something of the structure of ecclesial existence with its linguistic sedimentations is extant. In other words, the primary symbols and even some version of the mythos will have been gathered out of the plurality of historical details.

Second, if ecclesial *process* is underway, there will be some way in which faith, kerygma, and the subsequent traditions of interpretation will function in that process. And this function will not be through the quantity of discrete texts but by way of fundamental imagery: the Christ, hope, sin, God. If the underlying matrix is the experience of salvific transformation, then the primary images or symbols will already be intended as reality bearing by the theologian. In other words the theologian's world or context in which portraiture is attempted is not simply a plurality but a mythos, a world of primary symbols already graded in importance. This does not establish the symbols as "true," as universal in status, but it means that the theologian does not begin reflection with either a blank tablet or a mere aggregate of details. On the other hand we should not leave the impression that faith and the prereflective situation provide portraiture with a full set of criteria and guidelines in advance. The picture of ecclesial existence with its mythos is portraiture's task, not assumption. There is neither total clarity nor obscurity about the elements of that symbolic universe at the beginning of the task. Hence, the hermeneutic criteria, clues, and guidelines emerge with the task itself in a dialectical process.

A third clue is present when we recall that portraiture has an *ideal* element. Because it portrays ecclesial existence and because that existence itself occurs on a moving horizon never being completed and never coinciding perfectly with its historical actualizations, portraiture includes transactual elements of possibility. Idealities such as universality are responsible for the entelechaic aspect of existence. They lure the ecclesial community in some directions and not others. Therefore, given what ecclesial existence is in its very structures, it contradicts itself when it establishes racial and cultural conditions for salvation and divine presence and expresses itself when it actualizes itself toward new spaces, cultures, and situations without requiring such conditions. This ideal and entelechaic feature enters into hermeneutics as one of its guides and clues in using the three literatures to identify candidates for ecclesial universals. For this means that portraiture is not simply collecting historical information about or assembling the primary symbols of past periods of the actual community. Strictly speaking, the historian knows that the Mosaic Yahweh and the Yahweh of Second Isaiah are not identical, that, in fact, every linguistic sedimentation and symbol is strictly correlative to its historical context. At the same time, the community perpetually assessed itself and experienced its situation under primary symbols in their ideal status, symbols, and references which were obscurely grasped if at all. The portraitist is looking for dimensions and references of the symbolic universe of, for instance, the kerygma, which are "more" than explicitly intended, used, or understood by the community in which they occurred. For it is this "more" that indicates why the symbol is a candidate for an ecclesial universal and not simply an expression of a provincial situation in history.

We turn now to the three literatures themselves. I shall make no attempt at a theological hermeneutic itself but shall simply explore in a brief way the distinctive contributions of each to the discernment of ecclesial universals and the central hermeneutic problem portraiture faces in each literature.

The Kerygma, the literature of the initial transition to ecclesiality, has a certain primacy in relation to the other two literatures. Because it is, as a literature, an account by the ecclesial community itself of the events of transition to the new universal community and the nucleus figure of that transition, it contains in an explicit way the primary paradigm of ecclesiality, the paradigm of a strange, new universal availability of salvation. Portraiture cannot approach the other two literatures apart from this paradigm, hence, the paradigm of kerygma itself sets the interpretative standpoint of theological portraiture. This paradigm, present in such symbols as the kingdom of God and Jesus of Nazareth as the Christ, is a universalized mythos of salvation. The distinctive hermeneutic task this literature poses for theological portraiture is the discernment of this new, universal paradigm of salvation. And this, of course, involves an endless variety of specific tasks. For instance, what new primary symbols are introduced into the faith-world by this paradigm? What is the place of the nucleus figure, the Christ in this paradigm? Does the paradigm have elements of a new anthropology? What sort of community attends the universalizing of the conditions of salvation? These questions will be taken up from a historical base, that is, from the plurality of literatures and writings from within this literature and from the historical situation they represent. And this in turn generates the complex historical questions that recent generations of historians of early Christianity have struggled with: for example, the place of Jewish apocalypticism in the teaching of Jesus. It is only through such specific studies that the hermeneutical task of portraiture can be undertaken since the grasp of the new universal paradigm of salvation presupposes a hermeneutic distinction between the paradigm with its symbolic universe and the historical frameworks of Jewish and Hellenistic ethics, doctrines, and worldviews which are behind the plurality of expressions in this literature. It should be clear that without some understanding of this paradigm and its symbolic universe, the candidates for ecclesial universals cannot be identified. Their strange universality is due in part to this paradigm. I repeat, however, that the mode of this undertaking is ideal-historical. The paradigm is viewed as a distinctive *literature* expresses it, and, therefore, as it was attached to a specific time and language.

The literature of the faith of Israel offers the portraitist a very different hermeneutical problem. I have contended that this literature and the faith-world expressed in it is not simply a preceding antiquated phase of a later fulfillment, a law seeking fulfillment in Gospel. The only way teleology is retained in the view offered here is in the universalization of the mode of salvation to which kerygma testifies. Its contribution to portraiture is to express the symbolic universe of faith, a symbolic universe which constitutes ecclesial existence. Expressed in that literature is a vision of the human being trapped in a historical bondage of evil whose status is that of a corruption of an intrinsically good finite being and which situation is open to the transforming presence of the transcendent world maker. The transcendent, evil, justice, corporate salvation, and hope are all elements of this faith-world and they are just as immanent in ecclesia as a corporate historical existence as they were in Israel and Judaism.

And herewith is set the hermeneutic problem. The literature of that faith occurs in a territorial (landed) symbolism of divine presence where a universal element is implicitly present but not as the overall interpretative framework. The problem and task then for portraiture is, under the paradigm of universal salvation, to disengage the symbolic universe of faith from its territorial and landed meaning-framework. Obviously, this is not a purely historical-critical task. The historian's tendencies are all the other way, to ever more precisely locate the myths and symbols of a historic faith in specific historical contexts of situation, language, culture, author, and so on. Portraiture must begin there as it does with the Kerygma, but its aim is a disengagement. And the symbols of faith are disengageable only if their constitutive meaning is not exhausted by their territorial-landed setting and, therefore, only if they do have transterritorial references. Hence, as portraiture disengages the symbolic universe of faith, at the same time it apprehends that about the symbols which qualify them as ecclesial universals. Again, portraiture's work remains tied to the specific historical matrix with which it is concerned, in this case, Israel. It thus proposes the mythos and symbols, such as the Adamic myth, as having as-such and universal references, but does not attempt to expose the actual linkage to world structures which express that universality.

The third literature, Interpretation, presents portraiture with what seems to be a much more complex hermeneutical problem. As a literature it is not a single discrete collection, nor is it unified and bounded by a specific historical period of transition like the Kerygma or by the tradition of a single national people. Reflecting the universalization of salvation this literature embraces two thousand years of very different cultural settings, historical situations, nations, and epochs. It embraces different branches of the actual religious community. Occasional new symbolic elements appear in the course of development of this literature. The literature marks the community's unceasing attempts to formulate the Christian mythos at levels of belief, understanding, and even knowledge. Thus the literature has the character of doctrinalization. Even when its genre is biography or worship and prayer, it occurs in a framework when doctrines have become the units that carry the symbolic universe of ecclesiality. Furthermore, the doctrinalizations of most of this period occur within the house of authority. Hence, the doctrinalizations carry the status of a priori truth, engendering a built-in resistance to hermeneutical disengagement of symbols and doctrines. In the face of such a complex, the historian can only tremble at the prospect of portraiture making use of this literature. The task of tracking the debate concerning the meaning of *ousia* in third and fourth-century conciliar statements is complex enough. Portraiture from this total literature seems impossible.

And yet if portraiture is to be attempted at all, this literature is an unavoidable source. Ecclesiality as a *corporate historical* existence is spread out in time, and not identical with any one period or branch of the religious community including the period of the originating events of universalization. Attending its ever-new pervasion of spaces and times are potentially new insights into itself, new symbols, new doctrines. To portray its enduring contours, including the light and shadow of salvation and corruption, involves this historical reality in its temporal spread. And just as each of the other literatures poses a distinctive hermeneutical problem, so does the literature of Interpretation. This problem is not primarily a result of the historical variety and complexity of Interpretation. It arises from that which Interpretation is. For Interpretation as a literature receives its unity from the ongoing effort of the ecclesial community to understand the Christian mythos. Within the limits imposed by the way of authority, Interpretation reflects the continuing attempt to discern ecclesial universals. Therefore, it contains attempts to discover and set forth the linkage between the contents and symbols of ecclesiality and world structures as they are grasped in the sciences and philosophies of the time. In short, Interpretation as a literature has the character of doctrine and reflects doctrinalization. And this sets the distinctive hermeneutical problem in relation to it. For Interpretation's potential contribution to the ecclesial universal is in units which have already obtained the form of the ecclesial universal. The literature of Interpretation presents not just primary symbols such as sin but articulated relations between this primary symbol and world structure expressed in the *doctrine* of original sin. Portraiture, therefore, works with something which already has the form and character of the ecclesial universal it is attempting to identify. Furthermore, these doctrines, especially as they occur in branches of Christendom, come together as unitary expressions of the mythos as a whole. And the doctrines and myths as candidates to be ecclesial universals carry with them claims and arguments to that effect.

The hermeneutics of this literature must make several kinds of disengagements. First, it must disengage the doctrines and mythos from the house of authority. For theology cannot assess their candidacy as long as it gives them from the very beginning the a priori character of truth. Second, it must disengage them from strata of meaning and interpretative frameworks which depend on outmoded or discredited readings of world structures. For example, Platonic anthropology and pre-Copernican cosmology function as layers of meaning for eschatology and descriptions of human hope. Yet the doctrine itself may have insights not wholly dependent on these elements of *weltanschauung*.

Serving as guidelines for this work of disengagement and assessment are discernments into the structure of faith itself and the paradigm of universal salvation. In other words, hermeneutical work with the literature of Interpretation is not limited to criteria persisting from the prereflective world of faith but rather appropriately employs the discerned structures of ecclesial existence in the faith of Israel and Kerygma. The doctrines are thus submitted to the universal paradigm and their universal or antiuniversal import is tested. They are likewise submitted to the structure of the faith of Israel itself. The kerygma as a distinctive paradigm has a certain primacy and dominance over the other two literatures, which the very structure of ecclesial existence assigns. The faith of Israel has primacy as a cosmic myth of God and human being to which kerygma as a paradigm of the modality of salvation is subject. Both are potentially subject, though not in respect to their distinctive contributions, to ongoing doctrinalizations which articulate modes of understanding appropriate or inappropriate to faith and its universality.

Portraiture thus assembles sedimented symbols and doctrines from these three literatures, subjecting them to each other as is appropriate, to arrive at candidates for ecclesial universals. Insofar as it involves the third literature, Interpretation (doctrines), it is propounding insights that have attended former theological endeavors not only into the symbolic universe of ecclesia but the linkage between that and world structures.

FORMULATING THE ECCLESIAL UNIVERSAL: THEOLOGICAL JUDGMENT

Some recent theologies resist accounts of theology which retain the concept of theological judgment. The motives behind this resistance are praiseworthy for these theologies sense in the language of judgment scientific and objectifying modes of understanding which distort faith and its relations.[2] Furthermore, the judgment seems to be a literary unit which fences in and even captures its subject. The world of judgment is the world of the predicate, the assertion, the ostensive definition, the discrete object. We must acknowledge these warnings. On the other hand, the perils of theological understanding do not disappear with the eschewal of making judgments. Because of the strange dimensions of references of the ecclesial universal, all the appropriated linguistic helps, be they metaphors and stories or concepts and propositions, are placed under stress. In addition, when theological reflection occurs at all, judgments will be functioning at some level, even in the attempt to avoid them.[3] For theological reflection means more than simply historical portraits of a community of faith or personal existential appropriations expressed in personal and existential modes of discourse. The former alone is historicism and the latter pietism, and both, if they are driven by faith, mask discrete truth-intentions and claims about the relation between language and faith and how the world is. The fact that a symbol or narrative can be intertwined with one's own personal existence and story involves a claim even if it is unarticulated.

2. Three such works are John Dixon, *Art and the Religious Imagination* (New York: Seabury Press, 1978); Tom Driver, *Patterns of Grace* (San Francisco: Harper & Row, 1977); and John Dunne, *In Search for God in Time and Memory* (London: Macmillan & Co., 1967).

3. Wolfhart Pannenberg, strongly influenced by Anglo-Saxon empiricist philosophy, makes this same point of the inescapability of the judgment under the theme, the scientific status of propositions. *Theology and the Philosophy of Science* (London: Darton, Longman and Todd, 1976), pp. 326 ff.

Opposite to the pretension that theological judgment can and should be avoided is the view that makes theological judgments imitations of scientific judgments. When this is the case, theological judgment is seen as an explanation, and its structure is obtained from the move from hypothesis to verification. In this sense explanation can refer to any rational clarification and can occur in everyday life, in historical inquiry, even in philosophical reflection where it would mean "supplying the grounds for."[4] In a stricter sense and within the framework of natural and social sciences, the *explanandum*, that which is explained, is not just an entity or fact but something occurring in time, an event or happening. The eclipse of the moon, the Vietnam War, an hallucinatory episode all call for explanation. For this reason the explanation itself tends to have a causal element, the assigning of dependence of one occurrence in time to one or more earlier occurrences. This is why the route from hypothesis to verification attends explanation. In natural science, repeatability of results is required as verification or a generalizable causal pattern proposed by the hypothesis is not really established.

We can see that the move to theological judgment is not a move to explanation in this narrower sense. If theological judgment is a type of explanation at all, it is more the structural explanation of philosophy since the *explanandum* is not so much an event or occurrence as a type of situatedness in the world totality.[5]

And yet there are two senses in which the move to judgment may retain an etiological feature and the reference to causal explanation. First, because of the global dimension of ecclesial universals, theology has the world as its reference. We must acknowledge that theology's account of the human problematic focuses primarily on what appear to be structural features. For instance, Schleiermacher's notion of absolute dependence and Edwards's interpretation of human sin both concern perdurable structures. And yet the "structure" of historical existence, the context of all human life, has at the same time some causal efficacy. It is not only a structure but a power unleashed. The

4. See R. H. Weingartner's essay, "Historical Explanation," in *The Encyclopedia of Philosophy,* ed. Paul Edwards (London: Collier Macmillan, 1967), Vol. 4.

5. G. F. Woods, *Theological Explanation* (Welwyn, Eng.: J. Nisbet, 1958), is one of the few modern works in theology to retain the notion. To fill it out Woods offers his own revival of the natural theology tradition and describes Christianity or Christian theology as a defensible account of the world-whole when compared with rival accounts.

same could be said about the relation between the transcendent and the world. The transcendent in the Christian mythos is not merely a deep structure but a power with its own causal efficacy. Theology is reticent to formulate these relations in their causal efficacious dimension partly because of the easy relapse into mythical thinking and partly because it is a strange and elusive causality.

The second sense in which a causal element is present occurs especially in the third dimension of theological reflection, that dimension when one "looks through" ecclesial universals to uncover realities that are occurring in the present. In this interpretation of contemporary and discrete world situations, what are before us are political events, wars, trials, autobiographical situations, and the like. And when dimensions of these events are uncovered by viewing them through ecclesial universals, a causal connection is being assigned between the occurrence and the way the world is grasped in the ecclesial universal. Thus the universal structure of sin is discovered to be (causally) at work in political, racial, and sexist oppressions.

What, then, is the move from theological portraiture to theological judgment? We have said negatively that the structure of theological judgment is not primarily that of event-hypothesis-verification, although elements of causal efficacy are present in the Christian mythos. We can say, however, first of all that the theological judgment does retain general or formal features of judgments as such. Judgment, accordingly, is an activity in which something is affirmed or denied. In this act the person making the judgment is moving beyond mere images or contents to explicit interpretation of or claim about the contents attended by justifying reasons. Judgment is correlative with possible or intended evidence. The nature of this interpretation is that of a synthesis which connects the reference with something else—an attribute, an element in its setting, or another entity.[6] Thus the move to judgment means both a new level of cognition, a seeing into the reference, and a formulation of such in evidential mode.[7] Therefore, when we say that judgment is a constitutive feature of theology, we mean that theology *reviews the truth-intentions which attend*

6. Bernard Lonergan, *Verbum: Word and Idea in Aquinas* (Notre Dame: University of Notre Dame Press, 1967), pp. 59 ff.

7. I am making use here of Lonergan's very clear treatment of judgment in *Insight: A Study in Human Understanding* (New York: Philosophical Library, 1957), chap. 9.

faith as to their claims about how the world is and as to the evidence for those claims.

If judgment is an evidence-oriented and claim-making activity, the product and goal, at least of true judgment, is understanding. Understanding and the making of true judgments are correlative. Understanding in its full sense appears to have four moments or aspects. First, it is insight which attends the negative act of disengaging the reference in question from linguistic forms and categories and from worldviews and contexts inappropriate to or arbitrary to those references. Second, understanding means insight into the conditions of a reality's occurrence, and this can mean its historical origin, its ontological genesis, or its transcendental possibility. Third, understanding means grasping the matter at hand in its own interior constitutive structure, its aspects, their interrelationship, and their unity. Fourth, understanding means grasping the matter at hand in its place in its own "world," the environment proper to its being, function, and meaning, and also in its place in *the* world, the interrelationship between it and its "world" and other environments. These features of understanding disclose that understanding has a historical character. Correlated with the activity of making judgments, understanding resides in a continuing and never completed set of insights. Furthermore, different types of matters or references will evoke and require different emphases within these features. In the scheme of the present work, the archaeology of the house of authority displays an attempt to disengage ecclesial existence from a conceptual environment inappropriate to it. *Ecclesial Man* was an attempt to give an account of the "origin" of ecclesial existence in the sense of the matrix of its manifesting realities. It also included a brief account or portraiture of ecclesial existence in its aspects and unity. The present work offers a largely formal account of the relation between the faith-world and the larger environment.

The Problem of the Distinctiveness of the Theological Judgment

The course of the argument up to now is this: (1) Because of the truth-intentions of faith itself, ecclesial reflection (theology) cannot avoid the task of making judgments. (2) The general features of making judgments (conceptuality, evidentiality, understanding) persist in theological judgments. The references of all judgments have, accordingly, an as-such character, and theological judgments are no exception. In their own special way of describing how the world is, they lay claim to realities as such. And what gives this as-such character to the judgments is their concern with world structures, with persisting ways in which human beings are in the world and ways in which the world is a problem and a matrix of hope for human beings. (3) That which is discerned in the theological judgment is the ecclesial universal, a unity of truth which refers to world structure as discerned through the determinacy of the Christian mythos. To summarize the thesis of this chapter, the move to theological judgment is a *move from identifying potential candidates for ecclesial universals in their setting in ecclesial existence to a formulation (or abandonment) of these candidates as universals by uncovering their world structural (as suchness) elements*.

Manifest in this thesis is a version of that issue which structures most comprehensive theologies, the relation between the symbols and realities of the faith-world and the structure of being as such. This issue is present in the theological tradition in many forms: God and the world, faith (revelation) and reason, theology and metaphysics, symbol (*Vorstellung*) and concept (*Begriff*), Christ and culture. Further, the theological tradition offers several major ways of conceiving the relation. In Thomism and medieval theology, in which natural theology is very much operative, we have a part–whole approach in which reason goes so far in its apprehension of world structures and is then supplemented by revelation. The two are related to each other as supplementary avenues to reality and by the analogy of being. A second approach, one in the heritage of Kant and transcendental philosophy, begins in fundamental ontology of human being to uncover the need and possibility in human being for the faith-world.[8] A third approach recalls Hegel and contemporary hermeneutical and even analytic philosophies of religion. In this view the contents of the faith-world and of ontology are identical, but the forms of awareness

---

8. Karl Rahner's theology is an example of a transcendental program within the house of authority. That is, the structure of authority is retained and the dogmas which it yields, and each one is then probed for its transcendental conditions. See especially *Foundations of Christian Faith,* trans. W. V. Dych (New York: Seabury Press, 1976), where the themes of revelation, knowledge of God, sin, salvation, and Christology all have transcendental aspects. I am persuaded that Paul Tillich's method of correlation is within this tradition, that the dependent-interdependent question and answer is Tillich's version of relating the symbolic world of faith to transcendental conditions in the sense of an existentialist modification of Kant. If so, Tillich's method of correlation would be an example of a transcendental approach *outside* the house of authority.

and understanding differ. The faith-world comes to expression in the figure, a symbol, the metaphor, and calls for translation into forms of understanding. A refinement of this view acknowledges the autonomy and untranslatability of the metaphor and offers instead of translation hermeneutical uncovering of the metaphor's structure.

I offer this overly brief typology of selected ways of relating faith and world structure in order to clarify two issues which the present proposal attempts to resolve: (1) Are world structures to be regarded as *external* to the faith-world and its symbols and therefore as conditions of grasping the faith-world or states of affairs into which the faith-world matters can be translated? If so, world structure in the sense of something yielded by extra- or metatheological analysis (ontology) is the autonomous criterion for theological understanding. (2) Are faith-world and world structures (theology and ontology) terms from two different languages or avenues to express the *same* realities, thus posing a set of issues which concern epistemology, modes of understanding, uses and units of language, but in no way issues of being or reality? In the first alternative, world structures are the business of the sciences and philosophy, and the problem of theological judgment is to explore how the symbols, the portraiture of ecclesiality, are related thereto. In the second alternative, the same world structures are manifest in the faith-world, as in ontology, and the problem is to either translate the symbol into the concept or to coax the symbol into sharing its content.

The thesis I propose would avoid both of these alternatives. It has two parts. First, there is a distinctive ontological reality content in the faith-world and its symbols. The reason for this is that the world structures yielded by ontology are generic. Their as-suchness has to do with what is a priori to, constitutive of human being, process, world-occurrence, and so on. Faith and its reflective enterprise has to do with how the world is as it is opened up by the ecclesial universal. Second, the world structures are not something merely external to the faith-world. They are external only in the sense of generic predicates yielded by comprehensive ontological reflection. World structures thus are immanent in the experience and the language of the faith-world. Because faith-world realities and world structures are both distinguishable yet inseparable, the relation between theology and ontology cannot be simply translation of figures into concepts, either on the grounds that the reality content is identical or that it is grasped already by science and ontology.

From the Figure Through the Generic Universal
to the Ecclesial Universal

It should be clear from the preceding analysis why theological judgment is not simply a journey from the figure (symbol, metaphor) as yielded by portraiture to the universals of ontology. For although the universal of ontology, hereafter called generic universal, is comprehensive, it is not exhaustive. The sum total of generic universals does not amount to an exhaustive inventory of being but a generalized aspect of being. For this reason and because the figure or ecclesial universal itself has a distinctive reference, the making of a theological judgment cannot be simply a transition from the ecclesial universal to the generic universal. Because there is a distinctive as-suchness and universality immanent in the ecclesial universal itself, the task of theological judgment is to discern and formulate that immanent universality. How can this be done? We have criticized translation into the generic universal (generic hermeneutics). Its opposite (relevance hermeneutics) must also be avoided. That is the turn from ontology and generic universals to particulars and the view of theology as a journey from the figure to the particular. Translation is still the dominating model, but now one translates the figure (the symbol, the ecclesial universal) into the particularities of culture, human psychology, society, and the like—in other words into occasional, empirical, and cultural entities and realities. So goes the approach of the ever-popular relevance theologies. In rejecting this version of theological judgment, I do not want to suggest that ecclesial universals have no relation at all to the particular events and structures of human psychological and social life. Insight into that relation is in fact the task of the third dimension of theological reflection. Relevance hermeneutics omits the task of theological judgment in its rush to relate faith and world events. This move is premature because it ignores the ecclesial universal whose as-such and world structural element is that which discloses aspects of the determinate and the occasional which call for redemption. This is not to say that the world structural element is eternal, immutable, or unhistorical. Yet it is more enduring than an individual entity or a specific cultural predicate.

337

How then is the as-such or world structural element discerned and formulated? How can one discern a world structural, persisting element in the ecclesial universe which is neither a generic universal nor a particular? At this point we recall that if the realities immanent in the ecclesial universal are to endure at all, they must incorporate and instantiate universal features of reality. In other words, the realities grasped in ecclesial reflection, like all realities, are instantiations of generic universals. Thus, for instance, temporal process, vulnerability to change and demise, the capacity for response and adaptation which appear to characterize all living things also characterize human being. And they attend human being in distinctive ways, in modes of self-awareness, anxiety, and imagination. These are generic universals, that is, enduring features of a type and region of being. One way of discerning and exploring these features (existentials?) of human being is to see how these universals are modifications of universals which occur at more generic levels. For instance, temporality appears to be a comprehensive feature of all actuality but has a distinctive meaning as a feature of human being. The method of discernment which this suggests is the use of more general features of being as hermeneutical devices for exploring more determinate but still enduring modes or regions of being.

And this is the method we propose to discern and formulate the world structural content of the ecclesial universal. Generic universals can be employed as devices, even lenses, through which one can view the figure, the ecclesial universal, by means of which one can uncover the way that the generic universal has undergone modification in the ecclesial universal. When that modification is discerned, a world structural element of the ecclesial universal has come into view, something which gives the reference of the figure its enduring and as-such character and which is identical with neither the discoveries of fundamental ontology nor empirical science.

An example close at hand is sin as symbolized reality in the faith-world and as a candidate for the ecclesial universal. Translating this symbol into such concepts as anxiety, ignorance, or insecurity would replace its contents with the generic universals of philosophical anthropology. To translate it into psychopathology would replace its contents with the categoreal world of psychology. Thus proceeds relevance theology. However, an exploration of sin through the generic universal of intentionality would not mean translation of sin *into* intentionality. Rather, grasping the intentional structure of sin brings into view the peculiar intentional object and way of meaning the world involved in sin and therefore discloses the difference between sin and anxiety and sin and psychopathology. Yet what is discerned and formulated is nevertheless "how the world is," a world structural and enduring feature of human being, which is not a generic universal in the sense of something a priori to human being as such.

Here we have theological reflection making heuristic use of ontology in a way that does not violate the distinctiveness of the ecclesial universal and yet uncovers the world structural, as-such element, the feature which grounds the judgment as true. The journey, therefore, is from the figure through (by means of) the generic universal to the ecclesial universal. It should be clear from this that theology as "philosophical" is not simply an occasional hobby or idiosyncratic game. Accordingly, philosophy and other enterprises which discern generic universals (psychology, social sciences, and others) are intrinsic to theology.

The Nature of the Linkage Between the
Ecclesial Universal and the Generic Universal

The heuristic use of generic universals to uncover the world structural elements of the figures is only a very general account of theological judgment. What this means specifically depends on just how generic universals are linked to the ecclesial universals, how specifically they are incorporated. All that has been said is that these general features undergo modification in their instantiation in the faith-world. This means that the most general characteristic of the relation is that of analogy, because the generic feature, being present by modification, resembles but is not identical with itself in its generic sense. This could be said of the relation between generic universals and any situation of particularity. Does the faith-world give rise to some distinctive relationship between its realities and the general features of being? If so, that relationship will exercise a certain governance in the making of theological judgments. It would be unfortunate and misleading to put this question in such a way that two worlds, two realms, are indicated—that of the faith-world with its ecclesial universals and that of being with its generic universals. Theology and ontology are distinguishable enterprises of reflection and understanding and as such their cognitive environments, their references and realities, are not identical. But these references do not divide into two realms. Our problem then is not to formulate the relation between two side-by-side realms but to understand how generic universals persist, even if in modified form, in ecclesial universals. Or to express it differently, how do the world structures immanent in ecclesial universals reflect or mirror reality as it is discerned by ontology? To clarify this is to make a small step in indicating what gives theological judgment its evidential and as-such aspect.

The clue to the way in which the faith-world receives, instantiates, world structures is not present in ontology itself but in the comprehensive myth or story of creation and redemption which presides over ecclesial existence. The overall structure of the Christian mythos is the differentiation of transcendence and world process with the latter dependent on and subject in some way to the influence and creative power of the former. The result is that all being, that which is, which is actual, and has reality, is in itself proper and valid, having a proper and valid autonomy and self-originating powers.

We have here in this vision of world structure and world process as created being the first clue to the way world structures are immanent in the faith-world and its universals. With the exception of certain features of transcendence itself, the structure of this created, dependent, and proper being persists in everything with which theological reflection has to do. And this presence and persistence grounds the theological concern for how this world is, even as it grounds the reflective journey from the figure through the generic universal to the ecclesial universal.

Furthermore, the all-pervading presence of world structure as created and proper being means that ecclesial reflection views even the problematic character of human being, vulnerability, and sin, as built on or out of what is real and proper. Or, to express it in more classical terms, nothing that is, is in itself purely problematic or purely evil.

This motif has always been present in theology. More recently it has come to expression in what is called transcendental theology. The more Kantian form of transcendental theology, which tends to make primary the question of knowledge in theology, attempts to show that the structure of being grounds the (human) possibility of the knowledge of God, of true community, of salvation. Here the world structural element is resident in the ecclesial universal in the sense that a proper created being furnishes the ontological stratum presupposed by the primary symbols of the faith-world. A less Kantian form of this motif is the attempt on the part of correlation theology (such as Tillich) to avoid heteronomous or arbitrary relations between faith and reality. The focus here is not so much on being as the transcendental possibility of theological discernments as on theological realities pertaining to what is *constitutive* of (human) being. The Christian myth of creation and redemption dominates both forms insofar as they see the faith-world as built on and related to created being as proper and real.

But the Christian myth of creation and redemption is, as Ricoeur has pointed out, a theodicy myth. Thus its account of created being ascribes to that being vulnerability to the perils intrinsic to created being. In addition, it describes created being as possibly self-distorting and in fact self-distorted, not in the mode of fate but under the possibility and fact of redemption. This aspect of the myth adds a second feature of generic universals. Not only are they descriptions of created being, they attend realities which, because of their autonomy and self-determination, are subject to self-distortion. Thus, generic universals can and do occur in strata of created being that have undergone radical modification. Since the Adamic myth is our concern here, we especially have in mind the pervasive distortion of human historical being. And because generic universals are simply descriptions of realities at varying levels of generality, they are modified by whatever stratum or region they attend. Ontological anxiety as a universal attending human temporality in an insecure environment is structured by sin. We recall Kierkegaard's distinction at this point between anxiety as the presupposition of sin and anxiety as the consequence of sin.[9]

This presence by modification of generic universals in human, historical realities is the condition for the theological apprehension of the world structural elements in sin and redemption. For the realities set forth in the symbolism of sin and redemption are not intended as either a priori elements of created being or as utterly occasional occurrences. They are enduring realities of human, historical exis-

---

9. Søren Kierkegaard, *The Concept of Dread,* trans. W. Lowrie (Princeton: Princeton University Press, 1957), chaps. 1, 3, 4.

tence. The structures of world process (and therefore generic universals) are resident in them but not as mere abstract features of being as such. Rather, the openness of created being to self-distortion makes possible the presence of world structural elements in the mode of distortion. This is why ecclesial reflection, working under the myth of creation and redemption, can use generic universals to uncover and discern the world structural elements of the human, historical realities with which it is concerned.

No doubt there are philosophers, theologians, and social scientists who resist this whole line of inquiry. It may be, however, that the resistance is largely to the language, reminiscent of classical Western philosophy, of universals. It is important to clarify that we appropriate that language in order to avoid an utterly occasional and atomistic understanding of reality. Reality does not display itself as simply an aggregate of utterly distinctive atoms. It occurs in the mode of types, genera, and typicalities, which persist over periods of time, as continuities of types. And only the most extreme sort of idealism would explain those types totally by way of human epistemological requirements. We are using the term *generic universals* to express continuities, distinctive yet shared features, genera. And both natural and social science as well as ontology have to do with universals in this sense.

We are proposing a certain understanding of the relation of those universals to their concrete instantiations. Although it is a theological view, it has certain similarities to both Aristotle's criticism of what he understood to be Platonism and to Wittgenstein's critique of universals. These universals as *concepts* can be abstracted from their particulars for the sake of definition and analysis. But in their incarnate, instantiated state, they are open to influences. The incarnate typological, continuity aspect of the reality (and our primary example here is human being) is constantly affected by the determinacy itself, by its fragile, vulnerable condition, and even by distortion in the light of idealities. Aristotle and Wittgenstein are both correct in resisting an account which opposes unchangeable universals to changing particularities. In two senses, however, the "Platonic" view of unchanging universals must be retained. First, the universal as an abstracted *concept*, the unit of synthetic insight, does not change. Second, the instantiated universal retains features without which the reality is not what it is. Instantiation does not mean simply the loss or exchange of the universal's features. If that were the case, the universal (and the types and continuities) would disappear. And it is because of the features of the universal that reality can persist as types. For example, intentionality as a generic universal of human being itself has the constitutive feature of being an act of meaning which synthesizes the plural aspects of the object of experience into unified entities, such as chair, house, or person. As long as this universal is present, it will have this feature. What would we mean then in saying that it undergoes modification in its instantiated (rather than abstracted) state? The alternative to this view is the view which Aristotle and Wittgenstein oppose. According to this view the universal is so insulated from modification that the determinacy, fragility, and sin of the human being have no effect on the universal at all. The universal is thus something transcendent of human being, which suggests that the human being is composed of forms and matter sitting side by side. Such a view arises by permitting the cognizing, abstracting acts of apprehending, describing, and conceptualizing the universal to be all determinative. Ontologically speaking, the universals *are* the concrete human being as a distinguishable type and continuous reality. Human being's distinctive *historicity* requires universals in this sense. And if this is the case, the features of the universal will themselves take on features in instantiation. Thus, the abstracted concept of meaning as an essential feature of intentionality is an unchanging essence. The instantiated universal is, however, an activity of meaning and as such is an open field into which press all sorts of motivations, emotions, cultural legacies, and situationalities. Accordingly, it is correct to say that both the ancient Egyptians and contemporary Americans are in-the-world in the mode of intentionality and meaning activity. It would be incorrect to say that the intentionalities of these two historically different peoples were identical.

The primary point made in this philosophical analysis of the relation between generic universals and particulars is the openness of the instantiated universal to modification, and this itself is a generic insight. Our *theological* point is that this openness is one which reflects the determinacy, fragility, and sinfulness of the human being. At the same time it is also a field for redemptive modification and divine presence. And this is what grounds the theological discernment of a reality's redemptive possibilities. In more traditional language, it is the dimension of hope in theological reflection. According to this theological version of the relation, realities are redeemed not separately from what makes them types and gives them continuity (their generic universals) but *as* instantiated universals. For this reason it is not inappropriate to speak of fallen and redeemed intentionality, sexuality, masculinity, femininity, sociality, individual temporality, intersubjectivity, embodiment, linguisticality, and so on.

We return now to the theme of the chapter. We are arguing that theological judgments are "true" only if their claims can be grounded in as-such and world structural references. The myth of creation and redemption suggests three ways these references occur in the faith-world: (1) as the created reality presupposed by the theodicy myth itself and present in every faith-world reality both as the possibility of redemption and the reality behind the distortion; (2) as the distorted modifications of generic universals in sin; and (3) as a field open to redemption and divine presence.

I should clarify that this description of theological judgment is restricted to its most fundamental level, the level on which evidences occur more or less directly and world structural elements can be evoked by inquiry and presented to immediate insight. Much more complex is the question of judgments concerning appresented realities, realities such as the transcendent or the nucleus figure of ecclesial existence, the Christ.[10] Here the world structural elements which provide the judgment with evidential references are not directly present. I would still contend that these references are necessary whenever judgments are made, even in the case of appresentations. However, in that case certain manifest world structural elements would appresent as their required field of meaning other world structural elements.

10. For the appresented structure of faith's knowledge see Edward Farley, *Ecclesial Man* (Philadelphia: Fortress Press, 1975), chap. 9, sec. B.

The General Structure of
Social Duration

Parts 1 and 2 of the text attempted respectively an archaeological uncovering and criticism of the traditional presuppositional framework of theological judgment (the house of authority) and an ideal-theological recovery of ecclesial duration as the setting of that judgment. Both endeavors make use of but do not explicate an understanding of the general features and structures of social duration as such. The criticism argues that the Scripture principle violates that proper correlation between ecclesial duration and its vehicles (and their function). The recovery attempts to restore that proper correlation. In neither case is there any explication of the general relation between a distinctive historical community and the structures and realities required for its duration. Although the critical uncovering and recovering can be understood apart from such an explication, they will surely be clearer if a general account of social duration is attempted.

INTRODUCTION: ALTERNATIVE APPROACHES
TO THE PROBLEM

The term *structure* in the Appendix title may create the misleading impression that social duration is a matter of understanding how changeless entities, essences, or structures endure through time. This view would not be corrected if we surrounded the immutable core with changing processes to which it adapts but through which it persists. No actual human society has an immutable essence that endures, successfully resisting change by adopting different modes of appearance in altered historical situations. Social duration is itself a process, the structural aspects of which are certain continuities. These continuities enable us to differentiate one global society from another by grasping each one's distinctive structures, which in some sense persist over a period of time. But this persistence itself is an ever-adapting phenomenon and therefore a process. The concern of this Appendix is not so much with the adaptations and alterations but with the continuities, features, and vehicles. It should be clear, however, that such continuities are an abstract cross section of a larger entity (an actual society or community) which is itself in a constant, even if very slow, state of alteration. Nor should we see structure and process as simply alternative qualities of social entities. The *structural* or continuity aspect of a society must constantly change if it is to continue over time. Thus, without change and adaptation in new historical situations (such as the diaspora), Israel's continuity as a community of the Torah would have been severely threatened if not lost. Thus the vehicles of *continuity* must at the same time function as vehicles of adaptation and *innovation*.

A more serious ambiguity attends the term *social duration,* even as similar ambiguities characterize such terms as social time, social change, and the like. The ambiguity pertains to the sense in which "time" is being used, to the many different ways the problem can be formulated, and to the stratum or social entity to which the investigation pertains. When phenomenological anthropology provides the categories, social time tends to mean a social version of lived-time, a horizon of individual experience.[1] When sociology, even depth sociology in the tradition of Sorokin, speaks of social time, it differentiates it from biological, physical, or psychological time and propounds it as the temporal quality of social entity.[2]

Further, we find a multiplicity of ways of formulating and investigating the phenomenon of society in its temporal dimension, and most

---

1. Although Alfred Schutz does not use the term *social time*, he nevertheless describes the temporality of the social world of everyday life as a lived-time in the sense that that which structures the time of the social world, predecessors, contemporaries, consociates, and successors are present on the temporal horizon of the lived-experience of individuals.

2. Pitrim Sorokin, *Sociocultural Casuality, Space, Time* (Durham: Duke University Press, 1943), pp. 171 ff. When Sorokin discusses the three *planes* of social time, or the rate or flow of sociocultural time as even, interrupted, rapid, slow, or its finite divisibility into periods, he is speaking about temporality as a quality of human groups.

of these are not exclusive or competing but supplementary inquiries. Perhaps the most general approach is to focus on the dynamics (as over against statistics) of society as a whole.[3] A second approach focuses on the problem of generations, both in the sense of the typical development from an innovative generation to the fourth generation (Mariàs) and in the sense of the problem of how societies bridge generations and how to scientifically describe what a generation is (Mannheim).[4] A third approach, influenced primarily by Alfred Schutz and the literature of the sociology of knowledge, formulates social temporality as a matter of society's maintenance of its own world or social universe, and doing so by means of institutionalization and legitimation.[5] The older and more typical approach found in sociological literature lays emphasis on social change and social evolution, showing as a literature a curious lack of interest in social continuity and social identity. So vast is this literature that typologies of theories of social change are available.[6] A final approach to the problem is as much historical as sociological. It attempts to understand the major historical types of social duration from precivilization times to the present.[7] A variation on this approach is exemplified by Hannah Arendt who distinguishes between the premodern (Western Christian) mode of continuity comprised of tradition-authority-religion and the modern totalitarian systems in which that mode has been abolished.[8]

3. See Kenneth E. Boulding, *A Primer on Social Dynamics* (New York: Free Press, 1970), for a formulation so inclusive as to take up basic kinds of processes in history (teleological, mechanical, random, and so on), as well as general factors such as social exchange, productivity, and economic development.

4. See Julian Mariàs, *Generations: A Historical Method* (University: University of Alabama Press, 1970), and Karl Mannheim, "The Problem of Generations," in *Essays in the Sociology of Knowledge* (New York: Oxford University Press, 1952).

5. Peter L. Berger and Thomas Luckmann, *The Social Construction of Reality: A Treatise in the Sociology of Knowledge* (New York: Doubleday and Co., Anchor Books, 1967); and Peter L. Berger, *The Sacred Canopy* (Garden City, N.Y.: Doubleday and Co., 1967), chaps. 1 and 2.

6. See B. F. Ryan, *Social and Cultural Change* (New York: The Ronald Press Company, 1969); Robert A. Nisbet, *Social Change and History: Aspects of the Western Theory of Development* (New York: Oxford University Press, 1969); and J. A. Ponsioen, *The Analysis of Social Change Reconsidered* (Gravenhage: Mouton and Co., 1962).

7. See Margaret Mead, *Culture and Commitment* (New York: Natural History Press, 1970). She classifies types of cultural continuity into prefigurative, which models on the past; cofigurative, which models on contemporaries; and postfigurative, where the models seem to be lacking and discontinuity dominates.

8. Hannah Arendt, *Between Past and Future* (New York: Viking Press, 1968), chaps. 1 and 3.

The third ambiguity in the phrase social duration is rooted in the relativity of duration to the specific social entity or stratum within that entity. Does the inquiry concern *Gemeinschaft* or *Gesellschaft*? Are we talking about the duration of a global society such as a nation or a subgroup within such a group whose primary social relationship is face-to-face interaction? Are we talking about the duration of a political party, a religious denomination, a multinational corporation? Further, global societies and subgroups all have strata within them. Gurvitch finds a number of strata distributed between the surface, ecological level of a social entity where it interacts with its external environment, and deeper levels such as patterns present in organizations or collective attitudes.[9] Needless to say, a full account of social duration would treat both global and subglobal human groups as well as the different strata therein.

I mention these ambiguities in order to clarify the scope of this analysis of social duration. Obviously, that which prompts the inquiry in the first place, the social duration of a specific social entity, the ecclesial community, provides the principle for focus. Accordingly, I shall be concerned with social duration as it occurs in any identifiable, visible social grouping. On the other hand I shall not attempt to set forth a comprehensive description of all the features and processes involved in all the strata of a social entity. I shall concentrate instead on the depth (and most slow moving) level of duration, that in a social entity analogous to a "self," or the social entity considered as a social self. This focus is only in part based on my conviction that this level best exposes the distinctive duration of ecclesial existence. It is also based on the view that the *distinctiveness* of all human social duration lies exclusively at the depth level of intersubjective cointentions which occur under a dominant myth or paradigm and which determine how the past persists and the future is protended. An analogy taken from the way the human individual persists over time may be clarifying. A comprehensive description of that persistence would include, among other things, the duration-change of the physical organism at cellular and subcellular levels as well as patterns of observable behaviors. Yet that would not capture the distinctiveness of the human being's duration, missing as it does

9. Georges Gurvitch, *The Spectrum of Social Time* (Holland: D. Reidel, 1964), chap. 3.

the retentional-representional-protentional structure of time-consciousness. Something similar occurs in social duration since what
endures are human beings in interaction with each other.

THE CONDITIONS OF SOCIAL DURATION

I have attempted to narrow the problem of social duration to the
description of temporal processes of a social group. In the actual
description of this temporality (the following sections on the elements
and process of social duration), I set forth the features of the process
itself as they are distributed between objective and subjective poles,
followed by an account of the *vehicles* of social duration which turn out
to be social sedimentations, objects, institutions, and social activities.
At this point I would distinguish between the features of depth
temporality and their conditions. For the kinds of processes and
vehicles we find in social duration are possible only because the
human individual is the kind of being he or she is, a self-transcending,
embodied being whose experience is characterized by horizons of
lived-time and lived-space. Furthermore, a society's depth temporality
depends obviously on the society's very existence and therefore on all
the things the society does to survive successfully in its environment.
Finally, depth temporality's actual successful continuance is dependent on a great many complex "mechanics" of social maintenance. All
these are conditions of (depth) social duration in the sense that, apart
from them, it can never occur at all. Hence, prior to the direct
description of depth social temporality, I shall cursorily propose its
major types of conditions.

The Space-Time Horizons of Individual Experience

To propose individual human experience as one of the conditions
of social duration presupposes a major thesis which I want to argue
later, namely, that the human individual makes an indispensable
contribution to human social duration. This means, negatively, that
models of social duration (biological, physical-causal, mathematical)
which bypass the distinctive makeup and the contribution of the
individual are inadequate models. I shall postpone for now the
individual's actual contribution to social duration and shall begin with
the conditions of that contribution in the makeup of human being.

An extensive description of the distinctive makeup of the human being is neither possible nor appropriate here. That undertaking would be nothing less than a full-scale philosophical anthropology.[10] I shall focus briefly on four features of the human being which are especially pertinent as conditions of social duration. The first is that the human being experiences the world through acts of meaning. I say this with neither an idealist (world construction) nor realist (world reception) emphasis. This simply means that the human being is in the world by way of entertaining its objects through a variety of acts (perceiving, appreciating, making judgments, valuing, remembering, and so on), all of which attach significance to the objects as objects-in-their-setting. Because these entities are meant as *unities,* they are differentiated from other entities as types and can be selected by experience as important, perceived, peripheral, desired, and so on.

One kind of entity which all human beings apprehend in a specific kind of meaning-act is the other human being. However one solves the so-called problem of other minds, it is clear that human beings do in fact mean or intend each other as living, experiencing selves, and this results in the often-cited fact that human being is *intersubjective being,* living in a network of reciprocal intentions. It may even be argued that human beings are intersubjective before they are subjective, that their very individuality has intersubjectivity as its ontological matrix.[11]

A third constitutive feature of the human being which characterizes distinctive human experience and the human way of being in the world is that of *lived-time.* Lived-time is not merely world time according to which some objectively measured periods of time are experienced as passing faster or slower. In Calvin Schrag's language, lived-time is a horizon-form of world experience.[12] Negatively, this means it is not the *result* of the distancing act of objective measuring. Objective time is not a feature of experience at all. Rather, lived-time

10. See Michael Landmann, *Philosophical Anthropology* (Philadelphia: Westminster Press, 1974), for a summary of major types of philosophical anthropology. In the comprehensive sense the total corpus of writings of such philosophers as Sartre, Marcel, Jaspers, and Heidegger offer us a philosophical anthropology.

11. Maurice Merleau-Ponty, "The Child's Relation with Others," in *The Primacy of Perception* (Evanston: Northwestern University Press, 1964). See also Remy C. Kwant, *Encounter* (Pittsburgh: Duquesne University Press, 1960), chap. 2.

12. Calvin Schrag, *Experience and Being* (Evanston: Northwestern University Press, 1969), p. 56.

is the very structure of human consciousness as it experiences the world through retentions, presentations, and protentions. *All* experience has all three of these temporal dimensions, and because there is no objective limit of either retention or protention, relative as they are to the valuational posture of the human being, the metaphor *horizon* is an appropriate expression. Time-consciousness in this sense is one of the conditions of human imagination. Only because we can retain the past and protend the future we can live in the modes expressed by subjunctive moods and future perfect tenses, "if only it had happened thus," "if A occurs, B might come about," and "at that time I shall have done such and such." Hence, human beings can project intended goals of action, future states of affairs, idealities of past and future.

It is clear, however, that the retentions and protentions of lived-time are not simply acts of a disembodied temporal consciousness. They occur with reference to the here–there orientation established by the spatial embodiment of the self and to various locations in which the person was, might have been, wished it had been, hoped to be, and so on. The human being not only projects into the future any image of a musical concert he or she plans to attend but also its *place* even if it is only a typical place for that kind of event. *Lived-space* coordinated with lived-time is also a horizon of human experience.[13]

Universal Ecological Conditions of Social Duration

The social duration of a society reflects that society's attempt to survive. While it is true that the depth structures of social duration are conditions of any society's continuing existence, it is also true that these structures presuppose a society's successful struggle against internal and external threats.

Looked at in the most external way, that is, in modes of understanding that emphasize what the human being shares with animal life, two

---

13. Ibid., pp. 60 f. See also chap. 2, sec. 3, for an exceptionally clear portrayal of how lived-time and lived-space are coordinated. One of the few analyses of spatial sociality in coordination with temporality occurring in a theological work is Tom W. Boyd's *Contemporaneity and the Presence of Christ* (Nashville: Vanderbilt University, diss., 1973). Boyd studies this coordination in connection with a phenomenology of contemporaneity.

kinds of problems or areas of problems appear to be decisive. First, the human being is a mammal and primate and thus retains the primate's bisexual biological manner of perpetuating the species through sexual union, conception, and birth. Human society must so interact with its environment that this biological act of species transmission is not endangered. Further, human sociality is itself an environment in which mating continues to take place and the young are protected until maturity. Such things as the pollution of the natural environment which endangers the gene pool, societal chaos, or modes of sociality which reject mating altogether (such as the Shakers) endanger this condition.

Closely related to these biological requirements is the need of human society to be equipped to survive the challenge of its natural-social environment. Human societies must continue through all generations to locate sufficient food for survival and to persist in the face of catastrophic events of nature such as famine, plague, and other ecologically threatening changes in the environment. The *social* aspect of this challenge is intra- and intersocietal conflict. Thus from the dawn of civilization methods of warfare have been a component in almost all societies' struggle to perpetuate themselves.

Yet we only deal with very general and surface matters if we limit our account of ecological survival conditions to human biological transmission and struggle with the natural and social environment. Because of their temporal-spatial and imaginative way of being-in-the-world, human beings (and therefore their societies) anticipate future developments and produce means (tools, weapons, roads, and so on) to deal with them. So arises what Schutz calls the stock of knowledge which characterizes every society. Obviously, not all of the stock of knowledge is pertinent to survival, but much of it is. This means that a society not only must solve problems concerning food (plants, irrigation, fertilizing, and so on), but it must transmit the solutions over generations. It is at this point that society as a system of interrelated activities comes into view, society as composed of structures and processes as studied by sociologists and sociologists of knowledge. Thus to carry on warfare or to feed a rather large population requires processes and structures that involve the transmission of knowledge. These include the distribution of particular roles in the society, the accomplishment of communication, some regulation of explicit teaching and socializing processes in which knowledge is transmitted to the young, and symbolic legitimation of the goods of the society.[14]

The one distinction which has now emerged is between the bioecological conditions necessary for a society's survival and the patterns and processes which society originates in order to solve the problems of those conditions and to transmit that knowledge to subsequent generations. While both sets of conditions are necessary to the persistence of any society, they do not constitute the level of social duration which bears the society's distinctive temporality.

THE ELEMENTS OF SOCIAL DURATION

Having considered in the briefest way selected yet primary conditions of social duration, I turn now to the phenomenon itself. My concern is with society as a global unit but not viewed simply as a collection of empirically observable and quantifiable changes and processes. Like any real entity a society has a unity, and that unity is the *type* of unity it is because human beings and their distinctive way of being-in-the-world and relating to each other make up the society. In attempts to express this distinctive unity, philosophers and sociologists have used such terms as social self, collective unconscious, *Geist,* and *Weltanschauung.* I have no hesitation in using the term *social self* providing we understand its analogical nature.[15] In the strict sense of the word, a society is not a self nor does it have a self. It does not perpetuate acts of remembering, perceiving, anticipating, and so on in the concrete sense of processes of consciousness (*Erlebnisse*), or better, of experiencing. Mental acts and affectations attend or constitute the being of a human individual who is both an individual organism and a part of an intersubjective societal network. This network may well be a necessary condition of individuality and its

14. See Marion J. Levy, Jr., *The Structure of Society* (Princeton: Princeton University Press, 1952), chap. 4, for a list of functional requisites for any society's existence and persistence. See also Charles B. Loomis, *Social Systems: Essays on Their Persistence and Change* (London: D. Van Nostrand Co., Inc., 1960), for a similar listing of elemental processes and their correlative functional categories and elements which occur in any society.

15. For an exposition of this analogy see L. Gilkey, *Reaping the Whirlwind* (New York: Seabury Press, 1977), p. 40. Gilkey rejects the term *self* to interpret a society but does press the analogy of human being and social group quite far.

specific acts, but the network itself does not think, feel resentment, or suffer pain.[16]

On the other hand, many things characteristic of human society are closely analogous to the human self. The individual's continuity through time is unified in part by a relatively coherent value system, a dominant model and mindset. The past is present in the individual's memory in key turning-point events which stand out in the memory. The biographical past also is present by selectivity and interpretation in which the individual lets lie some things and resurrects others as his or her situation changes. Because the individual is embodied and spatial, the past is present as a past of spaces and places as well as events and time periods, and the future is protended and anticipated also in correlation with placed events. All these things we have observed about the persistence of the individual self have their counterparts in the society. For this reason I shall self-consciously employ the metaphor of the human self in the understanding of social duration.[17]

This metaphor is based on a real analogy between the human community and the individual human self. The analogy is only partly accounted for by the fact that individuals who have time and space as horizon forms of their experiences are the primary actors in the community. In addition, a society at its very foundation is not simply a collection of individuals but a *determinate intersubjectivity*.[18] More specifically, the depth stratum of a society is composed of individuals who are not only interacting with each other at behavioral and functional levels but who "mean" or intend each other in determinate ways. Constitutive for the very selves of these individuals are those

16. For the distinction between the personal and all collectivities, collective personalities, and so on see Nicolas Berdyaev, *Slavery and Freedom*, trans. R. M. French (New York: Charles Scribner's Sons, 1944), pp. 41–42.

17. Among philosophers and sociologists of the recent past, two especially have offered insightful formulations which find some parallel between the unity of an enduring society and the unity of an enduring individual person. See Josiah Royce's *The Problem of Christianity* (Chicago: Henry Regnery, Gateway Edition, 1968), vol. I, chap. 2, "The Idea of the Universal Community." In addition Karl Mannheim speaks about social remembering and forgetting, about both conscious and unconscious modes of the past's persistence into the present, and about an entelechy of a particular generation. See Karl Mannheim, *Essays in the Sociology of Knowledge* (New York: Oxford University Press, 1952), chap. 7.

18. I have described determinate subjectivity in a fairly extensive way in *Ecclesial Man*, pp. 93 ff.

reciprocal intentions or acts of meaning in which they are for each other male and female, establishment members or outsiders, anonymous passersby or friends. Constitutive for the society is this intersubjective network carried by language and surfacing in behaviors, typifications, and role assignments. A society, accordingly, has what might be called both subjective and objective poles.[19] Subjectively, a society is composed of individuals whose distinctive way of being-in-the-world founds a distinctive kind of sociality. In this sense society originates in certain capacities and distinctivenesses of the human being. At the same time a society is a preindividual, pregiven system of language, symbols, roles, institutions, and depth cointentions on which the individual draws to interpret himself or herself or the world. In this sense the individual originates in society. It is this polar structure of society that accounts for a society's resemblance to a self and for the presence of the distinctive spatiality and temporality (including memory) which resemble individual consciousness. This is the basis for the analogy and its metaphor, the social self. I shall, therefore, describe the process of social duration by distinguishing between the process viewed as a preindividual and objective matrix and also as something to which the individual contributes.

The Role of a Unifying Paradigm

The many possible ways of ordering the elements of social duration are overwhelming, and none of them is without its problems. Is it best to develop the themes in historical order beginning with a founding generation, or to present an ontology in which one traces each stratum

19. This language is explicitly the organizing structure of Berger and Luckmann's *The Social Construction of Reality*. After establishing "everyday life" as the matrix of knowledge, the authors investigate society as an objective reality, thus treating themes of institutionalization, legitimation, and then society as a *subjective* reality, in which are discussed themes of socialization and internalization. The primary origin of this polar analysis of society is Alfred Schutz's life-long investigation of the social world. Inheriting the problem from Max Weber of how a (social) *science* could investigate a realm that is not objectifiable since part of that realm is composed of actors, subjects, perpetrators of meaningful action, Schutz's thought attempts to put together in a coherent theory a view of the social world which does justice to such individual and personal contributions to sociality as typifying, experiencing through appresentation, experiencing by gradations of relevance, and also to the sedimented products of such which function as the stock of knowledge at hand, the symbolic structure, and the like. Schutz's articulation is not typically that of subjective and objective poles of society, but the Berger–Luckmann language does not do violence to his thought at this point.

of elements to its underlying presupposed stratum, or simply to set forth elements without consideration of order at all? What follows is a compromise, a combination of ontology and historical dependences. Four themes enter into this morphology of social duration. The first three, the dominant paradigm, the contribution of individual cointentions, and the development of vehicles of duration and transmission, suggest a loose sequential order, especially in the founding period of a society. That is, a new dominating paradigm tends to be responsible for new ways individuals come together into a community with new ways of meaning each other, and only after this does the new community develop institutions of survival and maintenance. All three together are presupposed by and are elements in social process itself which I take up as a fourth theme. One might say, then, that the first three themes are unified as elements of a developing new mode of social existence and also by serving as constitutive elements in social process. Thus, the relationship between the first three sections and the fourth section is not sequential. The fourth section simply attends to an already existing society in duration and attempts a direct description, drawing on the presupposed elements of the first three sections.

Any description of social duration or the depth temporality of the social self would make a false start if it attempted to go directly to the society's past, present, and future. It is true that the past does persist in the collective memory of a society and the future is anticipated in some way. Yet what persists is not the total past of the universe or even the society's total past. Nor is the anticipated future one of an infinite and ungraded number of possibilities. The past of any society persists into the present in a very determinate way, a particular set or stratum of remembered events and persons. Likewise, the future is anticipated in determinate ways. Generally speaking, we would be correct in saying that the particularity of the society's past and future is based on the kind of society we are talking about, and that means in part its basic value structure, its characteristic activities which reflect its aims as a society. Yet we are still pushed one step farther. A society's values and aims are not mere isolated pluralities. They tend to have a unity. Further, the values and aims of a society are located not merely in behaviors or even emotions but in the language and especially the recurrent (or continuing) symbols. And what unifies this plurality of values, aims, and priorities, deposited in language and symbol, is what might be called the society's unifying myth, model, *Weltanschauung,* or paradigm.[20]

At this point I grope for adequate terminology. None of these terms just mentioned is really suitable. The point is that every human society has its own distinctive way of interpreting reality and understanding itself. This may be more apparent in ancient tribal types of communities and also in the early civilizations of Egypt, Sumer, Peru, and China, than in the present highly pluralistic, technological societies. It may be, as some suggest, that a distinguishing mark of modern societies is the absence of a unifying myth or paradigm. Yet Russia, mainland China, and the United States, as well as all third world nations, possess a unifying paradigm in the sense of an overall interpretation of reality. In many of these cases the paradigm is rapidly changing due to the nation's transition from a pre-Communist to a Communist universe with a resulting mixture of the two, as in China. The clearest instance of a global group floundering in a pluralism devoid of a unifying paradigm is surely the United States. Yet even here a kind of civil religion keeps alive the dream of the new land, with attendant ideals of individual freedom and equal opportunity.

My point is that the past does not simply persist but persists in a particular way or in particularities of social memory under a dominating paradigm or reality-view. And it is this paradigm which is at work when the society remembers one part of its past and not another, when it focuses more on the past than on the future or vice versa, when its future expectation has the character of anticipation of a cyclical return of the past rather than steady progress.

When we look at these global, dominating paradigms of various societies, we find in most cases some relation between the paradigm or model and the *origin* of the society. It may be too strong to affirm an a priori relationship between a society's origin (or originating event) and its dominant myth, yet the relation seems to be a universal one, which includes not only primitive societies and the great ancient

20. Ernst Troeltsch uses the term *principle* in this same way when he speaks of a society's "religious principle." See his essay, "Religious Principle," in J. Pelikan, ed., *Twentieth Century Theology in the Making* (New York: Harper & Row, 1970), vol. II.

civilizations but contemporary nations or political systems. The theoretical and activist founders of the Russian and Chinese Communist revolutions are related to the overarching myths or reality-universes of these nations even as Abraham's migration and Moses and the Exodus play a role in the Jewish paradigm of self-understanding. Even though the societies' actual origins are part of the lost past in many myth-oriented societies, these societies still understand themselves and maintain their reality-universe by theogonic myths and stories of totemistic ancestors. Later I want to inquire further into the way the memory of origin engenders vehicles or bearers of social duration.

The Contribution of the Individual:
Cointending Under the Dominant Paradigm

It would be proper to say that human beings are the authors of paradigms and not the other way around. On the other hand, human beings are brought together by and under comprehensive paradigms which give expression to their reality universe. The paradigm does not, of course, occur de novo without sociocultural background. Yet if we focus on a society at the point of its origin, it seems that the paradigm, the new experience of and interpretation of reality, is that which produces gradually a new intersubjectivity. It is not the case that individuals first discover a new intersubjectivity and then extract from it a controlling myth or paradigm.[21] Under the paradigm (the Adamic myth, the Gospel, the Four Noble Truths, the Communist Manifesto), human beings begin to "mean" each other in different ways, as sinners, as good, as sufferers, as oppressed, as ordered toward the state. These prereflective reciprocal acts of meaning we shall call the cointentions of a society, and it is these acts that altogether comprise the society's specific intersubjectivity. Since my thesis is that these cointentionalities play a major role in any society's duration, its distinctive social space and social temporality, the task now is to

21. This may appear to contradict a basic thesis of *Ecclesial Man*, namely, that individuals apprehend the symbols and realities of the community of faith by means of participation in its determinate intersubjectivity. If that which presents itself is the already existing community, such an order seems correct. The point here is that determinate intersubjectivity with its many ways in which human beings mean and relate to each other is originally produced by a new paradigm for reality.

inquire how it is that cointentionalities of individuals function in the founding of a society's social duration.[22]

In treating the conditions of social duration I argued the general thesis that without the individual's experiential structure of lived-space and lived-time, social duration would not be possible. The present inquiry goes farther. The problem is how individuals under a dominant paradigm constitute or intend each other in such a way that they come to have a common past and future.[23] This problem does not presuppose the idealist view that individual consciousness is immediate and social being is problematic, thus setting the task of showing how social being is produced by individuals. The phenomenon before us is already a social one. What I am trying to understand is how the individuals who participate in the social reality come to have a common past and future. Nor is the "come to have" meant chronologically. What may appear to be sequential stages are not meant as such. If there is any order at all among the elements of the analysis, it is the logical and ontological dependence of one act of meaning on another.

I begin with the fact that an individual's actual existence comes to be unified and lived under the society's paradigm. This does not mean simply belief *in* the paradigm but a participation in the reality or realities expressed in the paradigm. In the case of the ecclesial paradigm, that reality is corporate redemptive existence. Sharing in the paradigm or its reality means self-meaning and meaning the other according to the basic elements of the paradigm. We should remind ourselves at this point that the paradigm we are talking about is not simply directed at the biography of an individual. Since it is a societal phenomenon which is before us, it is the paradigm under which that society lives.

Assuming that we have in fact a society composed of individuals

22. Reciprocal or cointentions should not be confused with Schutz's typifications. Although cointentionality is not explicitly a Husserlian term, it does presuppose Husserl's notion of preconscious meaning-acts and it does apply to the intersubjectivity constitutive of a determinate kind of corporate entity. Typifications are more tied to the visible acts and roles of the social world, and their rootage is specific patterns of experience which lead the typifier to expect certain behaviors and responses.
23. Royce's view is similar. He, too, is describing social being arising out of the individual's idealizing extension of the self into the past and future. *The Problem of Christianity*, vol. II, chap. 9, "The Community and the Time Process."

who share a common paradigm and reality, how is it that the commonality of such individuals is a temporal one, a sharing of past and future? One obvious and yet surface-level answer is that a society's paradigm will contain symbols and stories which not only carry the society's aims but also relate its origin, its past history, its outstanding events and personages. To be part of a society and to be aware of its paradigm will mean also to share in the society's stories about its past. What we have so far is simply a collection of individuals who have inherited the way the society remembers itself. Let us grant this empirical fact but move deeper to discover what it involves.

I submit that certain meaning-acts occur under the paradigm which express both subjective and intersubjective intentions. Looked at individually or subjectively the effect of the paradigm on an individual is to provide a framework of self-interpretation which reaches beyond the lived-space of the individual and beyond the lived-time of his or her biographical reach between birth and death. The paradigm and the society under the paradigm create a space far broader than simply the "here" established by the lived-body of the individual. Rather than being abolished, the individual's bodily "here" (place) is extended to mean the "here" (space) of the society, a here that includes the fellow members of the society distinguished from nonfellow members. These may or may not be face-to-face related fellow members. The here can be as narrow as a ghetto, as small as a tribe, as broad as a nation or international organization. The extension of the framework of self-interpretation also reaches beyond the bounds of one's own biographical life to include events, persons, even epochs which preceded the self's birth and outcomes which will succeed its death. This is simply a more detailed specification of what it means to say that an individual constitutes himself or herself in distinctive acts of meaning that attend participation in a specific society.

The intersubjective side refers to individuals in the society meaning or responding to each other according to the ruling paradigm. The foundational act of meaning (bypassing at this time the more universal reciprocal acts of meaning in which human beings intend each other as human) is simply meaning the other as sharing the paradigm and the realities it expresses. The other's existence is meant as like one's own, as in some sense concretized, unified, and transformed by the paradigm. If Royce had used the phenomenological concept of intentionality to express his own favorite theme, he would have said that the members of a community mean each other as *loyal* to the community.[24] Switching to the language of Schutz, we would say that the members direct typifications and expectations of community loyalty to each other. These acts of meaning involve both spatial and temporal references. Spatially, the other is meant as sharing my "here," the here of the society, which means the *kind* of space it is (migratory, national, ghetto, or other). For example, ghetto blacks will mean each other as occupying a social here and there which is the *here* of the confined and impoverished space as distinct from the *there* space of opportunity, resources, and power where the confiners reside.

Temporally, I constitute the other in the transbiographical mode of one whose being is oriented to the same events, epochs, and persons of the past that are determinative for my being. The other is meant as one who shares with me the same portion or route of events. Thus, Jews intend each other as having a past in which Abraham, the Exodus, the destruction of the temple, and the holocaust are decisive. Further, I mean the other as transcending the biographical limit toward the future by sharing in common expectations. While it may be said that at certain points Jews have a common empirical past (such as the holocaust), we cannot say they share the same empirical future since the future is a region of possibility. At the same time the future means for specific societies not mere mathematical possibilities, an ungraded infinite realm, but specific projects correlated with the society's paradigm. Hence, fellow members mean each other as sharing possible but determinate future outcomes. Needless to say all these acts of meaning, spatial, temporal-past, and temporal-future, establish and preside over the actual activities of the society.

In this section the focus has been on the cointendings or acts of meaning under the dominant paradigm in which the individuals come to share a common or societal space and time. The examples show that these cointendings, these ways of having a common space, past, and future, are specific and determinate. The paradigm itself

24. Josiah Royce, *The Sources of Religious Insight* (Edinburgh: T. & T. Clarke, 1912), pt. 5. See also *The Philosophy of Loyalty* (New York: Macmillan Co., 1908).

and the type of society it expresses are determinate. Hence, the common space is *this* space, the space of a tribe, or nation, or religious faith. The past is *this* past, the specific origin and decisive events and persons of that space. The future is *this* future with its projected outcomes. What this describes is not social duration itself but one aspect of it, the continuity aspect, the *what* that endures and changes. I turn now to a third feature of social duration, the means through which the society bridges generations, the bearers or vehicles of continuity.

The Vehicles of Social Duration

I am still not prepared to enter into a direct description of the actual process of social duration. I have been describing the elements of that process, a unifying societal paradigm, meaning-acts in which individuals comprehend each other in a common social space and social time. A third element goes beyond the level of meaning-acts between individuals. An actual society is far more than a collection of individuals meaning each other *as* this or that. These acts of meaning which persist in and structure relationships and responses are units of a society's continuity but they do not indicate how that continuity is maintained. Maintenance occurs more on the level of a society acting as a whole like a social self. Here we have something not simply dependent on whether this or that individual engages in certain acts of meaning. A transindividual social reality has arisen with institutions, repeated activities, and deposits of language. At the depth level of that society's continuity is its intersubjective network of meaning activities, but the means through which this occurs are the society's "self-conscious" attempts to survive as a society. If it is a new or founding generation, it needs more than a new distinctive space and time. It requires organization, institutions, and activities which perpetuate its space and time across the generations. These "means" of duration I am calling, following Sorokin, vehicles of social duration.[25]

To express the distinction in a slightly different way, the duration of a society is more than simply the duration into the present of an intersubjectively held common space and time. Social duration means

25. Pitrim A. Sorokin, *Society, Culture and Personality: Their Structure and Dynamics* (New York: Harper & Brothers, 1947), chap. 22.

that a society has not forgotten or lost its past due to indifference but that some stratum of its past continues to be remembered and revivified and this is part of the society's present. How does this happen? Granting that a society is not literally a self, how does it "remember" its past? The existence of distinctive cointentionalities does not answer the question. The persistence or "remembering" of those cointentionalities requires a bridging of generations of individuals whose individual memories are therefore lost. Hence, society must discover a way for its intersubjectively accomplished space and time to obtain generation-bridging vehicles. Unless that happens the cointentionalities of the first or founding generation will die with its members. To repeat the definition, the vehicles of social duration are the means through which the society's depth temporality bridges the generations. There seem to be two basic types of vehicles of duration: *activities* and *sedimentations,* and both possess transindividual structures and patterns (an objective pole) and individual contributions (a subjective pole).

Vehicles as Sedimentations

The distinction between activities and sedimentations as vehicles of social duration may be a forced one. I make it in order to call attention to vehicles that are primarily processes and vehicles that are primarily structures. But no concrete example is available that is totally the one or the other. Activities and sedimentations interact with each other and presuppose each other. The term *sedimentation* can refer to a feature of individual time-consciousness in which past dispersed experiences accumulate in units of feeling or memory thus disposing the self toward the future. I am speaking here of an analogous feature of the social self, social sedimentation, in which the past not only accumulates but does so by being deposited in entities in the society which have some duration. Historical analysis of what occurs between the first or founding generation of a historical innovation and its successor generation discloses clearly the initial sedimentations of what is originated. Only if this occurs will the innovation survive the first generation. Several kinds of sedimentation seem always present in the social duration of a society.

The most basic sedimentations are *linguistic.* It is one thing for new experiences to occur involving new insights or reality-apprehensions.

While experience and insight themselves are rarely if ever nonlinguistic, they may occur in an inherited framework and language. To capture the *innovation* in language which breaks with older linguistic sedimentations is an enormous task and accomplishment. The same words may be used but with altered meanings. Symbols will arise which synthesize elements of the new paradigm. Stories, parables, and metaphors may arise which become deposits of the new reality. All the other sedimentations (as well as activities) presuppose these initial sedimentations.

A second kind of sedimentation is that of the *social institution.* Human beings are not only linguistic but institutional. Yet institutions are enduring patterns or structures of human activities which persist over time in spite of changing individual membership and which themselves take on symbolic significance. Although the nature and purpose of the institution is to give some permanent status to a human enterprise or dimension of experience (making war, sexuality, education, leisure, and so on), and thus is ordered toward and subject to that enterprise, it can obtain an autonomy and objectivity of its own. Accordingly, a nation or state may express and protect certain values and, because of that function, become itself a value to be symbolized and protected. Thus institutions are generated which are ordered toward the state itself (patriotic groups, military institutions). Institutions are not mere structures, composed as they are of human beings. Individuals can and do contribute to institutions by fulfilling roles of distributed assignments, and, as charismatic leaders they can alter institutions.

A third kind of sedimentation which carries forward social duration and bridges generations is the deposit of the past in visible, space-time objects. Although human activities are involved in making and maintaining these objects, they do not comprise them. I have in mind here everything from cave paintings, amulets, and ritual objects of primitive societies to the massive architectural structures and computer storage of modern societies. While some of these may themselves be visible symbols (a totem pole), most are in some sense deposits of language. We have, therefore, in the sacred writings of a religious community a secondary sedimentation. The initial sedimentation occurred when the paradigm found expression in narrative, metaphor, and wisdom saying, such as in oral tradition or oral kerygma. The secondary sedimentation occurred when the initial sedimentation, usually in connection with some role in the cult itself, was reduced to writing (such as the Gospels).[26]

Vehicles and Activities

More is involved in a social unit's duration than simply sedimentations of its paradigm, its cointentionalities of space and time. Human beings preside over the sedimented deposits of language, institutions, and artifacts. Social duration, in addition to being the sedimented persistence of an entity, thing, or structure over time, is also an *activity* of transmission. Because of human mortality and the succession of generations, this involves a transmission to the young. Margaret Mead has rightly pointed out that such transmission occurs at both conscious and deliberate (teaching-learning) and preconscious (empathy, imitation) levels of socialization.[27] Important in both are a society's activities in which transmission occurs. To generalize, perhaps outrageously, ritual activity appears to dominate premodern cultures and educational activities modern cultures, although both ritualistic and educative activities occur in some sense throughout human history.

Transmittable activities like sedimentations fall into basic forms. One form is correlated with the institutions of the group which function as bearers of continuity. When we look at those institutions as processes and not just as structures, we find them to be routinizations of human life. The paradigm, the cointentionalities, are remembered and transmitted through repeated, routine, ritualized activities, and these are present whether a society is religious or secular.

In addition to routine and ritual activities, human social duration involves interpretative activities. The initial accomplishment of the sedimentation of a society's experience and paradigm was itself an interpretative act as was its secondary sedimentation (if it occurred) into writings. The objectified sedimentations persist in a human group not simply in a vacuum but as entities with significance: for

---

26. Granting that Geiselmann's description of the origin of the Christian tradition or *paradosis* occurs at a more specific level than this analysis, it aptly exemplifies this point. He describes the apostolic *paradosis* as funding units of transmission, thus obtaining a deposit or *paratheke*, first in the form of a living kerygma and then in the form of writings. Both the oral and written *paratheke* precede what he calls the ecclesiastical *paradosis* where the writings take on the status of Scripture and an interpretative institution arises. See J. R. Geiselmann, *The Meaning of Tradition* (London: Burns and Oates, 1956), p. 12.

27. Margaret Mead, *Communities in Cultural Evolution* (New Haven: Yale University Press, 1964), chaps. 3–5.

instance, a sacred tomb, a sacred writing, a preserved battlefield, a graveyard with monuments. These exist for the members of society through interpretative acts, some deliberately educational, some not. And as the society changes under external or internal duress, the interpretation is reinterpreted.

To summarize, the vehicles of social duration are both enduring sedimentations and activities which function to transmit the depth cointentionalities and the unifying paradigm from generation to generation. There is an *ideal* correlation between the kind of social group (the specific unifying paradigm, the specific space and time) and the kind of vehicles appropriate to its duration. Thus a modern state would not put forth vehicular activities such as rituals designed to recreate the world and which presuppose mythic space and time. While such an ideal correlation can be uncovered by phenomenological and descriptive analysis, and can serve as a criterion of a group's assessment of its own vehicles, an actual historical society is not an "ideal" entity. Like human beings themselves it can generate incoherences, contradictions among the elements of its duration, and it may not obtain the ideal correspondence between its own paradigm and its vehicles. The classical Christian criteriology is a case in point.

The Role of Remembered Origins in Social Duration

How a group's origin functions as an element in its social duration is an extremely complex matter. The a priori status of remembered origin in a society's duration is difficult to establish. Although almost all societies and social groups have some version of their origin in their ongoing self-interpretation and their dominant paradigm so as to suggest that remembered origin is found universally, it is conceivable that a society is so related to its past as to be indifferent to its origin, hence the memory of origin plays no role in self-interpretation. The latter possibility suggests that remembered origin is not an a priori element in social duration. I shall not attempt to settle this question. A second source of difficulty is the elusive character of the concept of origin. There are no "absolute" origins for historical and social entities but rather turns and shifts in already existing societies. Further, origin in ahistorical or mythically oriented groups is not a historical beginning point but a mythical beginning cyclically renewed.[28] Yet, however we account for it, reference to origin appears to be universal among comprehensive, developed societies. A society can legitimately speak of its beginning in the sense of a period or set of events that are decisive in the formation of its paradigm and determinate intersubjectivity while acknowledging that beginning as a successor to a previous period and society.

More important than simply the fact of remembered origin in a society's social duration is the important role it plays in the other elements of duration. If a society remembers its beginnings at all, it will do so not simply in a neutral act of dating, but in a periodizing, valuing, distinguishing between the time "before" and the time "after" its beginnings. Reference to beginnings is reference to events or persons connected causally with the realities presently constituting the society and determining its distinctiveness. This is why the paradigm of the society with its various expressions in symbols and stories contains references to the originating events or persons. Thus a society maintains its continuity not simply by revivifying its past. It revivifies its past by means of unifying the past under its founding events or persons. It was these events or persons that precipitated the "after," which produced the shift in history giving rise to the society in the first place. Thus the origin is not meant on the same level with all past events but as the interpretative clue to the meaning and significance of subsequent events.

Second, there seems to be some correlation between the kind of social space and time that characterize the society and the kind of origin recalled by the society. The mythical origins of cyclical or nature religions correspond with the sacred space and time of these religions. The origin of Israel has to do with events (visionary, migratory, military) and leaders (tribal, military) who established the space (the land) of Israelite religion, and the time of this community had to do with the past and future of this land (invasion, dispersion, return).

Third, we find a correspondence between the *mode* of remembered origin and the *vehicles* of social duration. Ritualistic acts on seasonal cycles clearly correlate with remembered mythical origin. If the origin

28. Mircea Eliade, *The Sacred and the Profane* (New York: Harper Torchbooks, 1961), chap. 2, and *Myth and Reality* (New York: Harper & Row, 1963), chap. 3.

is the origin of a territorial people with a common language, laws, and self-governance, then institutions and activities that perpetuate, protect, and order life in that territory will be necessary. Such correspondences are ideal correspondences. The impetus of a society attempting to perpetuate itself is toward rather than away from appropriate vehicles. But this in itself does not guarantee that a society's remembered origin will in fact correspond with the vehicles, the social space and time, and the paradigm of that society.

THE PROCESS OF SOCIAL DURATION

This brief treatment of the *elements* of social duration has addressed the following three questions. *What* is it which endures at the depth level of sociality? Answer: the cointendings or reciprocal meaning-acts of individual participants. What unifies the reality universe of the depth level? Answer: the dominating paradigm of the society. What carries this depth level from generation to generation? Answer: vehicles of sedimentations and activities. But these elements give us only a frozen cross section of social duration: individuals constituting each other under a common paradigm yielding a common space and a common origin, past, and future, and vehicles that carry this commonality to future generations. When we unfreeze the picture and attempt to grasp social duration as a process, we find the following.

Ontological and Intentional Dimensions of Social Process

Views of social process which rest on the analogy of the human self in its temporality stress the persistence of the past as occurring in the mode of memory.[29] I have followed a similar approach here, but it is a somewhat misleading one. The social self approach to duration highlights human intentionality. The past and future are present in a society by means of acts of meaning. Yet this valid point should not exclude the fact that the past persists *ontologically* into the present in the form of received data.[30] It is simply not the case that a society at any present or contemporary moment is so cut off from the past that a

---

29. For instance, Boyd, *Contemporaneity and the Presence of Christ;* Royce, *The Problem of Christianity,* part II, lecture IX; John Knox, *Jesus, Lord and Christ* (New York: Harper and Brothers, 1958), pp. 61 ff.

30. This is supplementation to the theory of social duration which would be characteristic of most process philosophers.

distinction is founded between the dead but remembered past and the living present. Rather, what the present itself is in content is an inheritor of data from the past. To think of time as a succession of discrete units, each of which totally replaces then remembers what it displaces, is simply an erroneous view. Thus, in Russia the Communist Revolution is a remembered past event and one which has been succeeded by other historic events. But the actual data of that event have accumulated, been brought forward, and are present still in Russia.

If we stopped at this point, we certainly would not be doing justice to the temporality characteristic of a human society. We would simply have described a universal feature of all temporality. But time itself not only has some universal features but is also a correlate of the mode of being it attends.[31] The depth temporality of a society is neither a flow of events measured quantitatively, nor internal time consciousness, nor lived-time in the sense of a horizon form of human experience. Yet societies as societies have pasts which accumulate with them by means of the vehicles of duration. The retention of this past occurs under the society's paradigm and in the face of changing situations, hence the past is perpetually reinterpreted and reshaped. Therefore, the metaphor *horizon* is applicable to social temporality, not in the sense of a horizon form of individual experience but as an indication that the (interpreted) past (and future) of a society is a changing and indeterminate one. It has a horizon of past events still operative (remembered) in the cointentions of its individuals and its vehicles. The past is thus a horizon form of the social self in the sense of the intersubjective structure which shapes and is shaped by participating individuals.

The future of a society is, like all futures, a realm of possibility. More specifically, a society projects for itself certain strata of hoped-for, feared, decided-upon possibilities and not others. And these specific projections express the dominant paradigm. Therefore, the future is also a horizon, namely, a horizon of possible events present in the cointentionalities which project idealities in the sense of aims, hopes, and the like. A society does not actually perpetrate acts of consciousness such as protention and anticipation, but the intersubjec-

31. William Earle, "Intersubjective Time," in W. L. Reese and E. Freeman, eds., *Process and Divinity* (LaSalle, Ill.: Open Court, 1964).

tive network of a society does contain future references. In this sense of a horizon of past and future which attends the society's cointentionalities, we can speak of social time at a depth level.

We must grant that most of the actual past, considered as data (at molecular and cellular levels, the trillions of events which have occurred each moment in both the human organism, its immediate environment, and the larger universe), is not a remembered past since it was never even a perceived present. But we cannot grasp the peculiarity of social time unless we include both ontological and social intentional features. The past does persist as data in a society, most of which data are too microscopic, macroscopic, or distant to be accessible. Thus a society's distinctive temporality refers to the data received from the past, interpretatively brought together by the society's own paradigm, intersubjectivity, sedimentations, and activities.

The Shaping of Space and Time

The most distinctive feature of a society's duration is that, like individual temporality, the past is retained and the future graded in a selective or sifting activity. This means that the vast multiplicity of actual and possible events must be restricted. Every human society is a determinate society with its own origin, paradigm, intersubjectivity, and vehicles. Not all the data of the past are remembered and not all future possibilities, even those pertinent to the society, are anticipated. The accomplishment of the particular grading and selection appropriate to a society is what I am calling the shaping of space and time. This begins with those events which so alter an existing society that they begin a new human social existence. As I have previously observed, almost all comprehensive societies in some way recollect and are tied to their events of origin, even if it is a mythical view of world beginnings. The community's comprehensive paradigm of self-interpretation tends to be generated in these events of origin, at least in postmythical societies. And this too plays a shaping role since the paradigm contains the reality-universe of the community and with that its understanding of its own spatiality and its past and future. Memory, therefore, is bound to the determinate space of the society (tribal, island, continent, ghetto, migratory, nomadic, and so on). And the memory sifts from the past key events, epochs, and biographies pertinent to that space and to that society.

Nor is the past the only thing subjected to shaping and sifting under the determinate aims and paradigms of the society. The future is likewise subjected to this process. We find an analogy to this shaping of the future in the individual self. In the sense of the intentional structure of consciousness, the future is both a preconscious protended stratum of possibilities and a realm of specific expectations, fears, desires, and the like, that is, possibilities projected through the grading of their value or disvalue. Ontologically speaking, the future is a set of possibilities graded to the *data* of the past which have persisted into the present. The future of a society involves both intentional and ontological dimensions. There are data inherited from the past which set possibilities. But, a society analogous to the individual subjects these possibilities to a grading or shaping process in accordance with its remembered origin and its paradigm. The future thus is a projected stratum of the society's feared, hoped for, planned for possibilities.

Only when space, past, and future are so shaped can a society inherit the data from the past according to its own determinacy. This is the first step of social process.

Innovation and Solidification as Responses to New Situations

I have described social process as a sifting of the past and future which requires a shaping of the society's space and time. What this shaping yields are the criteria for the selecting or sifting. So far, then, we have a society at its depth level of intersubjectivity persisting through time by way of a selective memory and expectation. But social process is not mere persistence through time. The setting of the persistence is a macroenvironment of the society which itself has a microenvironment (individuals, subgroups, and so on), both of which are in perpetual change. This change can be highly visible, rapid, traumatic, a future shock change, or exceedingly slow, repetitive, hidden, as in isolated, provincial, and highly stable societies. This variable aside, all social process is persistence in the face of changing situations. Uncovered here is an ever-present feature of social process which is that of continuity adapting to change. Adaptation may be too tame a word since it suggests a predominately past-oriented society. What in fact happens in the society which adapts to the new is *innovation*. Innovation becomes necessary when one kind of governing system fails to meet a new kind of crisis, when perpetual drought

371

threatens the existence of the tribe, when a people is transported from one land to another, when the population quickly expands.

Innovation both solves and creates problems for the society. It may solve the problem initiated by the new situation, but it may also threaten the society's continuity and its reality-universe. Hence, the society integrates or absorbs its innovation into its continuity, a moment we shall term *solidification*. Although solidification may be expected to occur under the criteria yielded by the society's shaping of its space and time, the society is not merely the same society after innovation and solidification. For now new events and interpretations have entered the society's history and this effects a new bounding of past and future. More far reaching, innovation and solidification, if significant enough, may effect the dominant paradigm itself, the depth intersubjectivity of the society, and the vehicles of transmission. An example ready at hand is the adaptation that occurred among the Jews as a result of the diaspora. The continuity (the paradigm, the cointentions, the vehicles) between the religion of Israel and later Judaism is apparent. On the other hand, new events were added to the corporate memory. A new space, a new set of institutions (synagogue) and activities (rabbinical teaching) arose as generation-bridging vehicles. When innovation and solidification occurs in a radical way within a society, the result may be a new paradigm, a new space and time, so that a new origin takes place. This occurred when early Christianity ceased to be a Jewish sect and became a community independent of Judaism. With that came a new depth temporality and continuity which nevertheless shared features with the community that preceded it.[32]

In this analysis I have stressed enduring, structural, and, in most cases, even a priori elements of the social duration of a human society. I hope this does not obscure what is more obvious and visible in everyday life, the variables that occur within societies because they are the kind of societies they are. Thus there are different modes of having the past and future. In Hannah Arendt's view, tradition is not an a priori element to social duration but a peculiarly Western and

32. The examples taken from the history of Judaism and Christianity should not give the impression that innovation-solidification as moments of social process are necessarily to be understood as "progress." A society may innovate in order to meet a new situation but in harmful or even catastrophic ways. Thus the technological innovations of the twentieth century, designed to meet some kinds of problems, may have eventually fateful consequences in military or ecological destructiveness.

now defunct historical mode.[33] Variables occur depending on how the past and future function in a society, whether one or the other is the society's primary focus. They occur depending on how the society's origin is grasped, and also on the particular role of origin as a criterion for shaping the past. There are many variables in the kind of vehicles of transmission that exist and how they function. I have avoided one whole dimension of social process, focusing as I did on eidetic and universal features, namely, the effect of human alienation on social process, and this too founds many variables.

However, the emphasis of this appendix is not on variables but on continuities. And even this emphasis is ordered toward that theme which both major parts of this text have made use of. This is the matter, touched upon briefly in a former section, of ideal correspondence between the elements of social duration. In order to survive at all, societies must have some unity and some entelechy. To originate at all and to successfully maintain themselves, there must be some successful integration of their paradigm, their cointentionalities, which render the elements of the paradigm into ways of being spatial and temporal, the vehicles of transmission, and the innovative and solidifying processes. If these are simply unrelated to each other or related in contradiction, the society's duration will be unstable and constantly threatened and its reality-universe easily eroded. This ideal correspondence among the elements of social duration was the primary object of the investigation of ecclesial duration. Only then could we test the coherence and adequacy of the actual vehicles, the actual mode of self-perpetuation, which have attended that form of corporate historical existence.

To summarize, social process, looked at with its various elements gathered together and stretched out temporally, is a persistence of the past into the present sifted through a society's determinateness, a determinateness defined by its origin, paradigm, space, and time. The process itself occurs as the society's depth continuity struggles to maintain itself in new situations, thus generating both innovations and means of reintegrating the innovations with its continuity. This in turn creates alterations in the elements of continuity themselves (the paradigm, intersubjectivity, vehicles); hence, social process is a matter of a depth continuity which undergoes minor or major alterations.

33. Arendt, *Between Past and Future*.

Index

Abelard, 96 n., 108
Ackroyd, Roger, 48 n.
Adamic myth, 21, 35, 39, 53, 71 n.,
    158 n., 198, 270
Ahlstrom, Sydney E., 181 n.
Aland, Kurt, 76 n.
Alsted, J. H., 39 n.
Althaus, Paul, 4 n.
Anselm, 115
Apocalyptic, 16, 23 n., 31–32
Archaeology, 3–5, 214
Arendt, Hannah, 34 n., 98 n., 347,
    372–73
Aristotle, 47 n., 297 n., 302 n., 308
Augustine, xvi, 92, 108, 115–16,
    232
Authority, 108 ff.

Bachelard, G., 219 n., 226 n.
Baeck, Leo, 16 n.
Baier, W., 122 n.
Barbour, Ian, 136 n.
Barr, James, 48 n.
Barth, Karl, xvi, xvii, xviii, 5, 99,
    187 n., 193, 231 n., 279, 309
Bauer, Walter, 76 n., 92 n., 120 n.
Baum, Gregory, 173 n.
Baur, F. C., 201 n.
Becker, Ernst, 138 n.
Bennett, John C., 30 n.
Berdyaev, Nicholas, 29 n., 232,
    354 n.

Berger, Peter, 347 n., 355 n.
Bettenson, Henry, 132 n.
Bokser, B. Z., 8 n.
Bornkamm, G., 17 n., 22 n.
Boyd, Tom W., 217 n., 226 n.,
    351 n.
Bracketing (Epoche), 263–64, 273
Brandon, S. G. F., 40 n.
Bright, John, 282–83 n.
Brown, William A., 131 n.
Bruce, F. F., 40 n.
Brueggemann, Walter, 8 n., 24 n.
Bruno, G., 136, 168
Buber, Martin, 24 n., 85 n.
Bultmann, Rudolf, 7 n., 91 n.,
    101 n., 234 n.
Burrell, David, 312 n.
Burtt, E. A., 135 n.

Care, 255 ff.
Cassirer, Ernst, 136 n.
Chadwick, Owen, 202 n.
Channing, W. E., xv
Chemnitz, Martin, 108
Childs, Brevard, 10 n., 28 n., 48 n.,
    52 n.
Christian, William, 302 n., 305 n.
Christianity, 194, 205, 214, 298
    beginnings, 12 ff., 64 ff., 148, 237
    essence of, 131–32, 146, 186,
        194, 200–5
Church, 97–105, 126

375

Index

Index

377

Index